AUGUSTINE ON WAR AND MILITARY SERVICE

AUGUSTINE ON WAR AND MILITARY SERVICE

PHILLIP WYNN

Fortress Press
Minneapolis

AUGUSTINE ON WAR AND MILITARY SERVICE

Cover design: Laurie Ingram

Cover image: Roman Helmet, from Judea, Israel Museum (IDAM), Jerusalem, Israel © Erich Lessing / Art Resource, NY

Library of Congress Cataloging-in-Publication Data is available

Print ISBN: 978-1-4514-6473-3

eBook ISBN: 978-1-4514-6985-1

The paper used in this publication meets the minimum requirements of American National Standard for Information Sciences — Permanence of Paper for Printed Library Materials, ANSI Z329.48-1984.

Manufactured in the U.S.A.

This book was produced using PressBooks.com, and PDF rendering was done by PrinceXML.

CONTENTS

Acknowledgments

With a work as broadly conceived as this, even the strictest detractors must, according to *their* measure of the material that should be in it but isn't, occasionally make allowances for mortal ignorance, while conceding the merest possibility that any particular something *they* mastered with their mothers' milk may be missing for lack of space, or relevance.

The best medicine I've known for treating mortal ignorance in these matters is the University of Notre Dame's Medieval Institute, its library, and especially the staff and my colleagues there. Call-outs to that scoundrel Roberta Baranowski, who, though she denies it, actually runs the place; colleagues Leslie Lockett, for providing me a place to live while much of this was written; David Mengel, for providing me with a job; and Jonathan Juilfs, for his help in keeping me sane—although in the end he failed.

One who succeeded was mentor and friend Tom Noble, whose intelligence and learning permeate these pages; he was, simply, indispensable to it.

Thanks are also due the folks at Fortress Press, particularly Will Bergkamp, all of whom I think—or at least hope!—will forgive me for sometimes claiming authorial prerogative in ladling out a spicy sauce or two.

A certain Pam and Charles are mostly relieved that a certain windbag now no longer talks about just war.

In the realms this work traverses, I must acknowledge three true pioneers whose footsteps I've encountered, and often followed: Herbert Deane, Peter Haggenmacher, and Bernard Verkamp.

Finally, the greatest thanks are due my critics who show me my errors and omissions.

Abbreviations

Barnes, *Constantine and Eusebius*. Barnes, T. D. *Constantine and Eusebius* (Cambridge, MA: Harvard University Press, 1981)

Barnes, *Constantine*. Barnes, Timothy. *Constantine: Dynasty, Religion and Power in the Later Roman Empire* (Chicester: Wiley-Blackwell, 2011)

Brown. Brown, Peter. *Augustine of Hippo: A Biography*, 2nd ed. (Berkeley and Los Angeles: University of California Press, 2000)

Cameron and Hall. Cameron, Averil, and Stuart G. Hall, trans. *Eusebius: Life of Constantine* (Oxford: Clarendon, 1999)

CCL. *Corpus Christianorum, Series Latina* (Turnhout, 1954–)

CDS. *Capitula diversarum sententiarum pro negociis rei publice consulendis*, Paris, Bib. nat. lat. nouv. acq. 1632, fol. 78v–89v

Cod. Theod. *Theodosiani libri XVI cum Constitutionibus Sirmondianis*, ed. T. Mommsen (Berlin, 1962 reprint)

CSEL. *Corpus Scriptorum Ecclesiasticorum Latinorum* (Vienna, 1866–)

DCD. Augustine, *De civitate Dei*, ed. B. Dombart and A. Kalb (*CCL* 47, 48)

Div. Inst. *L. Caeli Firmiani Lactanti Divinae Institutiones*, ed. S. Brandt (*CSEL* 19, Prague/Vienna/Leipzig, 1890)

DMP. *De mortibus persecutorum*, ed. & trans. J. L. Creed (Oxford: Clarendon, 1984)

Dolbeau. *Augustin d'Hippone, Vingt-Six Sermons au peuple d'Afrique*, ed. François Dolbeau (Paris: Brepols, 1996)

GCS. *Die griechischen christlichen Schriftsteller der ersten Jahrhunderte* (Leipzig, 1897–1918; Berlin, 1954–)

HE. Eusebius of Caesarea. *Historia Ecclesiastica* (*GCS, Eusebius Werke II*, ed. E. Schwartz [Greek], T. Mommsen [Latin] [Leipzig, 1903])

Hefele. Hefele, C. J. *Histoire des Conciles* (Paris, 1907)

Heim. Heim, François. *La Théologie de la victoire de Constantin à Théodose* (Paris: Beauchesne, 1992)

Mansi. Mansi, J. D. *Sacrorum conciliorum nova et amplissima collectio* (Florence: A. Zatti, 1759–98)

McCormick. McCormick, Michael. *Eternal Victory: Triumphal Rulership in Late Antiquity, Byzantium, and the Early Medieval West* (Cambridge: Cambridge University Press, 1986)

McLynn. McLynn, Neil. *Ambrose of Milan: Church and Court in a Christian Capital* (Berkeley: University of California Press, 1994)

Nixon. Nixon, C. E. V., and Barbara T. Rodgers, *In Praise of Later Roman Emperors: The* Panegyrici Latini (Berkeley, Los Angeles, & Oxford, 1994)

O'Daly. O'Daly, Gerard. *Augustine's* City of God: *A Reader's Guide* (Oxford: Oxford University Press, 1999)

Orosius. *Pauli Orosii Historiarum Adversum Paganos Libri VII, CSEL5, ed. Zangemeister (Vienna, 1882)*

PL. *Patrologia Latina* (Paris, 1844–1974)

PLRE **2.** Martindale, J. *The Prosopography of the Later Roman Empire 2: A.D. 395-527* (Cambridge, 1980)

RIC **9.** Pearce, J. W. E. *The Roman Imperial Coinage: Valentinian I to Theodosius I* (London, 1951)

Russell. Russell, Frederick H. *The Just War in the Middle Ages* (Cambridge: Cambridge University Press, 1975)

SC. Sources chrétiennes (Paris: Cerf, 1942–)

Stephenson. Stephenson, Paul. *Constantine: Unconquered Emperor, Christian Victor* (London: Quercus, 2009)

VC. *Über das Leben des Kaisers Konstantins* (GCS 1/1, ed. F. Winkelmann [Berlin, 1975])

Introduction

The early twenty-first century has witnessed a continued, heightened, and widespread interest in the idea of just war.[1] This renewal of interest began early in the twentieth century prior to and especially after the First World War, after a centuries-long period when the idea was largely banished to the realm of moral theology.

As the idea of just war gained increased visibility in intellectual discourse, it also acquired a history. In this account it emerged that the idea of Western just war was ancient, its origins traceable to statements made by St. Augustine in the late fourth and early fifth centuries. As James Turner Johnson recently expressed it, "the origins of a specifically Christian just war concept first appeared in the thought of Augustine."[2] This Augustinian just war was first systematized in Gratian's *Decretum* and received its classic formulation in Thomas Aquinas's *Summa Theologiae* in the late thirteenth century, from which point the just war idea became part of the Western Christian intellectual tradition.

What I have just outlined could be considered a summary of the standard narrative of the development of the just war idea in the West. Unfortunately, there are a number of serious interrelated flaws in this narrative. Like all such reductive narratives, it tends to efface the influence through time of ideas divergent from a privileged "main" line of development by ignoring or even attempting to appropriate what are actually opposing intellectual trajectories, an approach that has been termed "tunnel history."[3] The prevailing narrative of just war's development also tends to view the idea as a set of propositions transmitted by a series of intellectual "torch-bearers," a view that tends toward rendering the idea ahistorical, at its core little influenced by contemporary historical circumstances. This view also emphasizes the ideational aspect of the justification of war and largely ignores its reality as an expression of political culture.[4]

---

1. One measure of the idea's topicality is in the references to just war in President Barack Obama's Nobel Peace Prize acceptance speech in December 2009; for a transcript, see www.csmonitor.com/World/Global-News/2009/1210/text-of-barack-obamas-nobel-peace-prize-acceptance-speech (accessed 14 May 2013).

2. James Turner Johnson, "Just War, As It Was and Is," *First Things* 149 (January 2005): 14.

3. David Hackett Fisher, *Historians' Fallacies* (New York: Harper & Row, 1970), 142–44.

But the fundamental flaw in the prevailing narrative of the history of just war in the West, a notion that binds together the narrative with all its other flaws, is the role it assigns to Augustine. The African Father provides the authority necessary for privileging a core set of propositions on just war ascribed to him, a core that is always potentially recoverable by reverting to his original statements. Since by this view just war is an idea transmitted by a series of intellectuals, there must have been an originator of the idea, and that individual was Augustine. As will be shown, however, Augustine himself did not originate the Christian just war idea. This view of his role perverts what he thought and wrote about war and military service, and any subsequent scholarly interpretation of that material. More importantly, such a view tends to obscure and misrepresent what Christians in the first millennium, and later, actually thought about these matters.

This book's origin lies in work done for my article published in 2001 on the views of Gregory of Tours on war.[5] There I noted that Gregory seemed to have a conception of the justification of war that apparently did not stem from Augustine.[6] Subsequent reflection on the issues raised in that study, and research in the relevant texts and the body of scholarly interpretations intervening between Augustine's time and our own, led to my realization that the standard narrative linking Augustine to the origination of the Christian just war doctrine was fundamentally flawed and, in the most important sense, utterly wrong. Such considerations inform the background for the current work, which basically has two goals. First, I have attempted to determine the content of and the context for early Christian ideas on war and military service, having set to one side the erroneous notion of Augustine's magisterial influence on such thinking during this period. Second, I have tried to set Augustine's actual thinking on the matter in its original historical and literary context, and to illustrate how he began to become a Christian authority on war. What

4. On the tendency of intellectual history to treat ideas as "autonomous abstractions which, in their self-propelled journeyings through time, [happen] only accidentally and temporarily to find anchorage in particular human minds," see Stefan Collini, "What Is Intellectual History?," in *What Is History Today?*, ed. Juliet Gardiner (London: Prometheus, 1988), 106. Regarding the particular issue of Augustine and the just war idea, Robert Markus wrote in 1983 that "ideas do not lead a disembodied existence; they encourage individuals and groups to take very definite attitudes towards their cultural and social environment" (Markus, "Saint Augustine's Views on the 'Just War,'" *Studies in Church History* 20 [1983]: 1–2).

5. Phillip Wynn, "Wars and Warriors in Gregory of Tours' *Histories* I–IV," *Francia* 28, no. 1 (2001): 1–35.

6. Ibid., 34–35. Here I recant much of the conclusion of that article, as I now do not think of Gregory's ideas as reflecting an "underlying Christian tradition."

follows is therefore necessarily *not* the early history of the Christian just war idea, though the beginnings of that history could be derived from it.

Although the history of early Christian attitudes toward war and military service seems well-traveled ground, if one removes Augustine from the central role he has usually played in such works, there is a need to revisit the evidence used in many of the prevailing standard narratives on the subject. In attempting to construct anew the story of the intersection between early Christianity and war, this study will address the following questions, among others:

- What were Christian attitudes toward war and military service before Constantine's conversion?
- What accounts for those attitudes, and how and why did they evolve over time?
- How were Christian attitudes toward war and military service affected when the religion became dominant in the late fourth-century Roman world?
- How did "official" propaganda act to reflect and/or create the image, or the reality, of a normative Christian attitude toward war?
- What were the spiritual consequences of Christian participation in the army and in war, and how were such consequences addressed?
- What role did Scripture play in determining Christian attitudes?
- What are the terminological and ideological origins of just war?
- What is the history of the development of just war in the Roman republic and empire, both as an idea and as a term of political rhetoric?
- How did just war, as an idea and as a political practice, come to be associated with Christianity?
- Finally, since his statements were later—much later—used to construct him as a Christian authority on war, what did Augustine actually think about war and military service, once his relevant statements have been restored to their original historical and literary contexts?

In what follows, as much as anything I am trying to capture a mentality and an attitude. Such an approach is necessary, because nothing like a sustained intellectual engagement with the question of how Christianity should regard war and military service exists until centuries after Augustine's death. Significantly, no treatise was written specifically on the subject for the first thousand years of Christianity's history, and for some time thereafter. Why?

Indeed, anyone who confidently wades into the mass of Christian literature of the first millennium seeking to discover an authoritative early Christian attitude to war is bound for a frustrating dead-end. This is true for two reasons.

First, there is simply no singular, authoritative Christian attitude toward war to be found, then or later. Second, the sort of detached and theoretical rumination on issues today associated with theological disquisition is actually relatively rare at this period, and is never found applied to war. This is because surviving Christian literature of the first millennium is overwhelmingly pastoral in intent, even in such apparently non-pastoral genres as biblical commentary and *computus*. It is therefore unsurprising that as late as Gratian in the early twelfth century, the early Christian texts that we moderns privilege as related to war actually treat at greater length and in greater detail issues related to Christians serving as soldiers. Then and for some time to come, one cannot find even one Christian writer explicitly theorizing at length about war as a general proposition. More immediate pastoral concerns were paramount, and naturally when it came to war such concerns had to do with Christian military service. Since one must go where the evidence lies, this study will examine issues related to both war *and* military service in the writings of Augustine and other early Christian writers.

My attempt to engage sympathetically with the attitudes and feelings of early Christians toward war and military service also explains what at times might seem an uncritical approach to sources. In evaluating sources to determine the ideas and attitudes that inform them, it is possible to take the hermeneutics of suspicion too far, and to emphasize what rhetoric conceals rather than what it reveals. For example, the historicity of hagiographic accounts of events in their saintly heroes' lives is often justly suspect. It thus might seem naïve and credulous to use the life of Martin of Tours, for example, to uncover something of contemporary Christian views of war and military service. Yet it is precisely because such texts can present an overly idealized and overly simplified point of view that they are valuable for the historian of ideas: the events described in them may not have *actually* happened, but according to the hagiographer's ideology and worldview they *should* have. In accordance with the same sympathetic reading of the relevant texts is my use of the word *pagan* to denote non-Christians and their beliefs. For although the existence of a uniform pagan "Other" opposed to Christianity is itself a Christian construction, its usage accurately reflects the early Christian worldview, and is one of the more significant bipolarities in Christian thinking that conditioned developments in ideas connected with war.

The period under investigation is one that is notorious for its supposed scarcity of sources. Those familiar with those sources know better. Therefore, it has been impossible to treat everything. To give just one example: certain of the nave mosaics of the early fifth-century church Santa Maria Maggiore in Rome arguably provide a visual repertoire that can be interpreted to give information on how early fifth-century Christians in Rome regarded the military. Unfortunately, what I know of the scholarship on those mosaics has convinced me that more work needs to be done on them by art historians before such an interpretation can be safely made. I have therefore aimed at being comprehensive, while recognizing it is impossible to be exhaustive.

Part I lays out the historical and ideological backdrop for the modern view of Augustine's role in the development of the just war idea, and that for his actual ideas concerning war and military service. Chapter one surveys the modern construction of Augustine as the originator of the Christian just war idea. Chapter two pivots to a treatment of the development of Christian thinking on war and military service from the earliest extant writing on the matter in about 200 to the conversion of the emperor Constantine. Chapter three deals with the more immediate historical and ideological context for Augustine's own thinking in the late fourth century, when the scale of the "Christianization" of the Roman empire made more acute issues regarding Christianity's relationship to the state and its ideology. Chapter four then goes back to look at the origins of the Roman just war, emphasizing more its reality as a practice of political culture rather than simply a disembodied idea.

Part II examines in detail those passages in Augustine's writings that touch on issues of war and military service. Chapter five briefly addresses certain issues involved in the interpretation of what Augustine had to say on war and military service. Chapter six looks at what Augustine had to say about *militia*, a term that in that period encompassed both civilian and military service to the state. Chapter seven surveys what Augustine wrote on war, including his relatively few remarks on just war. Chapter eight treats Augustine's subversion and appropriation of the words "peace" and "victory," words of fundamental significance in contemporary imperial ideology. Chapter nine outlines the significant steps in the process whereby medieval ecclesiastics transformed Augustine into an authority on war.

The translations of original texts are my own unless noted. Often when I have used existing translations I have modified them slightly in order to bring out more clearly information central to the argument.

PART I

1

The Modern Construction of an Augustinian Just War

Although the assertion that it was St. Augustine who set out the foundational principles of Christian just war is only a century old, the beginning of the basis for that claim rests in the numerous citations from his works in the second part, *causa* 23 of Gratian's *Concordia Discordantium Canonum* or *Decretum* (c. 1140).[1] In response to the hypothetical there, which posits a defense led by orthodox bishops against the aggression of heretics, Gratian addressed issues related to sin and the conduct of war, and specifically the question as to what constitutes a just war. In *causa* 23, Gratian, by my count, cited Augustine no fewer than seventy-eight times, far more than the thirteen citations of the next most-quoted authority, Gregory the Great.[2] Yet Gratian nowhere explicitly denominated Augustine as the originator of just war.

Nor does the other most influential medieval writer on just war, Thomas Aquinas, ever describe Augustine thusly. In *quaestio* 40, article I in the *Secunda Secundae* of his *Summa Theologiae* (c. 1270),[3] Thomas countered criticisms that war violated the letter and spirit of Christianity, detailing there criteria for a just war which, given Thomas's subsequent reputation, have come to be regarded as constituting an authoritative core of Christian just war tradition.[4] Adding to the impression given by the *Decretum*, one of his sources, Thomas seemingly further cemented Augustine's position as the original authority on just war: other than once mentioning Jerome, his only cited authorities here are Augustine and the Bible.

---

1. *Corpus iuris canonici* I, *Decretum magistri Gratiani*, ed. Emil Friedberg (Leipzig, 1879).

2. *Decretum*, col. 889–965.

3. *S. Thomae de Aquino Summae Theologiae Secunda Secundae* (Ottawa: Commissio Piana, 1953), vol. 3, col. 1632a–34a.

4. E.g., Johnson, "Just War" (Introduction, note 2 above), 16.

In fact, in the subsequent centuries of canonical and theological commentary on the *Decretum* and the *Summa Theologiae*, Augustine is never explicitly named as the originator of a Christian just war idea, although he is mentioned frequently, sometimes in the company of other patristic authorities.[5] For this "prehistoric" period of international law before Grotius, I have found only two instances where the author could be interpreted as explicitly assigning Augustine a special place in the expression of a Christian doctrine of just war. Toward the end of the fifteenth century, the Spanish jurist Juan Lopez/Ioannes Lupus (d. 1496) wrote a brief treatise *De bello et bellatoribus*.[6] In a dialogue between *magister* and *discipulus*, the student at one point says:

> I acknowledge everything which you said and adduced, and I acknowledge the conclusion of the blessed Thomas, of Innocent and of Hostiensis and of the Archdeacon, who speak best on this matter, and of the others whom they seem to follow in everything, the blessed Augustine and the blessed Jerome and the blessed Isidore.[7]

Note, however, that Lopez here regarded Augustine as one member of a group of patristic authorities. The African Father is not singled out, but treated as one voice in a *consensus doctorum* on war. In the period before Grotius, the Spanish Jesuit theologian Gregorio de Valencia perhaps came the closest to conferring upon Augustine a uniquely authoritative status on the subject of just war. In his *Commentaria Theologica*, first published in 1595,[8] the author cited Augustine numerous times in his *quaestio* 16 on war.[9] In discussing the conditions required for a war to be just, he cited the relevant passage from Thomas and added: "Augustine wrote briefly but quite clearly on this matter . . . from whom almost

---

5. E.g., *Die Summa Magistri Rolandi*, ed. Friedrich Thaner (Innsbruck, 1874), 90, 91, 92; Giovanni da Legnano, *Tractatus de bello, de represaliis et de duello*, ed. Thomas Erskine Holland (New York: Oceana, 1964), 85–6; Franciscus Arias, *De bello et eius iustitia*, in *Tractatus universi iuris, duce, & auspice Gregorio XIII pontifice maximo, in unum congesti: additis quamplurimis antea nunquam editis* (Venice, 1584), tom. 16, 325ff.; *Summula Caietani* (Lyon, 1550), 32, s.v. *bellum*; *Summae Sylvestrinae, quae summa summarum merito nuncupatur, pars prima* (Venice, 1578), f. 66r, s.v. *bellum*; Lud. Molinae e Societate Iesu, primarii quondam in Eborensi academia sacrae theologiae professoris, *De Iustitia et Iure tractatus* (Venice, 1611), tom. 1, col. 365, 366, 367, 368, 369, 370, 374, 375, 381, 385, 390, 393, 401, 404, 412, 425, 428.

6. *Ioan. Lup. De Bello & Bellatoribus*, in *Tractatus* (previous note), ff. 320–22. On his date, see Walker (n. 30 below), 213, n. 2.

7. *De Bello & Bellatoribus*, f. 320v.

8. Regout (n. 56 below), 245.

9. *Gregorii de Valentia Metimnensis e Societate Iesu, sacrae theologiae academia Ingolstadiensi professoris Commentariorum Theologicorum* (Paris, 1609), tom. III, col. 829–63.

all the other authorities took that which they handed down concerning the very same matter."[10]

Regarding this statement, it is interesting that although Grotius often cites Valencia's work in his *De Iure Belli ac Pacis*,[11] he still did not thereby derive the conclusion that Augustine originated the just war. If Valencia's statement is taken as an acknowledgment of Augustinian paternity, it is curious that, Grotius excepted, for the next three centuries there seems little notice taken of Valencia's statement, let alone any conclusion derivable from it as to Augustine's role in developing the just war idea. Rather than an expression of Augustinian origination, Valencia's words are probably best regarded as a significant yet isolated assessment of Augustine's preeminent authoritativeness and clarity of expression on the subject of just war, which is not quite the same thing as suggesting that he authored the very idea.

Because of their influence on Grotius, a particular series of sixteenth-century writers on the just war stand more directly in the line of scholarship that ultimately led to the assertion of an Augustinian paternity, beginning with the great Spanish theologian Francisco de Vitoria (d. 1546). The pattern of Vitoria's selection of Augustinian citations on war clearly betrays the influence of the earlier canonical writers. As with the previous authors, Vitoria at points acknowledged Augustine's authoritativeness on the subject of just war without ever attributing origination to him. So, for example, in his *De iure belli*, based on lectures delivered in 1539,[12] Vitoria noted that the proposition that Christians could wage war was "Augustine's conclusion in many passages."[13] For one of Vitoria's successors at the School of Salamanca, the Jesuit Francisco Suárez (1548–1617), Augustine was only one of a number of earlier Christian authorities on war, including Vitoria himself, who helped to form a *communis sententia* on the subject.[14]

A similar approach to Augustinian authority on war is seen in the two most prominent lay precursors to Grotius in the field of the *ius belli*. Balthazar Ayala wrote his *De iure et officiis bellicis* in 1581 while serving as judicial advisor for the Duke of Parma's army operating in the Spanish Netherlands. For Ayala, as for his predecessors, Augustine was one of several authorities

---

10. *Commentaria Theologica*, col. 841–42.

11. Regout (n. 56 below), 245.

12. On the date, Oliver O'Donovan and J. L. O'Donovan, eds., *From Irenaeus to Grotius: A Sourcebook in Christian Political Thought* (Grand Rapids: Eerdmans, 1999), 610.

13. Francisco de Vitoria, *De Indis et de iure belli relectiones*, ed. H. F. Wright (Washington, DC: Carnegie Institution, 1917), 272–73.

14. *Francisci Suarez opera omnia* (Paris: L. Vives, 1858), tom. XII, 737–63.

on war who contributed to a *communis omnium consensus*; in addition, his citations of Augustine show his dependence on immediate predecessors such as Diego Covarruvias for his knowledge of the relevant passages from Augustine.[15] Likewise the Italian expatriate and sometime professor of law at Oxford Alberico Gentili, whose *De iure belli* was very influential for Grotius's later work on the *ius belli*,[16] often cited Augustine, but nowhere privileged the African Father as the originator of a just war doctrine.[17]

In both the juridical work of his youth, the *De iure praedae commentarius* (1605), and his classic *De iure belli ac pacis* published twenty years later, Hugo Grotius cited Augustine numerous times. Grotius more than most of his predecessors explicitly singled out Augustine as an authority in the field of the *ius belli*. Augustine was the "most outstanding of the theologians,"[18] the "greatest teacher of religion and morality,"[19] whose authority alone stood for that of all theologians.[20] Grotius recognized that the authority of the African Father, whose writings on war—possibly here echoing Valencia's appreciation—he characterized as universally known to be more numerous and clear than the earlier statements by Ambrose,[21] had been followed in almost everything in the law of war by writers of recent times.[22] As with those earlier writers, though, Grotius nowhere interpreted Augustine's preeminent authoritativeness on issues of war as proof of doctrinal originality.

Important for the development of the notion of an Augustinian paternity for the Christian idea of just war was the reputation that the work of Grotius acquired in subsequent generations. Grotius occupies a situation similar to that of Augustine in the realm of the history of ideas, inasmuch as later writers by the very fact of their attribution to him of the origination of international law ultimately created a conceptual reality.[23] Over time the jurisprudential

---

15. *Balthazaris Ayalae De iure et officiis bellicis*, f. 31r-v.

16. Walker (n. 30 below), 276.

17. *Alberici Gentilis De iure belli libri III* (Hanover, 1612).

18. Hugo Grotius, *De iure praedae commentarius, Vol. II, The Collotype Reproduction of the original manuscript of 1604 in the handwriting of Grotius* (Buffalo, NY: William S. Hein & Co., 1995), f. 146v: "praestantissimo theologorum Augustino."

19. *De iure praedae commentarius*, f. 3v: "summus ille doctor pietatis et morum."

20. *De iure praedae commentarius*, f. 25v: "Theologos poscimus? En unum pro omnibus Augustinum."

21. *Hugonis Grotii De iure belli ac pacis libri tres* (Amsterdam, 1646), I.3.2, 47: "Augustini multo etiam plura sunt & clariora, omnibus nota."

22. *De iure belli ac pacis*, III.1.17, 434: "Non placent haec scholae auctorum paulo ante seculorum, ut quae unum ex veteribus Augustinum ferme in omnibus sequendum sibi delegerit."

23. On the development of the reputation of Grotius as the father of international law, see Haggenmacher (n. 109 below), 3–8.

development of international law and the place assigned to Grotius in its origination had two effects on the perception of the idea of just war, effects certainly ironic given Grotius's dependence on and fundamental continuity with earlier sixteenth-century writers, writers explicitly indebted to the medieval canonical tradition. First, as a result of the self-conscious effort of Enlightenment writers to characterize a body of international law as independent of theological premises, the foundations of the *ius belli* and the idea of just war subsumed within it were located no further back in time than Grotius and his immediate predecessors, thereby effacing the putative role of Augustine in the development of the law of war. Thus in articles on war in his *Encyclopédie* of 1757, Diderot either cited Grotius or referred readers to him for more information,[24] and Ompteda in 1785 in his survey of the literature of the *Völkerrecht* began his discussion of the *ius belli* with Ayala, Gentili, and Grotius.[25] Second, the same perceived liberation of international law from theology supposedly effected by Grotius, and the accumulation over especially the nineteenth century of a body of conventions and decisions putting international law into practice, tended toward the relative devaluation of the practical applicability of the just war idea, as it became regarded as being more of a moral than a legal concept.[26] One late nineteenth-century learned perception of the just war idea was well expressed in the article "International Law" in the ninth edition of the *Encyclopaedia Britannica* in 1881.

> To the question whether a given war be just or unjust international law has no answer to give, or only a formal one. . . . The justice or injustice of any war is really a question of morality, and in proportion as international law has escaped from the merely ethical region it has abandoned the attempt to decide this question.[27]

But at almost the same time as this dismissive statement from the *Encyclopaedia Britannica*, historians of international law, by virtue of their very perception of Grotius as marking the turning point in the development of

---

24. Denis Diderot, *Encyclopédie* (Paris, 1757), *s.v.* "guerre," 985.

25. D. H. L. von Ompteda, *Literatur des gesammten sowohl naturlichen als positiven Völkerrechts* (1785), II, 615.

26. On the so-called "positivistic" era in the history of international law during especially the nineteenth century, Stephen Neff, *War and the Law of Nations: A General History* (Cambridge: Cambridge University Press, 2005), 161–275.

27. *Encyclopaedia Britannica*, 9th ed. (New York: Charles Scribner, 1881), *s.v.* "International Law," vol. 13, 193. See also the remarks of Joachim von Elbe, "The Evolution of the Just War in International Law," *The American Journal of International Law* 33 (1939): esp. 676–84 and the literature cited there.

international law from medieval moral theology to modern jurisprudential science, thereby acknowledged that the concept of a law of war had a "prehistory," and in the course of tracing out that history began the move toward the attribution to Augustine of the creation of a doctrine of just war. Compared with later assertions of Augustinian paternity, the initial remarks on Augustine's role among late nineteenth-century historians were hesitant, tentative, and much qualified. Furthermore, their appreciation of Augustine's role was often contextualized in a narrative that sought to explain a shift from a presumed generalized pacifism in early Christianity to an acceptance of war by the medieval church. Perhaps the earliest historian of international law who thus highlighted Augustine's role was Ernest Nys in his 1882 *Le droit de la guerre et les précurseurs de Grotius*:

> This aversion [of early Christianity toward war] went so far as to refuse military service. The accession of Constantine the Great and the radical transformation which this brought about in the relationship of church and state provoked a reaction against this extreme view. Under Constantine, a council condemned soldiers who out of religious motives abandoned their standards, and soon thereafter, especially as a consequence of the writings of St. Augustine, the idea of the legitimacy of war penetrated Christian consciousness. Not that the great thinker does not acknowledge and deplore the appalling calamities of war; not that he does not preach moderation in combat; but his pragmatic mindset overcomes any pacifist views and he admits that war can be just.[28]

In his own history of international law before Grotius, published the year after Nys's work appeared, Rivier pivoted the early course of development around Gratian, who "sanctioned the reasonable doctrine of Saint Augustine, in opposition to the ancient fathers of the church, who had unreservedly condemned war."[29] In the following years, other historians of international law continued to highlight both the role of Gratian in transmitting Augustinian thoughts on war and the supposed post-Constantinian pragmatism of the African Father.[30]

---

28. Ernest Nys, *Le droit de la guerre et les précurseurs de Grotius* (Brussels & Leipzig: C. Muquardt, 1882), 25.

29. Alphonse Rivier, *Note sur la littérature du droit des gens avant la publication du* Jus belli ac pacis *de Grotius* (Brussels: F. Ha, 1883), 12.

Late nineteenth-century legal historians were already prepared to see Augustine as a key figure in the development of a Christian *ius belli*. In the wake of these initial scholarly forays into the development of international law in the centuries before Grotius, and partly in reaction against the secular positivism among such legal scholars manifested in their unfamiliarity or discomfort with the theological tincture of the medieval law of war, there appeared in the early twentieth century the works of Alfred Vanderpol (1854–1915), who more than anyone was responsible for cementing the position of St. Augustine in modern historical scholarship as the founder of a Christian doctrine of just war.[31] Vanderpol was educated as an engineer and in the late 1800s became prominent at Lyon as a leading civil engineer and industrialist, but also as a charitable benefactor. Vanderpol's life was marked by hardship and tragedy. An active and vigorous man well into his forties, he suffered a months-long paralysis in 1900 and never fully recovered. He lost a three-year old son to a carriage accident in 1888, and his youngest son and son-in-law died in the First World War. Vanderpol himself did not live to see his son-in-law's death. In the early days of the war he had helped to establish and administer a hospital for the wounded in Lyon. Three months after his son had died at the hospital after having been evacuated there ill from the front line, Vanderpol, worn out by grief and overwork, on the way from Lyon to his country house suddenly collapsed and died on 18 June 1915, an indirect casualty of the war.

In the months while he lay bedridden after his attack of paralysis in 1900, Vanderpol had taken up again a youthful enthusiasm that the intervening years of adult work had caused him to abandon, an interest in the question of war and peace. Strongly influenced by his deeply held Catholic beliefs, he undertook an extensive reading program in the works of both modern pacifists and those of the church fathers. Ultimately Vanderpol became one of the leaders in the Catholic peace movement in the years immediately preceding the war. In attendance at an international congress of European pacifists at Milan in 1906 and inspired by encouraging responses to the movement from Pope Pius X,

30. Thomas Erskine Holland, *Studies in International Law* (Oxford: Clarendon, 1898), 42 ("St. Augustine was the champion of such a reasonable construction of the Bible as would allow the lawfulness of war, and his views seem to have been generally accepted.") and 43 ("The 23rd causa of the Second Part of the *Decretum Gratiani* contains a discussion *de re militari et de bello*, in which are embedded the theological conclusions of St. Augustine . . ."); Thomas Alfred Walker, *A History of the Law of Nations* (Cambridge: Cambridge University Press, 1899), vol. 1 [only volume published], 204 ("Augustine, who was destined to exercise a predominant influence in the West, adopted more practical counsels.").

31. A good appreciation of Vanderpol's influence and role in twentieth-century just war scholarship is in James Turner Johnson, *Ideology, Reason, and the Limitation of War* (n. 76 below), 3–4, 27–30.

Vanderpol went on the next year to help found and maintain the *Bulletin de la Société Gratry*, later the *Bulletin de la Ligue des catholiques français pour la paix*, to which he often contributed and which had the goal of propagating church doctrine on the law of war. Until the very outbreak of war, Vanderpol worked tirelessly at the *Bulletin* and at building up a Catholic peace movement among the countries of Western Europe.[32]

Vanderpol's friend Emile Chénon, professor of law at Paris, urged him in his studies to devote more attention to the writings of the church fathers, which were little known to his Catholic contemporaries, than to the works of the modern pacifists.[33] In his survey especially of the medieval canonists, of whom until then Vanderpol had known only their names, he was also assisted by the great French legal historian Paul Viollet.[34] As a result of these studies, Vanderpol became convinced that far back into the medieval period, many centuries before Grotius, there had existed a Christian doctrine of a law of war, transmitted as a coherent tradition by successive theologians.[35] While acknowledging the centrality of Thomas Aquinas's role in systematizing a just war doctrine in the *Summa Theologiae*, Vanderpol explicitly maintained that Thomas's doctrine was nothing other than the just war doctrine of St. Augustine, passed down through the intervening centuries.

Vanderpol first made his claim for the Augustinian paternity of such a doctrine in his 1911 *Le droit de guerre d'après les théologiens et les canonistes du moyen-âge*. He wrote in the foreword:

> The goal of the present work is to show that there was in the Middle Ages a doctrine of the law of war, and to make that doctrine known. This doctrine, universally and continually professed by theologians up to the seventeenth century, was regarded by them as being that of the fathers of the church and constitutes an authentic Christian tradition.[36]

---

32. These biographical details are found in Chénon's preface, vii–xxviii, to Vanderpol's *La doctrine scolastique du droit de guerre* (n. 40 below).

33. Vanderpol, *La doctrine scolastique*, xii, xviii.

34. Author's inscription in his presentation copy of *Le droit de guerre d'après les théologiens et les canonistes du Moyen-Âge* (see n. 36 below; property of Purdue University): "c'est vous qui avez guidé mes premiers pas au milieu de ces théologiens et de ces canonistes du Moyen-âge, dont je ne connaissais même pas les noms."

35. Vanderpol, *La doctrine scolastique* (n. 40 below), xviii, xx–xxi.

36. Alfred Vanderpol, *Le droit de guerre d'après les théologiens et les canonistes du moyen-âge* (Paris: Tralin, 1911), I.

Later, in his list of authorities, Vanderpol wrote of Augustine:

> It is in this work [*The City of God*] and in certain of his letters that
> St. Augustine treated the question of war and indicated the principles
> which served as the basis for the doctrine of St. Thomas and for the
> Christian tradition of war during the entire Middle Ages.[37]

The next year, in his book *La guerre devant le Christianisme*, Vanderpol gave
further details on the sources of Augustine's thought and its transmission and
relationship to the works of later authorities.

> [The scholastic doctrine of war] is the only one which has been
> professed in the church from St. Augustine up to the last years of
> the sixteenth century. All the theologians and all the canonists of this
> period, without any exception, made it the basis of their teaching.
> The principles of this doctrine are found in the works of St.
> Augustine, particularly in *The City of God* and in the book *Contra
> Faustum*. The principal passages from these works relative to war
> are reproduced in Gratian's *Decretum*, a fact which demonstrates the
> importance ascribed to them by the church during the centuries
> which preceded their appearance in the *Decretum*.[38]

The great synthesis of Vanderpol's interpretation of the history of a
Christian law of war in the centuries before Gratian, a work that the outbreak
of war forced him to abandon and that was published after his death due to the
efforts of his friend Chénon,[39] a work that became the foundational argument
setting out an Augustinian paternity of the doctrine of just war for twentieth-
century historical scholarship, is his *La doctrine scolastique du droit de guerre*,
published in 1919.[40] In this work Vanderpol attempted a summary statement
of his contention that a Christian doctrine of war had always existed in the
church, a doctrine systematized by various medieval scholastics, who in turn
had based their ideas of just war on the writings of Augustine. In an almost
scholastic manner, Vanderpol first presented an outline of the elements of just
war doctrine, showing throughout by the numerous citations of Augustine
where he thought the wellspring of those elements lay.[41] He then proceeded to

37. Vanderpol, *Le droit de guerre*, VI.

38. Alfred Vanderpol, *La guerre devant le Christianisme* (Paris: Tralin, 1912), 67–68.

39. Vanderpol, *La doctrine scolastique* (n. 40 below), vii, xiv, xxi.

40. Alfred Vanderpol, *La doctrine scolastique du droit de guerre* (Paris: A. Pedone, 1919).

a historical survey, in chronological order, that set out how that doctrine had manifested itself in successive Christian writings. There he wrote of Augustine's writings on war that "[t]hese are the fundamental principles defined by St. Augustine which served much later as the basis for the doctrine set forth by St. Thomas in his *Summa Theologiae*."[42] Later, after showing by nine citations Thomas's dependence on the African Father for the elements of his just war doctrine, Vanderpol went on to conclude:

> It can therefore be said that the doctrine of war contained in the *Summa Theologiae* was for St. Thomas nothing other than an exposition of the doctrine of St. Augustine, an exposition interpreted according to the church's practice in his period.
>
> But since all the texts upon which St. Thomas depended are found in the *Decretum*, and moreover since that work contains nothing in it which could contradict the doctrine of the holy doctor, it could equally be maintained that he simply laid out in a clear and precise form the canonical doctrine of the law of war just as it was taught in his time.
>
> All of which is to say that since two things equal to a third are equal to each other, then the doctrine of St. Augustine, the canonical doctrine and the scholastic doctrine of the law of war are in reality nothing other than one and the same doctrine, more or less developed.
>
> Furthermore, as this question of the law of war was not dealt with by any author in the centuries which immediately followed St. Augustine's death, it is possible to believe that the principles set forth by him were accepted by all and interpreted by the church in the same sense as they were interpreted much later by the canonists of the eleventh and twelfth centuries.
>
> At the very least it can be claimed that from St. Augustine until St. Thomas and—as has been seen in the first part [of the book]—from St. Thomas until the end of the sixteenth century, the only teaching given by the Catholic church on the subject of the law of war conformed to what we have called "the scholastic doctrine of the law of war," that is, to the doctrine developed by St. Thomas in the *Summa* according to the principles set forth by St. Augustine.[43]

41. Vanderpol, *La doctrine scolastique*, 15–158 ("Exposé de la Doctrine").

42. Vanderpol, *La doctrine scolastique*, 196.

43. Vanderpol, *La doctrine scolastique*, 213–14.

Vanderpol's thesis of a more or less consistent Christian law of war stretching from Augustine to the end of the sixteenth century, an argument culminating in the patient and exhaustive synthesis of medieval and early modern authorities detailing such a doctrine in his last great work, exercised an almost immediate magisterial influence among writers on the just war. Vanderpol's interpretation was seconded soon after the publication of his last work by a sort of companion volume to it, the 1920 *L'Église et le droit de guerre*, a volume that featured a posthumous contribution from him. Building on Vanderpol's earlier work and that of other contemporary Catholic pacifists, the authors sought to set out in chronological order the views of the fathers on the *ius belli*.[44] In the preface to that work, the authors explicitly argued that a traditional doctrine of just war, though first explicated by Augustine, went back to the very origins of Christianity.[45] Augustine played a role in this development as "the oracle of succeeding generations, the master of theologians."[46]

Shocked by the horrors of the First World War and by the apparent inability of international law to prevent or mitigate those horrors, even before the war ended a number of writers began to attempt a reformulation of the law, a venture that included a reconsideration of the historiographic interpretation that with Grotius and his successors international law had "escaped from the merely ethical region."[47] In such an intellectual climate, some historians were now prepared to take more seriously the "prehistory" of international law before Grotius. Even as the moral underpinnings of international law were being rediscovered, the first hints of unease with Vanderpol's arguments began to appear.

Both the rediscovery of the Christian roots of international law and a dissatisfaction with Vanderpol's arguments are seen in Geoffrey Butler and Simon Maccoby's 1928 *The Development of International Law*. The authors of this volume at one point admitted that the aftermath of the First World War

---

44. Vanderpol, *La doctrine scolastique*, xxiv.

45. P. Batiffol, Paul Monceaux, Émile Chénon, A. Vanderpol, Louis Rolland, Frédéric Duval, and Abbé A. Tanqueray, *L'Église et le droit de guerre* (Paris: Bloud & Gay, 1920), vi–vii. It should be noted that this strong version of the origins of a Christian *ius belli*, already implicit in Vanderpol, was ignored by later writers, who were largely content with seeking the beginning of the doctrine no earlier than the post-Constantinian church.

46. Batiffol et al., *L'Église et le droit de guerre*, 41.

47. L. Oppenheim, *International Law: A Treatise*, 6th ed. (London: Longmans, Green and Co., 1947), 4, n. 2; Beaufort (n. 51 below), vii, x; Elbe (n. 27 above), 687–88 and notes 169–71. On the "rebirth" of the just war idea in the wake of the First World War, see also Neff (n. 26 above), 285–313.

had "revived a conception [just war] which gives new interest to the musty tomes of Fathers and canonists and scholastic moralists."[48] Augustine here was singled out because he "gave a lead to subsequent Fathers of the Church by a statesmanlike exposition of the passages [of the Bible that could be cited in support of pacifism]." Too, Augustine had expressly sanctioned the profession of arms by Christians.[49] In their discussion of the just war, the authors relied without question upon the texts that Vanderpol had collected in *La doctrine scolastique*. But they went on to say that "[h]is deductions and conclusions, however, have not always been followed."[50]

The Franciscan legal scholar L. J. C. Beaufort explicitly wrote his 1933 *La guerre comme instrument de secours ou de punition* in reaction to "le cataclysme de 1914" and to the tendency of previous historians of international law to minimize the dependency of Grotius upon ancient and medieval authorities.[51] Although Beaufort wanted to see Augustine as not being completely original and as being somehow dependent on Ambrose for his views on war and peace, he thought that the African Father's rigorous argumentation nonetheless rendered him "the pioneer and guide for the generations coming after him."[52] Beaufort admitted that Augustine wrote no systematic work specifically devoted to issues of war and peace and that what can be extracted from Augustine on such matters constitutes incidental references in various works written for other purposes. Such, however, was Beaufort's confidence, or need, regarding Augustine's relevance for the development of international law that it seemed possible despite the lack of a systematic treatise to reconstruct an authentic Augustinian theory "without the aid of forced or arbitrary interpretations."[53]

Though his work was already well advanced when Beaufort's book appeared, Robert Regout was still able to use it in his 1934 *La doctrine de la guerre juste de Saint Augustin à nos jours*, a work that approaches Vanderpol's in terms of its significance for later historians of the just war idea[54] and that by

---

48. Geoffrey Butler, Simon Maccoby, *The Development of International Law* (London: Longmans, 1928), 119.

49. Butler, Maccoby, 108, 109.

50. Butler, Maccoby, 185, n. 1.

51. D. Beaufort, O.F.M., *La guerre comme instrument de secours ou de punition* (The Hague: Nijhoff, 1933), vii, x, 1.

52. Beaufort, 8, 14.

53. Beaufort, 14–15.

54. Regout's influence on later historiography of the just war idea can be seen, for example, in Joan Tooke's *The Just War in Aquinas and Grotius* (London: William Clowes & Sons, 1965), *passim*.

its very title betrayed the author's interpretation of Augustine's role. Regout's book was both an updating, with brief biographical and analytical treatments of successive authorities, of earlier histories of international law before Grotius, especially Carl von Kaltenborn's 1848 *Die Vorläufer des Hugo Grotius*,[55] and to some extent an engagement with Vanderpol's historiographic interpretation of the development of a Christian *ius belli* in all its particularities. Regout's motivations for writing were similar to Beaufort's insofar as he felt that the Great War had set in motion "new currents in the science of international law [that] burst asunder the confining dams of juridical positivism."[56] These new currents opened up to international jurisprudence the long-neglected yet ancient work on the moral criteria of the just war as *ius ad bellum*, as opposed to the hitherto prevailing focus on the laws of war after hostilities had commenced, the *ius in bello*.[57]

While little that Augustine wrote on the subject was new, according to Regout the scope of his arguments and the logic with which he developed his ideas were such as to justify regarding him as having laid "the foundations of a medieval doctrine of the law of war."[58]

> After a period of hesitations and of contradictory arguments, there occurred about the year 400 a crystallization of opinions on war, due especially to Augustine . . . whose ideas, brought to a completion by Isidore of Seville, exercised an absolute dominance (*un empire absolu*) at the beginning of the Middle Ages.[59]

Regout went on to attempt a deeper analysis of Augustine's ideas about war than had been found in earlier works such as Vanderpol's, with their long lists of Augustinian statements organized according to the traditional criteria of just war doctrine, finding a core principle to be Augustine's view of the just war as a means to obtain peace.[60] Regout was quite explicit about the important influence of Vanderpol's work in the historiography of the Christian *ius belli*.[61] But Regout was also critical of Vanderpol's work, arguing, despite "les nobles

---

55. Carl von Kaltenborn, *Die Vorläufer des Hugo Grotius* (Leipzig: Mayer, 1848).

56. Robert H. W. Regout, S.J., *La doctrine de la guerre juste de saint Augustin à nos jours* (Paris: A. Pedone, 1934), 16.

57. Regout, 16–17.

58. Regout, 39.

59. Regout, 15.

60. Regout, 39–44.

61. Regout, 9, 27–28, 30.

aspirations de cet ardent pacifiste,"[62] that his writings had not avoided the risk inherent in the anthologizing of authorities of being false to the original and of ignoring various "nuances d'interprétation."[63]

Buttressed by Vanderpol's exhaustive and seemingly convincing documentation, and by Regout's chronological contextualization of Augustine at the head of an unbroken stream of writers stretching to the present, the proposition that the African Father was the progenitor of the just war idea was taken as axiomatic by later twentieth-century theological and historical writers, and it would be idle to pile up examples of this tendency. In the United States, a good instance of an influential work in this regard is Roland Bainton's 1960 *Christian Attitudes Toward War and Peace*, a historical survey in which Bainton wrote of Augustine's developed code of war that "it continues to this day in all essentials to be the ethic of the Roman Catholic Church and of the major Protestant bodies."[64] In his commentary on the passages on the Catholic church's stance toward issues of war and peace articulated in the *Pastoral Constitution on the Church in the Modern World*, approved at a general congregation of the Vatican II council in December 1965, René Coste similarly wrote of "the unanimous tradition of Catholic doctrine since Augustine (who for his part reflects the view of the major part of the early Church)" and cites in support Regout, among others.[65]

Next to the works of Vanderpol and Regout in terms of its influence on recent scholarship,[66] but ultimately in accordance with their view of the Augustinian paternity of the just war, is the 1975 book *The Just War in the Middle Ages* by Frederick Russell.[67] Russell recognized that the work of his predecessors on the history of the just war lacked analytical depth and had often been written from a nonhistorical perspective, or had been excessively brief in treating the medieval period.[68] He therefore sought to provide a historically

---

62. Regout, 301.

63. Regout, 9–10.

64. Roland Bainton, *Christian Attitudes Toward War and Peace: A Historical Survey and Critical Reevaluation* (New York and Nashville: Abingdon, 1960), 99.

65. *Commentary on the Documents of Vatican II*, trans. W. J. O'Hara (New York: Herder & Herder, 1969), vol. V, *Pastoral Constitution on the Church in the Modern World*, 351, 355, n. 12.

66. A notable instance of Russell's importance in contemporary just war discourse is found in *The Challenge of Peace: God's Promise and Our Response, A Pastoral Letter on War and Peace, May 3, 1983* (Washington, DC: United States Catholic Conference, 1983), 27, n. 31, where Russell's work is listed first among "[r]epresentative surveys of the history and theology of the just-war tradition."

67. Frederick H. Russell, *The Just War in the Middle Ages* (Cambridge: Cambridge University Press, 1975).

68. Russell, vii–viii, 1–3.

contextualized account of the chronological development of the idea that "concentrates upon those theories of the just war elaborated by scholars of the high Middle Ages."[69] Although his focus was on this later period, Russell, following his predecessors, not only maintained that "[t]he die for the medieval just war was cast by St. Augustine"[70] but also devoted several pages to an analysis of the African Father's just war writings.[71] According to Russell, Augustine viewed a just war, when fought without vengeful hatred or sadism, as an act of Christian love exercised against evildoers to stop their wrongdoing and thus hopefully to mitigate their eternal damnation.[72] In Russell's analysis, Augustine elided the categories of crime and sin, making war an acceptable punishment for both and thereby justifying war against both foreign enemies and religious heretics.[73] Despite what seemed to have been the explicit formulations of specific just war criteria, in the immediately subsequent centuries of the early medieval period "[t]he genuine Augustinian opinions in all their complexity were neglected, and even his formula for the just war disappeared,"[74] not to be fully recovered until the appearance of Gratian's *Decretum* around 1140.[75]

In the same year as Russell's book was published there appeared another historical treatment of the just war idea by another American scholar, James Turner Johnson. In his *Ideology, Reason, and the Limitation of War*, the first of a number of books Johnson has written on the just war, he focused on the historical development of the individual elements constituting the classical Western just war tradition. In thus attempting, along with Russell, a more historically nuanced analysis of just war's development, Johnson made explicit what had mostly been implicit in Russell, that such a detailed historical examination revealed serious problems with the narratives and interpretations of Vanderpol and Regout. Johnson argued that the modern just war formulation is constituted of two general legal categories: the *ius ad bellum*, the criteria for determining whether it is justifiable to go to war, and the *ius in bello*, the ethics

---

69. Russell, 1.

70. Russell, 16.

71. Russell, 16–26.

72. Russell, 17; idem, "Love and Hate in Medieval Warfare: The Contribution of Saint Augustine," *Nottingham Medieval Studies* 31 (1987): 108–24. This idea of an Augustinian just war as an act of love is not original with Russell, but is already found, for example, in Herbert Deane's *The Political and Social Ideas of St. Augustine* (New York and London: Columbia University Press, 1963), 164. For another example of this war as love idea, this time applied to the Crusades, see Jonathan Riley-Smith, "Crusading as an Act of Love," *History* 65 (1980): 177–92.

73. Russell, 19–20, 23–26.

74. Russell, 27.

75. Russell, 56.

involved in the fighting itself. Because, as he saw it, medieval theologians and canonists had dealt only with the first category:

> Those authorities who have traced Christian just war theory back to its Augustinian and medieval roots have overlooked one simple yet devastating fact: *there is no just war doctrine, in the classic form as we know it today* [italics in original], in either Augustine or the theologians or canonists of the high Middle Ages. This doctrine in its classic form [incorporating both *ius ad bellum* and *ius in bello*] . . . *does not exist* [italics in original] prior to the end of the Middle Ages.[76]

In thus recognizing that the modern just war doctrine could not be linked in a simple linear fashion back to Augustine, Johnson came close to stumbling upon an important truth, that Augustine, in fact, originated no such doctrine. Yet Johnson was not prepared to go that far. Instead, he argued that Augustine was ultimately responsible for the elements in the *ius ad bellum* tradition, and that the original Augustinian formulations had come down through the ages via the vital intermediation of Thomas Aquinas, a position that Johnson continues to maintain.[77] With the passage of time, perhaps because of the different thematic orientations of his other works, or perhaps simply out of sheer weariness at having constantly to provide nuanced reservations, Johnson in his later works has come increasingly to characterize Augustine plainly as the father of the just war idea.[78]

A similar intellectual trajectory—from initially expressing reservations with the standard intellectual historical narrative to recasting the terms of Augustine's role as progenitor of the idea—seems visible in the important works of David Lenihan on the just war and Augustine. In 1988 in his "The Just War Theory in the Work of Saint Augustine," Lenihan practically undermined the entire house of cards making Augustine the founder of the just war idea . . . but not quite. He began by acknowledging how well established was the scholarly position that

---

76. James Turner Johnson, *Ideology, Reason, and the Limitation of War: Religious and Secular Concepts, 1200-1740* (Princeton: Princeton University Press, 1975), 7–8.

77. Johnson, *Ideology,* 32: "The three main requirements in the *jus ad bellum* of the classic doctrine come straight down from Augustine via Thomas Aquinas . . ." Cf. Johnson, "Just War, As It Was and Is," esp. 16.

78. E.g., *Just War Tradition and the Restraint of War* (Princeton: Princeton University Press, 1981), xxiv, xxix–xxxi; *Can Modern War Be Just?* (New Haven: Yale University Press, 1984), 1; *The Quest for Peace: Three Moral Traditions in Western Cultural History* (Princeton: Princeton University Press, 1987), 57–66; "Just War, As It Was and Is," 14.

Augustine stood at the head of the Christian just war tradition.[79] In evaluating this scholarly consensus, Lenihan did something that it seems to have occurred to few historians to do: he surveyed what Augustine had written on the just war *both* in its original literary *and* historical contexts. What he found through this relatively straightforward exercise was the utter fallacy of attributing to Augustine the origination of the just war idea as commonly conceived. One overwhelming fact alone points clearly to this conclusion:

> Migne's *Patrologiae Latinae* devotes twelve large tomes to Augustine, more than any other writer. . . . In this ocean of words the just war is mentioned in but a few scattered references. . . . The just war theory is clearly a minor aspect of Augustine's work. He did not perceive it as a major problem worthy of the fuller treatment he gave to issues of doctrine such [as] the Trinity, Grace, Original Sin, Predestination and Free Will.[80]

Even within the wide range afforded by this extensive corpus, "Augustine never had occasion to address the subject independently of other concerns."[81] Augustine himself therefore did not fashion what became the just war theory, but was instead made its originator by later writers: "the medieval just war is not a direct descendant, but a mis-interpretation and simplification by the decretalists who failed to see the full Augustinian position with its spiritual complexity."[82]

> It would seem that Augustine has been cast into this position by theologians who, like Thomas Aquinas, answered the moral question of whether it was always sinful for Christians to engage in warfare by ferreting, out of context, small proof texts from Augustine to justify Christian participation in warfare.[83]

Rather than the workaday acceptance of war's realities implied by making him the serene theoretician of just war, Lenihan, in characterizing Augustine's premier work addressing the nature of human society, wrote that "[t]he mood of the *City of God* is somber and resigned, accepting of a flawed and imperfect

---

79. David A. Lenihan, "The Just War Theory in the Work of Saint Augustine," *Augustinian Studies* 19 (1988): 37.

80. Lenihan, "The Just War Theory," 55.

81. Lenihan, "The Just War Theory," 42.

82. Lenihan, "The Just War Theory," 41.

83. Lenihan, "The Just War Theory," 38.

reality, as the necessary consequence of original sin."[84] Taking into account the historical context in which he wrote, Augustine's scattered thoughts on war actually show him to be "on a continuum with the pacifist tradition of the earlier fathers."[85]

Although Lenihan was dismissive of the prevailing narrative of Augustinian paternity of the just war idea, he also argued that "Augustine did recognize the possibility of just wars" and noted that he therefore did allow for wars waged under a legitimate authority for the purposes of defense or punitive redress—all features, incidentally, of the standard just war criteria.[86] As with Johnson, however, a few years later Lenihan explicitly and with little qualification ascribed to Augustine (and to Ambrose before him) the origination of a just war ethic.[87] A comparison of a 1988 remark and a similar comment eight years later seems to reveal a subtle though important shift. Whereas Lenihan had earlier written that later medieval theologians had justified Christian participation in war "by ferreting, out of context, small proof texts from Augustine,"[88] a few years later he wrote "that the Augustinian just war was ferreted out centuries later by the decretists who sought patristic approval of their doctrine,"[89] thus seemingly emphasizing more the presence of a coherent Augustinian idea to be ferreted out. Yet, curiously, the presence of this idea was for a long time conspicuous by its absence, since "after Augustine, the just war went largely ignored for centuries."[90] Curious, too, that neither Russell nor Lenihan drew the obvious conclusion from their observation of this centuries-long silence.[91]

Robert Holmes in his 1999 article "St. Augustine and the Just War Theory" echoed Lenihan in questioning the basis for making Augustine the father of just war, yet was thereby able to come to a conclusion diametrically opposed to Lenihan's on the stance of the African Father toward war. Holmes acknowledged that "[t]he prevailing view is that, at least within Christianity, the father of just war thinking is St. Augustine."[92] He continued:

84. Lenihan, "The Just War Theory," 51.

85. Lenihan, "The Just War Theory," 37.

86. Lenihan, "The Just War Theory," 56–57.

87. Lenihan, "The Influence of Augustine's Just War: The Early Middle Ages," *Augustinian Studies* 27, no. 1 (1996): 78, 79.

88. Lenihan, "The Just War Theory," 38.

89. Lenihan, "The Influence of Augustine's Just War," 76.

90. Lenihan, "The Influence of Augustine's Just War," 55. On Russell's observation of the same phenomenon, see n. 74 above.

91. For Vanderpol's even more curious explanation of this silence, see notes 38 and 43 above.

The extent of his influence is documentable. If that is all that is meant by his being called father of the just war theory (or of the just war tradition, as some prefer to put it), the claim is certainly correct. But if one means more than that, the claim needs closer scrutiny. For although Augustine clearly seeks to justify war, what is less clear is what he offers in the way of original thinking about war, and whether his views hold together in a coherent and consistent fashion. . . . Insofar as the just war theory is thought to provide moral criteria by which to judge whether to go to war (*jus ad bellum*), and how to conduct war once in it (*jus in bello*), there is, I maintain, little of such guidance in Augustine, hence little ground on that score for representing him as the father of the just war theory.[93]

Holmes went on to argue that "[w]hen one looks at the practical import of Augustine's account . . . one finds an acceptance of war, with only the frailest of constraints against entering into it." Holmes thus located Augustine in a tradition that would ultimately lead to political realists of the ilk of Machiavelli and Hobbes.[94] Whereas the incoherence of Augustine's views on war reflected pacifism in Lenihan, for Holmes the same incoherence bespoke an incipient militarism!

How difficult it has become in practice to sustain the proposition of there being a coherent, logical Augustinian just war is seen in the important 2006 book by John Mark Mattox, *Saint Augustine and the Theory of Just War*. Quite understandably given its prevalence in twentieth-century just war literature, Mattox maintains the position that despite "the fact that, of Augustine's 116 extant works, not one of them deals exclusively, or even particularly, with just war," that there is nonetheless detectable in Augustine "a consistent set of premises, which . . . reveal the presence of an underlying, if unstated, theory."[95]

92. Robert L. Holmes, "St. Augustine and the Just War Theory," *The Augustinian Tradition*, ed. Gareth B. Matthews (Berkeley: University of California Press, 1999), 323.

93. Holmes, 323, 324. For a similar assessment at about the same time, see the introduction to *Augustine: Political Writings, Cambridge Texts in the History of Political Thought*, ed. and trans. E. M. Atkins and R. J. Dodaro (Cambridge: Cambridge University Press, 2001), xxiv: "Here [on the question of war] too, Augustine is often seen as an innovator and described as 'the first Christian just war theorist.' In this case, the label is certainly misleading, for at least two reasons. First, no major Christian theologian since the time of Constantine had been a pacifist, and Christians had for a long time taken it for granted that war was permissible. . . . Secondly, Augustine had no systematic theory of what would count as a just war, or a just way of waging wars."

94. Holmes, 338.

95. John Mark Mattox, *Saint Augustine and the Theory of Just War* (London: Continuum, 2006), 4, 5.

Mattox's formulation of an "Augustinian complex" of doctrines, complicated by its origin as an amalgam of neo-Platonic and Christian ideas and influences, in itself demonstrates the intractable resistance of the Augustinian texts to being so systematized.[96] Surprising conclusions can sometimes follow from such a complicated theory, such as the idea that "Augustine finds in Jesus the perfect just warrior."[97]

One would think that theologians might have something to say on the subject of Augustine and the just war, and yet to my knowledge only one writer in recent years has made a sustained effort—an effort, in my opinion, that ultimately falls short—deliberately to integrate a supposed Augustinian just war idea into the African Father's more general theological perspective. Josef Rief in his 1990 *"Bellum" im Denken und in den Gedanken Augustins* proposed that for Augustine—perhaps reflecting a residual Manichaeism, or perhaps a biblically based dualism—*bellum* was a basic principle of the "divine plan of the world" (*göttliche Weltplan*),[98] a perpetual strife discernible not only in the external battles of human warfare, but in the internal human conflict between flesh and spirit.[99] According to Rief, only *boni homines* acting *Deo auctore* are capable of distinguishing the greater from the merely human interests involved in the issues of war and peace and thus of deciding whether it was justifiable to go to war.[100] Rief took as axiomatic the proposition that Augustine had an idea of just war peculiar to himself,[101] but ended up proposing an Augustinian theology of war that does not always seem immediately obvious in the sources.

Clearly something is wrong. By the beginning of the twenty-first century, it was becoming increasingly problematic to view Augustine as the progenitor of a coherent and consistent Christian just war doctrine. The absence in the Augustinian corpus of any systematic treatise or even ephemeral digression devoted to the subject remained the leading embarrassment for the advocates of such a position, and, *pace* Beaufort, it did seem increasingly difficult to construct an Augustinian just war "without the aid of forced or arbitrary interpretations."[102] There was also the disquieting circumstance that up until

96. Mattox, 92–154. I don't share Mattox's confidence that these two strands of influence on Augustine can be easily disentangled.

97. Mattox, 135.

98. Josef Rief, *"Bellum" im Denken und in den Gedanken Augustins*, Beiträge zur Friedensethik 7 (Barsbüttel: Institut für Theologie und Frieden, 1990), 7, 9. Rief even cites the Darwinian struggle for existence in supporting the idea of strife as a basic cosmological principle (15).

99. Rief, esp. 59–67.

100. Rief, 27–33, 73–77, 88–97.

101. Rief, 3, 60: "So unbestreitbar es ist, daß Augustinus vom gerechten Krieg spricht . . ."

Gratian's *Decretum* in the 1140s there was a period of over seven centuries during which Augustine's just war idea as a coherent proposition seems to have utterly vanished from view. Too, it seemed difficult to derive an Augustinian just war idea convincingly from the Father's known theological positions. Was even retributive war an act of love? Was strife a basic cosmic principle? Was Augustine more in line with earlier Christian pacifists, or, despite his expressed distaste for war, was he actually albeit perhaps unwittingly an intellectual father of militaristic realism, the fashioner of a just warrior Jesus? What had seemed a relatively straightforward and uncomplicated proposition in Vanderpol's writings at the beginning of the twentieth century had become by century's end a contradictory and unwieldy tangle of ideas. Especially in the works of Lenihan and Holmes, as well as others, there were intimations that the way to resolve the apparently insoluble issue of the Augustinian paternity of the just war idea was to cut the Gordian knot, and to recognize that Augustine himself never originated a distinctive just war idea, or ever intended to.

A significant step toward this realization was taken in 1983 with Robert Markus's article "Saint Augustine's Views on the 'Just War.'" Markus decried the tendency of writers since Vanderpol to view Augustine's thinking on the matter through the prism of the just war tradition as it had developed since the fifth century. "[Being] conscious that there is nothing that can obscure the true nature of an original thought as radically as the tradition to which it gives rise," Markus proposed "to turn the telescope the right way round" and to view Augustine's thought "in the immediate context of his own intellectual biography."[103] One interpretive criterion distinguished Markus's approach to Augustine's just war writings from that of any previous would-be synthesizer.

> The one thing which has emerged from almost all serious studies of Augustine in the last fifty years or so is that whatever can be said about almost any aspect of his thought is unlikely to be true of it over the whole span of his career as a writer and thinker.[104]

Building upon the conclusions of his earlier groundbreaking study *Saeculum*, Markus went on to argue that the notion, propounded at least since the late nineteenth century, that Augustine had sanctioned a Christian turn away from pacifism was clearly false. Such a shift, insofar as it had occurred at all, had already taken place a century earlier as witnessed by Eusebius of Caesarea,

---

102. Note 53 above.

103. R. A. Markus, "Saint Augustine's Views on the 'Just War,'" *Studies in Church History* 20 (1983): 1.

104. Markus, "Saint Augustine's Views," 2.

among others. "He did not need to check his contemporaries' 'pacifist inclinations'—few of them could have had any."[105] But Augustine *had* in the late 390s shared with contemporaries a certain Christian optimism verging on triumphalism, a conviction that the visible, often violently imposed dominance of orthodox Christianity in the Roman world at that period was nothing other than the fulfillment of biblical prophecy. Thus in the *Contra Faustum*, written at that time and containing important "proof texts" for later just war theoreticians, Augustine could hold something he did not a decade later, that the conversion of kings and submission of peoples to Christianity revealed the continuing and straightforwardly interpretable providential hand of the God of the Old as well as of the New Testament.[106] For by the time Augustine began writing *The City of God*, just war had become a regrettable necessity, a necessary evil that checked greater evils in a human society no longer considered "sacralized" by the mere prevalence of Christianity within it.[107] Markus had thus provided an interpretation that helped explain an apparent contradiction—an apparent contradiction further complicated by earlier synthesizers in their attempts to construct an internally consistent Augustinian just war theory—between Augustine's somewhat offhand acceptance of war in a Christian empire in the *Contra Faustum* and the passionate denunciations of war found later in *The City of God*. The appearance of an irresolvable contradiction between the views expressed in two works written at different times was more real than apparent, because in the interim Augustine had actually changed his mind. Yet in thus revealing and explaining a real contradiction in the writings of Augustine on war, Markus still could not quite bring himself to question the scholarly consensus making Augustine the father of the just war tradition.[108]

In 1983, the same year as Markus's article, in an apparently little-noted early section of his book *Grotius et la doctrine de la guerre juste*, Peter Haggenmacher provided what should have been the final blow to the notion of an Augustinian paternity for the just war. Haggenmacher declared that only by a sort of "optical illusion" can the three conditions for a just war delineated by Thomas Aquinas be seen to be prefigured in Augustine.[109] As Lenihan later argued, it was the excerpting of scattered citations by later medieval canonists

---

105. Markus, "Saint Augustine's Views," 11–12.

106. Markus, "Saint Augustine's Views," 8–9.

107. Markus, "Saint Augustine's Views," 10–11.

108. Markus, "Saint Augustine's Views," 1. I must mention that in a conversation with me in October 2004, Professor Markus seemed open to the argument that Augustine, in fact, did not originate the Christian just war tradition as commonly conceived, and indeed now saw his 1983 article as not inconsistent with such an argument.

and theologians that led to the "artificial construction"[110] imagined by later scholars of an Augustinian just war doctrine.

> We do not doubt that the work of St. Augustine includes many reflections on war, nor that the work demonstrates its familiarity with the Roman notion of just war, nor finally that his work will be decisive for the creation of the doctrine of just war. Rather, we only dispute that his work actually already contained this doctrine.

Insofar as Augustine played any role at all in the elaboration of a just war doctrine, that role was "indirect et passif."[111]

Augustine wrote no treatise *De bello iusto*. Even around 400, when he seemed most well disposed toward the idea of a Christian Roman empire, in one of the very works where this attitude appears and at a place in the work where such a treatment might have logically occurred, Augustine in the *Contra Faustum* explicitly declined the opportunity, characterizing such a discussion as too long and unnecessary for his purpose,[112] and there is not one scintilla of evidence to suggest that Augustine ever wrote such a treatment. Despite the statements of numerous twentieth-century writers, Augustine did not intentionally originate his own idea of just war, a conclusion that can be demonstrated with near mathematical certitude. If it is one's intention, it is of course possible to regard Augustine's statements on war as authoritative, given that such statements formed much of the later medieval synthesis that would ultimately become a just war doctrine. But if one looks at Augustine's statements on war in their original context a picture emerges far different in many key respects from what ultimately became that doctrine.

---

109. Peter Haggenmacher, *Grotius et la doctrine de la guerre juste* (Paris: Presses Universitaires de France, 1983), 13–14.

110. Haggenmacher, 17.

111. Haggenmacher, 13.

112. *CSEL* 25, *Aureli Augustini Contra Faustum*, ed. J. Zycha (Vienna: F. Tempsky, 1891), 22.74, 673: "et de iustis quidem iniustisque bellis nunc disputare longum est et non necessarium."

2

War and Military Service in Early Christianity, and the Constantinian Revolution

I. CHRISTIAN ATTITUDES TOWARD WAR BEFORE CONSTANTINE: TERTULLIAN AND ORIGEN

The most meaningful general statement to be made about early Christian attitudes toward war and participation in it[1] is that no such general statement

---

1. The secondary literature on the question of pre-Constantinian Christian attitudes toward war and military service is considerable and growing; consequently, what follows is summary. Andreas Bigelmair, *Die Beteiligung der Christen am öffentlichen Leben* (Munich, 1902), esp. 164–201; Adolf von Harnack, *Militia Christi: Die christliche Religion und der Soldatenstand in den ersten drei Jahrhunderten* (Tübingen, 1905) (translated by David McInnes Gracie as *Militia Christi: The Christian Religion and the Military in the First Three Centuries* [Philadelphia: Fortress Press, 1981]); James Moffatt, "War," in *Dictionary of the Apostolic Church*, ed. James Hastings (Edinburgh: T. & T. Clark, 1918), 2:646–73; C. John Cadoux, *The Early Christian Attitude to War: A Contribution to the History of Christian Ethics* (London: Headley Bros., 1919); Henri Leclercq, "Militarisme," in *Dictionnaire d'archéologie chrétienne et de liturgie* (Paris: Letouzey, 1933), 11:1, cols. 1108–81; Edward A. Ryan, S.J., "The Rejection of Military Service by the Early Christians," *Theological Studies* 13 (1952): 1–32; Jean-Michel Hornus, *Évangile et Labarum: Étude sur l'attitude du christianisme primitif devant les problèmes de l'État, de la guerre et de la violence* (Genève: Labor et Fides, 1960) (translated by Alan Kreider and Oliver Coburn as *It Is Not Lawful for Me to Fight* [Scottsdale, PA: Herald Press, 1980; cited here]); Anna Morisi, *La guerra nel pensiero cristiano dalle origini alle crociate* (Florence: G. C. Sansoni, 1963), 3–83; W. Rordorf, "Tertullians Beurteilung des Soldatenstandes," *Vigiliae Christianae* 23 (1969): 105–41; John Helgeland, "Christians and the Roman Army from Marcus Aurelius to Constantine," *ANRW* 23, no. 1 (1979): 725–834; John Helgeland, Robert J. Daly, and J. Patout Burns, *Christians and the Military: The Early Experience* (Philadelphia: Fortress Press, 1985); Enrico Pucciarelli, *I cristiani e il servizio militare: testimonianze dei primi tre secoli* (Florence: Nardini, 1987); Hanns Christof Brennecke, "'An fidelis ad militiam converti possit [Tertullian, de idolatria 19,1]?' Frühchristliches Bekenntnis und Militärdienst im Widerspruch?," in *Die Weltlichkeit des Glaubens in der Alten Kirche: Festschrift für Ulrich Wickert zum siebzigsten Geburtstag*, ed. Dietmar Wyrwa (Berlin: Walter

can be meaningfully made.[2] Such an observation is not merely the negativizing expression of a scholarly caveat, but the affirmative revelation of a fundamental characteristic of early Christian statements on the matter, a feature as much revelatory of the nature and structure of the early church as of the diversity of opinion within it. Christian attitudes toward war varied both synchronically and diachronically, sometimes in the latter respect in the same individual. Especially in the case of the earliest period, the impediments to setting out a simple storyline caused by the impossibility of generalization are also compounded by the fact that the relevant texts, with few exceptions, refer to war and military service only casually or obliquely.[3]

The contrary assumption, that there *was* a singular and authoritative Christian attitude toward war, is the central fallacy in Alfred Vanderpol's brave attempt to derive a Christian law of war from his medieval and early modern sources. If one assumes that such a consistent, authoritative body of doctrine existed, then it only makes sense that the doctrine had to have had an originator. Clearly for medieval canonists and theologians the most authoritative voice on matters of war was Augustine, and it was then only a matter of synthesizing an Augustinian system out of the citations made by later writers, and if necessary then further assuming the intention on Augustine's part of originating such a doctrine in the first place.

Finally, as has been the case repeatedly throughout the history of Christian attitudes toward war and military service, from very early the relevant sentiments were expressed in a context of contestation with other Christians,

de Gruyter, 1997), 45–100; John F. Shean, *"Militans pro Deo*: The Christianization of the Roman Army" (Ph.D. dissertation, University of Wisconsin-Madison, 1998); Alan Kreider, "Military Service in the Church Orders," *Journal of Religious Ethics* 31, no. 3 (2003): 415–42; A. D. Lee, *War in Late Antiquity: A Social History* (Malden, MA: Blackwell, 2007); Paul Stephenson, *Constantine: Unconquered Emperor, Christian Victor* (London: Quercus, 2009), 49–61, an excellent survey of attitudes in the pre-Constantinian church, and our sources for knowledge of them. I did not see Stephenson's fine book until after writing most of the present work, but am naturally gratified that his observations closely track my own, as seen here and throughout this chapter.

2. A fact well characterized by Shean (24): "When surveying the opinions of Christian authors on this topic, one is struck by the lack of unanimity on this issue," and Stephenson (49): "To attempt to discern one coherent Christian attitude to warfare in the centuries before Constantine is wrong-headed." This is also grudgingly and fleetingly conceded by Cadoux (118: "Christian conviction in regard to it [viz., the compatibility of Christianity with military service] was never absolutely unanimous."). For a summary statement of the "new [scholarly] consensus" on this and related issues, see David Hunter, "A Decade of Research on Early Christians and Military Service," *Religious Studies Review* 18, no. 2 (1992): 87–94, and idem, "The Christian Church and the Roman Army in the First Three Centuries," in *The Church's Peace Witness*, ed. Marlin E. Miller and Barbara Nelson Gingerich (Grand Rapids: Eerdmans, 1994), 161–81.

3. On the evidentiary problems, see especially Helgeland, "Christians and the Roman Army," 733.

whose opposing views are recoverable either explicitly from their writings or, as is often the case, implicitly from the propositions of their opponents. As a result, succeeding generations were unable to discover a clear and internally consistent view of war as a general phenomenon in the writings of early Christians. Anyone seeking to impose such a singular view on others was reduced to cobbling together a pastiche of authorities whose contradictions had to be smoothed out or obliterated.

One of the handful of early writers who did attack the matter directly is also an early witness to such disagreements with his co-religionists over these very issues of the proper Christian attitude toward the state, war, and military service. In his *De idololatria*, Tertullian complains of Christians who decked their doorways with lamps and laurel-wreaths to honor the emperor, and counters their scriptural justification of "render unto Caesar."[4] He also criticizes the claim that the biblical examples of Joseph and David showed that Christians could hold public office under pagan rulers.[5] Tertullian then logically turns to the question of:

> whether the faithful may become soldiers, and soldiers be admitted to the faith. . . . The divine and the human *sacramentum* [viz., the military oath],[6] the standard of Christ and the standard of the devil, the camp of light and the camp of darkness, are incompatible. One soul cannot be obligated to two masters, God and Caesar.[7]

Here again Tertullian's Christian opponents adduce biblical examples, mostly from the Old Testament, to support their contention that it was licit for Christians to bear arms and wage war. Tertullian counters that when Christ had disarmed Peter he thereby disarmed every soldier.[8]

---

4. Tertullianus, *De idololatria*, trans. and ed. J. H. Waszink and J. C. M. Van Winden (Leiden: E. J. Brill, 1987), 15.1, 3 (50–53).

5. *De idololatria* 17–18 (56–61).

6. On both the military and ecclesiastical *sacramentum*, see Harnack, 33–35 (Eng., 53–55); C. Mohrmann, "Sacramentum dans les plus anciens textes chrétiens," in *Études sur le latin des Chrétiens* (Rome, 1958), 233–44; Helgeland, "Christians and the Roman Army," 739 and n. 52; idem, *Christians and the Military*, 50–51.

7. *De idololatria* 19.1–2 (62). Discussion in Bigelmair, 166–67; Harnack, 59–60 (Eng., 76–77); Cadoux, 108–9; Leclercq, cols. 1124–25; Ryan, 17–18; Morisi, 44–46; Rordorf, 107–12; Helgeland, "Christians and the Roman Army," 738–40; idem, *Christians and the Military*, 22–23; Pucciarelli, 170–81; Brennecke, 82–84; Shean, 42–44; Stephenson, 55–56.

8. *De idololatria* 19.2–3 (62, 63).

Two aspects of Tertullian's discussion here bear emphasis in the context of the present inquiry. First, the arguments of some scholars that Tertullian based his opposition to Christian military service not on any ethical objection to killing in war per se but on the consideration that it was impossible for soldiers to avoid any contact with the pagan religious rites associated with Roman army life cannot in any way minimize Tertullian's categorical rejection of not only military but any public service for Christians.[9] This absolute rejection is echoed years later in his *De corona*, where Tertullian again questioned "whether military service is proper at all for Christians" and clearly concluded that it was not, even coming close to advocating desertion for anyone who converted while in the service.[10] Second, the arguments of Tertullian's Christian opponents show that already by about 200 some Christians had recourse to Scripture to justify their taking part in public life, and in particular cited relevant war-related passages from the Old Testament to support the notion of Christian participation in war.[11] Though Tertullian dismissed this last argument as a bad joke,[12] we see here the first appearance of an idea destined for a long future in Christianity.

Origen was another writer before Constantine who directly addressed the issue of Christian participation in war.[13] To the pagan Celsus's exhortation to Christians to fight alongside the emperor, Origen in his *Contra Celsum* replied that, as with the pagan priesthood, Christians had to keep their hands undefiled from bloodshed so that their prayers for the emperor and his armies might be more effective. In fact, Origen claimed that such Christian prayers aided the emperors in war more than did their armies.[14] Such Christian prayers for the

9. Shean, 44, rightly emphasizes Tertullian's categorical rejection.

10. Q. Septimi Florentis Tertulliani, *De corona*, ed. Jacques Fontaine (Paris: Presses Universitaires de France, 1966), 11 (132–46). Discussion in Bigelmair, 167–70; Harnack, 61–66 (Eng., 78-82); Cadoux, 110–13; Leclercq, cols. 1122–24; Ryan, 18–20; Morisi, 36–44; Rordorf, 113–19; Helgeland, "Christians and the Roman Army," 741–44; idem, *Christians and the Military*, 23–29; Pucciarelli, 181–82; Brennecke, 84–86; Shean, 44–48. Harnack thought that Tertullian outlined as a viable option a third choice, in addition to those of leaving the service or not joining in the first place: that of avoiding pagan contact as much as possible while remaining in the army (67; Eng., 83; echoed in Leclercq, col. 1124). Cadoux, to my mind successfully, casts doubt on whether Tertullian intended this to be a serious option (114): ". . . his third alternative must . . . be regarded as an ironical concession of a bare abstract possibility, which would be obviously impossible in practice, like his concession that a Christian may hold office, provided he has nothing to do with sacrifices, temples, public shows, oaths, judgment of capital or criminal cases, pronunciation and infliction of penalties, and so on."

11. Especially noted by Harnack, 60–61 (Eng., 77–78).

12. *De idololatria* 19.2 (62): "si placet ludere."

13. Discussion in Bigelmair, 170–71; Cadoux, 129–47; Leclercq, cols. 1128–29; Morisi, 53–61; Helgeland, "Christians and the Roman Army," 746–52; idem, *Christians and the Military*, 39–44; Pucciarelli, 130–39; Brennecke, 86–90.

emperor go back to the beginnings of the church.[15] Some idea of their content in Tertullian's day can be derived from his *Apologeticum*, where he declared that:

> we are always praying for a long life for all the emperors, for them to have untroubled dominion, a secure household, strong armies, a loyal senate, a virtuous populace, a world at peace, anything desired by man and Caesar.[16]

It may be impossible for a modern to comprehend fully the extent to which earlier Christians understood such prayers as being far more than the expression of a mere hope, however piously and sincerely voiced.[17] Christian writers repeatedly expressed for centuries thereafter, both in the action of historical narratives and in explicit statements, the idea that prayer, though increasingly only that of the clergy, could actually effect divine intervention in matters of war, and that in the end prayers were more effective in battle than weapons.

Although a strong current of Christian aversion to war and military service is readily apparent in the sources, there is also evidence just as easily found in them of Christians who not only justified war, but who actually served in the pre-Constantinian Roman army. Here again the supposedly "rigorist" Tertullian provides good evidence. In his *Apologeticum*, written about 200, Tertullian thus characterized the rapid spread of Christianity: "Here but yesterday, and already every place of yours we have filled: cities, islands, forts, towns, market-places—even the camp."[18] Even his treatise *De corona*, which explicitly declared military service incompatible with the faith, was itself written in response to the actions of a Christian soldier in the ranks, surrounded by other Christian soldiers, and the possibility and fact of Christian participation in the military are also implicit in Tertullian's very rejection of military service.[19]

There is more evidence on this point. A number of authentic *acta martyrum* as well as inscriptions prove that Christians were already serving in the ranks before Constantine. In addition, both the *acta martyrum* and the inscriptional evidence indicate that these Christians included officers, some of high rank. All this evidence paints a fairly consistent albeit very general picture of Christian

---

14. *Contra Celsum*, VIII.73 (*GCS, Origenes II*, 291).

15. 1 Timothy 2:1-2. See the discussion in Cadoux, 209–11.

16. *Apologeticum* 30.4 (*CSEL* 69, 79).

17. Moffatt (n. 1 above) chides Origen's prayer counsel as being "unreal" (666), and Helgeland, *Christians and the Military*, 43, dismisses Origen's idea as being "unrealistic."

18. *Apologeticum* 37.4 (*CSEL* 69, 88). Also 42.3 (101): "Navigamus et nos vobiscum et militamus."

19. *De corona* 1 (41–50); Helgeland, "Christians and the Roman Army," 765–66.

participation in the military before Constantine. No later than toward the end of the second century, Christians served in the army in numbers large enough to be visible. The recent archaeological find of a Christian place of worship within the fort of Dura Europos in Roman Mesopotamia indicates that by the early third century not only were there significant numbers of Christians in the army, but that to some extent their presence had received at least tacit "official" recognition.[20] In accordance with their growing proportion in the general population of the Roman empire, the proportion of Christians in the army increased thereafter, especially in the late third century, to the point where Christian soldiers are found serving in the emperor Diocletian's military retinue, the *comitatus*, in 295. A sign of pagan nervousness over the enhanced visibility of Christians in the military's highest ranks is the fact that Diocletian was persuaded to purge Christians from the army as an overture to the Great Persecution of 303.[21]

Why, then, despite the seemingly categorical rejection of military service by luminaries of the church such as Tertullian and Origen, did their contemporary Christians nonetheless serve in the army, and in increasing numbers? Certainly there were incentives to do so. Before Caracalla's extension of the right to all free men of the empire in 212, service in the auxiliaries was a way for even the lowliest provincial to secure Roman citizenship, and even afterwards there were real material and social benefits to be gained from military service.[22] Beside these very real inducements must be set the fact that neither Tertullian nor Origen was in a position either to prescribe norms or to effect their enforcement, in a church whose organization was loose even by fourth-century standards, and which besides had learned to keep its head down for fear that attracting too much attention could provoke violence against it.[23] When at the end of the second century even the bishop of Rome, despite supposedly having on his side the bishops of most of the Roman world, could not bring to heel the bishops of the province of Asia over such a fundamental element of Christian practice as the date of Easter,[24] why should we expect the likes of Tertullian and Origen to be any more successful in imposing their views on others concerning an issue on which there was demonstrably nothing approaching consensus, even supposing the unlikely circumstance that any

---

20. Shean, 104; Stephenson, 54–55.

21. Helgeland, "Christians and the Roman Army," 766–97.

22. A. H. M. Jones, *The Later Roman Empire, 284–602* (Norman: University of Oklahoma Press, 1964), vol. 1, 635–36.

23. *De corona* I.4, 5 (49–51).

24. Eusebius, *H.E.* V.23–24 (488–96).

particular would-be Christian army recruit in the provinces, of middling to no education, had so much as heard the name of either one of them?

Since the pattern for subsequent Christian attitudes toward war—insofar as there can be said to *be* a pattern—was set to a considerable extent even in this early period before Constantine, a word must be said about how modern scholarship has approached the issue, as the interpretive schemes in that literature have often tended to cloud or oversimplify how we view the currents of early Christian ideas regarding war. In his 1979 article on Christians in the Roman army before Constantine, John Helgeland attempted to construct a taxonomy of twentieth-century scholarship on the issue of the relationship between Christianity and the military. He argued that such scholarship tended to fall into one of three camps: Roman Catholic, Protestant of a state church background, and pacifist Protestant from a disestablished tradition.[25] As an understandable consequence of the century's two world wars, the discourse in this scholarship as it developed tended to crystallize around one central issue: Was the early church pacifist, or was it somehow accepting of military service and war?[26] After a brief survey of the "hawks" and "doves" on this issue in the scholarship, Helgeland himself tended somewhat to side with the "hawks," finding there to be in early Christianity no unanimity on the question of war or any specific injunction against killing in war.[27]

The full consequences of that lack of consensus for both "hawks" and "doves" aren't always appreciated in the literature. As Helgeland noted, much of twentieth-century scholarship on the matter was informed by primarily theological presuppositions as well as by contemporary concerns regarding the proper stance of Christians vis-à-vis war and the military.[28] There is also the largely unexamined assumption, visible in nearly all the writers cited to this point, that the view of the pre-Constantinian church on war should be determinative for the present.[29] This assumption among some Catholic writers was predicated on the idea of an inerrant tradition on the subject from antiquity that should be equally valid for present conditions, and among some Protestant writers on the idea that the Constantinian revolution defiled the pristine purity of the primitive church, the modern recovery of which would necessarily include a restoration of the church's original pacifist stance.[30] Such positions in

---

25. Helgeland, "Christians and the Roman Army," 725–33. See also now Stephenson, 49.

26. Helgeland, "Christians and the Roman Army," 725.

27. Shean, 10–12.

28. Helgeland, 733.

29. Brennecke, 98, criticizes this historical approach for the determination of present-day ethical norms.

turn depend on a further, questionable, assumption: that there is recoverable a central, normative view of war and military service in the early church.

The approach taken by modern pacifist writers on the subject was largely pioneered by Cadoux, who argued that the words of Jesus bespeak an ethical aversion to war and military service at the core of Christianity, and then went on to assess how "normative" subsequent Christian attitudes were by the extent to which they differed from this original aversion. Cadoux largely concealed any diversity of opinion on this subject, only conceding at one point "[i]f it is allowable to speak at all of a general position taken by the early Church in this matter." Cadoux argued that after Constantine, "[o]fficial Christianity was now committed to the sanction of war."[31] Of course, there was no such general position taken by the early church,[32] it being impossible in any case to see how such a position could have been effectuated, and by whom. Further, since Cadoux wanted to overstate the unanimity of views on war in the early church, he necessarily also failed to appreciate how problematic is his notion of an "official Christianity" after Constantine capable of enforcing a unitary view on the issue of war, and thus failed to appreciate the persistence of pacifistic currents of thought in the church even after Constantine's conversion.

The presence of Christians in the army before Constantine in and of itself proves a lack of unanimity on this issue in the early church, but those writers who have tended to emphasize Christian acceptance of war and military service at that time have the opposite problem of the pacifists in attempting to explain, or explain away, the pacifist-seeming statements of the likes of Tertullian and Origen. The "hawks" here have largely relied on two arguments. First, they contend that these writers were not true pacifists in that their objection to military service for Christians was not the result of an ethically based aversion to the taking of human life, but arose from the conviction that it was impossible for a Christian soldier to avoid having to participate in the pagan religious practices that permeated Roman military life. Second, there have been repeated attempts, especially in the case of Tertullian, to marginalize those who spoke most forcefully against Christian participation in the military.

The work of John Helgeland provides a good recent example of the argument that early Christian opposition to military service was based on religious grounds and not any supposed ethically based pacifism. Of Tertullian

30. Brennecke, 46 and n. 1.

31. Cadoux, 256, 262.

32. Shean, 7, justly notes that "Cadoux's arguments represent the most extreme pacifist position and are the least convincing historically since he assumes that all Christians would have interpreted the faith in exactly the same way."

he wrote that "the question of whether he was pacifist in principle still remains to be answered," and went on to deny "that Tertullian held a doctrinal pacifism."[33] He concluded that:

> [t]here is practically no evidence from the Fathers which would support the argument that the early church denied enlistment on the ground that killing and war were opposed to the Christian ethic . . . [those Fathers who opposed military service for Christians] based their reasons not on ethical but on religious grounds.[34]

Rather than any ethical aversion to bloodshed and war, Tertullian's concern was with the inevitable contamination by the idolatrous practices that a Christian would encounter in the Roman army.[35]

In thus adopting from writers such as Cadoux a definition of pacifism as being ethically based and then failing to find such a phenomenon in the pre-Constantinian church, Helgeland and others state less a discovery than a banal tautology, viz., that modern ethically based pacifism is missing from the premodern world. Allowing for a transposition of terminology, Helgeland and those who argued similarly also perpetuated a distinction popular in early twentieth-century anthropology between higher religion—i.e., ethics—and the fear of ritual contamination characteristic of primitive religions, here early Christianity. Now it has been argued that concern for pollution and the rules attendant to that concern can, in fact, be linked with morality.[36] In any case, a better approach to discovering how at least some early Christians viewed military service lies in examining certain aspects of the religious mentality that informed the arguments of someone like Tertullian, who was less concerned with war as a phenomenon in and of itself than the consequences of individual Christians being connected with it.

When Tertullian was writing in the decades either side of 200, as the themes of various of his works suggest, the number of Christians and the diversity in their status and occupation had grown to the extent that the problems inherent to their living among and working alongside the members of a largely pagan society had become more and more acute.[37] When Christians

---

33. Helgeland, "Christians and the Roman Army," 741.

34. Helgeland, "Christians and the Roman Army," 764, 765.

35. Helgeland, "Christians and the Roman Army," 738–44.

36. Mary Douglas, *Purity and Danger: An Analysis of the Concepts of Pollution and Taboo* (New York: Praeger, 1966) ch.1 and 130, 131.

37. T. D. Barnes, *Tertullian: A Historical and Literary Study* (Oxford: Clarendon, 1971), 93–101.

ate the same food and wore the same clothes as their pagan neighbors, when like and alongside pagans they frequented the forum, the butcher's shop, the bath, the tavern, and the market, there was a very real danger that the normal intercourse of daily life would tend to efface the distinctive identity of a Christian.[38] It is thus no coincidence or contradiction that the very author who sought to convince pagans that Christians were enough like them to be no threat at the same time addressed his fellow Christians on issues of demarcating a distinctive identity consciously set apart from pagan society. It is in the context of this delineation of a separate identity that Tertullian's evident anxiety regarding bodily purity must be viewed, explained by the idea of concern for bodily integrity as a reflex of fears for maintaining the wholeness of one's society, inasmuch as the body is a symbol of society.[39] Viewed in this light, religious contamination can be regarded as anything conceived of as properly belonging to the pagan realm transgressing the carefully delineated boundaries of the Christian group and upsetting the consciously created order within that group, a contamination that can be expressed in terms of bodily elements.

The issue of purity and contamination in the works of Tertullian is too broad and too far afield from the present work to be treated in detail here, but since the mentality that underlay in particular his strictures against Christian participation in the military continues to be found in some currents of Christian thinking for centuries to come, it would repay elucidating some of the broader elements related to the issue of purity and its maintenance that informed his statements on military service. For something of the nature of Tertullian's abhorrence of the idea of Christians in the army can be gleaned from looking at the two bodily symbols he used in this broader context of his descriptions of the pagan contamination of the Christian community: that of blood and of the hand.

Although as a Eucharistic element the blood of Christ conveyed blessing rather than contamination, and Tertullian himself is the source for the statement that "the blood of Christians [as martyrs] is seed,"[40] these two exceptions, both fundamental to Christian identity at that time, demonstrate how central to such identity the symbol of blood had to become in order to overcome its usual association with paganism and death. More typically, Tertullian mocks the pagan who is horrified by the sight of the corpse of someone who has died a natural death and yet in the amphitheater gazes with complacency on mangled bodies smeared with blood,[41] and devotes an entire chapter of the

---

38. *Apologeticum* 42.1,2 (*CSEL* 69, 100–101).

39. Douglas, 116.

40. *Apologeticum* 50.13 (*CSEL* 69, 120).

Apologeticum to the blood shed in the public shows of paganism, in a passage that can still today elicit horror and revulsion.[42] As with their pagan devotees, the unclean spirits, the demons, relish the blood and smoke and carcasses of sacrificial animals.[43] Though as in the Eucharist blood was the source of life, its effusion both signified the evil associated with death and the violation of bodily integrity, the symbolic essence of the pagan contamination of Christian identity.

If blood embodied the potential pagan pollutant of Christian society, the hands were the avenue whereby the contaminant could be communicated across the boundary between Christianity and paganism. In a mixed community where Christians and pagans together sailed, fought, farmed, and transacted business,[44] it was the hands involved in Christians' activities in the pagan world that literally and of necessity touched that world, and thus had to be purified from the consequent contamination, or prevented from participating in certain activities in that world in the first place, lest with defiled hands the Christian return to his society as a carrier of contagion. This concern with the hands as a potential means of contamination is especially evident in Tertullian's *De idololatria*. At one point in that treatise he derides the argument that those who sign an oath (to the gods) as a pledge in obtaining a loan from a pagan do not thereby sin since they did not pronounce the oath aloud, arguing that nonetheless the hand silently conveyed the sinful intent of the soul.[45] At another point Tertullian argues that no Christian should work in the manufacture of idols, since he would thus use the same hands defiled by the making of idols in prayer to God and to receive the Eucharist.

> Nor does it stop with this. The hands of the idol-makers are not content to receive from other hands something which they defile, but they themselves even transmit to others what they have defiled: makers of idols are chosen into the ecclesiastical order. What a crime! The Jews only once laid violent hands on Christ, but the makers of idols ill-treat his body daily.[46]

---

41. *De spectaculis* 21 (*CSEL* 20, 22).

42. *Apologeticum* 9 (*CSEL* 69, 23–27). In the same chapter he explained Christian dietary restrictions as based on the principle "lest we be contaminated by blood" ("ne quo modo sanguine contaminemur").

43. *Apologeticum* 23.14 (*CSEL* 69, 66–67).

44. *Apologeticum* 42.3 (*CSEL* 69, 101).

45. *De idololatria* 23.1–3 (66).

46. *De idololatria* 7.1–3 (32, 33; I use here the translation by Waszink and Van Winden, n. 4 above).

Nor is this concern with hands merely the fetish of an eccentric heretic. In his treatise *On Prayer*, Tertullian mentions the practice among his co-religionists of washing their hands before using them in prayer. Here Tertullian actually plays the rational theologian, arguing "that after baptism hands are clean enough for prayer," and criticizes the practice as an "empty observance."[47] Nonetheless, his incidental mention of this practice proves that a concern regarding hands as liable to contamination and contagiousness from even everyday contact in the pagan world—a concern here to be alleviated by purification—was of general currency in the North African Christianity of Tertullian's time.

In the thought-world of his time, then, the association of blood with paganism and death and the view of hands as embodying the potentiality of the transmission of pagan contagion help elucidate for moderns better than any dispassionate theological consideration or proto-pacifist sentiment the anti-militarism evident in Tertullian's *De idololatria* and *De corona*. Such an interpretation also explains an interesting parallel between the two treatises. In both works Tertullian asks whether a Christian could put anyone in chains, or imprison or torture them. In *De idololatria* he is speaking of what a Christian magistrate would have to do, and mentions just previously that he would have to judge in capital cases; in *De corona* he is speaking of a Christian soldier, and writes just previously of such a soldier having to use a sword in battle.[48] In both cases a Christian with the power of life and death is pictured as acting—thus necessarily using his hands—in a sphere associated with blood, death, and paganism. In a world where the difference between a pagan and a Christian was not immediately evident to the eye, it was all the more necessary that sharp and rigid boundaries be delineated and enforced. In the case of serving in the army or even in public office, the extent of contamination involved in those occupations rendered them impossible as options for Christians. For how could the defilement that necessarily accompanied such occupations possibly be removed, when even the pollution occasioned by the ordinary intercourse of daily life had to be washed off one's hands before prayer? This concern with blood-defilement is as much as anything an affective and traditional rather than purely theological characteristic of early Christianity, and as such persisted into the early medieval period, where it was manifested in penitential literature.[49]

47. *De oratione*, 13, 15 (*CSEL* 20, 188–89).

48. *De idololatria* 17.3 (56, 58); *De corona* 11.2 (135–36).

49. See Kreider (n. 1 above), 423: "It is *killing* [my emphasis] that the *Apostolic Tradition* expressly proscribes." A good example of an early medieval penitential work evidencing concern for blood pollution, including from killing in battle, is the so-called Penitential of Theodore (c. 700), on which see

As to the attempted marginalization of those before Constantine who opposed Christian participation in the military, the pattern was set early by Moffatt. In 1918 he wrote:

> Both he [viz., Tertullian] and Origen after him are the protagonists of the extreme position in the Church which now frankly disavowed the military profession. . . . It is significant that several of the "pacifist" writers, from Tatian onwards, were or became eccentric and heretical. So it was in Tertullian's case . . . his great contributions to the doctrines of Christology and the Trinity . . . are unspoiled by Montanist aberrations. It was not so, however, in the field of ethics.

Moffatt goes on to write of "the fanatical anti-civic repudiation of force voiced by Tertullian and Origen," and writes of Tertullian's *De corona* and *De idololatria* that they reveal "specimens of his special pleading at its best—or at its worst . . . a fanatically anti-social bias," containing "arguments . . . scornful and fantastic."[50]

Bigelmair had already earlier, in speaking of Tertullian's position, written of "the rigorous idealism of the Carthaginian Montanist."[51] But it was Henri Leclercq's depiction of Tertullian's position on war in 1933 that led to the image of the radical heretic on this issue, which still predominates in much of recent scholarship. Leclercq termed Tertullian an extremist ("*ultra*") as well as an innovator. He also insisted that the two treatises in which Tertullian had rejected military service for Christians were written after he had become a Montanist heretic, arguing that *De idololatria* was written after *De corona* and that the later work shows that his more pronounced Montanism led to an even more extreme position on Christians in the army.[52] Later writers in this vein showed less certainty on the relative chronology of *De idololatria* and *De corona*, and on the question of whether Tertullian became more or less rigorous with time, while continuing to link Tertullian's position to his Montanism.[53] Brennecke in his 1997 article provides a good recent restatement and summation of this argument, writing "it is obvious that on this question the African theologian cannot be regarded as representative of the church at the

---

P. W. Finsterwalder, *Die Canones Theodori Cantuariensis und ihre Überlieferungsformen* (Weimar: Hermann Böhlaus, 1929).

50. Moffatt (n. 1 above), 664, 667.
51. Bigelmair (n. 1 above), 180.
52. Leclercq (n. 1 above), cols. 1122–25.
53. E.g., Rordorf (n. 1 above), 106, 119 n. 25.

turn of the third century, but rather as taking a radical position of an outsider" ("eine radikale Außenseiterposition").[54]

On this question of early Christian attitudes toward war and military service, it is difficult to see how one can successfully, from a modern perspective, marginalize the anti-military stance of certain pre-Constantinian writers, even that of the supposedly radical heretic Tertullian. For if the presence of Christians in the army at that time shows that Tertullian's position was not determinative and hence that there was a diversity of opinion on the subject, how can one then turn round and in this diversity of opinions single out Tertullian's as being outside a nonexistent mainstream? Put briefly, *pace* Brennecke, Tertullian's position was not that of an outsider, for on this question there was no inside to be outside of! And one cannot save the view of Tertullian's supposed radicalism on this point by recourse to his being a Montanist heretic, for such a brilliant insight was denied his contemporaries, and only became visible in the blindingly bright sunshine of hindsight.[55] The recent editors of *De idololatria* note that "[i]n his Montanist works Tert[ullian] is by no means always more rigorous than in earlier treatises," and go on to argue that Tertullian's aggressive temperament often led him, depending on the line of argument, to focus on the object immediately before him to the exclusion of all else, thus leading at times even to the expression of contradictory views within the same work.[56] Besides, unless one is or lets oneself be deceived by Tertullian's ironical concession in *De corona* to those who convert to Christianity while in the army, there is really no difference, argue the editors, between Tertullian's stance in *De idololatria* and in *De corona*: in both he is equally and utterly intolerant of Christians serving in the military.[57] Taking into consideration the diversity of opinion among pre-Constantinian Christians on the question of military service, as well as the anachronistic special pleading of modern writers who seek to marginalize those who utterly rejected such participation, the idea that Tertullian and Origen were on the fringes of a nonexistent center seems insubstantial at best.

The interpretations of both "hawks" and "doves" of a set of interrelated ancient church orders, the texts of which are attested in translations of a much later date into various Eastern vernaculars and in part in a Latin palimpsest

54. Brennecke (n. 1 above), 83.

55. On this, see the remarks of T. D. Barnes in his *Tertullian* (n. 37 above), 83: "Montanists and Montanism were still acceptable in 203, perhaps a full decade after the bishop of Rome condemned them. And they remained acceptable for some time beyond 203."

56. Waszink and Van Winden (n. 4 above), 11.

57. Op. cit., 271. On Tertullian's irony here in *De corona*, see n. 10 above.

of the late fifth century, provide yet another apt illustration of the special pleading and contradictions that often bedevil the scholarly discussion of early Christian attitudes toward war. Some of this material has been traced back to a putative Greek work titled the *Apostolic Tradition* and attributed to Hippolytus of Rome in the early third century. Although scholars in recent decades have understandably become more skeptical as to questions of authorship and even whether there was ever an original document as such by that name, there remains broad agreement that some third-century material can be found in some of these texts, especially in the so-called Egyptian church order.[58] Among the list of occupations forbidden to Christians in this third-century material was that of soldier. A Christian soldier was told that he could not kill a man and had to refuse an order to do so. He could not swear the military oath, and would be rejected if he did. Anyone already a Christian who wanted to join up was to be cast out as having thereby shown contempt for God.[59]

Certainly any interpretations of the origins, dates, and interrelationships of such a set of texts, let alone determination of their exact purpose and authoritativeness, necessarily to some extent must always partake of speculation and thus would justify the wary tread of any student seeking to penetrate such a maze. Such necessary caution has not prevented the "hawks" and "doves" from making sweeping generalizations regarding what the ancient church orders do and do not tell us about early Christian views of the military. On the pacifist side, Cadoux argued that the wide diffusion of these texts and their authoritativeness meant that the injunction against Christians serving in the military "was widely held and acted on in the Churches up and down Christendom," and Hornus even regarded the *Apostolic Tradition* as "the basic disciplinary law of the primitive Church."[60] It is understandable that pacifists would tend to emphasize the authoritativeness of texts that support their contentions. Unfortunately, the state of the evidence does not permit much to be said about how such texts could have acted authoritatively, especially

58. Recent comments with bibliography on the ancient church orders are found in C. Jones, G. Wainwright, E. Yarnold, and P. Bradshaw, *The Study of Liturgy* (New York: Oxford University Press, 1992), 87–90; Allen Brent, *Hippolytus and the Roman Church in the Third Century* (Leiden: E. J. Brill, 1995); Alan Kreider, "Military Service in the Church Orders" (n. 1 above), 415–42; Susan Weingarten, *The Saint's Saints: Hagiography and Geography in Jerome* (Leiden: E. J. Brill, 2005), 127 and n. 160. My thanks to Susan Weingarten for providing me with these references. The relevant texts are edited in *La tradition apostolique de saint Hippolyte*, ed. B. Botte (Münster: Aschendorff, 1963), and there is an English translation by Gregory Dix, *The Apostolic Tradition of St. Hippolytus* (London: SPCK, 1968).

59. Botte (previous note), 16 (36).

60. Cadoux (n. 1 above), 128; Hornus (n. 1 above [English translation cited here]), 167.

in view of the evident fact that such prohibitions seem to have been widely ignored by the many Christians joining and serving in the military in the course of the third century.[61] Among the "hawks," some embarrassment is visible regarding how best to explain such early pacifistic sentiments. In his 1979 article on "Christians and the Roman Army," Helgeland dealt with the issue largely by ignoring it, devoting only two, somewhat confusing paragraphs to the matter.[62] Perhaps realizing this to be insufficient, in the 1985 book on *Christians and the Military* Helgeland employed a strategy of minimalization and marginalization that dates at least as far back as Bigelmair, who associated the texts in question with rigorist "Tertullianist" circles of uncertain—and probably relatively little—general influence in the church as a whole.[63]

I bear here no brief for pacifism. Although I have devoted more space to a critical examination of the opponents rather than the proponents of the pacifist interpretation, this is due on the one hand to the relative ease of refuting the overly broad claims of authoritativeness for Tertullian and those like him made by pacifists. On the other hand, the special pleading of the pacifists' opponents often arguably has more to do with the longstanding and today well-nigh orthodox current of interpretation that would tend to put in the forefront of Christian thought at this period those ideas and individuals, including Augustine, that seem most to harmonize with later church doctrine. It has been shown, however, that such an ahistorical approach does not get us very far in understanding, as it both leads us to marginalize that which was not then marginal and to misconceive the very material that seems to support such an interpretive approach. Such an ahistorical approach also posits a false distinction between ethics and fears of idolatrous contamination in the early Christian community, since across cultures and times pollution rules are seen buttressing and enforcing moral prohibitions.[64]

This section ends as it began, with an emphasis on the plurality of Christian views toward war and military service in the pre-Constantinian church. It is probably too schematic to conceive of these views as distinct and separately progressing currents of thought, since not only did Christians of different minds necessarily interact with each other on this point of contention as on others, but in the case of Tertullian someone can be seen in one treatise emphasizing Christian participation in the military[65] and in others categorically rejecting

---

61. A theme in Kreider (n. 1 above), *passim*, esp. 434: "We cannot know what authority the *Apostolic Tradition* and the subsequent church orders had in the churches."

62. Helgeland, "Christians and the Roman Army," 752.

63. Bigelmair (n. 1 above), 171; Helgeland, *Christians and the Military*, 35.

64. Douglas (n. 36 above), 130–40.

such participation.[66] We must certainly on this question expunge any notion of a single, authoritative view of the matter in the early church: no one current of thinking can be thus privileged above any other. That said, it is also notable that where in Tertullian, Origen, and the ancient church orders we do have explicit pronouncements on the question of whether Christians can serve in the military, the answer is uniformly and categorically negative. In the case of the church orders, those who question the relevance of those texts for this discussion because of the post-Constantinian date of some of them can be accused of looking in the wrong end of the microscope. However we may want to conceive of the authoritativeness of the ancient church orders in practice, the continued copying and revision of them into the fifth century and later shows that at the very least claims were being made then for their authoritativeness. Their preservation also illustrates a tendency not to be ignored or minimized, that pacifistic currents of thinking persisted in the church up to the time of Constantine, and beyond.

II. The Constantinian Revolution

As it happens, an excellent example of the early Christian pacifistic strain of thought is seen in a work written during the very period of Constantine's reign, a work authored by an individual who may even have exercised some influence at Constantine's court.[67] Sometime in the latter years of the first decade of the fourth century, while the Great Persecution still raged, the Christian rhetorician Lactantius wrote his *Divine Institutes*, a work in which he continued the trend in apologetic pioneered by his fellow African Tertullian of aiming less at a defense of Christianity than at a thoroughgoing critique of pagan religion and society.[68] The pagan philosopher Carneades, in seeking to expose the insecure foundations of common conceptions of justice, had argued for the incompatibility between the inherent wisdom of self-preservation and the demands of justice, which in certain circumstances can amount to folly. If a shipwrecked sailor takes a floating plank from a weaker man or if a soldier in a routed army takes a horse from a wounded fellow-soldier, they have wisely saved themselves but acted unjustly; if they refuse to save their own lives at the expense of the lives of others, they have acted justly but foolishly.[69] Lactantius

---

65. *Apologeticum* 37.4; 42.3 (*CSEL* 69, 88, 101).

66. *De idololatria* 19 (notes 7, 8 above) and *De corona* 11 (note 10 above).

67. An argument in Elizabeth DePalma Digeser, *The Making of a Christian Empire: Lactantius and Rome* (Ithaca, NY and London: Cornell University Press, 2000).

68. On the chronology for Lactantius, see now Barnes, *Constantine*, "Appendix A: The Career of Lactantius," 176–78.

countered that the truly just man, i.e., a Christian, would never find himself in such a circumstance to begin with, since the truly just are enemies to no one and want nothing of the possessions of others. "For why would he put to sea, or what would he whose own land suffices for him want from another land? Why would he in whose heart dwells perpetual peace with all men wage war and get entangled in the furious passions of others?"[70]

Lactantius also attacked the very notion of patriotism. The poet Lucilius had written that it was a virtue to put the interests of the *patria* before those of one's family or of oneself, and to defend good men against the wicked.[71] But Lactantius argued that since good men are as often as not vanquished in war, it was no virtue to defend the good against the wicked, because true virtue cannot be subject to the vagaries of chance. Putting the interests of one's country first is a "virtue" that only comes into play when there exists discord among men. Anything advantageous to one's own country in such a circumstance is necessarily disadvantageous to other states and peoples; expansion of one's territory at the expense of others, increase of power, and the imposition of tribute are no virtue, but virtue's overthrow. For not only are the bonds of human society in such situations torn apart, but justice herself takes flight wherever there is the flash of arms.[72]

Lactantius came out most directly against Christian participation in war in the context of an attack on the gladiatorial games of the arena. Such games, according to Lactantius, should be abolished, as they are an incitement to vice and corruption. Anyone who enjoys seeing even deservedly condemned criminals die in the arena pollutes his conscience as much as if he were to witness and participate in a murder committed in secret. How can they be considered pious and just men who not only demand the death of the condemned as they lie prostrate begging for mercy, but even call for the fatally wounded to be butchered with repeated strokes?

> So it is not appropriate for those who try to keep to the path of justice to be complicit in this public murder. For when God forbids killing, He not only prohibits us from killing by stealth (*latrocinari*), which is illegal even according to the public laws, but also admonishes us not to do things which are nonetheless considered legal among men. Thus the just man, whose true service is justice herself, is not

69. *Div. Inst.* V.16 (449–52).
70. *Div. Inst.* V.17.11–12 (453–54).
71. *Div. Inst.* VI.5.3 (495).
72. *Div. Inst.* VI.6.12–24 (501–4).

permitted to serve as a soldier, or indeed to accuse anyone of a capital crime, because it makes no difference whether you kill with a sword or a word, since it is killing itself which is prohibited. Therefore no exception whatsoever should be made regarding this commandment of God, in that it is always wrong to kill a human being, who by God's will is a sacrosanct creature.[73]

Here Lactantius, like a modern pacifist, explicitly links his anti-military stance to the biblical commandment "Thou shalt not kill," which in his mind constitutes a total and absolute rejection of killing of any sort.[74] As in Tertullian, Origen, and the third-century church orders, there can be no question about Christians fighting in war.

Less than a decade later—perhaps much less—Lactantius wrote *On the Deaths of the Persecutors*, a work in which he described with obvious relish the deaths of the emperors who had authored the persecutions of Christians, especially those responsible for the Great Persecution.[75] The writer who had decried the inhumanity of the gladiatorial games now dwelt at length on the last days of Galerius, as his stinking body was consumed internally by worms, and made sure to stress the terrible and painful nature of the death of Maximin Daia.[76] The writer who had argued that the defense of the good against the wicked was no virtue, and that successful leadership in war could not be reconciled with true piety,[77] now praised his hero Constantine's *industria militaris*.[78] The writer who had denied any effective human agency in the obtaining of divine favor in battle and who had emphasized the role of superior numbers in victory now described the decisive battle between Licinius and Maximin Daia in terms of a contest between Christianity and paganism, in which Licinius obtained a heaven-sent victory for his smaller army after his soldiers had chanted a thrice-repeated prayer to "summus Deus."[79] The writer who had objected to the execution of even guilty criminals as a violation of the sacrosanctity of man now complacently reported the executions of Maximin Daia's supporters in the East.[80] At one point in the *Divine Institutes* Lactantius

73. *Div. Inst.* VI.20.15–17 (558).
74. *Div. Inst.* VI.20.9–17 (557–58).
75. Lactantius, *De mortibus persecutorum*, ed. and trans. J. L. Creed (hereafter *DMP*) (Oxford: Clarendon, 1984). On the date, intro., xxxiii–xxxv.
76. *DMP* 33, 49 (50–53, 74/75).
77. *Div. Inst.* V.10.1–9 (429–31).
78. *DMP* 18.10 (28/29).
79. *DMP* 45.7–47.4 (66–69).

had criticized the Romans for so admiring the ability of regal prowess to work widespread harm as to think that brave and warlike leaders were to be found amidst the very assembly of the gods, and for believing that:

> there is no other way to immortality than to lead armies, to devastate the territories of other peoples, to destroy cities, to overthrow towns, to slaughter free peoples or enslave them. In fact, the more of humanity they have oppressed, plundered and killed, the more noble and glorious they think they are: captivated by the empty illusion of glory, they term their crimes a virtue. . . . If anyone has killed one man, he is considered defiled and wicked, nor do they think it right for him to be admitted into the earthly house of the gods. But he who has slaughtered countless thousands, who has flooded fields with blood and fouled the very rivers, he is not only admitted into the temple, but even into heaven.[81]

Yet now only a few years later the same Lactantius wrote in triumphalist tones that in the battle that Licinius had won through divine favor, Maximin Daia's

> army was cut to pieces without resistance, his large and powerful legionary force mown down by a handful of men . . . as if they had come not to fight, but as victims destined for slaughter, the supreme God delivered them to their enemies to be butchered.[82]

There is yet more evidence of a change with Lactantius. Some years after the composition of *On the Deaths of the Persecutors*, and at least a decade after writing the *Divine Institutes*, Lactantius summarized his *magnum opus* in his *Epitome Divinarum Institutionum*.[83] In the *Epitome*, there is nothing on the wickedness of war leaders and their responsibility for widespread havoc and slaughter. In the *Epitome* Lactantius does repeat the examples from Carneades of the shipwrecked sailor and the fleeing soldier in arguing for the incompatibility

80. *DMP* 50 (74–77).

81. *Div. Inst.* I.18.8–10 (68). Here at times I have liberally borrowed from all three English translations of the *Divine Institutes*, those being that of the Ante-Nicene Fathers series, vol. 7, 31 (trans. William Fletcher); *The Divine Institutes*, trans. Sr. Mary Francis McDonald, OP, *The Fathers of the Church*, vol. 49 (Washington, DC: Catholic University of America Press, 1964), 72; and *Divine Institutes*, trans. Anthony Bowen and Peter Garnsay, *Translated Texts for Historians*, vol. 40 (Liverpool: Liverpool University Press, 2003), 100–101.

82. *DMP* 47.2, 3 (69; Creed's translation).

83. *L. Caeli Firmiani Lactanti Epitome Divinarum Institutionum*, CSEL 19, 673–761 (hereafter *Epit.*).

of justice and wisdom.[84] But in the next chapter Lactantius refutes the argument without recourse to the idea that Christians would not be fighting wars in the first place.[85] In *Epitome* 58, as in the earlier work in the context of criticizing the public games, Lactantius asks: "What is as horrible, as ugly as the slaughter of a human being?" Again as in the earlier work, he goes on to mark the spectator as equally complicit in the public murder of a defeated gladiator. But in the *Epitome* Lactantius then immediately proceeds to criticize the vices of the stage,[86] whereas in the *Divine Institutes* the criticism of the theater is preceded by the rejection of military service for Christians, and an attack on the practice of infanticide.[87] It is true that in *Epitome* 59 Lactantius returns to the issue of killing. "Not killing is an old commandment, which should not be understood as though we were enjoined to abstain only from murder, which is even punished by the public laws." But rather than as in the *Divine Institutes* proceeding directly to the prohibition of Christian military service, Lactantius only repeats the injunction against accusing anyone of a capital crime ("nec verbo licebit periculum mortis inferre") and his critique of infanticide, nowhere repeating his original condemnation of all killing whatsoever.[88] Of course, it could be argued that the summary nature of the *Epitome* sufficiently explains these omissions. But that there was deliberate intent involved here is indicated not only by what Lactantius omitted, but by what he added. Whereas in the *Divine Institutes* he had argued that patriotism is no virtue,[89] in the *Epitome* he writes that "if you are fighting for your country, courage is a good thing."[90]

Between the years of Lactantius the pacifist in the *Divine Institutes* and Lactantius the apologist for Constantine's wars in *On the Deaths of the Persecutors* and the *Epitome* there lie the dramatic years of the emperor's rise to supremacy in the West of the empire and his battlefield conversion to Christianity. Despite Constantine's turn to the Christian God and his decisive intervention on behalf of his church, the example of the first Christian emperor had surprisingly limited purchase in later centuries on the imagination of writers on royal power and war. It would not be Constantine, but Theodosius I who would become for Christian writers of his own time and later the model of a Christian prince in war and peace. It is rather the changes Constantine effected—often, it would

84. *Epit.* 51 (56), 730–31.
85. *Epit.* 52 (57), 731–33.
86. *Epit.* 58 (63), 741–43.
87. *Div. Inst.* VI.20.15–26 (558–60).
88. *Epit.* 59 (64), 744.
89. *Div. Inst.* VI.6.18–22 (502–3); note 71 above.
90. *Epit.* 56 (61): "et sicut fortitudo, si pro patria dimices, bonum est."

seem, as a result of his personal, direct initiative—in the ideology, institutions, and cultural practice associated with the Roman legitimation of war that are relevant to this study, for those changes resulted in an enduring political context for "official" Christian affirmations of the wars of the state. It is telling that the first wars so sanctioned were civil wars.

In turning to the Christian God for success in war, Constantine was very much a man of his age, as even the persecutors in their edicts linked the favor of the gods with the public weal and success.[91] Whatever may be made of the differing stories of the battlefield conversion, the stories do represent an authentic impression of Constantine the visionary, a man who also loved "allusions, riddles, and secret messages in poetry and art."[92] Constantine also actively managed and doubtless at times personally initiated themes in the products of an ongoing, sophisticated, inventive, and more or less effective propaganda "machine" presenting the official image of his regime, including much regarding Christianity and war.[93]

Constantine the visionary and the dexterity of his regime's propaganda are both evident in a speech delivered by a Gallic panegyrist in 310. The speech made two bold assertions in the service of Constantine's current political needs. First, it was claimed that Constantine was actually descended from the third-century emperor Claudius, who had inflicted a crushing defeat on barbarian invaders. Second, it was said that Constantine had recently seen a vision of Apollo accompanied by the goddess Victoria.[94] Constantine was now advertising his rule as deriving its legitimacy from sources independent of and more powerful than those of his imperial rivals. Not only could he stake a claim superior to any other in terms of hereditary right, he was also now declaring that his rule was directly favored by a god, a god who also promised Constantine victory. This twofold assertion of divine support and the bestowal of divine *victoria* is neatly exemplified in the appearance on Constantine's coinage from this period of Sol Invictus, whose very name comprises the linkage of god and victory. Thus already two years before his showdown with Maxentius, Constantine was advertising his closeness to divinity and his consequent possession of *victoria*'s "lucky star."[95]

91. H. A. Drake, "The Impact of Constantine on Christianity," in *The Age of Constantine*, ed. Noel Lenski (Cambridge: Cambridge University Press, 2006), 122–23.

92. Noel Lenski, "Introduction," *The Age of Constantine* (previous note), 4.

93. T. Grünewald, *Constantinus Maximus Augustus: Herrschaftspropaganda in der zeitgenössischen Überlieferung* (Stuttgart, 1990), *passim*; and recently Barnes, *Constantine*, 2–6, 17, 61–63, 72–74, 82, 100–102, 105.

94. Nixon and Rodgers, 248; Barnes, *Constantine*, 74–80.

A final contest between Constantine and Maxentius over the rule of the West had been in the cards since they had both become emperors in 306. In the years since, Constantine's adroit diplomacy and propaganda had backed Maxentius into an alliance with the Eastern emperor Maximin Daia, much hated and feared by the Christians for his persecuting zeal. In 312 Constantine assembled a relatively small but mobile army and invaded northern Italy. The morale of his men must have soared as they marched to victory after victory against Maxentius's forces. In the fall Constantine, moving with a celerity that bespeaks a growing confidence in divine favor, suddenly advanced to Rome.[96] With a flair for the dramatic, at this point Constantine now announced to his soldiers encamped outside of Rome that he had been told in a dream to mark the *chi-rho*, the sign of the Christian God, on the shields of his men. In his account written two or three years later of the battle of the Milvian Bridge on 28 October 312, Lactantius told how the hand of God hung over the field and inspired terror in the army of Maxentius, who drowned in the Tiber in the ensuing defeat and rout. At a stroke, Constantine had become the undisputed master of the West.

If the changes Constantine initiated in the next few months were judged solely by their effects in the spheres of Christianity and war, for that reason alone what his victory began can be called revolution, or else nothing can.[97] Constantine himself drove the revolution, a politician shrewd enough to know where to "make haste slowly," and in what areas to press ahead, and where there was no compromise possible. In the last category falls his Christianity, for while the emperor with deliberate ambiguity continued for some years in documents to refer to his divine patron as "the Divinity" (*divinitas*), his dexterous propaganda machine immediately sought to maximize the effect of his victory, and to emphasize his connection with that victory's ultimate source. From the time his triumphal procession, led by Maxentius's severed head aloft on a pike, entered the city the day after the battle, the victor let it be known that he owed his success to no pagan god but to the High God of the Christians, to whom he offered up a prayer of thanksgiving as the author of his victory.[98]

95. Barnes, *Constantine and Eusebius*, 35–37; Noel Lenski, "The Reign of Constantine," in *The Age of Constantine* (n. 91 above), 66–68; Grünewald (n. 93 above), 50–61.

96. On Constantine's growing confidence in divine patronage at this point, see Stephenson (n. 1 above), 134.

97. The Constantinian revolution in its religious aspects became especially visible in the East after Constantine's conquest in 324, as Barnes has again argued, with new evidence, in *Constantine*, 16, 107–43.

98. *VC* I.39.3 (36); Barnes, *Constantine and Eusebius*, 44–47; idem, *Constantine*, 80–83.

Military was followed by political success. After a speech confirming the body in its traditional prerogatives and forgiving its members who had supported Maxentius, the Senate decreed Constantine "Maximus Augustus." Sometime later, a statuette of Victoria was consecrated in Constantine's honor in the senate-house.[99]

In January 313 Constantine left Rome for northern Italy and a summit with Licinius, his Balkan ally against Maximin Daia of the East, the last of the persecutors. The allies at Milan in February announced a political and religious program that was diplomatically sealed by a marriage alliance. Persecution was to end, the Christians to regain lost property, and all religions were to be tolerated. From Milan Licinius marched east to confront his rival, who reportedly on the eve of battle vowed to Jupiter that if victorious "he would obliterate and utterly destroy the Christian name."[100] Perhaps for the first time, though certainly not the last, Christianity became entangled with the politics of civil war in the fourth-century Roman empire. Pagan and Christian soldier alike may have prayed to the High God for victory, and Licinius after his victory may have massacred the loser's supporters in the East more for being on the losing side than for being persecutors, yet Christians such as Lactantius might be forgiven for seeing the just judgment of their God in the defeat and death of Maximin Daia and his persecuting followers.[101] In any case, the effect on the church in the East was immediate and electric: "now henceforth a day bright and radiant with rays of heavenly light, overshadowed by nary a cloud, shone down upon the churches of Christ throughout the whole world."[102] Surely it is a historical irony that the one battle that more than any other assured the success of the Christian cause was won not by Constantine but by his ultimate pagan rival Licinius.

During the winter of 312/313 Constantine issued a series of enactments, not all of which survive, that sought to define and elevate to a privileged status the legal position of the church as a corporate entity in the Western provinces.[103] Of particular relevance for this study is the presumption that it is at about this time, if not earlier, that the emperor decreed or in some manner effectuated the immunity of Christian clergy from military service, thereby

---

99. Barnes, *Constantine and Eusebius*, 46: Grünewald, 86–92. On Constantine's adoption of *invictus* as part of his imperial titulature, Stephenson (n. 1 above), 138f.

100. *DMP* 46.2, 66/67.

101. *DMP* 52, 76–79.

102. *HE* X.1.8 (76–79).

103. Barnes, *Constantine and Eusebius*, 50, on the series of laws issued by Constantine at this time and the fact that not all survive; also, idem, *Constantine*, 131–36.

granting the clergy the same immunity traditionally reserved for the pagan priesthood. The closest we come to such a statement is probably in a letter in March 313 from Constantine to Anulinus, the proconsul of Roman Africa. In it the emperor gave to the African clergy immunity from public liturgies (*munera civilia* such as serving in city government, collecting taxes, or providing public entertainments), and it can be safely presumed that he conferred the same benefit on all the clergy in the areas he then ruled.[104] It seems prima facie unlikely that Constantine would have provided such a benefit to the Christian clergy without also granting them immunity from the most onerous and personally dangerous public service, that of serving in the military. It may be that such a law, if one ever existed, does not survive because the issue of Christian clergy serving in the military had not been pressing even under pagan emperors, let alone Constantine, whereas the issue of clerical civic immunities continued to bedevil Constantine's successors.[105]

Nonetheless, that Constantine at about this time granted exemption from military service to the clergy is suggested by canon 3 of the Synod of Arles on 1 August 314, a meeting that the emperor himself summoned and at which he was present. The canon reads: "Concerning those who throw down their weaponry in peacetime, it has been decided that they are to be excluded from communion."[106] For centuries there have been scholars who have struggled to interpret this canon in some way other than what seems its plain meaning, even seeking to emend "in pace" to "in bello," a reading with literally marginal manuscript support.[107] In 1935 Carl Erdmann went so far as to deny the canon's authenticity.[108] Now there can be little doubt that the canon concerns Christians who, as soldiers, renounce the profession of arms. Further, as noted by Helgeland, the proposed reading "in bello" would have been superfluous, since Roman military law already covered such an eventuality, prescribing death in such instances.[109]

---

104. *HE* X.7 (891). *Cod. Theod.* XVI.2.2 of 21 Oct. 319 (835), directed to the *corrector* of Lucania and Brittia [?], seems to preserve just such another grant of immunity to the clergy of that region *ab omnibus omnino muneribus*.

105. *Cod. Theod.* XVI.2 (835–52).

106. *Concilia Galliae*, ed. C. Munier, *CCL* 148, 9: "De his qui arma proiciunt in pace, placuit abstineri eos a communione."

107. On the scholarly discussion before the twentieth century, see C. J. Hefele, *Histoire des Conciles*, I1 (Paris, 1907), 282–83 and notes. On the manuscripts, *CCL* 148, 9 *apparatus*.

108. Carl Erdmann, *The Origin of the Idea of Crusade*, trans. Marshall W. Baldwin and Walter Goffart (Princeton: Princeton University Press, 1977), 5, n. 4. For a good later discussion, Jean Gaudemet in *SC* 241, 48–9 and notes.

109. Helgeland, 806 and n. 388.

Inasmuch as the canon seems to concern Roman military discipline, it does seem to fit with evidence indicating serious problems with disciplinary issues in the army in these years of violent persecutions and recurring civil war. Diocletian just before the Great Persecution had required all soldiers to sacrifice on pain of dishonorable discharge or worse, thus abrogating a century-old "policy" tacitly allowing Christians to serve in the army.[110] Besides the consequent executions of Christian soldiers recorded in *acta martyrum*, one must presume some further turmoil in the ranks corrosive to discipline, as soldiers of various grades were themselves forced—or aided others—to compromise their religion or in some way to evade compliance in order to remain in the army. More to the point, it is clear that canon 3 of the Arles synod, with the expression *in pace*, is only explicable in the context of Christian soldiers rejecting *any* service in the military, in conformity with the longstanding pacifistic current prohibiting such service, as indicated by the near contemporary *Acta Marcelli*, which recounts how the centurion Marcellus was executed in 298 for throwing down his military insignia because of his Christianity. The same text also suggests that the term *arma proiciunt* of the Arles canon must be understood as involving some act symbolizing the renunciation of military service, here the casting aside of the military sword-belt, the *cingulum militare*.[111]

But why did the Synod of Arles deal with this issue only in 314, and what, if anything, did Constantine have to do with such a canon? What seems to have happened is that upon Constantine's publicizing his conversion to Christianity and his acts favoring the religion's adherents, some Christian soldiers, now emboldened to reject the "don't ask, don't tell" policy of the previous century, not only openly advertised their Christianity, but in the period of peace after Maxentius's defeat, now that the religion was licit, sought to leave the service on the grounds of its incompatibility with their religion. Constantine could not afford to accept the loss of military manpower and erosion of discipline such actions would entail, and prevailed upon the bishops assembled at Arles to prevent Christian soldiers from attempting to resign.[112] That Constantine at this period sought to reconcile Christianity with military service is also indicated by the examples cited above from Lactantius's near contemporary *On the Deaths of the Persecutors* and the somewhat later *Epitome*, where the former pacifist now praised *industria militaris*, military discipline and courage in

---

110. Helgeland, as n. 1 above.

111. *The Acts of the Christian Martyrs*, intro., text and trans. Herbert Musurillo (Oxford: Clarendon, 1972), 250, 251. Discussion in Helgeland, 780–83.

112. As also suggested by Helgeland, 806.

battle, not repeating his earlier categorical rejection in the *Divine Institutes* of the killing of any human being.[113] That Constantine had to respond to such attempted resignations from the army at this time is made understandable by his grant to Christian clergy at this same period of immunity from military service. Both actions can be seen in the broader context of providing for the first time definitional distinctions in the secular law between clerical and lay Christians, as exemplified in the already-mentioned letter to Anulinus, which in extending immunity from civic duties to the clergy necessarily had to define who the clergy were.[114] In exempting the clergy from military service so that by their performance of divine worship they could "confer incalculable benefits on the state,"[115] Constantine had, in effect, acceded to Origen's argument of over a half-century earlier,[116] but with the crucial difference that whereas Origen had apparently argued that *all* Christians should have the same immunity from military service as the pagan priesthood, Constantine intended that privilege to apply *only* to Christian clergy. Christian laymen in the army were quite another case. Thus the long argument in Christian circles as to the compatibility of the religion with military service was finally settled, at least in Constantine's mind. Not only could Christians licitly serve in the army, but any who attempted to resign as a conscientious objector faced excommunication.

It need hardly be stressed how significant Constantine's actions in this regard were for later ideological, cultural, and institutional developments, since from this point on clerical immunity from military service ran alongside the "official" sanction, by both secular and ecclesiastical authorities, of Christian laymen serving under arms. Yet even Constantine could not completely dam the pacifistic currents in Christianity, and such ideas continued to circulate. The pacifistic argument had at least in part been accepted, though restricted in its application, and the not-much-later example of Martin of Tours shows that Christian laymen in the army continued to object to military service on religious grounds.

Constantine was not content with merely preventing Christian soldiers from leaving the service. As with any effective leader who appreciates and knows how to create and manage the intangibles of rule, the emperor also initiated in the Roman military measures of a ritual and symbolic nature that

113. Notes 73, 74, 78, 90 above.

114. *HE* X.7 (891). Later laws in the *Codex Theodosianus* on clerical immunities show that precise secular legal definitions of the clergy and who among them were eligible for immunities continued to vex subsequent emperors; see n. 105 above.

115. *HE* X.7.2 (891).

116. Note 14 above.

not only sought to institutionalize in the army imperial allegiance to the High God of the Christians but also set the pattern for similar ritual and symbolic expressions of a Christianized military in subsequent centuries. Certainly the best example of an effective Constantinian symbol in this regard is the *chi-rho* monogram he had ordered to be put on his soldiers' shields before the battle of the Milvian Bridge. In addition, Sunday was set aside as a day of worship when Christians in the ranks had leave to attend church. Constantine also decreed that pagan soldiers on that day had to recite with arms extended heavenward a monotheistic, though not necessarily and exclusively Christian, prayer as follows:

> You alone we know as God,
> You are the King we acknowledge,
> You are the Help we summon.
> By you we have won our victories,
> Through you we have overcome our enemies.
> To you we render thanks for the good things past,
> You also we hope for as giver of those to come.
> To you we all come to supplicate for our Emperor Constantine and for his
> Godbeloved sons:
> That he may be kept safe and victorious for us in long, long life, we plead.

According to Eusebius of Caesarea, the emperor himself wrote this prayer and personally led his soldiers in its recitation. By his personal participation Constantine underlined a key assertion made in the prayer, that those standing about the emperor with their arms raised heavenward in soldierly solidarity owed not only past but future successes to the numinous *victoria* inherent to the emperor's person, an assertion that both commemorated the past association of brothers in arms and promised future victories to Constantine's fraternal faithful.[117] Besides providing us with the prayer itself and the physical and temporal context of its ritual performance, Eusebius gives his own interpretation of the prayer, declaring that the soldiers by participating in it acknowledged that their hope for success rested not on weapons or physical strength, but upon God as the giver of victory itself.[118] This assertion that ruler and ruled were bound together by successes that both owed to the Christian God would come to constitute an important element in the ideological

---

117. On this bond between emperor and soldiery and how that bond was cemented by *victoria*, see Stephenson (n. 1 above), 71–75, 228–31.

118. *VC* IV.19–20 (127); Cameron and Hall trans., 160.

substratum of Christian rulership in not only medieval but also modern times. Especially for the late antique and early medieval periods, Eusebius's statement is also one of the earliest examples in a Christian context of what came to be a cliché in narratives of war, that success in battle was more dependent on prayer than arms.

Perhaps the strangest element in Constantine's symbolic repertoire for Christianizing the Roman army was the *labarum*.[119] Some idea of its form is derived from Eusebius's description of it and a coin of 326/7, from which it is clear that the *labarum* resembled, and was certainly used as, a Roman military standard. A gold-plated pole had attached to it a crosspiece, from which hung a gold-embroidered banner bearing bust portraits of Constantine and his sons. The standard was surmounted by the *chi-rho* monogram.[120] More important for our purposes than the physical appearance of the *labarum* is the symbolic resonance it bore. Constantine appointed an honor guard for it of fifty men distinguished for their strength, courage, and piety. Eusebius wrote that victory ensued wherever in battle this guard carried the *labarum*, even in instances where a unit was in difficulties.[121] Seen in this light, the *labarum* was nothing other than the visible and tangible manifestation of Constantine's "lucky star," his *victoria*, a sign both of his personal charisma and of the High God who granted him such power. One need not credit the symbol with any "real" supernatural power to recognize that with Constantine, as is common in human affairs, success bred success, and the *labarum* thereby acquired a very "real" power over both soldier and subject. Each of his victories enhanced the morale of his forces, further bound to his regime not only his immediate followers but all the subjects of his realm, and—as we will see in works authored by the emperor himself—increased the conviction in himself as well as in others that God favored his efforts. Whether we believe the *labarum* to have had actual divine power or only a power invested in it by men's beliefs, it is not at all difficult to credit that when hard-pressed soldiers saw that battle-tested banner come into view, a surge of enthusiasm enabled them to turn the tide. At least in the army, the God of the Christians had now become the arbiter of war.[122]

Constantine's measures to Christianize his army seem to have been particularly on display in the final showdown with his Eastern rival Licinius.

119. On Celtic origin of name, see Barnes, *Constantine and Eusebius*, 306, n. 150 and literature cited there. On the *labarum* itself, see now Stephenson, 182–87, 338.

120. For a description of the *labarum*, *VC* I.31 (30–31), with translation and commentary of Cameron and Hall, 81–82, 211–12.

121. *VC* II.7–9 (51–52).

122. On the *chi-rho* and *labarum* as symbolic of Constantine's *victoria*, see esp. Heim, 98–104.

Already in 316 the two had fought a brief civil war.[123] The subsequent years have been aptly termed a "cold war" between East and West, as each emperor maneuvered politically, especially using propaganda, to secure their own bases of support and undercut the other's.[124] In the East Licinius, in contradistinction to Constantine's policies favoring the Christians, sought to placate both Christian and pagan subjects, though to little ultimate advantage. As one writer has put it, "[n]o pagan subjects of Constantine are known to have turned against him through a desire to have a pagan emperor. But many Christian subjects of Licinius (as he well knew) were potentially or actively disloyal."[125] Whereas Constantine adroitly moved to assure his pagan subjects that his Christianity posed no threat to them, Licinius felt compelled to purge his administration and army of Christians, going so far as to revoke the immunities from taxation and civic responsibilities earlier granted to the clergy.[126]

Eusebius's later description of the decisive war fought in 324 is vague on details but suffused with an ebullient ideological interpretation.[127] Constantine had supposedly provided himself with a retinue of priests who aided him on campaign in his sequestered tent in supplications to the Deity. From this tent Constantine would emerge to lead his army to certain victory.[128] Eusebius seems on firmer ground in assigning a prominent place to the *labarum* in this civil war. According to the account in his *Life of Constantine*, Licinius, aware of the *labarum*'s power, ordered his officers to avoid direct encounters with it on the field of battle and even to avoid looking at it.[129] It is certainly plausible that Licinius and his soldiers respected and even feared such a potent symbol of Constantine's God-granted *victoria*, a divine power that had secured for him one success after the other on the battlefield. Constantine's eventual defeat of Licinius was yet one more proof that he enjoyed divine favor, and to mark the event he assumed the title *Victor*, a title that in the circumstances of the times advertised his closeness to God.[130]

Among Constantine's new Christian subjects in the East was the accomplished scholar-bishop Eusebius of Caesarea.[131] The writings of Eusebius,

123. Barnes *Constantine and Eusebius*, 67–68; idem, *Constantine*, 103.

124. The useful term "cold war" for this period is in C. M. Odahl, *Constantine and the Christian Empire* (London and New York: Routledge, 2004), 165.

125. Barnes, *Constantine and Eusebius*, 70.

126. Barnes, *Constantine and Eusebius*, 70–71; idem, *Constantine*, 105; *VC* 2.20.2; 30.1 (56, 61).

127. Stephenson (n. 1 above), 179–82.

128. *VC* II.4.1; 12; 14 (49, 53, 54).

129. *VC* II.16.1 (55).

130. *VC* 2.19.2 (56); Barnes, *Constantine and Eusebius*, 77, 326 n. 165; Stephenson, 215–17.

especially his historically minded works the *Ecclesiastical History* and the encomiastic *Life of Constantine*, have done more both to illuminate and to obscure the reign of Constantine than any other contemporary authority.[132] An important issue in evaluating Eusebius's picture of Constantine is that his view of the emperor evolved with time, especially from that witnessed in the various editions of the *Ecclesiastical History* from 314 to 324 to the image presented in the *Life*, written shortly after Constantine's death in 337.[133] The general trend of this interpretive evolution was in the direction of Constantine's own estimation of his piety toward God and the favor accordingly bestowed upon him, so much so that François Heim has written that "it can be questioned whether Constantine converted to the religion of Eusebius, or Eusebius to that of Constantine."[134]

Yet despite our having evidence from Constantine himself as to his own view of things, one must not exaggerate its uniqueness for the time. As noted earlier, even the pagan persecutors had believed that only by securing divine favor could they ensure their success.[135] It would be more accurate, then, to regard Eusebius as our best witness to a certain contemporary Christian mentality that he had in common with the emperor, a view of matters in which he may have been anticipated by Constantine but that also has points of similarity with ideas expressed by his contemporary Lactantius. For Eusebius expressed a Christian ideology of victory in war, a view of the nature of divine and human agency in the event of war and of how that viewpoint should be normatively contextualized within the framework of providential history.

Years before Eusebius himself came into contact with Constantine, the first Christian emperor had broadcast the idea that it was essential for a ruler to obtain the favor of the Christian God. Already in February 313 Constantine had expressed the hope that "the divine favor toward us, which we have experienced in such important matters, will continue for all time to prosper our successes along with the public weal."[136] Conversely, contempt for the Christian God leads to disaster: in his letter to Anulinus about a month later, Constantine contrasts the prosperity and success he enjoys with the dangers to the state brought about by pagan rulers.[137] This simple calculus, that a Christian emperor

131. Barnes, *Constantine and Eusebius*, 77; Heim, 57–58.

132. On Eusebius as a source for Constantine, see now Barnes, *Constantine*, 9–13.

133. T. D. Barnes, "The Editions of Eusebius' *Ecclesiastical History*," *Greek, Roman and Byzantine Studies* 21, no. 2 (1980): 191–201.

134. Heim, 52.

135. Note 91 above.

136. *DMP* 48.11 (72/73; Creed's translation, modified).

enjoys as God's gifts success and victory, whereas misfortune is the lot of the pagan persecutor, is in sum total the historical theory underpinning Lactantius's *On the Deaths of the Persecutors* written shortly thereafter.[138] Boilerplate propaganda to be sure, but propaganda of the most effective sort since it seems to reflect the actual beliefs of the propagator-in-chief. The idea that God's favor brings success and his disfavor disaster is, of course, to be found in the Old Testament as well. Although he was the first Christian ruler to express the idea, Constantinian precedent need not be invoked to explain the persistence and appeal of this ancient, simple notion from antiquity to the present.

What was for Constantine equally simple would in later times become more complicated—and contested—in the ideas regarding the position to be taken by a Christian ruler vis-à-vis the Deity and what might be expected as a result. In his circular addressed to his new Eastern subjects after his defeat of Licinius, Constantine had written that God had "examined my service and approved it as fit for His own purposes."[139] Foremost among the divine benefits conferred on God's imperial servant was victory in war. In another circular to his Eastern subjects written in 325, Constantine claimed that by "making Your seal my protection everywhere, I have led a conquering army."[140] His unbroken succession of victories constituted obvious and manifest proof of divine favor, and in sum had strengthened Constantine's faith in his divine mission.[141] Such a view of things cannot be squared, of course, with Lactantius's observation in the *Divine Institutes* that the better side in war often loses,[142] and has to be seen as reflecting Constantine's belief that he had a unique and special relationship with the Deity.

Though Constantine may have seen his relationship to God as unique, his view of that bond was not peculiar to himself. In his earlier account of Constantine's victory over Maxentius in the *Ecclesiastical History*, Eusebius had stressed Constantine's role as an instrument of providence, and had attributed his success to a God-given power that seems to operate largely independently of Constantine's personal qualities.[143] It is Eusebius's subsequent movement to the idea that the emperor was directly favored and inspired by God which Heim

---

137. *HE* X.7.1 (891). For a later expression of this idea, see Constantine's letter of 324 to the Eastern provincials (n. 139 below), *VC* II.24–27 (58–59).

138. Heim, 52–53.

139. *VC* II.28.2 (60).

140. *VC* II.55.1 (70).

141. *VC* II.42; 55.2 (65–66, 70).

142. *Div. Inst.* VI.6.15–17 (501–2).

143. Heim, 93–94.

has characterized as the bishop's conversion to the religion of Constantine.[144] As already in the *Ecclesiastical History*,[145] God was Constantine's "Champion and Guardian God in battles,"[146] who "by the law of combat" had defeated the enemies of truth.[147] All of Constantine's enemies, both foreign and domestic, fall before him in defeat,[148] for "God Himself, the Supreme Sovereign, stretches out His right hand to him from above and confirms him victor over every pretender and aggressor."[149] This Christianized conception of divinely sent victory thus retained the numinous quality of its pagan counterpart, but especially after the defeat of Licinius was now regarded as the fruit of Constantine's personal piety.[150] According to Eusebius, when on campaign Constantine would sequester himself in a secluded tent with a few men of like piety to offer up prayers. Eventually he would receive a revelation directly from God, rush from the tent, and summon his troops to a quick and certain victory over his opponents.[151] Besides Eusebius and Constantine himself, the general currency of the idea that God intervened directly in battle on the emperor's behalf is proved by its appearance in Lactantius's *On the Deaths of the Persecutors*, which also has the image of God's hand bringing victory from heaven.[152]

What sort of language could best be used to describe this new and unique relationship of the emperor to the divine and its consequences, especially as it related to war, in the world? The new dispensation seemed to require a new language to describe Christian *victoria*, a vocabulary peculiar unto itself. It is natural, inevitable, and completely unsurprising that Christians derived such a language from the Bible, and thus only a century after Tertullian had mocked those who attempted to make such connections, Christian writers began to place accounts of war within a biblicized framework of typical narratives and types.[153] A key, almost foundational biblical text for such narratives was that of the Crossing of the Red Sea and the ensuing canticle of Moses (Exod.

144. Heim, 52; 93–98.

145. *HE* IX.9.9 (830); *VC* I.39.3; 46 (36, 39–40).

146. *ΕΥΣΕΒΙΟΥ ΤΟΥ ΠΑΜΦΙΛΟΥ ΕΙΣ ΚΩΝΣΤΑΝΤΙΝΟΝ ΤΟΝ ΒΑΣΙΛΕΑ ΤΡΙΑΚΟΝΤΑΕΤΗΡΙΚΟΣ*, ed. I. A. Heikel, *GCS*7 (hereafter *Triak.*), 18.3 (259). Translation by H. A. Drake, *In Praise of Constantine: A Historical Study and New Translation of Eusebius' Tricennial Orations* (Berkeley and Los Angeles: University of California Press, 1976) (hereafter Drake), 127.

147. *Triak.* 2.3 (199); Drake, 86.

148. *Triak.* 3.3 (201); Drake, 87.

149. *Triak.* 10.7 (223); Drake, 102; *VC* IV.6.2 (122).

150. *HE* X.9.1 (898); Heim, 87.

151. *VC* II.12 (53).

152. *DMP* 44.9 (64); Heim, 55.

153. Notes 11, 12 above.

14:5–15:19). The association of this text with what in certain instances amounts to a positive Christian perspective on human warfare goes back to what is, along with that found in Lactantius's *On the Deaths of the Persecutors*, the earliest account of Constantine's victory over Maxentius, that found in Eusebius's *Ecclesiastical History*, an account copied decades later into his *Life of Constantine*. Maxentius, though no persecutor himself, is portrayed as a pagan tyrant, and thus when he and his bodyguard drown in the Tiber while fleeing Constantine's victorious army it is perfectly understandable that Eusebius would think of the earlier overthrow of the pagan tyrant Pharaoh and his host in the waters of the Red Sea. The eerie similarities between the two events prompted Eusebius to liken Scripture here to the ancient pagan oracles, a comparison advantageous to the former because Scripture is prophetically accurate and true.[154]

But the significance of the Exodus story for positive Christian narratives of war relies on more than this one case of accidental similarities between events. The story of the Crossing of the Red Sea and the canticle of Moses are central elements in what had been considered by Christian exegetes since apostolic times as probably the most symbolically resonant of all Old Testament texts. The Crossing of the Red Sea in particular was identified from the earliest times as a type of Christian baptism. In this interpretation Egypt typified the world, Pharaoh and his army the devil, and the Red Sea the baptismal font through which the faithful must pass. The departure of the Israelites from Egypt signified the newly baptized Christian's rejection of sin, and just as the mighty hand of the Lord had freed his earthly people from an earthly tyrant, so baptism freed his spiritual people from a spiritual tyrant.[155] The association of baptism with the Crossing of the Red Sea influenced or was influenced by the use of the Exodus text in the Easter vigil, when baptism normally took place in the early church. The reading of the Passover story in the Jewish prototype for the Christian celebration as well as other evidence suggest a great antiquity for the lection of the Exodus account at Easter.[156]

To appreciate fully the awesome significance of the Exodus story for early Christians one must keep in mind that for all the symbolic resonances of the story, they regarded the Crossing of the Red Sea as a concrete and very real historical event. Far from being overshadowed and rendered historically suspect

154. *HE* IX.9.4–8 (828/830) = *VC* I.38 (34–35).

155. Jean Daniélou, *From Shadows to Reality: Studies in the Biblical Typology of the Fathers* (Eng. trans. of *Sacramentum Futuri* [Paris: Beauchesne, 1950] by W. Hibberd) (London: Burns & Oates, 1960), 153–201.

156. Gregory Dix, *The Apostolic Tradition of St. Hippolytus* (London: SPCK, 1968), 338.

by its typological valence, the reality of the event guaranteed and magnified the power of the antitype fully realized in the present.[157] An indication of how concretely Christians then viewed the Crossing of the Red Sea is seen in the early fifth-century historian Orosius, who claimed that the ruts made by Pharaoh's chariots were still visible on the shore of the Red Sea.[158]

This historical event's verification of God's awesome power extends its symbolic field beyond that of baptism alone. So how did Eusebius use the Red Sea motif here? Although the story was familiar to him from exegesis and liturgy and was certainly suggested by the manner of Maxentius's death, the ancient event of the Crossing of the Red Sea must have also appealed to him here because of the context of the event in the present, in which the defeat of Maxentius must have seemed to him to constitute nothing other than the incontestably direct intervention of God in the course of history. Like similar divine interventions in the Old Testament, Constantine's defeat of Maxentius was sudden, dramatic, and decisive. After suffering the trials of persecution, when God had seemingly abandoned his people, the suddenness of Constantine's victory in the West and Licinius's defeat of the great persecutor Maximin Daia in the East understandably seemed wholly miraculous. Understandable, too, is Eusebius's use of the Exodus story at this point in his narrative, since a symbolic valence common to his use of this story and its interpretation as a type of baptism in both exegesis and liturgy is the deliverance of God's people from bondage, a bondage in the one case earthly and in the other spiritual, by a mighty act of divine power. It must have seemed natural for him to turn to the story of the Crossing of the Red Sea and the exultation of the Israelites over the destruction of Pharaoh and the Egyptians as the most appropriate biblical framework for an event that in its sudden and decisive reversal of fortune bore the distinguishing characteristics of an actual divine intervention in the course of human affairs. That such an intervention was the outcome of battle and war was by no means inappropriate for the Christian God; rather, the Exodus story appropriately prefigured the divine and well-nigh miraculous overthrow of an earthly tyrant's army, and the deliverance of God's people from pagan persecution. Although Rufinus faithfully recorded the Exodus text in the account of Maxentius's fall in his Latin translation of the *Ecclesiastical History*,[159] rather than because of Rufinus's direct influence it seems more probable that the use of this story in later narratives of war in the

157. Daniélou, 190.

158. Paulus Orosius, *Historiarum Adversum Paganos Libri VII*, ed. C. Zangemeiter(*CSEL* 5), I.10.17–18 (58–59).

159. *HE* IX.9.5 (829/831).

Latin West was in like manner suggested by events that in their suddenness and decisiveness bespoke divine intervention in history, and by the intimate familiarity of the writers through exegesis and liturgy with a biblical text that appropriately framed an account of such events.[160]

The use of biblical language to frame accounts of divine intervention in the world did not simply signify a species of literary embroidery, the Christian equivalent of a classical tag line from Homer or Vergil. Christianity required the adoption of a totalizing worldview.[161] In terms of the consequences of this worldview for the Christian conception of history, the New Testament and the period it described had already from the beginning been regarded as the fulfillment of prophecies and types from the Old Testament.[162] With the historical work of Eusebius one sees for the first time in a Christian author a comprehensively worked-out schema that extended this divinely actuated history diachronically to the present, and by implication synchronically to contemporary pagan kingdoms and empires, especially in the last case as seen in his *Chronicle*, a Christian universal history that by way of Jerome's translation became one of the most influential works in Western historiography.[163] The theology of history underlying such works, that human events are the visible manifestation of a providential progression leading to the Last Judgment, was a proposition to which all Christians subscribed. And it seemed to follow naturally that present-day events could be recognized as constituents of this constantly unfolding providential plan and correctly interpreted by regarding them as the realization in the present of past biblical prophecies and types. Eusebius's view seems to have been common among late antique Christians, and he saw no difficulty in regarding contemporary events as the fulfillment of biblical prophecy.[164] In the *Life of Constantine* he went further and not only interpreted the defeat of Maxentius as the realization of a biblical event, an interpretive move already in place in the *Ecclesiastical History*, but also now depicted Constantine himself as the realization of the biblical type of Moses.[165]

---

160. On the fourth-century Christian sarcophagi carved with the Red Sea scene, a subject relevant to but too far afield for the present purpose, see Stephenson, 210–11.

161. A phrase adapted from Averil Cameron's "totalizing discourse" in *Christianity and the Rhetoric of Empire: The Development of Christian Discourse* (Berkeley: University of California Press, 1991), 2, 58, 123, 220.

162. The theme of Jean Daniélou's work on typology (n. 155 above).

163. See Hervé Inglebert, *Les Romains chrétiens face a l'histoire de Rome* (Paris: Brepols, 1996), 153 and the literature cited there.

164. Barnes, *Constantine and Eusebius*, 249.

165. See Cameron and Hall, 35–39, and the literature cited there, and now Stephenson, 209.

Like Moses, Constantine had grown up in the palaces of the pagan persecutors of God's people, a people whom he would ultimately come to lead. Too, like Moses Constantine had delivered his people from oppression, and with divine assistance had exacted vengeance upon his people's persecutors.[166] Given that Moses was regarded as a type of Christ, an interpretation made elsewhere by Eusebius himself,[167] such a comparison would not be sustained in later Christian writers, and it would be another biblical type who would come to represent the ideal for Christian royalty in the West.[168] Rather than establishing an interpretive precedent that in any case was not followed in this instance, for our purposes Eusebius, again, should be seen here instead as the best early witness to a broader Christian worldview regarding the events of battle and war, in which such events bespoke a God who continued to act through them in the course of human history. If one correctly contextualized such events within the perspective of salvation history, one could not only securely identify such events but even correctly determine their providential significance.

One of the more remarkable aspects of the years of the Constantinian revolution was the apparent ease and celerity with which Christianity became involved in the politics of Roman civil wars. The impetus for this development was Constantine's. Whether prompted by dream, vision, or something else, his adoption of the *chi-rho* monogram in October 312 literally pushed the Christian cause to the foreground of civil war politics. Although other motivations were certainly involved, a few months later Constantine and Licinius's joint statement from Milan publicized to the world the Christian cause as a war aim. Maximin Daia's ending of persecution in late 312 was undoubtedly intended to appease a discontented population in his rear, an action incidentally revealing the considerable political clout of the more numerous Christian population of the East.

The Christian cause was in the years to come interwoven into the tensions of the Constantine-Licinius "cold war," as again the Christian population in the East proved a political force to be reckoned with, as Constantine bid for its support and Licinius began to equate Christianity with disloyalty. We have an indication of contemporary Christian opinion regarding the contest between the two emperors during these years in a dedication to Constantine inserted into a second edition of Lactantius's *Divine Institutes*. After praising Constantine as the first emperor to worship the one true God, Lactantius warns the wicked

---

166. *VC* I.12; 19.1; 20, 38 (21, 25, 26, 34–35).

167. *Demonstratio Evangelica* 3.2.6–7 (*GCS, Eusebius Werke VII*, ed. I. A. Heikel [Leipzig, 1913], 97).

168. Marc Reydellet, "La Bible miroir des princes," in *Bible tous les temps* 2: *Le monde latin antique et la Bible*, ed. J. Fontaine, C. Pietri (Paris: Beauchesne, 1985), passim.

men "who still rage against the just in another part of the earth" that their punishment would be all the harsher for being delayed. "Wanting to defend His religion and divine worship, to whom better might I appeal, to whom speak, save him through whom justice and wisdom have been restored to human affairs."[169] In the eyes of a Christian viewing the imperial standoff, Constantine's exalted role as the divinely commissioned restorer of justice was significantly linked to a promise of punishment for persecutors: there was little doubt as to who would be God's agent in executing such punishment. In his circulars to the provincials and Christian leaders in the East after his victory in 324, Constantine portrayed Licinius as a persecutor, a dragon who had been driven out by divine power. Expressing sentiments that have been attributed to the influence of Lactantius himself, who made similar statements in both the *Divine Institutes* and *On the Deaths of the Persecutors*, Constantine viewed Licinius's fate as a condign punishment for his wicked acts against the Christians.[170] Not only were Christians to be recalled from exile and their property restored, but Christian soldiers who had been dismissed from the service by Licinius were given the option of restoration of rank or honorable discharge, the last a telling concession in that it bespeaks the persistence of pacifistic sentiments in the religion.[171] Christians had been on the winning side in the recent civil war, and now they were to enjoy victory's rewards.

CONCLUSION

Pacifists and others have asked and will ask, how could the religion of the Prince of Peace so quickly and so profoundly have gone over to a God of war? The question presumes *a* religion united on this issue, which as we have seen and will see is not true. In any case, regardless of their internal disagreements on the subject, it is an observable fact that Christians throughout the empire were involved and deeply invested in the outcomes of the civil wars of 313 and 324. In the one instance they had just endured as much as a decade of the worst persecution the church had ever suffered; in the other a persecution was begun or feared. Within a matter of months in both instances, in a surge of violence releasing the tension of years, in decisive battles deliverance had come suddenly and dramatically. As Constantine would put it, who could not see that the events themselves bespoke the power of God? As Jehovah God had

169. *Div. Inst.* I.1.15 (4).
170. *VC* II.24–27, 42, 46.2 (58–59, 65–66, 67).
171. *VC* II.33 (62).

defended his people Israel, so would he defend the Christians in war and battle. The working-out of this idea in practice would not be as simple, though, as the emperor and many of his Christian followers seem to have imagined.

However we conceive the changes in these years in the relationship between Christianity and war, many of those changes themselves were effected by Constantine. General and visionary, he was also a shrewd politician and consummate propagandist.[172] He believed himself to be favored by God with numinous *victoria*, a personal charisma that was somehow linked to God's willingness to intervene directly in history on behalf of his imperial servant. At least to his own satisfaction, and that of many of his prominent Christian supporters, the argument as to the compatibility of Christianity with military service and war was now settled. Any unease that someone like Lactantius may have felt in compromising the ideal of the absolute rejection of killing and war was doubtless assuaged, in his case, by his appointment to be tutor of Constantine's eldest son Crispus.[173] Bishops now mingled with the emperor and his court, helped to propagate the idea of Constantine's closeness to God, and were ready to assist him with prayer on his campaigns. Christian supporters also began to frame the events of the reign, and the emperor himself, within the contours of ongoing salvation history, another pattern for Christian royalty that would persist for centuries. More than any other individual, Constantine was responsible for creating a Christianity intertwined with politics and war.[174]

172. According to Barnes, *Constantine*, 2, 173, Constantine was "a highly skilful politician . . . a political genius of the highest order."

173. Jerome, *Liber de viris inlustribus* 80, ed. E. C. Richardson, in *Texte und Untersuchungen zur Geschichte der altchristlichen Literatur* 14 (Leipzig, 1896), 43: "Hic in extrema senectute magister Caesaris Crispi, filii Constantini, in Gallia fuit, qui postea a patre interfectus est."

174. So also Stephenson, 189: "Constantine fought no crusades, but his wars did transform how Christians viewed war, and allowed the transformation of the Roman army into a Christian army in the century following Constantine's victory over Licinius."

3

Accommodating the State: Ambrose of Milan and Martin of Tours

Periods of civil war have often in Roman history been fruitful in the production of historical works; one thinks of the writings of Caesar and Sallust under the Republic, and those of Tacitus for the Principate. The contenders for the purple seconded their arms with the weaponry of propaganda, which was often reflected in panegyric and in contemporary and later historiography. Just as civil wars earlier in the fourth century had generated official justifications for the resort to war, so too did the civil wars of Theodosius I in 388 and 394, though now with a Christian coloration. In the late fourth century and early fifth, after decades of imperial favor and experience in working with the secular power, there is increasingly evident among some Christians the more or less clear lineaments of a "Christian" way of waging war, especially in the case of a prince of impeccable orthodoxy. This synthesis owes much in influence and origin to contemporary Theodosian propaganda. Some of the themes of this "Christian way" of war-making can also be seen in non-Christian sources, reflecting a more general late-antique mentality regarding war: there is much pouring of old wine into new bottles.

Unlike with the cheerleading of a Eusebius, however, there persisted among many Christians of this period—even in the case of someone like Ambrose of Milan, often cited as an example of a Christian "accommodationist"—a certain sense of disgust with the idea of *any* public service, and especially that of the army. There is the same horror of blood pollution manifested most clearly in Tertullian and the ancient church orders, but also in Origen and Lactantius (of the *Divine Institutes*).

THEODOSIAN WAR PROPAGANDA

The propaganda broadcast by the Emperor Theodosius I (379–395) and his supporters that pushed the justification for and a would-be authoritative interpretation of especially his wars against the Western "usurpers" of the late fourth century has left traces in the historiography of the period, though its influence can be traced in other genres as well, even in the realm of pictorial representation. Certain themes in this propaganda were to recur in accounts of war for centuries into the medieval period, and were also already present in Constantinian propaganda earlier in the fourth century, though Theodosian war propaganda seems more assured and widespread than its Constantinian counterpart.[1] Undoubtedly this reflects the increased pace of Christianization in the late fourth-century empire, necessitating the creation of the lineaments of a "Christianized" way of waging war, or at least of its representation. The extent to which this aspect of Theodosian political culture fathered later medieval ideologies of war is open to debate, but clearly some connections can be shown. In any case, Theodosian propaganda and its themes are a prominent part of the thought-world that backgrounded Augustine's views on war and military service, and thus deserve our close attention.

One motif in Theodosian propaganda involved the use of prophecy to signal divine approbation and intervention. Writing a few years after Theodosius's death in 395, the translator and continuator of Eusebius's church history, Rufinus of Aquileia, wrote that by divine providence the monk John of Lycopolis had been filled with a prophetic spirit, so much so that Theodosius had consulted him as to the prospects of success before proceeding against the usurper Maximus and, later, Eugenius.[2] According to the mid-fifth-century church historian Sozomen, before the last of those wars against Eugenius, Theodosius had dispatched the court eunuch Eutropius to get John's response, an event apparently verified by the poet Claudian.[3] In both cases Theodosius received assurance of victory from the prophetic monk.[4] The conception that the new dispensation provided a surer alternative to the pagan oracles regarding the event of war had already been voiced by Eusebius, who had been anxious to

1. Barnes, *Constantine*, 2, 4, reflects on the role of Constantinian propaganda "in shaping the surviving evidence for his reign," and on how the resulting image of Constantine has deceived many modern historians. Much the same could be said of Theodosius I and his regime's propaganda.

2. *HE* XI.19 (1023–24).

3. Sozomen VII.22.7–8 (*GCS* 50: *Sozomenus Kirchengeschichte*, ed. J. Bidez [Berlin, 1960 (reprint)]), 336; *Claudii Claudiani Carmina*, ed. J. B. Hall (Leipzig: Teubner, 1985), *In Eutropium*, ll. 312–13 (155).

4. *HE* XI.32 (1036); Augustine, *DCD* 5.26 (*CCL* 47, 161).

prove the oracular superiority of Scripture, and who had framed Constantine's defeat of Maxentius as the fulfillment of biblical prophecy.[5]

Another motif seen in the reported picture of Christian warfare at this period is that of the relative smallness of the forces of the "good guys." Sympathy for the underdog seems to be a universal human attitude connected with war. In accounts with this feature, the audience's sympathy for the smaller contender is engaged. Such stories often portray the outnumbered victor of such an encounter as possessing some virtue that enabled him to overcome his material inferiority, and point to this virtue as a sign of divine support. One need only mention David and Goliath to recognize the persistence and metaphorical potency of such stories and how they function to identify who is on God's side in war, while keeping in mind that classical antiquity also had its own fund of such stories (e.g., Leonidas and the Spartans at Thermopylae). *Post bellum* official propaganda in the fourth century, and later, often emphasized how the victorious emperor's army had been outnumbered by his evil opponents, thereby indicating that the victory could only have been obtained with divine assistance.

The instances of this motif in various works of the fourth century are so numerous that to recount them all would belabor the point. A significant illustration of the idea appears in a panegyric delivered at Trier before Constantine in 313, where the orator devotes a section of the speech to the fact that Constantine was outnumbered by the forces of Maxentius. Despite the disadvantage, Constantine's virtue outweighed his opponent's numbers. The source of that virtuous power was obvious: having a smaller army proved that Constantine "sought no doubtful victory, but one divinely promised."[6] The origin of this notion in Constantinian propaganda is indicated by its appearance eight years later in Nazarius's panegyric,[7] and decades later in the *Life of Constantine* by Eusebius, who reports that both Maxentius and Licinius had relied on their superiority in numbers, while Constantine had trusted to God for victory.[8]

The same motif also appears in Orosius's account of the wars of Theodosius against the Western usurpers. Theodosius's war machine was much inferior to that of Maximus in every respect: only in his faith was he superior.[9] When Arbogast and Eugenius marched to encounter Theodosius at the battle of the

---

5. *HE* IX.9.4–6 (828/830) = *VC* I.38.4 (35); see Cameron and Hall commentary, 186.

6. *XII Pan.* 3–5.2, esp. 3.3 (272–74); Nixon and Rodgers, 297.

7. *IV Pan.* 23 (160–61); Nixon and Rodgers, 368.

8. *VC* I.27, 37.2, 58.3.

9. Orosius VII.35.2 (525): "sola fide maior, nam longe minor universa apparatus bellici conparatione."

Frigidus in 394, their army "overflowed" with Gallic and Frankish troops, "innumerable and unconquered forces."[10] In both wars the smaller army was victorious, and Orosius knows why: "Theodosius had always been victorious through the power of God, not reliance on man."[11] Ambrose had voiced the same sentiment earlier to the emperor Gratian, assuring him in the *De Fide* as he marched to fight the Goths that victory was less dependent on military strength than the faith of the emperor.[12]

Closely associated with the preceding idea is the assertion that the divine assistance necessary for the attainment of victory was obtained through prayer. Already in the mid-third century Origen had claimed that Christian prayers had aided emperors in battle more than did their armies.[13] In 313, Licinius had had his army recite a prayer before the climactic battle with the notorious pagan persecutor Maximin Daia, and as far as Lactantius was concerned that had been sufficient to bring victory.[14] Constantine himself had led his army in weekly prayers to the same, victory-bringing Deity.[15] But neither Licinius's nor Constantine's prayers were exclusively Christian, and for some decades thereafter there seems little contemporary evidence for prayer in the Roman military.[16]

Eight or nine years after the event, Rufinus of Aquileia gave an account of Theodosius's war in 394 against the Western usurper Eugenius, who was charged with being responsible for the death of Valentinian II and with having sponsored a pagan revival in the West.

> [Theodosius] prepared for war not so much with the aid of arms and weapons as [with the aid] of fasts and prayers; he was guarded not so much by sentinels as by nightlong supplications. He made the rounds of all the places of prayer accompanied by priests and people, and lay

---

10. Orosius VII.35.12 (529): "collectis Gallorum Francorumque viribus exundavit"; VII.35.11 (528): "contraxit undique innumeras invictasque copias."

11. Orosius VII.35.12 (528): "potentia Dei non fiducia hominis victorem semper extitisse Theodosium."

12. *De Fide ad Gratianum Augustum* (*CSEL* 78, 5): "Nosti enim fide magis imperatoris quam virtute militum quaeri solere victoriam."

13. Above, chapter 2, note 14.

14. Lactantius, *DMP* 46.6, 66: "Summe deus/te rogamus//Sancte deus/te rogamus//Omnem iustitiam/tibi commendamus//Salutem nostram/tibi commendamus//Imperium nostrum/tibi commendamus//Per te vivimus//Per te victores et felices existimus//Summe sancte Deus, preces nostras exaudi//Brachia nostra ad te tendimus//Exaudi, sancte summe Deus."

15. Above, chapter 2, note 118.

16. A. D. Lee, *War in Late Antiquity: A Social History* (Malden, MA: Blackwell, 2007), 182–83.

prostrate in sackcloth before the reliquaries of martyrs and apostles, calling upon them to aid him through the faithful intercession of the saints.

In contrast, Eugenius's pagan supporters indulged in blood sacrifice and the inspection of entrails to determine the outcome of the war. When in the ensuing battle Theodosius's forces began to give way, the emperor, like Moses in the battle against the Amalekites in Exodus 17, climbed atop a rock where he could be seen by both armies.

> Casting down his weapons, he turned to his accustomed help and prostrated himself before the gaze of God, saying: "Almighty God, Thou knowest that in the name of Christ thy Son I undertook this war as what I believe to be a justified vengeance. If this be not so, punish me; but if I came here in a good cause (*cum causa probabili*) and trusting in Thee, stretch out thy right hand to thine own, lest perchance the Gentiles should say, 'Where is their God?'"

Theodosius's generals, "certain that the supplication of the pious prince had been acceptable to God," returned with renewed inspiration to the battle and ultimately gained the victory.[17]

Whence originated this image of Theodosius praying in battle? On 1 January 383 the pagan orator Themistius, a "spin doctor" for the Theodosian regime,[18] delivered a speech before the senate of Constantinople and the imperial court in celebration of the consulship of his longtime patron Saturninus. In speaking of Theodosius's elevation to the throne in order to deal with the aftermath of the Roman disaster at Hadrianople in 378, Themistius asserted that Theodosius had been the first emperor to recognize that "the power of the Romans did not now lie in steel, nor in breastplates, spears and innumerable hosts," but that it was necessary for an emperor to rule in accordance with the mind of God, whereby he was enabled to subdue not only the Goths, but all the barbarian nations.[19] In the immediate political context of the oration's delivery, wherein a peace treaty had been recently concluded with the Goths on terms that were, out of necessity, not altogether advantageous to

17. *HE* XI.33 (1037–38).

18. On this characterization of Themistius, see the introduction to *Politics, Philosophy, and Empire in the Fourth Century: Select Orations of Themistius*, trans. Peter Heather and David Moncur (Liverpool: Liverpool University Press, 2001), esp. 38–42.

19. *Themistii orationes quae supersunt* (Leipzig: Teubner, 1965), 16.207c (297).

the Roman government,[20] the assertion privileging Theodosius's access to the mind of God over mere military capacity could be regarded as a fig leaf to cover his inability to overcome the Goths in battle. But from a Christian perspective, there was also here a claim of the emperor's intimacy with the Christian God that echoes similar assertions in earlier, Constantinian propaganda.

Given Themistius's closeness to the imperial regime, it looks as though he is here putting forth a theme of contemporary Theodosian propaganda, a theme that was later picked up in official pronouncements on the emperor's wars against the Western usurpers, which asserted that in battle Theodosius's access to divine power, manifested through successful prayer, counted for more than weapons or numbers of soldiers. It is significant that Rufinus echoed this assertion in his account of the victory over Eugenius in 394, the last act of a campaign that seems to have involved relatively large forces on both sides and was certainly far bloodier and more uncertain of outcome than the defeat of Maximus six years earlier. Surely in this instance imperial propaganda would have had scope to trumpet the valor and skill of the emperor and his army in overcoming the large forces arrayed against them. Yet it was for precisely this campaign that imperial propaganda claimed that it was solely because of Theodosius's intimacy with God that the tide of battle had turned in his favor at a critical moment.

The claim that Theodosius had obtained victory through prayer seems to have caught the imagination of later Christian writers, who tended to regard him and not Constantine as the ideal Christian warrior prince. This image of Theodosius is already seen in Orosius, who fleshes out Rufinus's account by having the emperor pray all night during a pause in the battle, leaving behind a veritable pond of tears "as the price he paid for heavenly assistance." The next morning "he gave as the signal of battle the sign of the cross" and launched an ultimately victorious attack.[21] Here again, as with the account in Rufinus, there is a nod toward Christian religious practice, and thus likewise a sacralization of the ensuing battle. Almost two centuries later, Gregory of Tours noted that Theodosius—one of the few Roman emperors, Christian or otherwise, to escape censure in his historical précis in Book I of his *Histories*—had gained victory not by the sword, but by vigils and prayer.[22] It was perhaps Augustine who summed it up best: "[Theodosius] fought against this very strong army [viz. Eugenius's] more by praying than by striking blows."[23]

---

20. On the treaty and Themistius's efforts to conceal how much had been given away, see Heather and Moncur (n. 18 above), 259–64.

21. Orosius VII.35.15 (529, 530).

22. *Gregorii episcopi Turonensis Libri Historiarum X*, ed. B. Krusch (*MGH: srm* I/1), I 42 (28).

What are we to make of this reiterated theme of Theodosius's reliance upon prayer in battle? If this theme is reflective only of propagandistic bombast, with no basis in fact, then it would seem so patently mendacious that one would think the fiercely anti-Christian Zosimus would have made something of it in his later account of Theodosius's reign, which in turn was in this portion of his work largely based upon the contemporary history of Eunapius.[24] And what does this repeated assertion say about the value placed on traditional military virtues? What about the steadfastness in adversity and courage in battle expected of the ordinary soldier, or the skill and cleverness expected of the successful commander? Are we really supposed to believe that Theodosius thought that what had brought victory to Roman arms over the centuries was now to be cast aside in favor of prayer alone? Were Theodosius's actions, especially in the war against Eugenius, merely a private eccentricity with little relevance to the actual prosecution and outcome of the conflict?

Theodosius's well-publicized reliance on prayer in war was certainly exploited for propaganda purposes, but it also is an early witness to what was to become increasingly an almost standard concomitant of war in the Roman empire of this period and in its successor states: the overt use of Christian liturgical forms, especially prayer, in the wars of Christian polities. Although Eusebius mentions prayers in the campaigns of Constantine, there seems little evidence that such a phenomenon became more or less general until the age of Theodosius and his immediate successors. We do not have to rely upon inference alone to know that this period witnessed the generalization of such practices. The poet Claudian in verses written about the year 400 teases the *magister equitum* Jacobus about his reliance in battle upon a whole series of Christian saints, expressing the concern that barbarian enemies have less to fear from the general than the pages of poetry that mock him. There is even a hint here of the liturgical content of contemporary war prayers in Claudian's mention of the drowning of Pharaoh's army at the Crossing of the Red Sea, a likely inference given Eusebius's earlier use of the example and its appearance in later liturgy.[25] The intimate penetration of a Christian mentality into the Roman army of this period, again expressed in quasi-liturgical language, is also indicated by Vegetius's citation of the phrase "Deus nobiscum" as a possible battle-cry.[26] More to the point, in one of the letters in the Augustinian corpus

23. *DCD* 5.26 (*CCL* 47, 161): "magis orando quam feriendo pugnavit."

24. *Zosime: Histoire nouvelle*, ed. and trans. François Paschoud (Paris: Société d'Édition Les Belles Lettres, 1979), II: 1, x.

25. Claudian 50(77), esp. ll. 7–8 (note 3 above, 402–3): "Sic quicumque ferox gelidum transnaverit Histrum,/mergatur volucres ceu Pharaonis equi."

recently discovered by Johannes Divjak, the *comes Hispaniarum* Asterius[27] in the year 419 or 420[28] asks the monk Fronto during a tense ecclesiastical standoff at Tarragona to "accompany me, and the army that you see before you hastening off to battle, with the power of your prayers."[29]

We may even have part of the text of a prayer related to war from about this period:

> God, who hath prepared the Roman empire for the preaching of the Gospel of the eternal kingdom, hold out to these Thy servants, our emperors, heavenly arms, so that the peace of the churches be not disturbed by any tempest of wars.

Gerd Tellenbach noted the similarity of this prayer in the Roman Leonine sacramentary to the idea and the text in a sermon of Pope Leo I (440–461).[30]

Christian times were no better than pagan if the end result of battle was the same as it had been before, with the bodies of the slain in their thousands, as Lactantius had put it, flooding and fouling the rivers and fields.[31] The intervention in battle by the Christian God required a different kind of war, and so the idea began to be propagated that the victories thus won were decided with scarcely a battle fought, and were bloodless, or nearly so.[32]

This idea appears first in propaganda originating with Constantine, whose victories over his enemies, according to Eusebius, were usually bloodless.[33] François Heim has also shown how the fourth-century *Passio Typasii*, the *Vita*

26. *Flavii Vegeti Renati Epitoma Rei Militaris*, ed. Alf Önnerfors (Stuttgart and Leipzig: Teubner, 1995), III.5.4 (114).

27. *PLRE* 2, 171, Asterius 4.

28. On the date of this letter, *Saint Augustine Letters 1*-29**, trans. Robert B. Eno, *Fathers of the Church* 81 (Washington, DC: Catholic University of America Press, 1989), 83.

29. Divjak 11.12.2 (*CSEL* 88, 60).

30. Gerd Tellenbach, "Römischer und christlicher Reichsgedanke in der Liturgie des frühen Mittelalters," *Sitzungsberichte der Heidelberger Akademie der Wissenschaften Philosophisch-historische Klasse* 25 (1934/35), 10 and note 1, 55 (text). Discussion in Anna Morisi, *La guerra nel pensiero cristiano dalle origini alle Crociate* (Florence: G. C. Sansoni, 1963), 142.

31. *Div. Inst.* I.18.10 (*CSEL* 19, 68).

32. François Heim, who subsumes this idea under the theme "victoire sans combat," has done important work on the subject in "Le thème de la 'victoire sans combat' chez Ambroise," *Ambroise de Milan: XVIe Centenaire de son élection épiscopale* (Paris, 1974). See also Giuseppe Zecchini, "S. Ambrogio e le origini del motivo della vittoria incruenta," *Rivista di Storia della Chiesa in Italia* 38, no. 2 (1984): 391–404, and Alan Cameron, *The Last Pagans of Rome* (Oxford: Oxford University Press, 2011), 97–98.

33. *VC* IV.53 (142).

Martini, and Ambrose's praise of the deceased Bishop Acholius of Thessalonica all involve to some degree the idea of a Christian "victoire sans combat."[34] It is Orosius's account of the wars of Theodosius and his son Honorius, however, where the idea is most fleshed out. His apologetic aim in *Against the Pagans*, to indict the bloodiness of earlier pagan times in order to palliate the shock of the recent Gothic sack of Rome in 410 under a Christian emperor, caused him to maximize the slaughter involved in ancient civil wars while minimizing the bloodshed of the civil wars of his own day. Orosius is especially insistent on the near bloodless nature of the war against Magnus Maximus in 388. As terrible as the war had been, victory had been obtained without bloodshed and with the death of only two men. "With God attending to matters, Theodosius received a bloodless victory."[35] Orosius is aware that his pagan critics can charge that the subsequent civil war against Eugenius in 394 was not quite so bloodless,[36] a fact also appreciated by Rufinus, who had earlier written that whereas John of Lycopolis had prophesied a bloodless victory against Maximus, on being consulted again he assured the emperor that the war against Eugenius would unleash a torrent of blood.[37] Orosius therefore claimed that only Theodosius's Gothic auxiliaries had suffered losses in the battle of the Frigidus: "surely to have lost *them* was a boon, and their vanquishment victory."[38] Other than in this one instance, though, in numerous wars foreign and domestic both Theodosius and his son Honorius had secured "holy victories" with little or no bloodshed.[39]

By far the most significant product of Theodosian war propaganda was the interpretation put out by Theodosius's supporters of the battle of the Frigidus in September 394, in which it was claimed that the piety of Theodosius had merited direct divine intervention in the course of his victory over the forces of the Western "usurper" Eugenius and his pagan supporters. More than one source, in a couple of instances written soon after the event, mention a wind during the battle that discomfited Eugenius's forces and contributed to their defeat.[40] Some modern historians have found this evidence unpalatable, despite

34. Heim, esp. 270–74.

35. Orosius VII.35.5 ("Theodosius incruentam victoriam Deo procurante suscepit"), 7 (526, 527).

36. Orosius VII.35.20 (531).

37. *HE* XI.32 (1036).

38. Orosius VII.35.19 (531): "quos utique perdidisse lucrum et vinci vincere fuit."

39. Orosius VII.35.9 (527). These wars included that of Honorius's general Mascezel against the African rebel Gildo, in which through prayer and fasting he "earned victory without war and vengeance without killing" (Orosius VII.36.5 [534]), and the defeat of Radagaisus, likewise effected without bloodshed or killing (Orosius VII.37.14 [541]).

40. On the sources for the battle, see François Paschoud, *Zosime: Histoire nouvelle* (n. 24 above), II.2 (Appendice C: La bataille du Frigidus), 474–503 (with map), to which add Matthias Springer, "Die

the fact that by the usual canons of source criticism such evidence has a strong initial claim to credibility, and despite the fact that it has long been known that a strong wind, the Bora, occurs in the very Alpine region where the battle was fought, at the very time of year when the battle took place.

In September 1994 a conference was held in Slovenia near the site of the battlefield to mark the battle's 1600th anniversary.[41] Mirko Kovač there presented a paper that argued that the Bora of September is always preceded by a thunderstorm with heavy precipitation, which historically can lead to flooding in the Vipava river valley where the battle occurred.[42] In the chapter on the battle in his 2011 book *The Last Pagans of Rome*, Alan Cameron relied on Kovač's argument to cast doubt on the accounts of the wind during the battle, reasoning that since no source mentioned rain, there must have really been no wind either. Cameron goes on to argue that all the contemporary sources mentioning the miraculous wind go back to certain texts authored by Ambrose of Milan, thus undercutting the veracity of such accounts by reducing the number of actual contemporary literary witnesses to one individual, who made it all up.[43]

Cameron's argument in this chapter of his impressive work strikes me at times as special pleading.[44] Not only is all this debunking of the Frigidus's miraculous wind irrelevant to Cameron's larger, valid point—that Christian sources then and later mischaracterized the battle as one between paganism and Christianity—but it also doesn't take into consideration the decidedly nonsupernatural and quite sufficient alternative explanation for the apparent congruence of a number of contemporary sources regarding the wind, their common origin in Theodosian war propaganda.[45]

We first hear of divine intervention in the battle in a letter from Ambrose to Theodosius written as soon as the bishop had learned of the latter's victory. At one point Ambrose writes:

Schlacht am Frigidus als quellenkundliches und literaturgeschichtliches Problem," in R. Bratož, ed., *Westillyricum und Nordostitalien in der spätrömischen Zeit* (Ljubljana, 1996), 45–93. See also the discussion by François Heim, "Victoire sans combat" (n. 32 above), 274; idem, *La théologie de la victoire*, 154–56.

41. François Paschoud, "Pour un mille six centième anniversaire: le Frigidus en ebullition," *Antiquité tardive* 5 (1997): 275–80.

42. Mirko Kovač, "Bora or Summer Storm: Meteorological Aspect of the Battle at Frigidus," in Bratož (n. 40 above), 109–17.

43. Cameron (n. 32 above), 107–17, 126.

44. Esp. 115–16.

45. This failure to give Theodosian propaganda its due in influencing accounts of the battle of the Frigidus is puzzling especially in Cameron's case, who wrote a book situating certain works of the poet Claudian precisely in the context of Theodosian propaganda, on which book see note 54 below.

Thanks be to the Lord our God who has responded to your faith and your piety and has brought back a model of ancient holiness, so that we see happening in our own time what we marvel at when read in the Scriptures.[46]

In a second letter written to Theodosius soon after, Ambrose returned to the subject:

Your victory, like the miracles of old such as those of holy Moses and holy Joshua the son of Nun, of Samuel and of David, is reckoned to be of the ancient sort, not because of any human judgment but because of the outpouring of heavenly grace [it manifested].[47]

Clearly something extraordinary had happened during the battle, something so miraculous that it seemed a divine intervention on Theodosius's behalf comparable to those recorded in the Bible in favor of war leaders such as Moses and Joshua. In a homiletic commentary on Ps. 36:15 ("let the spear of the sinners enter into their heart and let their bow be broken")[48] given soon thereafter, Ambrose was more specific.[49] He spoke there of the recent battle between the sacrilegious pagans and the pious emperor, in the course of which a wind had suddenly sprung up "which knocked the shields out of the hands of the infidels and turned all the shafts and missiles back upon the army of the sinner." Besides the wounds they suffered, the hearts of Eugenius's soldiery sank, according to Ambrose, at the thought that God was thus manifestly fighting against them.[50] In Rufinus's similar account written eight or nine years after the battle, the miraculous wind is placed on the second day, after the first day's battle had gone against Theodosius and after the emperor's prayer as noted earlier.[51] Slightly later accounts added that the spears of Theodosius's army were accelerated to lethal effect by the same wind that discomfited their opponents,[52] Orosius adducing in support the pagan poet Claudian, who in his panegyrical

---

46. *Epistulae extra collectionem* 2.3 (*CSEL* 82:3, 178–79). Translation of J. H. W. G. Liebeschuetz, *Ambrose of Milan: Political Letters and Speeches, Translated Texts for Historians* 43 (Liverpool: Liverpool University Press, 2005), 217 (modified).

47. *Epistulae extra collectionem* 3.4 (*CSEL* 82:3, 181).

48. *Framea peccatorum intret in cor ipsorum et arcus eorum confringatur.* Ambrose here uses, of course, an Old Latin text, which I have translated.

49. On the date of this sermon, Cameron, 114, n. 110.

50. *Explanatio psalmorum XII* (*CSEL* 64, 91).

51. Above, note 17; *HE* XI. 34 (1039).

52. Augustine, *DCD* 5.26 (*CCL* 47, 161–62); Orosius VII.35.17–18 (*CSEL* 5:530–31).

poem on the third consulship of Theodosius's son Honorius (begun 1 January 396) does in fact write:

> With icy gales from the mountain the north wind
> Overwhelmed the enemy's battle lines, and their own reversed missiles
> Turned upon their originators, and the whirlwind thrust back their
> spears.[53]

A skeptic has grounds for doubt, both as to the miracle itself and its supposed confirmation by the pagan poet. And though the aid of natural forces can always be attributable to coincidence, the similarity of Christian and pagan reports on the battle of the Frigidus cannot. As Cameron has conclusively argued, Claudian was an official propagandist for Stilicho, the true master of the West after the death of Theodosius in 395, whose verses on the battle cast reflected glory on Theodosius's son and Stilicho's imperial puppet Honorius.[54] The similarity in the accounts of the miraculous wind is due to their all stemming from the same source: official propaganda from the court of Theodosius and his son.

Such doubts of the miraculous in this battle, despite the dramatic suggestiveness of the sudden wind, could have been voiced at the time, as perhaps suggested by Rufinus's comment that the pagans (*impii*) could scarcely credit what had happened.[55] But it was the politico-religious context of the battle as it was depicted in contemporary Christian circles that elevated a chance meteorological occurrence to the level of divine intervention. Christian authors emphasize the piety of Theodosius, ranged against the pagan hopes that rode with the army of Eugenius. Once again, the logic of civil war led to a climactic and decisive encounter, and here as with the battles of 312 and 313 the stakes were elevated to the sacral, pitting Christian against pagan, and thus necessarily glossing over the fact that Eugenius, though supported by pagans, seems himself to have been Christian.[56] Given the politico-religious context, it is understandable that Orosius concluded his account of the battle

---

53. Claudian, *Panegyricus dictus Honorio Augusto tertium consuli* (n. 3 above, 56), ll. 93–95: "Te propter gelidis Aquilo de monte procellis / obruit adversas acies revolutaque tela / vertit in auctores et turbine reppulit hastas."

54. Alan Cameron, *Claudian: Poetry and Propaganda at the Court of Honorius* (Oxford: Clarendon, 1970), 42, 59.

55. *HE* XI.33 (1039): "vix fortasse ab impiis credantur quae gesta sunt."

56. Ambrose, *Epistulae extra collectionem traditae* 10.8 (*CSEL* 82:3, 209); Sozomen VII.22.4 (335). In this respect, Cameron provides a good corrective to the contemporary Christian interpretation of the battle in his chapter on the Frigidus.

by characterizing it as a duel between a party that relied on idols and its own strength and a party that placed its hopes in God alone, a duel decided by a heavenly judgment.[57]

The events and outcome of the battle were so striking to the imagination of Christian writers that in the East the mid-fifth century church history of Theodoret of Cyrrhus told of a vision during the battle in which Theodosius saw John the Evangelist and the Apostle Philip amidst his army dressed in white on white horses,[58] and in the West in the 410s Augustine, who as we will see was otherwise skeptical of the ability to recognize providence in contemporary history, seems convinced nonetheless that the hand of God was manifested in the battle.[59] Happening as it did on the very eve of what would prove to be the irrevocable division of the empire, the battle of the Frigidus provided both East and West assurance that God really did intervene in the course of war, and an exemplary portrait of what that would look like.

The imperial propaganda of the House of Theodosius seems to have been at pains to show that God provided direct and immediate support for the emperor's deeds, including his actions in war. In 383 Theodosius revived the *manus Dei* motif seen most prominently earlier in consecration coins of Constantine, here showing the hand of God reaching down to crown the emperor's young son Arcadius with a wreath.[60] The application of this image to contemporary representations of war is also seen in a curious fragment surviving from the history of the fiercely anti-Christian Eunapius of Sardis. In commemoration of an imperial victory, the urban prefect at Rome assembled a series of illustrated panels in the Circus Maximus. Upon one of the panels was painted a hand stretching downward from heaven, marked with the caption, "the hand of God driving off the barbarians."[61] One can probably get a good idea of the appearance of this painting from one of the nave mosaics in the Roman church of Santa Maria Maggiore, dedicated by Pope Sixtus III (432–440), which illustrates Josh. 10:11, where the Lord sent from heaven great

57. Orosius VII.35.22 (532).

58. *Theodoret Kirchengeschichte*, ed. L. Parmentier, *GCS* 19 (Leipzig, 1911), V.24.5–10 (325–26).

59. *DCD* 5.26 (*CCL* 47, 161–62).

60. On the *manus Dei* theme, especially in Theodosian coinage, see *RIC* 9, 153, 183, 194, 196, 222, 229, 242, 256, 282, 299; John D. MacIsaac, "'The Hand of God': A Numismatic Study," *Traditio* 31 (1975): 326; Sabine MacCormack, *Art and Ceremony in Late Antiquity* (Berkeley: University of California Press, 1981), esp. 11, 189, 191–92, 202–3.

61. Eunapius 68 (= *Excerpta De Sententiis* 72), in R. C. Blockley, *The Fragmentary Classicising Historians of the Later Roman Empire: Eunapius, Olympiodorus, Priscus and Malchus* (hereafter Blockley) (Liverpool: Francis Cairns, 1983), vol. II, 108/109.

hailstones to destroy the army of the Amorites fighting Joshua. In a scene showing Joshua leading a group of Israelite soldiers against the enemy, the mosaic shows stones falling onto the Amorites from a hand appearing in the sky.[62]

Much of the recent scholarship on this Eunapian fragment has centered on determining the time and place of the event described in it, a discussion bedeviled by the fact that the tenth-century Byzantine excerptor who preserved the fragment in *De Sententiis* apparently garbled the transmission of the text, and by the inability to identify the mysterious "Πέρσης" said to be the prefect here (an ethnic designation? a proper name? a nickname?). Based on its placement in the order of the fragments in *De Sententiis*, most commentators date the event described in the fragment to about the year 400. Recently David Woods has argued that we cannot exclude the possibility here of a retrojected Eunapian digression, and identifies the event in the fragment with the triumphal celebration held in Rome by Constantius II in 357.[63]

By contrast, relatively little attention has been paid to Eunapius's characterization of the display as being an occasion for mockery and laughter. Whatever may be the reason for Eunapius's scorn here, his description does seem to suggest that such a public display of an image of the hand of God intervening in battle was something of a novelty in Rome, an indication that the image is to be associated with Theodosius's revival after a long absence of the *manus Dei* theme in imperial iconography. We see here made visible the idea that the Almighty Christian God intervened from heaven on behalf of his faithful Christian rulers fighting in battle, an idea and an image that constituted a prominent theme in Theodosian propaganda. This image, made part of a public display that is the late antique version of a propaganda film, was so striking in its presentation and so successful in its propagation that Eunapius, who at one point complained of his inability to get accurate information from the west,[64] even in the east of the empire had heard of it. In the increasingly Christianized empire of the late fourth century, the emperor was no longer ambiguous and reticent in the advertisement of his religious allegiance and the favor bestowed upon him, in war and peace, by the God of the Christians.

62. Aldo Nestori and Fabrizio Bisconti, eds., *I mosaici paleocristiani di Santa Maria Maggiore negli acquarelli della collezione Wilpert* (Vatican City: Pontifical Institute of Christian Archaeology, 2000), table 33.

63. David Woods, "A Persian at Rome: Ammianus and Eunapius, *Frg.* 68," in Jan Willem Drijvers and David Hunt, eds., *The Late Roman World and Its Historian: Interpreting Ammianus Marcellinus* (London: Routledge, 1999), 156–65, which includes a good summary of earlier scholarship.

64. Eunapius 66.2 (= *Excerpta De Sententiis* 64); Blockley, vol. II, 102/103.

CHRISTIAN VALORIZATION OF WAR AND THE MILITARY:
AMBROSE OF MILAN

What I have termed Theodosian war propaganda, as well as contemporary works influenced by it, often seem to present a new vision of war transformed by Christian values, which, sometimes explicitly, rejects the classical reliance on one's own strength and the grimly heroic glorification of the carnage of battle, and instead refers the ultimate attainment of success to a pious connection with God. The fact that this new picture of war emanated to a large extent from imperial propaganda arguably in a way only magnifies its significance for the period. If emperors now touted less the valor of their armies and more their intimacy with the divine, there was a risk, as Eunapius had seen and lamented,[65] that the skill of commanders and the bravery of soldiers would be denigrated to the detriment of Roman arms. A long scholarly tradition, going back to antiquity itself, has held that the Christian take on war and the military increasingly ascendant in the fourth-century empire enervated the will and sapped the morale of the Roman army and citizenry, leading to the destruction of the Western empire.[66]

Those moderns who suppose that the Western empire fell due to the tranquilizing effects of Christianity are not only embarrassed by the continued existence of the Eastern empire, where the lotus-eaters of the ascendant religion were more numerous and concentrated, but also ignore the evidence of fourth-century Christian accommodation to war and the military. The late fourth century in particular witnessed a consolidation and even the beginnings of a regulation of Christian mores related to war, the culmination of a process that had begun with deliberate policy to that end instituted by the emperor Constantine many decades earlier. The older prohibitions in Christian writings against military service were now modified or ignored. Military virtues, especially courage, were now potentially praiseworthy. The killing of the enemy in war was not to be considered murder. And it was even possible now that war itself could be an agent of justice. The extent to which the sensibilities of Christians shifted on this subject over time is illustrated by the move from

65. Eunapius 68 (= *Excerpta De Sententiis* 72); Blockley, vol. II, 108/109,where Eunapius complains that the paintings in the Roman Circus nowhere credited the victory to the valor of the emperor and his soldiers.

66. Such sentiments asserting the baleful effects of Christianity on the morale of Romans facing the threat of Germanic barbarians often appear, oddly, in French historians such as C. Jullian, *Histoire de la Gaule* (Paris, 1926), t. 8, 358 and André Piganiol, *Le sac de Rome* (Paris, 1964), 84.

the era of Constantine, when Christian service in a still largely pagan army was first openly tolerated, and the situation almost exactly a century later, when in 416 it was decreed that *only* Christians could serve in the army.[67]

It has already been shown how Lactantius in his *Epitome* of the *Divine Institutes*, written about 320, modified his earlier categorical condemnation of war.[68] The loyal subject of an emperor who won battles thanks to God, and who relied upon the continued service of Christians in the ranks, now omitted his earlier prohibition of Christian military service. Although salient features of the late fourth-century Theodosian paradigm for Christian warfare seemed to minimize the activity of soldiers in battle, merely earthly actions overshadowed by divine disposition, Lactantius had already decades before in the *Epitome*, in what seems a deliberate refutation of his own earlier criticism in the *Divine Institutes*, praised military virtues either implicitly by omission or explicitly by addition. There was no more talk of the bloody horrors attendant to the exercise of successful military leadership. Instead, the failure to preserve military discipline was now cited as one of the calamities of the end times. Whereas in the *Divine Institutes* Lactantius had plainly stated that patriotism was no virtue, he now in the *Epitome* wrote that courage (*fortitudo*) was a positive good precisely in the circumstance of one fighting *pro patria*.[69]

Patriotism and the exaltation of courage in war also appear in works of Ambrose of Milan. Already mentioned as a source for Theodosian war propaganda, Ambrose had been near Ground Zero of its most spectacular manifestation, and his witness to the battle of the Frigidus is the most "hot off the press" of all the extant accounts.[70] As scion of a prominent family, Ambrose flew the colors of a type of late Roman patriotism, tinged with nostalgia for the heroes and virtues of the ancient Republic, that was characteristic of his time and class.[71] As a Christian, Ambrose at times seemed to equate loyalty to Rome with adherence to Nicene orthodoxy, and correspondingly to identify heresy with treason. For him, the fact that the Gothic depredations in the Balkans occurred in the same areas where heresy had been rampant was not a coincidence: "the cause of divine displeasure goes back earlier, in that wherever the bonds of faithfulness to God were broken, those to the Roman empire broke

67. *Cod. Theod.* XVI.10.21 (904).

68. Ch. 2, notes 85 to 90.

69. *Epit.* 56 (61); ch. 2, note 90 above.

70. See Paschoud's Appendice C, note 40 above.

71. On Ambrose's not untypical nostalgic patriotism, see, for example, J.-R. Palanque, *Saint Ambroise et l'Empire romain* (Paris: Boccard, 1933), 327–35; Clementina Corbellini, "Il problema della *militia* in Sant' Ambrogio," *Historia* 27 (1978): 630–36 and esp. 630, n. 1 and the literature cited there.

at the same time."[72] In the report to the emperors from the bishops attending the Council of Aquileia in 381, a report generally assumed to have been written by Ambrose, there is recounted the deeds of one Julianus Valens, a heretical bishop in the Balkans, who had refused to attend the council "lest he be compelled to account to the bishops for the overthrow of his country (*patria*) and the ruin of his fellow citizens." This man had been seen dressed in Gothic attire, "which without any doubt is sacrilege, not only in a bishop, but in anybody who is a Christian, since even if the priests of Gothic idolatry usually appear this way, it is far removed from Roman custom."[73] In Ambrose's dismay at a Christian donning tribal dress, one glimpses his antipathy to the barbarian enemies of Rome, an antipathy witnessed in other comments in his writings and shared by many of his contemporaries, Christian and pagan alike.[74] Such sentiments bespeak a shared sense of peril and a certain huddled defensiveness in the turbulent conditions of the late fourth-century empire.[75]

Ambrose spoke most directly to love of *patria* and the courage necessary for its defense in his work *De officiis*, written sometime after 386.[76] In this work Ambrose sought to transform his literary model, Cicero's classic treatise of the same title on the civic virtues, into a learned Christian exposition of the proper ethical stance and consequent public behavior required by the new dispensation. The work was directed primarily to Ambrose's immediate clerical entourage and his fellow bishops and followers in northern Italy, but prominent cultured laypeople—among the few certain to appreciate the Tullian echoes—certainly formed part of its audience as well.[77] Rather than attempting to Christianize Cicero or "Stoicize" Christianity, Ambrose in *De officiis* aimed to demonstrate the inherent superiority of the Christian message, especially as it was embodied in Scripture, over the inferior and outdated classical teachings on ethics, and in so doing incidentally "despoiling the Egyptians."[78]

72. *De Fide* II 16, 139 (*CSEL* 78, 106).

73. *Epist.* 4.9 (*CSEL* 82:3, 322–23). Liebeschuetz's translation (modified).

74. Palanque (note 71 above), 331–32; L. C. Ruggini, "Preguidizi razziali, ostilita' politica e culturale, intolleranza religiosa nell'impero romano," *Athenaeum* 46 (1968): 139–52 (on Ambrose, 148–49); Corbellini (n. 71 above).

75. M. Meslin, *Les Ariens d'Occident* (Paris, 1967), 4.

76. Much of the important earlier scholarship on Ambrose's *De officiis* is incorporated into, if not superseded by, the recent edition and translation by Ivor J. Davidson, *Ambrose:* De officiis (Oxford: Oxford University Press, 2001), vol. 1, introduction, text and translation; vol. 2, commentary.

77. Davidson, vol. 1, 61–64.

78. Davidson, vol. 1, 54–61, whose conclusions I follow in the text, gives an excellent summary of the scholarly debates over the purpose of *De officiis*. On *spoliatio* as a stock idea in contemporary and later Christian literature, 59.

For Cicero, as with Ambrose, patriotism ranked high in the scale of moral obligations. Of all types of human fellowship (*societas*), "none is more serious and none dearer" than the attachment to one's country. "Parents are dear, and children, relatives; and acquaintances are dear, but our *patria* has entwined together into one all the affections of them all."[79] Cicero goes on explicitly to rank patriotism as highest on the scale of proper individual obligations:

> *Patria* and parents would be first; for we are obliged to them for the greatest kindnesses. Next our children and our whole household, which looks to us alone and can have no other refuge. Then our relations, who are congenial to us and with whom even our fortunes are generally shared.[80]

Later in his work, however, perhaps following a different Greek model,[81] Cicero ranks the highest human obligations as being "prima dis immortalibus, secunda patriae, tertia parentibus."[82] Ambrose seems to have preferred this last formulation, for in his own work he wrote that "the piety of justice is first towards God, second, towards our *patria*, third, towards our parents, and lastly towards all."[83]

This seems to be a more or less straightforward transposition of Cicero's valuation of patriotism into Ambrose's own scale of values.[84] But arguably more than that is at play here. As noted in the previous chapter, many decades earlier Lactantius in the *Divine Institutes* had criticized the poet Lucilius's ranking of the virtues which had placed patriotism first, arguing that such a "virtue" only emerged in the context of war, a circumstance that necessarily involved the eclipse of true virtue amidst the greed, hatred, and violence stirred up by conflict among men.[85] Though Lactantius himself soon thereafter came to esteem those fighting *pro patria*,[86] there is nonetheless evidence sufficient to show that his earlier sentiment opposing patriotism was shared by many Christians throughout the fourth century.[87] The pagan senator Symmachus

---

79. Cicero, *De officiis* I 17, 57 (23). I use here the translation by M. T. Griffin and E. M. Atkins, *Cicero: On Duties* (Cambridge: Cambridge University Press, 1991), 23 (modified).

80. Cicero, *De officiis* I 17, 58 (24); Griffin and Atkins translation modified, 24.

81. Davidson commentary, vol. 2, 567.

82. Cicero, *De officiis* I 45, 160 (67).

83. Ambrose, *De officiis* I 27, 127 (*CCL* 15, 46): "Iustitiae autem pietas est: prima in Deum, secunda in patriam, tertia in parentes, item in omnes."

84. Palanque (n. 71 above), 328.

85. Lactantius, *Div. Inst.* VI.5.3, 6.12–24; ch. 2, notes 71, 72 above.

86. *Epit.* 56 (61), 739: "fortitudo, si pro patria dimices, bonum est."

seems to have taken note of such Christians in his *relatio* to Valentinian II in 384 asking for the restoration of the altar of Victoria to the senate house. In that work Symmachus asks rhetorically, "Who is so friendly with barbarians as not to need the altar of Victoria?" He answers the question by referring as follows to his opponents, presumably Christians of a Lactantian stripe: "Let those reject her power [viz. Victoria's] for whom it has proved no boon."[88] Symmachus here seems to refer to those Christians who had "opted out" of Rome's struggle to defeat her barbarian enemies.[89]

A straightforward and unthinking transposition of Cicero's esteem for patriotism into Ambrose's *De officiis* seems unlikely, especially given his repeated insistence in that work on the superiority of Christian over pagan values.[90] The supposition that statements *pro patria* simply reflect his actual sentiments,[91] while undoubtedly true, is also insufficient to explain the appearance of such passages in *De officiis*, for surely Ambrose also thought to be true other unmentioned things as well. Besides, he elsewhere degraded one's *patria* to the third rank of goods behind those of the soul and of the body, linking it with other characteristics of an individual that are the result of happenstance such as money, power, friends, and fame.[92] Certainly part of the explanation for Ambrose's exaltation of patriotism in *De officiis* lies in his previously mentioned equating of loyalty to Rome with Nicene orthodoxy, and the resulting equation of heresy with treason.[93] This identification of Rome's enemies with those of the church is seen in a passage where Ambrose writes that it is a harmful act to give money to someone "who is plotting against the *patria*, who wants to use your money to gather a band of desperadoes to attack the church."[94] It is therefore natural that the bishop of Milan would appeal to the patriotic sentiments among his fellow clergy so as to stoke their zeal in the defense of orthodoxy. But in writing on patriotism in *De officiis* Ambrose

---

87. E.g., note 196 below on Crispinianus.

88. *CSEL* 82:10 (23, 24), *Epist.* 72a (Maur. 17a).

89. On the interpretation of this passage as linking Christians with Rome's barbarian enemies, Richard Klein, *Symmachus: Eine tragische Gestalt des ausgehenden Heidentums* (Darmstadt, 1971), 101–4.

90. E.g., Davidson, vol. 1, 21: "Ambrose constantly insists that biblical truth and biblical exemplars are intrinsically superior to anything offered by the classical tradition."

91. On this see Heim, 138.

92. *De Abraham* II 6, 33, *CSEL* 32:1, ed. C. Schenkl, 590: "tertia sunt quae accidunt, hoc est divitiae potestates patria amici gloria."

93. Notes 72, 73 above.

94. Ambrose, *De Officiis* I 30, 144 (*CCL* 15, 52). Davidson, commentary, vol. 2, 585, speculates that Ambrose had Julianus Valens in mind in this passage.

was also addressing fellow Christians, clerical and lay, who followed Lactantius and others in thinking patriotism no virtue, and was also thereby countering the claims of pagan critics such as Symmachus that Christians were unpatriotic. Ambrose would make it clear in *De officiis* that Christians were second to none in their love of country.

Ambrose's effort in *De officiis* to counter both pacifistic Christians and pagan critics of such pacifism also helps to explain his lengthy treatment of courage (*fortitudo*), especially in Book I. There he writes that courage "stands out in loftiness and greatness of mind in both the military and domestic spheres," and introduces his discussion of courage proper with the observation that courage is "loftier than the other virtues."[95] Cicero had in his work also ranked courage among the cardinal virtues, but rather than simply adopting that virtue in the spirit of a Christian Stoic, Ambrose "ends up extolling martial courage with greater enthusiasm than Cic[ero]."[96] That his determined praise of even martial courage was directed both to Christian and pagan critics is patently indicated by at least two passages in *De officiis*. So, to Christians who followed Lactantius in arguing that justice was incompatible with war and the supposed virtues connected with it, Ambrose retorted that "courage, which in war protects the *patria* from barbarians and in the domestic sphere defends the weak or one's friends from robbers, is full of justice."[97]

Likewise, in the midst of his discussion of courage Ambrose pauses to take note of pagan critics who charged that Christians were pacifists and therefore incapable of participating in war, writing that "perhaps there are those so obsessed by the glory of it that they think there is courage only in war, and for that reason I had digressed, since courage is lacking among us [Christians]."[98] Ambrose goes on to refute such a perception by praising the courage in war of a succession of Old Testament heroes, as he in fact had already done previously in Book I, where he wrote of Abraham's valor in standing up against hordes of enemy kings,[99] and of Moses' fearlessness in undertaking wars against powerful enemies of his people.[100] Christians had no reason to feel inferior to pagans in matters of war, since "our ancestors, men such as Joshua son of Nun, Jerubbaal, Samson and David, also attained the highest glory in war."[101] In his subsequent

95. *De officiis* I 115, 175 (*CCL* 15, 41, 64).
96. Davidson, vol. 2, 605.
97. *De officiis* I 129 (*CCL* 15, 47).
98. *De officiis* I 196 (*CCL* 15, 73).
99. *De officiis* I 109 (40).
100. *De officiis* I 135 (49).
101. *De officiis* I 175 (64).

listing of martial heroes of the Old Testament, Ambrose notes the bravery and exploits of Joshua, the triumph of Gideon with only three hundred men over an enormous enemy army, and Jonathan, who made a name for himself while still a young man. "Why should I even mention the Maccabees?"[102] Repeatedly outnumbered, they had defeated one enemy after the other with tremendous slaughter. In one battle, the bravery of Eleazar in stabbing an elephant from beneath, thereby encompassing his own destruction as the animal fell on top of him, had so impressed King Antiochus that he immediately sued for peace. The courage of the Maccabees was displayed not only in success but in adversity, as when Judas Macabaeus had died in a valiant but doomed struggle of 900 men against 20,000. "What can I say about his brother Jonathan? Fighting with a small band against the royal armies, deserted by his own men, with only two left he resumed the battle, drove back the enemy, and recalled his fleeing men to share in his triumph."[103] Ambrose concludes this discussion by writing of martial courage that "in it there is no middling model of what is honorable and seemly, for it prefers death to slavery and disgrace."[104]

Ambrose's foremost biblical exemplar of martial courage is David, who "as king was second to none in war, a partner of his soldiers' toils, and brave in battle."[105] David had since the church's beginning served as a typical prefiguration of Christ, but Davidic symbolism subsequently proved to be quite plastic and polysemic. In particular, David came to be seen as the model par excellence for Christian kings, and although a consideration of early Christian ideas regarding royalty largely exceeds the concerns of the present work, it is worth noting that Ambrose seems to have been the first Latin writer to use David as a model for Christian rulers. Ambrose at points made an explicit comparison between David and the emperor Theodosius, and the apparent dedication of his *Apologia David* to the emperor confirms that work's status as an early form of *Fürstenspiegel*, the "mirror of princes."[106] David, who "was brave in war, patient in adversity, peaceful at Jerusalem, mild in victory,"[107] does also in

---

102. *De officiis* I 196 (73).

103. *De officiis* I 197–201; here, 201 (*CCL* 15, 75).

104. *De officiis* I 202 (*CCL* 15, 75): "in quo non mediocris honesti ac decori forma est quod mortem servituti praeferat ac turpitudini." Ambrose here echoes his model, Cicero, *De officiis* I 23, 81 (33): "But when time and necessity demands it, one must fight it out even hand-to-hand and prefer death to slavery and disgrace" ("sed cum tempus necessitasque postulat, decertandum manu est et mors servituti turpitudinique anteponenda.").

105. *De officiis* II 32 (*CCL* 15, 109).

106. On this especially see Marc Reydellet, "La Bible miroir des princes," in *Bible de tous les temps* 2: *Le monde latin antique et la Bible*, ed. Jacques Fontaine and Charles Pietri (Paris: Beauchesne, 1985), esp. 435, 438–39.

De officiis exemplify an ideal for a Christian king. And of all his characteristics as a leader, it is David's courage that is preeminent. David was

> victor in all his battles, sword in hand until a ripe old age, a warrior in the midst of fierce fighting in a war waged against Titans, eager for glory, heedless of his own safety.[108]

One cannot mistake the unqualified and almost enthusiastic approval of courage in battle exhibited in this passage. Considering especially the *literati* among the intended audience for *De officiis*, who were familiar with the classical examples of martial courage in Ambrose's Tullian exemplar, we are entitled to see in this passage not only the replacement of pagan with Christian models, but also the authentic admiration of a late fourth-century Christian and Roman patriot for the soldierly qualities of those defending the empire against its barbarian enemies.

Ambrose would have perhaps preferred that all wars end as had that with Eugenius, with direct divine intervention. He was certainly cognizant that such was usually not the case. Although he ascribed Theodosius's military successes to his faith,[109] the bishop of Milan had, as we have seen, a realistic appreciation of the courage in war exhibited by soldiers. This realism regarding the nature of battle surfaced in 384 in Ambrose's reply to Symmachus's *relatio* on the restoration to the senate house of the altar of Victoria. Whereas Symmachus argued that the cult of Victoria had contributed to Roman success,[110] Ambrose derided the idea that this success had anything to do with pagan cultic practices, and attacked especially the notion of a goddess with the power to effectuate victory. If Victoria was so powerful, why did soldiers claim victory for themselves? Why did there even have to be a battle, the outcome of which, not a goddess, would determine who won? Indeed, "the trophies of victory are not to be found in the entrails of cattle, but in the strength of warriors . . . it is due to the power of legions, not religions."[111] Admittedly, for polemical purposes Ambrose's "rationalist" approach here to the question of the responsibility for

107. *De officiis* I 114 (*CCL* 15, 41): "David etiam fortis in bello, patiens in adversis, in Hierusalem pacificus, in victoria mansuetus."

108. *De officiis* I 177 (*CCL* 15, 65): "in omnibus victor proeliis, usque ad summum senectutem manu promptus, bello adversus Titanas suscepto, ferocibus bellator misceretur agminibus, gloriae cupidus, incuriosus salutis."

109. *De obitu Theodosii* 6, 8 (*CSEL* 73, 374, 375).

110. *Epist.* 72a.3 (Maur. 17a), *CSEL* 73, 23–24.

111. *Epist* 73.7, 30 (Maurist 18), 36, 50.

victory emphasizes the human agency—which he certainly believed played a significant role in the final outcome—in a chain of causation ultimately traceable back to God.[112]

A more concrete indicator of the new realism toward war visible in late fourth-century Christian writers and the necessity of making some accommodation to Christian participation in it is found in one of the so-called canonical letters of Basil of Caesarea, written in 374. In the course of replying to certain questions posed to him by his friend Amphilochius of Iconium, Basil noted that earlier church fathers had not equated killing in war with the crime of murder, a position that he ascribed to their excusing wars in defense of morality and religion.[113] The fact that Amphilochius asked such a question does indicate the relative novelty in 374 of Christians having to come up with authoritative statements on the question.

In the writings of Ambrose of Milan, especially his *De officiis*, we see more clearly than in perhaps any other late fourth-century Christian thinker a grappling with the new issues confronting a church that was increasingly ascendant in a state that had to fight, and kill, in order to defend itself. But if one merely paints a picture of a powerful prelate imbued with Roman patriotism who exalted courage in war as a laudable virtue even for fellow Christians, as Louis Swift put it, "we run the risk of oversimplifying his approach."[114] This supposed theoretician of just war, who, basing himself on Cicero's dictum regarding the first priority of justice,[115] seemingly conceded to political leadership the right to fight back against aggressors,[116] elsewhere in *De officiis*

112. Richard Klein, *Symmachus* (Darmstadt, 1971), 126 and n. 8 on Ambrose's "rationalist" approach. Heim, 136, argues that Ambrose's defensive strategy here in opposing Symmachus led to statements unrepresentative of the bishop's actual assessment of human *virtus*. Even in the heat of his polemic against Symmachus, Ambrose does seem to be reserving a role for God when he writes that victory "munus est, non potestas; donatur non dominatur." But in his zeal to deny the existence of the goddess Victoria, Ambrose overemphasizes human agency, and his rhetoric, if not his actual estimation of the relative causative roles of human and divine agency in victory, produces an irresolvable contradiction here between the conception of victory as a divine gift and its attribution to the result of human activity. Cf. *De Abraham* I 16 (*CSEL* 32:1, ed. C. Schenkl, 513), "qui vincit non debet adrogare sibi victoriam, sed deferre deo." On this controversy over the restoration of the altar, see now Cameron (n. 32 above), 33–51, and Peter Brown, *Through the Eye of a Needle* (Princeton: Princeton University Press, 2012), 103–8.

113. *Saint Basile: Lettres*, ed. and trans. Yves Courtonne (Paris: Budé, 1961), v. 2, E188.13 (130).

114. Louis J. Swift, "St. Ambrose on Violence and War," *Transactions and Proceedings of the American Philological Association* 101 (1970): 535.

115. Cicero, *De officiis* I 7, 20 (9).

116. Ch. 4, notes 85, 86 below.

specifically forbade individual Christians from exercising the right of self-defense.

> But that very thing is excluded with us which philosophers think to
> be the duty of justice. For they say that the first expression of justice
> is that one should harm no one unless provoked by injury. This is
> nullified by the authority of the Gospel. For the Scripture wills that
> the spirit of the Son of Man should be in us, who came to confer
> grace, not to inflict injury.[117]

Therefore Ambrose in resolving Carneades's paradox as to whether a wise man
is justified in saving his life at the expense of a fool's goes even further than
had the pacifist Lactantius, who had finessed the question by positing that a
Christian would never find himself in a situation requiring such a choice.[118] For

> a Christian man, just and wise, ought not to save his own life by the
> death of another, so that even if he should happen upon an armed
> robber, he cannot, struck, strike back, lest by defending his life he
> defile his own sanctity. The verdict on this is plain and clear in the
> books of the Gospel: "Put back thy sword: for all who hath struck
> with the sword shall be slain by the sword [Matt. 26:52]."[119]

Even in his appeal to the elements of the Theodosian model for Christian
warfare, a model broadcast by historiography and contemporary state
propaganda, Ambrose reveals continuities with the longstanding pacifistic
current in Christianity. The reliance upon divine disposition for the outcome
of battle manifests if nothing else a disinclination to exercise that very courage
in war which Ambrose had praised in *De officiis*. The notion of obtaining a
bloodless victory may evidence a Christian slant to war, but it also obviously
shows distaste for the shedding of blood. And even though Basil of Caesarea
acknowledged that killing in war was not murder, he nonetheless prescribed
penance for those who had done so.[120] The pacifistic current in Christianity had
not ceased with the conversion of Constantine, to which current of thinking
we now turn.

---

117. *De officiis* I 28, 131 (*CCL* 15, 47). Translation by H. De Romestin in *A Select Library of Nicene and Post-Nicene Fathers*, 2ndseries, vol. 10, 22–23 (modified).

118. Ch. 2, note 70 above.

119. *De officiis* III 4, 27 (*CSEL* 15, 163). De Romestin's translation, 71 (modified). On the meaning of *pietas* in this passage, Swift, n. 114 above, 537.

120. *E*188.13 (n. 113 above).

Stirrings of Conscience: Penance and the Pollution of State Service

At some time in the first years of the fourth century, nineteen bishops and twenty-four priests, mostly from southern Spain, met in council at the town of Illiberis (Elvira), the present-day Granada. Most of the canons issued by this council dealt with matters of sexual delicts and clerical discipline, but canon 56 stated that "it has been decided that a magistrate is under the prohibition that he be kept away from church during the one year in which he acts as *duumvir*."[121] In provincial Spain at this period, *duumvir* was the most common designation for a municipal magistrate, called to service on a town council for one year by rotation or election.[122] The evident distaste felt for such service by the clergy assembled at Illiberis is thought by some to be due to the requirement of the *duumvir* to participate in the idolatrous ceremonial attendant to civic ritual.[123] A. W. W. Dale was, however, doubtless correct in 1882 in seeing such participation as a subsidiary reason for the canonical prohibition, and instead hearkened back for an explanation to the sentiments of Tertullian a century earlier, who had expressed repugnance at the idea of a Christian official imprisoning or torturing individuals in the performance of civic duties.[124] Though in the context of other punishments decreed by the council the exclusion from church for a year was relatively mild,[125] that such a prohibition existed at all bespeaks the persistence over the intervening century of a Christian sensibility that regarded secular service as inherently contaminating. Not only was the council's distaste for the holding of civic office congruent with Tertullian's earlier sentiments, but its decree that charioteers and pantomimes could enter the church only if they irrevocably renounced their professions aligns the council's fear of outside contamination with the sensibility evident

---

121. J. D. Mansi, *Sacrorum conciliorum nova et amplissima collectio* (Florence, 1759), 2:15; C. J. Hefele, *Histoire des Conciles*, I1 (Paris, 1907), c. 56, 252: "Magistratum vero uno anno quo agit duumviratum, prohibendum placet ut se ab ecclesia cohibeat."

122. A. W. W. Dale, *The Synod of Elvira and Christian Life in the Fourth Century* (London: Macmillan & Co., 1882), 233–35; A. H. M. Jones, *The Later Roman Empire, 284–602* (Oxford: Blackwell, 1964), vol. I, 725.

123. Hefele I:1, 252–53; Samuel Laeuchli, *Power and Sexuality: The Emergence of Canon Law at the Synod of Elvira* (Philadelphia: Temple University Press, 1972), 42.

124. Dale, 231–35; *De idolatria*, 17–19; *De corona*, 11; ch. 2, note 48 above.

125. Laeuchli, 69, 73.

in the ancient church orders, which had also prohibited charioteers and pantomimes from entering the church.[126]

The council did not mention the issue of Christian participation in the military. Of course, since it is clear that its canons did not aim at a comprehensive delineation of a Christian way of life, but rather dealt with matters on a somewhat ad hoc basis, the lack of any direct reference to Christian military service is arguably of no significance one way or the other. Dale speculated that the council's silence was due to a division of opinion on the subject among the assembled clergy, and Laeuchli even supposed that "[t]he synod apparently saw no conflict" between being a Christian and military service.[127] Though at first glance it seems an equally perilous *argumentum e silentio*, the parallel in mentality between the council's canons on municipal officers and the professions forbidden to a Christian with that seen in Tertullian and the church orders suggests that the assembly at Illiberis did not treat the issue of Christians serving in the military because such service, with the sin and blood pollution that inevitably accompanied it, was considered quite beyond the pale in terms of its appropriateness for Christian participation. Service on a town council, which hopefully at least did not involve the shedding of blood, was bad enough. Although Laeuchli is surely correct in supposing that the clergy at Illiberis knew that Christians were serving in the military,[128] from their perspective the less said on that subject, the better.

For our purposes it is worthwhile examining the evolution in Christian attitudes toward state service over the course of the fourth century, since military service proper even today falls under the general rubric of service to the state. Military service was similarly regarded in the late imperial period, as indicated by the expansion in meaning then of the noun *militia* and the verb *militare* to include a designation for any state office and service in that office respectively.[129] Tertullian had found both military and civil service equally abhorrent, in that both involved violence and bloodshed.[130] In the specific

---

126. Mansi 2:16; Hefele I:1, c. 62, 256: "Si auriga aut pantomimus credere voluerint, placuit ut prius artibus suis renuntient, et tunc demum suscipiantur, ita ut ulterius ad ea non revertantur, qui si facere contra interdictum tentaverint, proiiciantur ab Ecclesia." See the discussions by Hefele, 256; Laeuchli, 85 and n. 61.

127. Dale, 236–37; Laeuchli, 85, n. 61.

128. Laeuchli, 85, n. 61.

129. For the use of *militia* in late antiquity to denote state service, especially in the army or civil service, see A. H. M. Jones, *The Later Roman Empire, 284-602* (Norman: University of Oklahoma Press, 1964), vol. I, 377–78.

130. Especially in *De idololatria*, 17–19; see discussion, chapter 2, note 48 above.

case of civilian office, imposition of the death penalty became conceptually associated with the bloodshed of war, since both involved the state-sanctioned killing of human beings, the exercise of the *ius gladii*,[131] and this association was to persist on into the medieval period. Thus when fourth-century Christian texts use the words *militia* and *militare*, and it is unclear from the context whether military service per se is meant or is subsumed under the more capacious rubric of state service, it is a safe bet that the evolution in Christian attitudes toward *militia* in general that is visible in such texts throughout the fourth century parallels changing attitudes vis-à-vis military service in particular, and for much the same reasons.

Just as the Council of Arles in 314 had by denying conscientious objector status to Christians serving in the army thereby tacitly acknowledged the licitness of such service,[132] so the same council also recognized that Christians could now serve in high ranks of the imperial civil service. Less than a decade after the synod at Illiberis, bishops in the West had moved from a reluctant and conditioned acceptance of Christian service on a town council to acknowledging the possibility of a Christian serving as a provincial governor, a *praeses*.[133] Even so, such service was still regarded with deep suspicion, as indicated by the requirement that any *praeses* had to take with him to his appointed province *litterae ecclesiasticae communicatoriae* to certify his good standing in the Christian community. Wherever the *praeses* exercised his office, the local bishop was to monitor his activities, and excommunicate him if he acted contrary to the teachings of the church.[134]

As a direct consequence of the Constantinian revolution, the bishops of the Latin West, albeit with reservations, had here conferred a sort of probationary status upon Christian laity who served as officials in the imperial regime. But as the pace of conversions accelerated and individuals of elevated social and political status entered the church, there is evident in the late fourth century an increasing tension between the obvious opportunity thus afforded the church to exploit the talent and ambition of such former imperial officials, especially within the ecclesiastical hierarchy, and the traditional aversion to any Christian

---

131. Lactantius, *Div. Inst.* VI.20.15–17 (*CSEL* 19, 558).

132. Above, chapter 2, notes 106 to 116.

133. Jones (n. 129 above), I, 45.

134. *CCL* 148, 10, c. 7: "De praesidibus qui fideles ad praesidatum prosiliunt, ita placuit ut, cum promoti fuerint, litteras accipiant ecclesiasticas communicatorias, ita tamen ut, in quibuscumque locis gesserint, ab episcopo eiusdem loci cura illis agatur, et cum coeperint contra disciplinam agere, tunc demum a communione excludantur." On the meaning of *litterae communicatoriae*, Du Cange, *Glossarium mediae et infimae latinitatis* (Graz, 1954 [reprint]), II, 456.

participation in state service.[135] As a result of this tension, there are indications in the late fourth century of a growing debate within Christian circles as to whether former officers of the state could enter the ecclesiastical hierarchy, and under what conditions. In a letter sent to the bishops in Gaul from, so it has been argued, Pope Damasus (366–384),[136] the pontiff specified why former imperial officials were generally unfit to become bishops.

> It is clear that those who administered secular law after obtaining secular power cannot be free from sin. For so long as the sword is bared, or an unjust judgment handed down, or tortures employed out of legal necessity, or they attend to the preparation of public entertainments, or are even present at the production of such entertainments, once again associating themselves with those things which they had renounced [at baptism], they have forsaken any regard for the teachings transmitted to them. They would be better off not aspiring to the episcopacy. But after doing penance for all these things, once a certain period of time has elapsed they may merit to be associated with the holy altars.

In delineating the sins inherent to state service, it is noteworthy that Damasus first mentioned acts involving violence and bloodshed—including capital punishment ("gladius exeritur")—and only then activities linked to pagan practices.[137]

If a former imperial official, a baptized Christian, ambitious to advance within the ecclesiastical as he had earlier the secular hierarchy, could only with difficulty aspire to the highest rank of bishop, could he not at least more modestly hope to become a priest, or a deacon? By no means, according to some. In a letter to the bishops of Africa dated 6 January 386, Pope Siricius conveyed the decisions of a recent council held at St. Peter's that had aimed at rendering the church "free from every stain of this world."[138] One ruling

---

135. Charles Pietri, *Roma Christiana* (Rome: Bretschneider, 1976), I, 686.

136. Pietri (previous note), 764–72, on the dating of this document.

137. E. Ch. Babut, *La plus ancienne décrétale* (Paris, 1904), 81–82 (c. 13): "Eos praeterea qui saecularem adepti potestatem ius saeculi exercuerunt, inmunes a peccato esse non posse manifestum est. Dum enim et gladius exeritur, aut iudicium confertur iniustum, aut tormenta exercentur pro necessitate causarum, aut parandis exhibent voluptatibus curam, aut praeparatis intersunt, in his quibus renuntiaverunt se denuo sociantes, disciplinam observationis traditam mutaverunt. Multum sibi praestant si non ad episcopatum adfectent; sed propter haec omnia agentis [*leg.* agentes] poenitentiam, certo tempore impleto mereantur altaribus sociari."

138. *PL* 13:1156B: "ut ab omni labe saeculi istius immunes ad Dei conspectum securique veniamus."

of this council, repeated almost verbatim eighteen years later in a letter from Innocent I to Victricius of Rouen,[139] stated that "if anyone after the remission of their sins [i.e., baptism] had the belt of secular service (*cingulum militiae saecularis*), he should not be admitted to the clergy."[140] Now since *cingulum* has the specific meaning of "sword-belt" and is a metonym for military service,[141] it has been supposed by some that this canon refers to prohibiting former solders from entering the clergy.[142] But that Siricius had civilian office in mind here is indicated in another letter, where he wrote that only

> those be permitted to enter upon the ecclesiastical order whom apostolic authority enjoins, not those who formerly prided themselves in being bound by the belt of secular service ("cingulo militiae saecularis astricti"). They, who after having reveled in worldly pomp, or who wished to serve (*militare*) the needs of the state or to deal with the cares of the world . . . [their supporters] are constantly pouring into my ears that they could be bishops who by tradition and the teaching of the Gospels cannot be.[143]

These papal letters only imply what other evidence plainly shows, that a strong current of distaste for state service is visible in certain late fourth-century Christian circles. Any attempt to schematize this attitude within the framework of a consistent, teleological development of church doctrine, consistently applied or violated throughout the provinces of the Roman empire, would yield a misleading and oversimplified view not only of the realities of church governance at this period, but also of the complexities of contingent circumstances involved in the few cases we know of where the prior state service of an individual in church office was an issue. The only consistency

---

139. *PL* 20:472 (15 Feb. 404): "si quis post remissionem peccatorum cingulum militiae saecularis habuerit, ad clericatum omnino admitti non debet."

140. Jaffe, *Regesta Pontificum Romanorum* (Graz, 1956 [reprint]), I, 41; Mansi, 3:670; Hefele, II:1, 69; *PL* 13:1158–59: "Item, si quis post remissionem peccatorum, cingulum militiae saecularis habuerit, ad clerum admitti non debet."

141. Lewis and Short, *A Latin Dictionary* (Oxford: Clarendon, 1879), 332, *s.v.*

142. E.g., Hornus, 190.

143. *PL* 13:1165A (*epist.* 6): "ut tales videlicet ad ecclesiasticum ordinem permitterentur accedere, quales apostolica auctoritas iubet, non quales dico, vel eos qui cingulo militiae saecularis astricti olim gloriati sunt. Qui postea quam pompa saeculari exsultaverunt, aut negotia reipublicae optaverunt militare, aut curam mundi tractare, adhibita sibi quorumdam manu, et proximorum favore stipati, his frequenter ingeruntur auribus meis, ut episcopi esse possint, qui per traditionem et evangelicam disciplinam esse non possunt."

apparent is an ongoing negative attitude, expressed by some Christians for at least two centuries now, toward state service, an attitude that might be variously articulated and contested in its application and that might vary according to individual, time, and circumstance, but an attitude nonetheless that continued to nourish the roots of the Christian thinking of some on state service in general and war and military service in particular in the late fourth-century Roman empire.

Thus although a Roman synod early in the pontificate of Siricius had held that no Christian who had served in public office could enter the clergy, only fifteen years later, at a council in Toledo in September 400, the assembly declared that if any Christian had been admitted to the clergy after he had worn the *chlamys* or the *cingulum*—by such terminology perhaps distinguishing civil and military service—he could not rise to the diaconate "even if he perpetrated nothing worse."[144] A relaxation of a blanket prohibition, to be sure, but not exactly a ringing endorsement of state service either.

One excellent example of an apparent inconsistency in applying the traditional exclusion of former officials from the ranks of the clergy is provided by the elevation to the episcopate of no less a personage than Ambrose of Milan. Ambrose, who had administered the provinces of Liguria and Aemilia as *consularis* since 372/3,[145] was acclaimed bishop by the Nicene party at Milan in 374 upon the death of the semi-Arian Auxentius. Ambrose's biographer Paulinus records that the governor, who had not yet even been baptized, sought to avoid his election by erecting a tribunal and commencing criminal proceedings, including the use of torture, which was "against his usual practice."[146] Despite such attempts to avoid his fate, Ambrose was baptized and rushed through the ranks of ecclesiastical office, becoming bishop one week after his acclamation.[147] Ambrose himself later admitted that he had been "called to the priesthood from the clamor of legal wrangling and the terror of public administration . . . snatched from tribunals, abducted from the vanities of this world."[148] The irregularity of Ambrose's elevation to the episcopate may have

---

144. Mansi 3:1000, c. 8: "Si quis post baptismum militaverit, et chlamydem sumpserit, aut cingulum, etiamsi graviora non admiserit, si ad clerum admissus fuit, diaconii non accipiat dignitatem."

145. Neil McLynn, *Ambrose of Milan: Church and Court in a Christian Capital* (Berkeley: University of California Press, 1994), 42.

146. Paulinus of Milan, *Vita Ambrosii* 7, ed. M. Pellegrino (Rome, 1961), 58.

147. *Vita Ambrosii* 9 (62).

148. *De paenitentia* II 67, 72 (*CSEL* 73, 191, 192–93): "qui de forensium strepitu iurgiorum et a publicae terrore administrationis ad sacerdotium vocatus sim . . . raptus de tribunalibus, abductus vanitatibus saeculi huius." On this passage as revelatory of Ambrose's sentiments on being elevated to the episcopate from public administration see A. Lenox-Conyngham, "The Judgement of Ambrose the

been forgiven at the time, since his election seems to have been the result of political and ecclesiastical maneuvers at the highest level.[149] In this case political and ecclesiastical exigencies had trumped an ideal, but Ambrose's attempt to disqualify himself by violating it, as well as his later regrets over his past life, only proves the contemporary potency of a Christian ideal of nonviolence.

Given his background and especially the nature of the machinations by which he sought to forestall his election as bishop, it was certainly fitting that the former governor Ambrose was called upon by the Christian magistrate Studius to pronounce upon the question of whether it was licit for a Christian in authority to exercise capital punishment. In his reply, Ambrose began by acknowledging the dilemma faced by a Christian governor, torn between the impulse to mercy and the duty to safeguard the laws, a duty that St. Paul had sanctioned by writing that a judge "beareth not the sword without cause, for he is God's avenger upon those who do evil [Rom. 13:4]."[150] It was understandable, then, that there was disagreement and uncertainty in Christian circles on this question. There were, it is true, heretical clergy who denied communion to those magistrates who carried out the death penalty.[151] Though for his part Ambrose recognized that judges had full authority, sanctioned by law human and divine, to impose such sentences, his true feelings on the matter are revealed by the fact that most of the letter is devoted to a commentary on the Gospel story of the woman taken in adultery. In refusing to condemn the woman and admonishing her to sin no more, Jesus provided an example for a Christian magistrate faced with carrying out the death penalty. As Jesus had done, it was possible for a magistrate to hold out the hope of correction to a convicted criminal. A non-Christian could through baptism obtain forgiveness, and a Christian could do penance for his crime.[152] After all, there were even pagan governors who had acted mercifully while in office. "I know of many heathens

Bishop on Ambrose the Roman Governor," *Studia Patristica* 17, no. 1 (1982): 62–65, who, however, on the matter of the unsuitability of public officers for the clerical state emphasizes Ambrose's personal scruples and the appearance of contemporary papal pronouncements without seemingly being aware of the deeper historical roots of this sentiment in the church.

149. On the political context for Ambrose's election, see D. H. Williams, *Ambrose of Milan and the End of the Nicene-Arian Conflicts* (Oxford: Clarendon, 1995), 114–15. On the ecclesiastical aspects of Ambrose's swift and irregular elevation to the episcopate, see McLynn (n. 145 above), esp. 39–44, who in stressing the behind-the-scenes importance of Pope Damasus in Ambrose's election somewhat undercuts his own contention (4) that his elevation had *not* been engineered, as stressed by earlier scholars, by higher-ups "in an attempt to ensure a reliable tenant for this important see."

150. *CSEL* 82:2, ed. M. Zelzer (Vienna, 1990), *Ep* 50.1 (Maur. 25), 56.

151. *Ep.* 50.2 (56).

152. *Ep.* 50.8 (59).

who were wont to boast that they had brought back from the administration of their province an executioner's ax unstained by blood. If heathens do this, what should Christians do?"[153]

Years later the same issue of the proper Christian attitude toward capital punishment surfaced again in a letter from Bishop Exsuperius of Toulouse to Innocent I, in which among other questions regarding church discipline the bishop had asked "about those who had served in the civil administration after baptism, and either employed torture only, or even passed a death sentence." Innocent's reply, dated 20 February 405, stated:

> Concerning them we read nothing definitive in the fathers. For they [the fathers] remembered that these powers had been granted by God, and that they [the officials] were entrusted with a sword for the punishment of the guilty, and appointed to be an avenging agent of God in such matters [cf. Rom. 13:4]. How then would they censure that which they perceived was granted by the authority of God? Therefore, our view now toward them [the officials] is just as it has been observed toward them previously, lest we appear to undermine discipline, or go against the Lord's authority. But in rendering a judgment toward these individuals all their actions will be scrutinized.[154]

From the wording of Innocent's reply it would appear that Exsuperius had asked specifically whether a Christian judge had to abstain from communion or do penance for having ordered torture or the death penalty. Innocent's reply shows that, like Ambrose, in the absence of any unambiguous guideline in earlier authorities he was wary of seeming to go against the clear Pauline sanction in Romans 13 of the legal authority to punish wrongdoers, and thereby perhaps unwittingly endorse an unorthodox position.

For our purpose here the most significant aspect of these letters of Ambrose and Innocent is that they reveal the dilemmas of holding office at this period in an increasingly Christianized empire. Now Christians were becoming implicated in the contaminating violence of the business of the state, and in cognizance of the sins such individuals necessarily committed in exercising state power, especially the taking of human life, there were now increasingly urgent questions as to how Christians should act while holding public office.

---

153. *Ep.* 50.3 (57).
154. *PL* 20:499 (*E6*).

For Christians desirous to recover the pristine innocence of their postbaptismal state, now sullied by the sins of public affairs, the only remedy available was that of performing penance.[155] Performing acts of penance in order to expiate major sins had been practiced in the church since at least the second century. Ideally, those guilty of major sins would come on their own to the bishop and publicly confess the sins committed in the presence of the assembled faithful. The bishop fixed the period of the ensuing penance in proportion to the seriousness of the offense. During this period, the penitent was expected to manifest by outer actions and appearance the inner contrition of the heart. In Ambrose's Milan wealthy penitents were expected to put off their expensive robes and precious jewels, and put on cheap, shabby clothing that would soon become dirty and foul-smelling from being worn continually.[156] Fasting, tearful prayers and abasement, and acts of charity marked the penitents' outward behavior. An especially grievous deprivation for those in the penitential state was exclusion from the Eucharist. Only those who provided clear external proofs of an internal conversion could eventually hope to rejoin the Christian community in the rite of reconciliation, performed on Holy Thursday before the entire church. The bishop would lay his hands on the penitent, and after a prayer the penitent would be readmitted to communion. Having done penance once, in theory the reconciled Christian could not repeat the act, and was thereafter debarred from taking on certain specified occupations and positions, including state service, but above all the clergy.

In practice, it seems there was actually a range of behaviors for those manifesting their contrition, and such actions could be and were repeated. In his reply to Studius, Ambrose had found praiseworthy Christian judges who, having inflicted the death penalty, on their own initiative abstained from the sacraments.[157] In the obsequies for Theodosius, Ambrose noted of the deceased that even after his miraculous victory at the Frigidus, "because the foe had been laid low in battle, he refrained from participation in the sacraments." Just as he and not a bishop had imposed upon himself a penitential behavior, so

---

155. Much of what follows in this paragraph is based on C. Vogel, "Le péché et la pénitence: aperçu sur l'évolution historique de la discipline pénitentielle dans l'Église latine," esp. 147–216, in Ph. Delhaye, J. Leclercq, et al., *Pastorale du péché* (Tournai: Desclée, 1961), an excellent survey that draws upon much of the older scholarship. But among recent challenges to this "standard narrative" of the early history of penance, see now especially Mayke de Jong, "Transformations of Penance," in *Rituals of Power: From Late Antiquity to the Early Middle Ages*, ed. Frans Theuws and Janet L. Nelson, The Transformation of the Roman World 8 (Leiden, 2000), 185–224. Good work is currently being done on this topic, so I caution that the observations offered here on early penance are more provisional than usual in this book.

156. *De paen.* I 37 (137); II 88 (198).

157. *Ep* 50.2 (Maur. 25), *CSEL* 82:2, 56.

also it was Theodosius himself who determined when his state of contrition could end, taking the arrival in Italy of his son and niece from the East to be a sign of God's renewed favor.[158] It is true that Ambrose elsewhere criticized those who by abstaining on their own from the Eucharist took penance only part way. "They who prescribe a punishment for themselves but refuse the remedy [of not only penance but ultimate reconciliation] are very cruel judges of themselves," and by excluding themselves from the Eucharist in the end have defrauded themselves of divine forgiveness.[159] Yet what is significant here is that *all* these penitential behaviors resulted from the initiative of *the penitents themselves*. Lactantius may have adduced the moral code of the Decalogue, and Tertullian evoked the horror of blood pollution. But in this spontaneous reaction of Christian magistrates and commanders, who as Christians considered themselves as having been washed clean of their sins by the waters of baptism, one experiences over the gulf of centuries a thrill of recognition that such behaviors betokened a human conscience troubled and tormented by the taking of human life, an anguish compounded in a Christian by the fear that he had thereby imperiled the very salvation of his soul, leading him to seek somehow to alleviate the burden of a mortal sin the necessities of his office had rendered him unable to avoid committing. "A guilty conscience is so heavy that absent a judge it punishes itself, and longs to be covered up, and yet it is naked before God."[160]

The most spectacularly public and justifiably famous manifestation of contrition in this period springing from the pangs of a guilty conscience is the penance performed by Theodosius for his role in the judicial massacre at Thessalonica in 390.[161] In his recent survey and analysis of the incident, Neil McLynn almost embarrassedly acknowledges "the deep religiosity and abiding sense of human frailty that (we need not doubt) he [Theodosius] shared with his Christian contemporaries,"[162] preferring instead to emphasize the roles of Ambrose and Theodosius in stage-managing what amounts to an act of public relations. However much one wants to demystify an event overlaid with

158. *De obitu Theodosii* 34 (CSEL 73, 388–89): "Quid quod praeclaram adeptus victoriam, tamen, quia hostes in acie strati sunt, abstinuit a consortio sacramentorum, donec domini circa se gratiam filiorum experiretur adventu?"

159. *De paen.* II 89 (198).

160. *De paen.* II 103 (203): "Ita gravis culpa est conscientiae, ut sine iudice ipsa se puniat et velare se cupiat, et tamen apud deum nuda sit."

161. A good recent analysis of this incident, incorporating and evaluating the most important of the older scholarship, is in McLynn (n. 145 above), 315–30. But see the criticisms of Liebeschuetz (n. 46 above), 19 n. 3, 262–63.

162. McLynn, 329.

encrustations of pious interpretation, the central fact remains that the core of Theodosius's penance consisted of an act of utter humiliation, performed in public, which aimed to manifest by outer self-abasement the inner anguish of a conscience racked by guilt. McLynn is on much firmer ground in emphasizing the novelty of this act. The august ruler of the Roman world, whose person was regarded as almost god-like by pagan and Christian alike, "subordinated his royal power to God and performed penance, and having confessed his sin, besought pardon."[163] Theodosius "threw to the ground all the royal attire he was wearing, he wept publicly over his sin in church . . . with groans and tears he prayed for forgiveness."[164]

In an earlier age, Christians had led more modest lives, and their penitential acts of contrition for mortal sins had played out on a correspondingly more modest stage. But now Christians served openly in the army, governed provinces, and sat on the very throne of Caesar. War in particular, with its brutality and violence, with its blood and death, now in the late fourth century more than ever before was impinging upon the inner lives of Christians. Penance, what had before taken place in the conclaves of a minority religion, now occurred in imposing basilicas, and what had been expected of the huddled members of an obscure cult was now required of the soldiers, governors, and emperors of the Roman empire. Since in the late fourth century most of a Christian congregation would have been fairly recent converts, it is no wonder, as Ambrose informs us, that Theodosius in 390 did something that ordinary Christians blushed to do,[165] and no wonder that contemporary pagans were at a loss to understand his act.[166] If a Christian emperor was so tormented in conscience by an act he had initiated, however atrocious, which was yet perfectly within his royal prerogative as the ultimate arbiter of justice, it is also understandable that a Christian soldier would feel guilt for having killed another human being in battle, despite the fact that such an act was perfectly legitimate according to the standards of the state. So Basil of Caesarea in 374, while admitting that killing in war did not constitute murder, nonetheless advised that soldiers who had defiled their hands by the shedding of blood abstain from communion for three years.[167] The relative novelty in the late

163. *De obitu Theodosii* 27 (385): "Bene hoc dicit, qui regnum suum deo subiecit et paenitentiam gessit et peccatum suum confessus veniam postulavit."

164. *De obitu Theodosii* 34 (388): "Stravit omne, quo utebatur, insigne regium, deflevit in ecclesia publice peccatum suum, quod ei aliorum fraude obrepserat, gemitu et lacrimis oravit veniam."

165. *De obitu Theodosii* 34 (388): "Quod privati erubescunt, non erubuit imperator, publicam agere paenitentiam . . ."

166. McLynn (n. 145 above), 328–29.

fourth century of the requirement of penance for those among the mass of recently converted Christians who had done things once considered perfectly legitimate is illustrated by what his biographer told of Ambrose's conduct toward the emperor, or usurper, Magnus Maximus. When on an embassy to Maximus, Ambrose had supposedly kept the emperor from participating in the Eucharist until he did penance for having shed the blood of Gratian, the ruler he had overthrown. But "with a proud spirit" Maximus refused, thereby ensuring ultimate failure for his imperial adventure.[168]

Pride also figures much as an excuse for avoiding the practice in Ambrose's treatise *De paenitentia*, which provides not so much evidence for the formalities of penance as it was practiced in fourth-century Milan as penetrating insights into the psychological and emotional aspects of the penitential regime.[169] If one wants to get an impression of the sights and sounds, and even the smells, of what it would have been like to be in one of Ambrose's churches in the late fourth century, one could hardly do better than to read *De paenitentia*, and thus experience something of the wrenching emotional fever pitch involved in the actions of penance required of those who had once striven for office, but who were now expected to renounce the world, and interrupt their sleep with groans, sighs, and prayers.[170] It was expected that a penitent's prayer be

167. *Epist.* 188.13 (n. 113 above).

168. *Vita Ambrosii* 19 (n. 146 above, 76/78).

169. The existing scholarship on Ambrose's *De paenitentia* does not accord with its importance both in providing us a vivid picture of Ambrose's Milanese church "in action" and for giving us some of the most self-revealing passages in the Ambrosian oeuvre. Works that significantly discuss or touch upon *De paenitentia* include: S. M. Deutsch, "Des Ambrosius Lehre von der Sünde und der Sündentilgung," *Jahresbericht über das Königl. Joachimsthalsche Gymnasium* (Berlin, 1867), 1–58; M. Magistretti, "Il sacramento della confessione secondo S. Ambrogio," *La Scuola cattolica* 30 (1902): 493–512; E. Goeller, "Analekten zur Bussgeschichte des 4. Jahrhunderts," *Römische Quartalschrift* 36 (1928): 262–90; B. Poschmann, *Die abendländische Kirchenbusse im Ausgang des christlichen Altertums*, Münchener Studien zur historischen Theologie 7 (Munich, 1928); Galtier, *L'Église et la rémission des péchés aux premiers siècles* (Paris, 1932); H. Frank, "Ambrosius und die Büßeraussöhnung in Mailand: Ein Beitrag zur Geschichte der mailändischen Gründonnerstagsliturgie," in *Heilige Überlieferung: Ausschnitte aus der Geschichte des Mönchtums und des heiligen Kultes* (Münster, 1938), 136–73; G. Odoardi, *La dottrina della penitenza in S. Ambrogio* (Rome, 1941); V. Monachino, *La cura pastorale a Milano, Cartagine e Roma nel sec.* IV, Analecta Gregoriana 41 (Rome, 1947); Roger Gryson, *Le Prêtre selon saint Ambroise* (Louvain, 1968), 275–90; idem, ed. and trans., *Ambroise de Milan, La Pénitence*, SC 179 (Paris, 1971), intro., 11–14 (a review of the earlier literature); Raimondo Marchioro, *La prassi penitenziale nel IV secolo a Milano secondo S. Ambrogio* (Rome, 1975). It should be possible to show that *De paenitentia* was not, as usually argued, primarily an anti-Novatian treatise, but rather a sort of apologetic for penance intended for those Christians, many recent converts, who, though in need of it, were reluctant for whatever reasons to enter the penitential state.

accompanied by deep groans, wailing, and much weeping—the greater the sin the greater the weeping[171]—and *De paenitentia* is practically awash in tears from beginning to end. A penitent must make tears his bread and drink,[172] and if, after a period of penance, communion was still denied him, increase his weeping, and as a pitiful wretch embrace the feet of others, kiss them, and wash them with his tears.[173]

> I have known penitents whose countenance was furrowed with tears, their cheeks worn with constant weeping, who lay down their body to be trodden under foot by all, who with faces ever pale and worn with fasting bore about in a yet living body the likeness of death.[174]

Although, humans being human, crocodile tears must have occasionally flowed, any interpretation that would regard all this weeping and wailing as largely, or even in some significant measure, a sham and a show fails to reckon with the stricken conscience that impelled many penitents to undergo the process in the first place, and especially fails to appreciate the emotionally charged atmosphere alive in the church when penitents bewailed their sins. For it is made explicit in *De paenitentia* that *all* the congregants were expected to join with the penitents in tearful prayer. The penitent "by certain works of the whole people is purged, and is washed in the tears of the people, and redeemed from sin . . . and cleansed in the interior man."[175] "The whole church takes up the burden of the sinner, with whom she has to suffer in weeping and prayer and pain."[176] "Let Mother Church weep for you, and wash away your guilt with tears."[177] As pastor of the flock, the bishop himself was expected to lead the congregation in communal weeping. In a prayerful aside as nakedly self-revealing as anything in Augustine's *Confessions*, Ambrose admits his difficulty in performing this role: he prays that Jesus would "wash me with Thy tears, since in my hardened eyes I possess not such tears as to be able to wash away my offense."[178] Weeping, like laughter, is contagious in groups, and both the

---

170. *De paen.* II 96 (201).

171. *De paen.* I 10 (124).

172. *De paen.* I 59 (147).

173. *De paen.* I 90 (160).

174. *De paen.* I 91 (160–61). De Romestin translation, *On Repentance*, as in note 117 above, 344, slightly modified.

175. *De paen.* I 80 (156–57).

176. *De paen.* I 81 (157). De Romestin translation, 342.

177. *De paen.* II 92 (199).

authentic, anguished remorse of the grieving penitents and the compassion and pity of their fellows in the congregation would have fed off each other. When Ambrose's sometime congregant Augustine tells us how he was moved by the music in the church at Milan—"How greatly I wept, shaken to the core by the voices of Thy church sweetly singing in hymns and canticles! Those voices flowed into my ears, and the truth was distilled into my heart, and then the feelings of devotion boiled over, and tears ran down, and I was happy at them"[179]—can it be doubted that Ambrose's hymnody was at least in part deliberatedly crafted to inspire among his penitents the piercings of anguished contrition and the exciting of congregational weeping, in an emotionally gripping liturgical drama that was produced and directed by such a formidably talented bishop?

The pitch of emotional intensity in Ambrose's church could only have been heightened on Holy Thursday, when the anguish of penance was succeeded by the joy of reconciliation. By his penance, the penitent had been restored to the complete integrity of his postbaptismal innocence.[180] In a moving passage, Ambrose compares the readmission of the former penitent to full participation in the Eucharist to the joyous return of the Prodigal Son from exile in a foreign land.[181] When Jesus returns in body in the Eucharist, "he who had been dead is found as one among those reclining at table with Christ."[182] It is certainly explicable that when the penitents put off their foul-smelling rags, "where the dead stank the day before, now the whole house is filled with good odor . . . the whole house filled with the odor of the sweetness of grace."[183]

How a Christian conscience troubled by the state-sanctioned taking of human life, both in war and in the infliction of capital punishment, could manifest itself in a particular individual in the late fourth-century Roman empire is dramatically evidenced by events in the life of Martin of Tours. Although the writings of Sulpicius Severus, from which is derived almost all our contemporary information about Martin, may have done as much to obscure

---

178. *De paen.* II 71 (192). Ambrose's biographer Paulinus, however, was so protective of his hero's reputation in this respect that he has the bishop's ready tears forcing otherwise dry-eyed penitents to weep (*Vita Ambrosii* 3 9)!

179. My translation of Augustine, *Conf.* IX, 6, 14 (*CCL* 27, 141): "Quantum flevi in hymnis et canticis tuis suave sonantis ecclesiae tuae vocibus commotus acriter! Voces illae influebant auribus meis et eliquabatur veritas in cor meum et exaestuabat inde affectus pietatis, et currebant lacrimae, et bene mihi erat cum eis."

180. *De paen.* I 83 (158).

181. *De paen.* II 18 (171).

182. *De paen.* II 60 (188).

183. *De paen.* II 63, 64 (189).

as to illuminate our picture of him, nonetheless flashes of the real man shine through the hagiographic haze.[184] For our purpose here, particular interest attaches to Sulpicius Severus's account in the *Life of Martin* of his hero's service in the army and his ultimate renunciation of military life. Our view of both is to some extent dependent on the solution of a chronological knot in Martin's career. If one accepts the so-called "long chronology" in which Martin was born c. 316, entered the army in about 331 and left the service in 356, then Martin served out a full twenty-five-year term of service and there is nothing especially remarkable about his departure from the army.[185] On the other hand, if one accepts the "short chronology," in which Martin was born in 336 and entered the army in 351, then his departure in 356 after only five years of service[186] is more capable of being presented realistically as a courageous act of defiance against a wicked pagan ruler, viz., Julian the Apostate, which is how Sulpicius Severus portrays it:

> Meanwhile, with barbarians invading Gaul, the Caesar Julian, after assembling an army at the city of Worms, began to pay out a donative to the soldiers. As was the custom, they were called up one by one, until it came to Martin. Then, indeed, judging it an opportune moment to ask for his discharge—for he did not think it would be fair for him to accept the donative if he were not going to continue in military service—he said to the Caesar: 'Until now I have soldiered for you. Let me now be God's soldier. It is not licit for me to fight.' Then, indeed, the tyrant growled at his words, saying that Martin was rejecting military service out of fear of the battle that was about to happen the next day and not because of religion. But Martin was not only undaunted but even more steadfast in face of the terror put before him. He said: 'If this is ascribed to cowardice, not faith, tomorrow I will stand unarmed in front of the battle-line, and in the name of the Lord Jesus, protected not by shield or helmet but by the sign of the cross, I will safely penetrate the ranks of the enemy.' So he is ordered to be thrust into custody to see if he would be true to his words and expose himself unarmed to the barbarians. The next day the enemy sent envoys concerning peace, surrendering

---

184. On what we can know of the "real" Martin, see the balanced judgment of Clare Stancliffe, *St. Martin and His Hagiographer: History and Miracle in Sulpicius Severus* (Oxford: Clarendon, 1983), 315–62.

185. On the "long chronology," E.-Ch. Babut, *Saint Martin de Tours* (Paris, 1912), 166–96; J. Fontaine, "Vérité et fiction dans la chronologie de la *Vita Martini*," *Studia anselmiana* 46 (1961): 189–236.

186. The best recent proponent of the "short chronology" is Stancliffe (n. 184 above), 111–48.

themselves and all they had. As a result, who can truly doubt that this had been the blessed man's victory, it having been granted to him that he not be sent into battle unarmed? And although the good Lord could have kept his soldier safe even among the swords and missiles of the enemy, instead, lest the eyes of the saint be polluted by the deaths of others, He removed the need for a battle. For Christ would not grant any victory for His soldier other than one in which, because the enemy had been subdued without bloodshed, no one had to die.[187]

It has been noted that this account closely parallels, both thematically and verbally, the acts of African soldier-martyrs, especially the *Passio Typasii*. The literary stylization evident here caused Jacques Fontaine, for example, to question the historicity of the incident.[188] Sulpicius Severus certainly had motivations for dramatizing the circumstances of Martin's discharge. Since Martin had been baptized at the age of eighteen, he had as a Christian continued to serve in the army for at least two years—or, even worse, twenty-two years, according to the "long chronology"—before he finally realized and acted upon the incompatibility of his military service with the state of postbaptismal innocence. Sulpicius Severus is unquestionably defensive about Martin having served in the army, insisting that his hero had played the saint with his fellow soldiers and even his body-servant before his baptism.[189] This defensiveness is doubtless a reaction against the sentiment, as we have seen widespread in the Christian ecclesiastical hierarchy at the time, which regarded state service as so polluting as to prevent any ex-soldier from becoming a cleric, let alone a bishop.

That Martin's military service was held against him by his opponents among the Gallic clergy is proved by an incident Sulpicius Severus recounted in his *Dialogues*. Angry at having been reproved by the saint the day before, Brice, then a monk and later Martin's successor to the bishopric of Tours, burst into a furious rage against his bishop, "asserting that he was holier than his mentor Martin, since he from his earliest years had grown up in the monastery amidst the holy teachings of the church, whereas Martin, a fact which he could not deny, had been befouled from the beginning by his actions in military service."[190] It should be noted that it was apparently unnecessary for Brice to

---

187. *Vita Martini* 4 (*CSEL* 1, 114–15).

188. J. Fontaine, "Sulpice Sévère a-t-il travesti Saint Martin de Tours en martyr militaire?" *Analecta Bollandiana* 81 (1963): 31–58. On this passage see also Stancliffe (n. 184 above), 141–48.

189. *Vita Martini* 2 (111–12). In connection with Martin's Christian behavior as a soldier there is also, of course, the celebrated incident with the beggar of Amiens (*Vita Martini* 3, 113–14).

charge Martin specifically with having shed blood, since the actions inherent to being a soldier were in themselves sufficiently defiling ("militiae actibus sorduisse"), a sentiment shared by Sulpicius Severus himself, who wrote of Martin's behavior as a soldier that he was "untainted by those vices in which that breed of men [viz., soldiers] are usually implicated."[191] The same suspicion of soldiers, along with some detail as to what was considered objectionable in military life, is found in a closely contemporary sermon of Maximus of Turin. There Maximus speaks of certain Christian brethren "who are either bound by the belt of military service or have been appointed to public office" ("qui aut militiae cingulo detinentur aut in actu sunt publico constituti"), thereby apparently distinguishing between holders of military and civilian office respectively. These Christians, complains Maximus, are in the habit of excusing the sins they commit by the mere fact that they hold such offices. He counters that service to the state is not in itself sinful. Rather, soldiers do wrong when they get drunk and pillage the property of others, or even kill someone, and then turn round and say: "What was I to do, a man in secular office or a soldier? Am I a monk or a cleric?"[192]

Regardless of the extent to which Sulpicius Severus stylized his account of Martin's discharge from the army, or even if he made up whole cloth the incident with Julian, it is clear that the hagiographer was at pains to put a fine gloss on Martin's military service, which may have even extended to shortening in the *Life of Martin* his actual term of service. But that Christian soldiers in this period were self-motivated and encouraged to abandon the army before their term of service had expired, even at peril of their lives, is proved by two letters of Paulinus of Nola. In a letter to Victricius of Rouen in the late 390s,[193] Paulinus wrote of *exitus tuus a militia et ingressus ad fidem.*

> You marched on to the parade ground on the day designated for military assembly. You were clad in all the adornment of the armor of war which by then you had mentally rejected. All were admiring your most punctilious appearance and your awe-inspiring equipment, when suddenly the army gaped with surprise. You changed direction, altered your military oath of allegiance, and before the feet of your impious commanding officer you threw

190. *Dial.* 3.15.4 (*CSEL* 1, 214).

191. *Vita Martini* 2.6 (112).

192. *CCL* 23, *serm.* 26, 101.

193. On the date, *Letters of St. Paulinus of Nola*, trans. P. G. Walsh, *Ancient Christian Writers* 35 (London: Longmans, Green, 1966), 248.

down the arms of blood to take up the arms of peace. Now that you
were armed with Christ, you despised weapons of steel.

Victricius's commander, furious, ordered him to be beaten with rods and
tortured. When he still refused to yield, Victricius was threatened with
execution, which, miraculously, he avoided.[194]

The utter incompatibility of the demands of military service with one's
striving for the Christian ideal is starkly presented in a letter of about 400[195] to
the soldier Crispinianus, who is urged to quit the army and devote his life to
God. Although he was in the army, Crispinianus tried to lead a religious life,
going so far as to assist and protect civilians, probably from the depredations
of his fellow soldiers. Such behavior of a Christian soldier incidentally shows
that Sulpicius Severus's characterization of Martin's saintly behavior during his
military service is not necessarily all hagiographic hyperbole. Although striving
to be a good Christian, Crispinianus was ambitious of promotion in the ranks,
and Paulinus wondered whether his aim was to complete his term of service,
marry, and raise children, and only then turn to God's service. But Paulinus
points out that even if a soldier does not fight and kill in battle, his salary is
nonetheless derived from taxes that have to be extorted from the provincials by
violence. Crispinianus is urged not to put his patriotism before God. And, of
course, there is a dark reality at the heart of military service.

> He who is a soldier with the sword is the servant of death, and when
> he sheds his own blood or that of another, this is the reward for his
> service. He will be regarded as guilty of death either because of his
> own death or because of his sin, since it is unavoidable that a soldier
> in war, even if he is fighting not so much for himself as for another,
> either finds his own death when defeated or is the cause of death
> when victorious, for he cannot be victorious unless he first sheds
> blood.

Anyone who prefers this world and Caesar's service to Christ's is going to
hell.[196]

Sulpicius Severus provides us in the *Dialogues* with a vivid illustration
of the casual violence against civilians perpetrated by servants of the state in
the late fourth-century empire. Some *militantes viri*, perhaps connected with

---

194. Paulinus of Nola, *Epist.* 18.7 (*CSEL* 29, ed. G. de Hartel), 133–35 (Walsh trans.).

195. On the date, *Ancient Christian Writers* (as in note 193 above), 36, 316.

196. *Epist.* 25 (*CSEL* 29, 223–29; Walsh trans.).

administration of the imperial fisc,[197] were riding in a carriage along a public highway when their horses shied and got tangled up in their harness upon encountering Martin, who was walking along the road clad in his usual long, black cloak. Perhaps taking him for a peasant, who dressed similarly, the men leapt down from the carriage and began to beat Martin with whips and clubs. When Martin endured their blows in silence and seemed almost to be offering his back to them to be beaten, rather than being mollified, the men fell into a frenzy of furious blows, leaving Martin lying on the ground half-conscious and covered in blood. When the men later learned, after Martin's companions had come upon him and carried him away, that the man they had beaten senseless was the bishop of Tours, they rushed to find him.[198] "Suffused with shame, weeping, and with their heads and faces spattered with the dust with which they had sullied themselves, they prostrated themselves before Martin, imploring his forgiveness."[199]

Sulpicius Severus has here presented us a vignette encapsulating the life curve of those who served the state in the late fourth century, moving from the arrogant infliction of casual violence to the abasement of the penitential state. That he intended his audience to regard those imploring Martin's forgiveness as performing an act of penance is proved by the men's assertion that their pangs of conscience at their deed had alone been punishment enough.[200] Could it be that Martin's mute endurance of the blows rained upon him also bespeaks the remnants of an ex-soldier's guilty conscience, willing and even eager to suffer a penitential punishment in a situation similar to what he must have witnessed, if not himself participated in, more than once during his own military career? In any case, it is certain that Martin had been known to intervene, at least once at some personal risk, on behalf of those victimized by state-sanctioned violence. When the governor Avitianus, whose barbaric cruelty was so extreme that it seemed credible he was provoked by a demon,[201] one day entered Tours followed by troops of chained prisoners, sheer misery written on their faces, who were destined to be the victims of the "sad work" of torture and execution on the morrow, Martin went that night to the governor's *praetorium* and persuaded him to release them all.[202]

197. *Dial.* II.3.2 (*CSEL* 1, 183) says the men were riding in a *fiscalis raeda*.

198. *Dial.* II.3.2–9 (183–84).

199. *Dial.* II.3.9 (184).

200. *Dial.* II.3.9 (184).

201. *Dial.* III.8 (205). On Avitianus, see F.-L. Ganshof, "Saint Martin et le comte Avitianus," *Analecta Bollandiana* 67 (1949), *Mélanges Paul Peeters* I, 203–23.

202. *Dial.* III.4 (201–2).

The most famous example of Martin's standing against the state machinery of death, when his actions are seen compounded of an all-too-human admixture of hesitancy and courage, compromise and integrity, is provided by his role in the Priscillianist controversy, which came to a head in about the year 385. Priscillian, who in Spain had preached a species of ascetic renunciation flavored with a penchant for slightly dualistic apocryphal writings,[203] at an episcopal synod at Bordeaux held to investigate his teachings had appealed from the judgment of the bishops to that of the emperor Magnus Maximus at his capital Trier. Thither many bishops of Spain and Gaul traveled, including Martin.[204] Sulpicius Severus later observed that of all the assembled bishops there, many of whom were wealthy and powerful men, who disgraced their episcopal dignity by their abject fawning before the emperor and his court, only Martin by his steadfastness of character "maintained an apostolic authority." Martin at first refused repeated invitations to the imperial table, until, according to Sulpicius Severus, he was finally persuaded to come to a banquet when Maximus declared to him that his unlooked-for victory over Gratian showed that he had become emperor by divine will, and that none of his enemies had been slain except in battle. At the banquet itself, when a servant offered a bowl of wine to the emperor and he ordered it to be given first to Martin, thinking that he would then be graced by receiving the bowl back from the bishop, Martin instead gave the bowl to his accompanying priest, an action in upholding the episcopal dignity that won even the emperor's admiration.[205]

Years later it was Sulpicius Severus's opinion that in the trial before the emperor at Trier, the accusers of Priscillian, by his lights admittedly a heretic, were as bad as the accused. Their ringleader was Bishop Ithacius of Ossonuba (in today's southern Portugal),[206] and according to our source there was nothing holy about him. Although it led to his being charged with heresy himself, Martin repeatedly pressed Ithacius to withdraw the accusation, or at least prevail upon Maximus not to shed the blood of the heretics. Besides, it would be an unheard-of, unholy barbarity for an ecclesiastical matter to be judged by a secular authority. According to Sulpicius Severus, Martin before he left Trier went so far as to elicit a promise from Maximus that he would not inflict any punishment of blood upon Priscillian and his followers. But after Martin's departure, the prosecution of Priscillian was resumed. He was eventually

203. On the content of Priscillian's teachings, Henry Chadwick, *Priscillian of Avila* (Oxford: Clarendon, 1976), 57–110, and now Peter Brown (n. 112 above), 211–15.
204. *Chron.* II. 46–50 (99–103).
205. *Vita Martini* 20 (129–30).
206. Chadwick (n. 203 above), 20 on the identification of Ithacius's see.

convicted on a charge of *maleficium*, and in 385 or 386 he and six of his associates were beheaded, while others were sent into exile.[207]

The execution of Priscillian and his followers was a type of event still novel for its age: the participation of ministers of Christ in the judicial killing of fellow believers who thought and taught something at variance with what ecclesiastical authorities had deemed orthodox. Although the Priscillianists were widely regarded as heretics, many bishops in the West were shocked and appalled at what had happened. If one makes allowances for the exaggerations of panegyric, something of the contemporary opinion on the matter in secular circles can be derived from the speech given before the emperor Theodosius by the Gallic rhetor Pacatus in 389 in the aftermath of Maximus's suppression. There Pacatus sarcastically admits that the Priscillianists had been guilty of "too much religion and too assiduous a worship of the divine." He reserves special scorn for the bishops, unworthy of the name, who had instigated and encouraged the execution of the Priscillianists, bishops derided as toadies (*satellites*) and butchers (*carnifices*). After their participation in torture and execution, "they brought back to the sacred rites hands polluted by contact with capital punishment, and the ceremonies which they had defiled with their minds they also contaminated with their bodies."[208] And it seems ecclesiastical censure was likewise severe, and immediate. Ambrose of Milan, for his part, when on an embassy to Trier from the court in Italy would have nothing to do with the bishops involved in the Priscillianists' prosecution.[209] Pope Siricius in a letter to Maximus complained of ecclesiastics being tried before a secular tribunal, and of Bishop Ithacius's role in making an accusation involving a capital charge.[210]

One can well imagine the reaction of the ex-soldier bishop of Tours, who had left the army out of a conscientious aversion to bloodshed, to the news of the execution and exile of the Priscillianists. A synod of Gallic bishops was held at Trier soon afterwards, at which among other matters a successor to Bishop Britto of Trier had to be ordained. Maximus had put under royal protection Ithacius, who by acting as Priscillian's accuser had rendered himself liable, in an ecclesiastical forum, of being charged with having played a role in the execution of human beings, this being regarded as sinful no matter what they had said or done. When Ithacius and his episcopal allies learned that Martin was

207. *Chron.* II. 50–51 (103–4).

208. II *Pan.* 29.2–3 (105). Pacatus's language here, which stresses blood pollution and the hands as the transmitter of its contagion, would to my mind indicate that he is, indeed, a Christian.

209. *Epist.* 30.12 (Maur. 24), CSEL 82:1, 214–15.

210. Chadwick (note 203 above), 147–48.

nearing Trier, they became anxious that the renowned bishop of Tours would refrain from communion with them for their role in the executions and by his example encourage others to the same course. They had Maximus send out to meet Martin imperial functionaries forbidding him to enter the city unless he swore to share peace with the bishops at Trier, but Martin fobbed them off by declaring that he was coming "with the peace of Christ." True to his initial resolution, Martin at first had nothing to do with the other bishops at Trier, but instead went to the palace to petition Maximus to rescind his plan to send imperial agents armed with capital authority ("cum iure gladiorum") into Spain to prosecute the Priscillianists there, seeking thus, as Sulpicius Severus tells us, "to save not only Christians . . . but even the heretics themselves."

Meanwhile the bishops associated with Ithacius had gone to the emperor to complain of Martin's refusal to have communion with them. In a private interview with the stubborn bishop, Maximus assured him that the heretics had not been the victims of an episcopal witch-hunt, but had been justly convicted by the laws of the state, and that therefore there was no good reason not to share peace with Ithacius, who in any case had been declared free from blame in the affair in an episcopal meeting a few days earlier. Martin was not swayed by Maximus's arguments. But upon learning that the emperor was proceeding with his plan to prosecute the Priscillianists in Spain, the bishop rushed to the palace and promised that he would communicate with the other bishops if the emperor called off any further prosecutions. Maximus agreed to the compromise. The next day Martin shared communion with his fellow bishops at the ordination of Felix as bishop of Trier, although he could not be induced to attach his subscription to a document attesting to his communication.

Martin instantly regretted his action. On the way home the next day he was visibly depressed. At one point he sat down dejectedly on the road in anguished torment over what he had done, being persuaded to go on only after an angelic visitation, according to our source, convinced him that, considering the circumstances, he had had no choice. When afterwards he cured the possessed with more difficulty than he had previously, he confessed with tears that since "the evil of that communion" he had sensed a diminution of his spiritual powers. Despite his actions at Trier, however, in the end it was not the well-connected courtier-bishops who had connived at the execution of the Priscillianists who are remembered as being a friend to humankind. And lest Sulpicius Severus be thought to have exaggerated Martin's subsequent regret at communicating with Priscillian's executioners in order to blunt the effect of what many then, and later, must have regarded as a disgraceful compromise, a blot on his reputation for integrity, the saint's disciple refers to what must have been at the time a well-known fact, that for the rest of his life Martin never went to another synod, and kept his distance from any meeting of bishops.[211]

Jean-Michel Hornus, who was in the twentieth century probably the most scholarly student from an avowedly pacifist perspective of the history of attitudes toward war in early Christianity, noted with approval Saint Martin's anti-militarism, but bemoaned what he considered to be the fourth-century church's restriction of what had originally been a generalized Christian pacifism to the prerogative of a relatively small clerical elite. As a Protestant, Hornus felt keenly what he regarded to be Catholicism's betrayal of the primitive church's call to universal sanctity.[212] As we saw in the previous chapter, it is certainly true that Constantine had attempted to prevent Christians from leaving the army on religious grounds.[213] But the examples of Martin, Victricius, and Crispinianus show that Christian soldiers nonetheless later in the fourth century did exactly that, or were encouraged to do so. Clearly the Constantinian revolution had not successfully muted the pacifistic strains in Christianity, and the idea persisted from the early church that service to the state, especially in the military, was inherently contaminating.

Nor was the force of this anti-military sentiment restricted to some late fourth-century spiritual elite, as shown by its appearance in literature and art. Certain late fourth-century poetic productions attest to a veritable cult of military martyrs, playing upon stories and legends of Christian Roman soldiers executed during the persecutions. In these works the martyrs exhibit a horror of bloodshed and an aversion to military service, leading to their attempted departure from the army, with fatal results. The longest such work is Prudentius's hymn in his *Peristephanon* on the martyrs Emeterius and Chelidonius of Calahorra. Although they had served loyally and courageously as soldiers, "they forsake Caesar's banners, choosing instead the standard of the cross."[214] For they now no longer consider it a glorious act, but rather contemptible "to defile [what had been] infidel hands with bloody slaughter."[215] Likewise, on a poetic inscription in Rome to the martyrs Nereus and Achilleus commissioned by Pope Damasus (366–384), the soldiers had once served in "a violent office," but as *conversi* they now "flee, forsake the irreligious camp of

---

211. *Dial.* III. 11–13 (208–11).

212. Hornus (ch. 2, note 1 above), 195, 198.

213. Above, chapter 2, notes 106 to 116.

214. *Prudentii Carmina, Peristephanon* I (*CSEL* 61), 292, l. 34: "Caesaris vexilla linquunt, eligunt signum crucis."

215. *Peristephanon* I, 292, ll. 37–39: "Vile censent expeditis ferre dextris spicula, / machinis murum ferire, castra fossis cingere, / inpias manus cruentis inquinare stragibus."

their general, throw down their shields, medals, and bloody spears."[216] Similar wording appears in a hymn doubtfully ascribed to Ambrose, but certainly of Milanese origin, which speaks of the military martyrs Victor, Nabor, and Felix as having been "snatched from the irreligious camp."[217]

Jacques Fontaine in a penetrating article on the late fourth-century cult of military martyrs has linked their appearance at this time to the contemporary spread of a new ideal of Christian asceticism, reflected particularly in the beginnings of Western monasticism as in the case of Martin of Tours, which emphasized ideals of the apostolic church such as nonviolence.[218] Their similarity in sentiment to the motivations that drove Martin and Victricius of Rouen to abandon the standards and embrace a religious life proves that these poems, then, did not reflect a mere antiquarian nostalgia. Indeed, it has been suggested that Prudentius may have been partially inspired to write his poem on the martyrs of Calahorra as penance for his earlier government service.[219] Furthermore, Fontaine has argued that the cult of military martyrs cannot be regarded, as would Hornus, as the preserve of a relatively small, select group, a spiritual elite. It would seem that the authors of these poems intended them to be widely diffused, and they apparently were. The works of Damasus and Ambrose in particular were part of their episcopal endeavors to further the interests of the two greatest sees in Italy, and pilgrims to Rome and to the basilica in Milan which housed their relics could only have served to spread the fame of the military martyrs, and as well the ideals, including nonviolence, for which they had given their lives. As Fontaine concluded, their story was a call to *conversio* to *all* the Christians of the age of Theodosius, and not only monks.[220] But I cannot follow Fontaine when he maintains that the ideal of nonviolence in the stories of the military martyrs was only apparently incompatible with the contemporary norms of Christianized warfare.[221] It is inarguable, as Fontaine points out, that certain soldierly values such as courage, loyalty, endurance,

---

216. *Epigrammata Damasiana*, ed. A. Ferrua (Vatican City, 1942), no. 8, *Elogium SS. Nerei et Achillei*, 103, ll. 2–3a, 6–7: "Militiae nomen dederant saevumque gerebant / officium . . . conversi fugiunt, ducis inpia castra relinquunt, / proiciunt clipeos, faleras telaque cruenta." On these marbles commissioned by Damasus, see now Brown (n. 112 above), 252–53.

217. *Hymni Latini antiquissimi LXXV*, ed. Walther Bulst (Heidelberg: F. H. Kerle, 1956), 48, l. 15: "castrisque raptos impiis."

218. Jacques Fontaine, "Le culte des martyrs militaires et son expression poétique au IVè siècle: l'idéal évangélique de la non-violence dans le christianisme théodosien," in his *Études sur la poésie latine tardive d'Ausone à Prudence* (Paris: Société d'Édition Les Belles Lettres, 1980), 331–61; here, 344–46, 356–59.

219. Fontaine, 341–43.

220. Fontaine, 359–60.

221. Fontaine, 339.

and fraternal solidarity exhibited in these poems were treated positively and as transferable from the *militia Caesaris* to the *militia Christi*. But what we know of the careers of Martin and Victricius rules out any view of their military service as some sort of seemingly contradictory preparation for their subsequent religious life, for in both cases they had rejected military life with what seems a visceral horror, and the idea of a conflict in ideals being merely apparent cannot be saved by referring it to an elegant paradox.[222] The contradiction between the ideas expressed in the context of promoting a Christianized view of warfare in the age of Theodosius and the contemporary evidence for some Christians' aversion to war and military service bespeaks a real, not an apparent conflict within Christian circles at this period.

CONCLUSION

Although already by the year 200 Christians were to be found in some numbers serving in the Roman army, that same period is also witness to a deep-seated repugnance among other Christians toward service to the state and the violence and bloodshed that often accompanied such service, particularly in the military. Undoubtedly the pagan religious elements pervasive in Roman military life could not have made the prospect of such service attractive to Christians, but pagans and Christians alike agreed that divine disposition could, and did, govern the outcome of battles and wars. Constantine attempted a synthesis of old and new by adopting Christian symbolism and forms for his forces and by referring the outcome of war to the Christian God, who could be effectively supplicated by his faithful followers to bestow the divine gift of *victoria* upon those fighting for the right.

Theodosius I and his supporters further elaborated in his and his dynasty's service Christian themes in narratives of war, themes already present earlier in the fourth century in Constantinian propaganda. Even if outnumbered, a pious Christian prince like Theodosius could count on his closeness to God, an intimacy manifested through prayer, to ensure victory over his enemies, such a prince even meriting in one instance direct divine intervention on his behalf in the course of battle itself.

Christian spokesmen such as Ambrose of Milan, responsible leaders in a polity, now led by Christian rulers, that had to fight in order to defend itself, appreciated traditional Roman values such as patriotism and bravery in war. But Ambrose in particular was also keenly aware that service to the state put

222. Fontaine, 351–59.

Christians at risk of committing mortal sin. This aversion to state service went at least as far back as Tertullian, and is found over a century later in Lactantius, though there is evidence for a weakening of such a rigorist stance over the course of the fourth century. But even if Christians could now attain the heights of secular power, it was incumbent upon them that when they had completed such service, or whenever they had sinned grievously in carrying it out, to atone for their deeds by performing penance. The need for Christians to perform penance became associated with new currents of ascetic spirituality that upheld perceived traditions of the apostolic church, and in this context particularly the ideal of nonviolence, which spoke so strongly to Roman soldiers such as Martin of Tours and Victricius of Rouen that they were willing to risk imprisonment or death by quitting the service in order to follow the call of their conscience.

4

The Roman Just War and Early Christianity

I. BELLUM IUSTUM ET PIUM

Then conquer we must, when our cause it
is just,
    And this be our motto—"In God is
our trust."

These lines from the last stanza of the American national anthem, penned by
Francis Scott Key in 1814, illustrate strikingly the persistence across time and
space in the Western world of the fundamental and interrelated elements of
the just war concept of the ancient Romans, that a war fought for a just cause
ensures divine support and consequently victory.[1] This concept of divinely

---

1. Important recent discussions on this theme include: Hans Drexler, "Iustum Bellum," *Rheinisches
Museum für Philologie* 102, no. 2 (1959): 97–140; Herbert Hausmaninger, "'Bellum iustum' und 'iusta
causa belli' im älteren römischen Recht," *Österreichische Zeitschrift für öffentliches Recht* 11 (1961): 335–45;
Sigrid Albert, *Bellum Iustum: Die Theorie des "gerechten Krieges" und ihre praktische Bedeutung für die
auswärtigen Auseinandersetzungen Roms in republikanischer Zeit*, Frankfurter Althistorische Studien 10
(Frankfurt am Main: Michael Lassleben, 1980); Silvia Clavadetscher-Thürlemann, Πόλεμος δίκαιος und
bellum iustum:Versuch einer Ideengeschichte (Zürich, 1985); Helga Botermann, "Ciceros Gedanken zum
'gerechten Krieg' in *de officiis* 1, 34–40," *Archiv für Kulturgeschichte* 69 (1987): 1–29; Mauro Mantovani,
Bellum Iustum: Die Idee des gerechten Krieges in der römischen Kaiserzeit (Bern: Peter Lang, 1990). See also
the works cited in Clavadetscher-Thürlemann, 135, n. 44. Despite its title, Mantovani's work, though
valuable, contains relatively little as a whole on the use of the just war idea in the imperial period, as a
good part of his treatment deals with the Augustan period or literature written then, especially Livy's
history, which deals with the Republican period.

sent victory as a consequence of fighting in a just cause appeared not only in antiquity, but in the medieval period as well. It is of course possible to overemphasize the role of cultural conservatism in explaining this phenomenon. Such an explanation would suggest a continuity of ideas over millennia. Another, perhaps more credible explanation for this apparent continuity was advanced in the early twentieth century by Joachim von Elbe, who remarked that "the states in their practice, that remained constant over a period of several centuries up to recent times, always attempted to justify their wars with cogent reasons of law or equity, in obvious response to *a deep-seated spiritual need of human nature to base political actions on just and equitable grounds* [italics mine]."[2] This need of polities to justify their wars on the grounds of equity seems well nigh universal, and is not restricted to the West.[3] Although the impetus to justify war may be universal, its verbal expression is culturally specific, and there is often observable a continuity in its verbal expression over the centuries. The reflection of just war rhetoric not only in Augustine, but also in both the ancient and the medieval Western world, justifies a brief look at the ancient Roman concept of just war.

Questions surrounding the archaic fetial ritual of declaring *purum piumque duellum*[4] against Rome's enemies such as the history and ultimate disappearance of that ritual and the extent to which Cicero's later theoretical formulation of the *bellum iustum* was influenced by Stoicism have been treated exhaustively elsewhere and have limited relevance for the purposes of this study.[5] Other

2. Joachim von Elbe, "The Evolution of the Concept of the Just War in International Law," *American Journal of International Law* 33, no. 4 (October 1939): 685.

3. See von Elbe, 686, n. 164, on the declaration of war against China by the Japanese emperor in 1894. On ancient non-Western examples of just war, Paul Christopher, *The Ethics of War and Peace: An Introduction to Legal and Moral Issues* (Englewood Cliffs, NJ: Prentice Hall, 1994), 8–12. On the ancient Greek "laws of war," both in terms of *ius ad bellum* and *ius in bello*, see op. cit., 10–12, and Frederick H. Russell, *The Just War in the Middle Ages* (Cambridge: Cambridge University Press, 1975), 3–4. Despite its being usually coupled with the ancient Roman just war in discussions of the origins of the Western just war idea, the Roman *bellum iustum*, demonstrably the *fons et origo* of the idea in the West as a practice and as a term in political culture, owes nothing functionally to the Greek idea, and hence the discussion here need not address the latter.

4. Livy 1.32.12 (I, 42): "Puro pioque duello quaerendas censeo" (the formula given for the approval of a declaration of war in the fetial college).

5. On the fetial rite, Tenney Frank, "The Import of the Fetial Institutions," *Classical Philology* 7 (1912): 335–42; F. W. Walbank, "Roman Declarations of War in the Third and Second Centuries B.C.," *Classical Philology* 44 (1949): 15–19; J. W. Rich, *Declaring War in the Roman Empire in the Period of Transmarine Expansion*, Collection Latomus No. 149 (Brussels: Latomus, 1976); William V. Harris, *War and Imperialism in Republican Rome, 327–70 B.C.* (Oxford: Clarendon, 1979), 166–75; Thomas

aspects of the ancient Roman idea continued to condition the cultural and verbal expression of just war for centuries to come. First, there has long been debate over exactly what Livy—far and away the surviving classical Roman writer who most used the terminology—meant by denoting a *bellum* as being both *iustum* and *pium*.[6] The last term seems largely unproblematic, indicating a war somehow religiously sanctioned. It is the meaning of *iustum* that has proved troublesome. Its close coupling with *pium* here, in what seems to be verging on if not actually hendiadys, caused Coleman Phillipson a century ago to argue that *iustum* only meant that war had been initiated in correct accordance with the formalities of the fetial ritual, and in this, with some added nuances, he has been followed by subsequent scholars.[7] Recently Mauro Mantovani has written that whereas *pium* emphasizes the congruence of a war with divine law, *iustum* stresses a war's consonance with human conceptions of what is right: *iustum et pium* thus covers both the celestial and the terrestrial bases for war.[8]

Given the close coupling of the two terms, it seems unlikely that *iustum* can be so neatly differentiated from *pium* in this context. Arguably a better approach in understanding what *iustum* connotes here is briefly to follow out the course of the Roman procedure for going to war, originally connected with the fetial college, as it was several times reported in Livy. First, Livy tells of the Romans as going to war in response to *iniuriae* inflicted upon them by outsiders, a term which can be regarded quasi-legally as referring to a tort perpetrated against the Roman people that required restitution. By the early second century BCE, such *iniuriae* in and of themselves could be regarded as "quite sufficient grounds for war,"[9] especially in the case of foreign invasion, *incursio hostilis*.[10] Thus

Wiedemann, "The Fetials: A Reconsideration," *Classical Quarterly* 36 (1986): 478–90; Alan Watson, *International Law in Archaic Rome: War and Religion* (Baltimore: Johns Hopkins University Press, 1993). On the influence of Stoic ethics on Cicero's conception of the just war, see especially Hausmaninger, 342–45 and Botermann, 3f. (note 1 above).

6. Livian instances of the linking of *iustum* and/or *pium* with *bellum, arma*, etc. include 1.32.12 (note 4 above); 9.8.6 (II; no page number: "iustum piumque . . . bellum"); 30.31.4 (IV, 437: "pia ac iusta . . . arma"); 33.29.8 (V; no page number: "iusto pioque . . . bello"); 39.36.12 (VI, 251: "iustum piumque bellum"); 42.23.6 (*Titi Livi ab urbe condita*, ed. J. Briscoe [Stuttgart: Teubner, 1986], 81: "pio iustoque . . . bello"); 42.47.8 (op. cit., 120: "iusto ac pio . . . bello").

7. Coleman Phillipson, *The International Law and Custom of Ancient Greece and Rome* (London: Macmillan and Co., 1911), vol. 2, 179–80. On the persistence of this interpretation, see, e.g., Hausmaninger (n. 1 above), 342. Frank (n. 5 above), 340, gives a different interpretation more in line with that given here.

8. Mantovani (n. 1 above), 63, n. 22.

9. Livy 34.22.9 (V, 198)

10. Albert (n. 1 above), 18.

any Roman war of self-defense, whether under the Republic or the empire, was *iustum* ipso facto.[11] Nonetheless, Livy reports the Romans as continuing for centuries the practice in some instances of demanding restitution from the external wrongdoer before going to war, originally the *repetitio rerum* proffered by the fetial envoy.[12] Only after observing these formalities could the Romans proceed *iuste* to war. Given the emphasis in this procedure on the claim for damages, the term *iustum* must surely here simply relate to the basic human sense of fairness, in accordance as well with a core meaning of the adjective.[13] Satisfaction of a demand for restitution would restore the *status quo ante* and thus equity. Further, simple fairness also dictated that the wrongdoer be given the opportunity to make restitution.[14] Having done everything that fairness demanded, a resort to war when satisfaction was denied was itself also fair.

That a war was *iustum* at the least implied it had been entered upon in accordance with equity, but the close terminological coupling with *pium* also meant that the sense of *iustum* in this context was inseparably bound up with matters divine. In the original fetial ritual as reported by Livy, if the people who committed the *iniuria* had not made restitution, the fetial envoy declared them to be "unfair" (*iniustum*) and called the gods as witnesses to their unfair dealings.[15] It was a longstanding Roman notion, a notion that persisted in the

11. Albert, 25; Mantovani, 25.

12. Livy's use of variants of *res repetere*, and particularly the formulaic *ad res repentendas* (e.g., 1.22.4; 4.30.13 [I, 27, 281]; 7.6.7; 7.32.1; 8.22.8; 10.12.1; 10.45.7 [II; no page numbers]; 42.25.1 [Teubner edition as above, note 6, 82]), points to his annalistic source or sources and thus some antiquity in at least the understanding of its usage in the context of the fetial ritual. See Harris (n. 5 above), 166f.

13. Lewis and Short, *A Latin Dictionary* (Oxford: Clarendon, 1980), 1020, *s.v. justus*. Frans de Waal, *The Age of Empathy: Nature's Lessons for a Kinder Society* (New York: Harmony Books, 2009), 182–93, discusses his experiments with primates which show that capuchin monkeys and apes demonstrate a sense of fairness, which he terms "inequity aversion" to emphasize how there are strong self-interested motives for social animals to act fairly. As his experiments also showed that apes further seem to have a "fairness norm" like that of their close human relatives, one must presume a sense of fairness to be a basic element in human nature, a conclusion reinforced by the similarities cross-culturally in the results of the "ultimatum game" (on which see op. cit., 185–86). Definitions of what the "just" in just war actually means have to stop somewhere, and to stop with the basic human sense of fairness seems as good a place as any.

14. On the term *repetitio rerum* in Roman law, see Adolf Berger, "Encyclopedic Dictionary of Roman Law," *Transactions of the American Philosophical Society* 43 (1953): *s.v.*, 675.

15. Watson's recent argument (n. 5 above, 10–11), based upon his interpretation of the verb *testari*, that the phrase "ego vos [viz., the gods] testor" in the fetial ritual as reported by Livy calls upon the gods not to witness but to judge the offending nation as *iniustum*, and further that the gods were not originally understood as being responsible for actively ensuring Roman success in a *bellum iustum* (27–28), seems strained and indeed contradicted, at least in Livy's understanding, by later usage in his history such as in

West at least into the medieval period if not later, that having done what fairness demanded (originally in accordance with a particular religious ritual), the Romans had thereby ensured the support of the gods and hence success in the ensuing war.[16] The Romans could, and did, claim that their victories were the inevitable consequence of the equity involved in their reasons for going to war in the first place, their *iusta causa*.[17] When a Rhodian delegation came to Rome in 167 BCE to plead for peace before the senate, Livy reports that one of the envoys told the senators "surely you are the same Romans who as such proclaim yourselves to be successful in your wars because they are just."[18] That the gods favored the Romans in war was thus proved by their ultimate victory over their opponents, making of war a sort of divine judgment.[19]

Success in war being a gift of the gods, it was inevitable that the Romans personified victory itself as a goddess. By the early third century BCE there was a temple dedicated to Victoria at Rome, and she already appeared on coins minted during the First Punic War.[20] But Victoria really took its central place in imperial ideology under Augustus, who placed a statue of her in the senate house at Rome, the heart of the Roman state. As a basic element of imperial ideology, *victoria* came to be associated solely with the emperor's person and to be seen as a legitimation of his rule.[21] This *Victoria Augusti* could be regarded as an autonomous divinity who brought success in war, but also as a sort of charisma inherent in the emperor himself, his "lucky star."[22] The potent mystique of *victoria* was destined to retain its significance for the presentation and legitimation of imperial and royal rule far into the Middle Ages.

Certain questions regarding the Roman *bellum iustum* discussed in the literature on the subject remain relevant for the later development of the just war concept—answers to these particular questions also turn out to be interrelated. To what extent was the just war idea an actual, "living" cultural phenomenon as opposed to a purely intellectual one? Why did the concept

3.2.4, where the consul Quintus Fabius in chiding the Aequi both cites the gods as witnesses (*testes*) of the latter's perfidy and predicts a divine role in the consequent punishment of the offenders ("Quorum id perfidia et periurio fiat, deos nunc testes esse, mox fore ultores" [I, 155]).

16. That the Romans associated fighting a *bellum iustum* with divine favor is noted by several historians who address the Roman concept, including Drexler (n. 1 above, 109–10); Harris (n. 5 above), 170; Albert (n. 1 above, 13); Mantovani (n. 1 above, ix, 1).

17. On *iusta causa*, see the discussion in Clavadetscher-Thürlemann (n. 1 above), 129–32.

18. Livy 45.22.5 [Teubner edition as in n. 6, 313].

19. Harris (n. 5 above), 170.

20. Harris, 123–24.

21. McCormick, 4, 13.

22. Jean Gagé, "La théologie de la victoire impériale," *Revue Historique* 171 (1933): 1–43, esp. 20.

seem to have fallen into desuetude during the imperial period? And why, although civil wars were widely regarded as *impia*, were so many of them described as *iusta*?

As to the actual Roman practice of just war in the Republican period, the invaluable testimony of Polybius is of great significance, for although he does not speak of a Roman just war in so many words, he does, first, speak of the Roman practice in his time of making a formal declaration of war before initiating hostilities.[23] Second, Polybius in reporting the famous interview between Hannibal and Scipio Africanus before the battle of Zama has the latter claim that the gods themselves had granted victory to the Romans in their battles against the unjust actions of the Carthaginians.[24] Taken together, these statements certainly support the assertion that the Romans in the late third and early second centuries BCE had made claims for the justice of their wars and the consequent dispositive role of the gods in granting victory to them.

Polybius also helps to explain why the powerful Romans even bothered to justify themselves, and to whom. This issue of the "practical" operation of the idea and the audience to whom such claims of justice in war were addressed has perennial significance for the just war concept. In reporting on the discussions in Roman political circles during the run-up to the Third Punic War, Polybius noted that the Romans were divided on the question of what to advance as an appropriate cause for war against Carthage that would be acceptable to public opinion in other countries, particularly those, it would seem, of the Hellenistic East.[25] A later fragment of Polybius even preserves some of the content of the public discourse that occurred in Greece after the fall of Carthage and the defeat of the pseudo-Philip, a discourse that clearly shows that the international conduct of Rome in the Mediterranean world of the mid-second century BCE was discussed and evaluated by non-Romans on the basis of principles of justice and equity that the Romans themselves claimed had guided their actions and had led to their successes.[26] This evidence from Polybius indicates that the claim to be fighting for a just cause does seem to have been at this period a feature of Roman war propaganda exhibiting a certain sensitivity to public, especially foreign, opinion.[27] In that respect there can be no question but that the just war

---

23. Polybius 13.3.7 (Büttner-Wobst, 237).

24. Polybius 15.8.2 (Büttner-Wobst, 275).

25. Polybius 36.2 (Büttner-Wobst, 438). On this passage, see F. W. Walbank, *A Historical Commentary on Polybius* (Oxford: Clarendon, 1979), III, 653.

26. Polybius 36.9 (Büttner-Wobst, 446–50).

27. On Roman concern for foreign "public opinion" at this period, see Harris (n. 5 above), 171.

idea was actualized in the context of a public discourse that had "real world" effectiveness, or at least aspired to it.

The question of the audience for the Roman claims to fight just wars also helps to explain why the notion seems to have ultimately fallen into desuetude. As Rome came to conceive of itself as an empire embracing the entire civilized world—with the possible exception of Parthia[28]—there was less of a need felt to consider the tenderness of public opinion in other polities, as there were no polities left whose opinions needed to be considered. Certainly the sensibilities of barbarians could be ignored, since they had none.[29] It was also the case that since *pietas* came to be considered as an imperial attribute,[30] any war initiated by the emperor—that is, any war of the empire—was just ipso facto,[31] and it would have verged on lèse-majesté to suggest otherwise. With the disappearance of the fetial ritual and the lessening of any pragmatic value in Roman self-justification to outsiders, the rhetoric of just war thus tended to fade from Roman propaganda.[32]

But it by no means disappeared entirely. There remained under the Late Republic and the empire one category of war in which it was still necessary to appeal to a body, however small in comparison with the modern period, of opinion-makers—civil war. It is true that civil wars per se had a bad reputation among the Romans, so that Florus, for example, could speak of *iusta et pia bella* against foreign peoples, but termed wars of citizens with each other *impiae pugnae*.[33] Nonetheless, the passions attendant to civil wars, especially evident in those of the Late Republic, and the intense bidding of the parties to win over public opinion tended to override any scruples about the use of just war rhetoric

---

28. A recognition that conceivably only Parthia remained as an organized polity outside the Roman orbit might help explain the appearance of just war rhetoric with reference to Parthia in the early years of Augustus' principate, on which see Mantovani (n. 1 above), 123–24.

29. On this, see the discussion in Clavadetscher-Thürlemann (n. 1 above), 130–31 and the literature cited there in note 20.

30. Mantovani (n. 1 above), 7, n. 41.

31. Mantovani, 47, citing the Pseudo-Aurelius Victor's assertion that Augustus "had never declared war against any nation except for just causes."

32. The lack of an appropriate foreign "audience" for just war claims under the imperial regime, along with the other factors noted in the text—not to mention the general lack of sources in the third century—seem to me a better explanation for an apparent decline in just war rhetoric regarding foreign wars during the imperial period than the explanation given by Mantovani (summarized on 131), who argues that such rhetoric was discredited by its use in civil wars and by the evident failure of Marcus Aurelius to defeat the Marcomanni despite his revival of the fetial ritual (66–67).

33. Cited in Mantovani, 16 and note 25. See also Albert (note 1 above), 26, n. 77 and Clavadetscher-Thürlemann (note 1 above), 133 and n. 35.

in the context of civil war.[34] Mark Antony and Octavian, for example, seem to have employed the rhetoric of just war in their propaganda against Brutus and Cassius, as did Octavian later in his campaign against Cleopatra and Antony.[35] A century later, Galba's revolt against Nero was described by Suetonius as a *iustum piumque et faventibus diis bellum*.[36] The most evidence for the use of just war terminology in the context of civil war appears in certain writings and speeches of Cicero. In his second Catilinarian oration, Cicero had called the war against Catiline a *bellum iustum*. Over a decade later in letters to Atticus he wrote of just war as a partisan of Pompey in the struggle against Caesar, and a few years later in his *Philippics* he termed the senate's fight against Antony a *iustissimum bellum*.[37]

Cicero is also important in the history of the just war for his discussions of the idea in his works *De republica* and *De officiis*.[38] Especially influential was a definition of just war apparently derived by Isidore of Seville from a lost section of *De republica*: "Just war is that which . . . is waged for the purpose of the recovery of property or the repulse of enemies."[39] This definition of the just war appeared centuries later in the canonical collections of Ivo of Chartres, whence it came into Gratian's *Decretum*, thereby becoming part of the later medieval just war synthesis.[40] Augustine himself, who termed Cicero "one of a number of very learned men, and at the same time the most eloquent of them all," is the sole witness to another passage on war from the lost third book of *De republica*, which states that "the best state undertakes no war except either to keep faith [with its allies] or for its own security."[41]

---

34. Clavadetscher-Thürlemann, 178–83, demonstrates conclusively, despite high-sounding Roman assertions to the contrary, that the Romans not only used just war rhetoric in civil wars but apparently felt urgently compelled to do so in precisely such circumstances.

35. Mantovani, 122, 123.

36. Mantovani, 124.

37. Clavadetscher-Thürlemann, 156–59.

38. *De Re Publica* II.17 (31) (*M. Tulli Ciceronis de re publica*, ed. J. G. F. Powell [Oxford: Clarendon, 2006], 67); III.24 (34); 25 (35) (107); *De Officiis* I.11 (34)–13 (40) (*M. Tulli Ciceronis de officiis*, ed. M. Winterbottom [Oxford: Clarendon, 1994], 14–18).

39. Isidore of Seville, *Etymologiarum sive Originum libri XX*, ed. W. M. Lindsay (Oxford: Clarendon, 1911), t. II, *lib.* XVIII.1: "Iustum bellum est, quod ex praedicto geritur de rebus repetitis, aut propulsandorum hostium causa. Iniustum bellum est, quod de furore, non de legitima ratione initur. De quo in Republica dicit Cicero: 'Illa iniusta bella sunt quae sunt sine causa suscepta.'"

40. Ivo of Chartres, *Decretum* X.116 (*PL* 161:727); *Panormia* VIII.54 (*PL* 161:1315); Gratian, *Decretum*, causa 23, q. 2.1 (*Corpus iuris canonici* I, *Decretum magistri Gratiani*, ed. Emil Friedberg [Leipzig, 1879], col. 894).

41. Augustine, *DCD* 22.6 (*CCL* 48, 812, 814).

If described in the preceding manner, it is easy to see how the history of the just war idea can be constructed as a sort of intellectual relay-race, where the baton is like the idea, passed in chronological succession to a series of intellectual "runners."[42] But the history of the just war idea especially illustrates how much more complicated is the actual process of the transmission of ideas. Regardless of how well we understand its earliest manifestation among the Romans, on the one hand the just war as it was discussed in Cicero and later writers is the expression of an idea derived from an ongoing *practice of political culture*. The fetial ritual of the Early Republic sought to secure divine support and hence success for Roman wars fought in pursuit of equity, i.e., for a just cause.[43] By about 200 BCE, just war rhetoric was a staple of Roman propaganda used to justify their actions to non-Roman public opinion.[44] In civil wars during both the Late Republic and the empire, claims to be fighting in a just cause were part of the propaganda used in the intense bidding of the parties for support among the Romans themselves.[45] So, in a panegyric for his imperial cousin Constantius, Julian noted that the emperor had undertaken and fought the war against the Western usurper Magnentius in the early 350s "with justice on his side," even at one point styling the conflict a "holy war" (πόλεμος ἱερός), and the "official" origin of such propaganda is only proved by the speech's manifest insincerity.[46] The intrafamilial nature of his own revolt against Constantius in 361 had Julian in his letters to the notables of various cities—only that for Athens survives, but others are known to have been sent—justify his conduct at length, concluding that he deemed his conduct "just." Here is an instance of official late-Roman civil war propaganda, as well as an idea of the mechanisms and audiences for its dissemination.[47] In these circumstances just war was a claim made in the context of a living political culture that sought to have, and presumably at times did have, a "real world" effect.

By contrast, the context of an ongoing practice of political culture illuminates the details of a just war *idea* as it appears in the writings of Cicero and others, details that can otherwise seem extraneous or obscure from the standpoint of the "relay-race" model of intellectual history, which in its linearity

---

42. Russell's book is probably the best example of the "relay-race" model of the history of ideas when applied to the history of the medieval just war, even though he criticized Vanderpol for failing to correlate the medieval just war theories "with the historical context whence the theories sprang" (2).

43. Above, notes 4 to 19.

44. Above, notes 23 to 27.

45. Above, notes 33 to 37.

46. *L'empereur Julien: Oeuvres complètes*, ed. and trans. J. Bidez (Paris, 1932), I *To Constantius* 33c (86).

47. Julian, *To the Senate and People of Athens*, esp. 269d–270a, 286d (as previous note, 214–15, 234).

tends to efface and smooth out dead-ends and contestations. For example, not only did Cicero in both *De republica* and *De officiis* explicitly link the Roman notions of law and justice (*ius*) in war to the ancient fetial ritual, he also insisted that no war could be just unless it had been publicly declared.[48] It is understandable that later Christian writers had no use for the fetial ritual (though this religious rite was clearly *not* a minor consideration for Cicero in his discussion of just war). So although Isidore copied from Cicero the necessity for a public declaration of war,[49] the different political culture of late eleventh- and early twelfth-century Western Europe clearly saw no utility in transmitting this particular just war requirement, since it does not appear in the canons of either Ivo of Chartres or of Gratian.

Even from this standpoint of regarding the history of just war as the transmission of an intellectual proposition, the transmission of the idea in antiquity seems to have been less direct and more complicated than the notion of linear intellectual inheritance suggests. It has already been noted how there were doubts expressed in the mid-second century BCE as to whether the Romans were living up to their own just war propaganda.[50] The early third-century Roman historian Cassius Dio reports that Calenus, a partisan of Mark Antony, had accused Cicero of insincerity and opportunism in his support of Pompey during the civil war with Caesar, claiming that after Pharsalus Cicero had defected to the winning side, as though by his victory alone Caesar had sufficiently proven to Cicero the justice of his cause. Mauro Mantovani has argued that Calenus here probably expressed the historian's own opinion, and further suggests that Cassius Dio is voicing ironic skepticism regarding Cicero's just war idea itself.[51] If the last is true, it indicates that Cicero had already been recognized as an authority on the idea in the arena of intellectual discourse two

48. *De Re Publica* II.17 (31) (67): "[Tullius Hostilius] constituit ius quo bella indicerentur, quod per se iustissime inventum sanxit fetiali religione, ut omne bellum quod denuntiatum indictumque non esset, id iniustum esse atque impium iudicaretur."; III.25 (35) (107): "Nullum bellum iustum habetur nisi denuntiatum, nisi indictum."; *De officiis* I.11 (36) (15): "Ac belli quidem aequitas sanctissime fetiali populi Romani iure perscripta est, ex quo intellegi potest nullum bellum esse iustum nisi quod aut rebus repetitis geratur aut denuntiatum ante sit et indictum."

49. Isidore (n. 39 above), XVIII.1.3: "'Nam extra ulciscendi aut propulsandorum hostium causa bellum geri iustum nullum potest.' Et hoc idem Tullius paucis interiectis subdidit: 'Nullum bellum iustum habetur nisi denuntiatum, nisi indictum, nisi de repetitis rebus.'"

50. Notes 25, 26 above.

51. Mantovani (n. 1 above), 52. That Cicero's own just war theory is here being criticized may be doubted, especially since Cicero seems nowhere to assert *ipsissima verba* that just wars are invariably successful. In support of Mantovani's suggestion is the fact that Cassius Dio *did* choose Cicero to be the butt of his criticism.

centuries before Augustine. In any case, the story in Cassius Dio does prove that not everyone in antiquity believed that the just party in war was revealed by victory.

It should be noted that the claim to be fighting in a just cause was thought by some to have another "real world" effect in antiquity, that of boosting the morale of the troops as they proceeded to combat. The first-century writer on strategy Onasander argued that soldiers are encouraged to battle by a general who invokes the aid of the gods in a war fought for justice.[52] Three centuries later Ammianus Marcellinus has Constantius II inspire his troops marching against Julian with a speech claiming to be fighting for equity and justice.[53] Of course, it is arguable that the assertion of fighting for a just cause was more encouraging to a commander than to his soldiers. It is certainly possible that, as when Shakespeare's Henry V invoked a just cause to encourage his troops before Agincourt, Roman soldiers might have similarly answered "[t]hat's more than we know . . . for we know enough if we know we are the King's subjects."[54]

II. Early Christian References to Just War before Augustine

The earliest Christian references to just war were incidental, at most conceding that it was a secular value acceptable to Christians out of necessity but inferior to the values expressed in a perfected religious life. This view of the just war was, as we will see, later reflected in Augustine. Moreover, it is questionable how much significance should be assigned to these initial Christian references to the just war idea. After all, that Christians of this period would find more or less acceptable a secular notion described by the adjectives δίκαιος and *iustus* seems in itself quite unremarkable, given especially the ubiquity and theological significance of those adjectives in the Bible. If the Lord is just,[55] if his "right hand is full of justice,"[56] if "the just shall inherit the earth, and dwell upon it forever,"[57] and if it is the just who are to be dismissed into life eternal at the Last Judgment,[58] why should one wonder at, or assign any special significance

---

52. Ὀνοσάνδρου Στρατηγικός, ed. Arminius Koechly (Leipzig: Teubner, 1860), IV, 9–10. On the spelling of the name, see W. A. Oldfather in his introduction to the Loeb text (*Aeneas Tacticus, Asclepiodotus, Onasander* [Cambridge, MA: Harvard University Press, 1928], 345–47).

53. Ammianus Marcellinus 21.13.13–15 (*Ammiani Marcellini rerum gestarum libri qui supersunt*, ed. C. U. Clark [Berlin: Weidmann, 1910–15], 242–43).

54. *The Life of King Henry the Fifth*, act 4. sc. 1, lines 126–33.

55. Exod. 9:27; Deut. 32:5; Ps. 10:5; 114:5; 118:137; Rev. 16:5.

56. Ps. 47:10.

57. Ps. 36:29.

to—let alone seek to contextualize within a supposedly intentional development of doctrine—the fact that some early Christians considered just war to be a good in this inferior world?

The earliest surviving Christian mention of just war is in Origen's *Contra Celsum*, in the same passage in which he argued for Christian exemption from military service.[59] Origen writes that Christians fight with their prayers to God:

> on behalf of those fighting justly (δικαίως) and on behalf of the emperor ruling justly, in order that everything which is opposed and hostile to those acting justly may be destroyed.[60]

This passage has elicited a number of comments and interpretations in the literature.[61] For our purpose it is sufficient to note that Origen here is clearly speaking of the Roman just war, insofar as he seems to be referring to a just cause and opponents acting unjustly. Origen here also seems to imply that Christians would pray for emperor and army *only* in the case of just wars, indicating that by no later than the mid-third century some Christians had valorized the idea at least to the extent that it was legitimate to pray for those fighting in a just war. Still, Origen's few words on the just war, when viewed within the full context of the *Contra Celsum*, are not to be regarded reductively as merely the earliest in an unbroken series of statements ultimately leading to an authoritative Christian doctrine, as Clementina Mazzucco has cogently argued that Origen was less concerned here with just war than with not having war at all.[62]

A sentiment similar to Origen's is seen in the anonymous early fourth-century *Dialogue on the True Faith in God*. In this work the orthodox champion Adamantius refutes the charge of his Gnostic opponent that the orthodox God is inconsistent on the matter of killing human beings by noting that even the Gospels recognize the necessity for slaying evil men, concluding that "it is just to wage a just war against those who go to war unjustly."[63] It would be

---

58. Matt. 25:46.

59. Noted especially in Clementina Mazzucco's valuable study, "Origene e la guerra giusta," *Civiltà classica e cristiana* 9, no. 1 (1988): 67.

60. *Contra Celsum* VIII.73 (291): "υπερ των δικαίως στρατευομένων και υπερ του δικαίως βασιλευοντος, ινα τα εναντία πάντα και εχθρα τοις δικαίως πράττουσι καθαιρεθη." The translation is that of Henry Chadwick in his *Origen: Contra Celsum* (Cambridge: Cambridge University Press, 1965), 509 (modified).

61. On this, see Mazzucco (n. 59 above), 68 and n. 4.

62. Mazzucco (n. 72 above), 84.

63. Adamantius, *GCS* 4, *Dial.* I.10 (24).

wrong to see this passage as part of the working-out of a distinctively Christian idea of just war, especially since Adamantius goes on immediately after this passage to praise those who preach not war but peace, even here quoting the famous passage from Isaiah on beating swords into plowshares.[64] Even the "accommodationist" Eusebius of Caesarea seems to have regarded just war as a lesser good, for when in his *Demonstratio Evangelica* he wrote of military service in the exercise of justice, he did so in the context of a discussion of the two ways of life available to a Christian, associating military service with that form of life granted as a concession to human weakness which also includes marriage and the acquisition of property, to be contrasted with the perfected form of Christian living which rises above the things of this world.[65]

As to what Lactantius thought of the Roman just war, in his *Divine Institutes* he directly attacked the idea that the just side in war thereby earned divine support and consequently victory. According to Lactantius, victory in war falls completely within the sovereignty of God, and has nothing to do with the will of man. Because oftentimes the wicked are more powerful than the good in both numbers and internal cohesion, success in war is more a matter of luck than the justice of one's cause, and history is replete with examples of the defeat of the side that was better and more just.[66] Besides, the fetial declaration of war at the heart of the ancient Roman practice of just war had masked with a show of legality the unjust seizure of the property of others: it was sheer greed, not the pursuit of justice, that had caused Roman armies to ravage and conquer the entire world.[67]

By contrast with earlier Christian references to just war, the remarks of Ambrose were not always incidental and at times show an intentional effort to confront the issues engendered by the church's social and political ascendancy in a state threatened by enemies internal and external, an approach one might expect from the assertive and courageous bishop of a capital city who valued many of the old-time Roman virtues, including patriotism. Because such an important figure in the history of Western Christianity did speak to issues of war, a number of twentieth-century writers on the development of the just war doctrine have made out Ambrose to be Augustine's John the Baptist in the

---

64. Adamantius, loc. cit.; Isa. 2:3-4.

65. Eusebius, *Demonstratio Evangelica* I.8 (*GCS* 6, 39).

66. *Div. Inst.* VI.6.15–17 (*CSEL* 19, 501–2).

67. *Div. Inst.* VI.5.15; 9.4 (498, 510). C. Ingremeau, "Lactance et la Justice," *Autour de Lactance: Hommages à Pierre Monat*, ed. J.-Y. Guillaumin and S. Ratti (Paris: Presses Universitaires de Franche-Comté, 2003), 45, argues that Lactantius is here criticizing the just war as an element of the supposed justice of the Roman state outlined in the lost third book of Cicero's *De republica*.

course of that development. One irony in this view of Ambrose's role is that the relative lack of an interpretive investment in his case, in comparison to the originative role assigned to Augustine, has led oftentimes to a more nuanced, and, in my opinion, more accurate assessment in the scholarship of the Milanese bishop's views on war than is the case with the African Father.

For instance, both Pierre Batiffol in 1920 and L. J. C. Beaufort in 1933 emphasized the brief and summary nature of Ambrose's comments on war.[68] Whereas Batiffol saw Ambrose's moral stance on war as reflective of natural law principles emanating from his "Christianized Stoicism"[69]—here following a trend in scholarly interpretation of De officiis represented for Batiffol by the work of Raymond Thamin[70]—Beaufort concurred in seeing Ambrose as a Christian Stoic while denying that De officiis constituted a synthesis of Christianized natural law.[71] Both writers, however, agreed that Ambrose was the most important precursor to Augustine in the development of a Christian ius belli.[72]

Later twentieth-century American historians were less restrained in how they regarded Ambrose's place in the development of Christian views on war. One of the most influential writers in this respect was Roland Bainton, who in 1960 stated flatly that a "Christian ethic of war appears first to have been formulated by St. Ambrose."[73] Frederick Russell in his influential 1975 work situated Ambrose firmly within the history of the development of a Christian just war theory, even to the point of his desiring "a sort of perpetual holy war" rooted in the bellicose virtues of Old Testament warrior heroes.[74] While formative, Ambrose's "diffuse analysis" was nonetheless too unsystematic to form a solid foundation for a Christian ius belli, a task left to his successor Augustine.[75]

68. Pierre Batiffol, ch. 1, "Les premiers chrétiens et la guerre," in Batiffol et al., L'Église et le droit de guerre (Paris: Bloud & Gay, 1920), 34; D. Beaufort, O.F.M., La guerre comme instrument de secours ou de punition (The Hague: Nijhoff, 1933), 9.

69. Batiffol, 35.

70. Raymond Thamin, Saint Ambroise et la morale chrétienne au IVe siècle (Paris: G. Masson, 1895) (cited in Batiffol, 38, n. 2). A good summary of this scholarly interpretation of De officiis, along with citations of the most important literature, is in Ivor J. Davidson, Ambrose: De officiis (Oxford: Oxford University Press, 2001), vol. 1, 46–47 and notes 108–16.

71. Beaufort, 10.

72. Batiffol, 34; Beaufort, 14. Seconded by Robert H. W. Regout, La doctrine de la guerre juste de saint Augustin à nos jours (Paris: A. Pedone, 1934), 40.

73. Roland Bainton, Christian Attitudes Toward War and Peace (New York and Nashville: Abingdon, 1960), 89.

74. Russell, 12, 14.

Probably the best interpretation of Ambrose's stance on war is found in two works of Louis Swift.[76] Although he follows Bainton in seeing Ambrose as "the first to formulate a Christian ethic of war," even spelling out the conditions for a just war supposedly derivable from *De officiis*,[77] Swift insisted that Ambrose's formulation did not constitute a "simple baptizing of the Roman tradition of the just war."[78] More than any other writer, Swift recognized and stressed the ambiguities and limitations inherent in the bishop's attempts to reconcile Christian ethics as they had been traditionally understood with the necessities thrust upon the church by its newfound preeminence in the fourth-century Roman empire.[79]

This is not the place for a thoroughgoing critique of the scholarship on Ambrose's view of war that can fairly delineate and assess the ideas of the various writers on the subject and all the nuances of their various positions. It has to be noted, though, that all these writers share the idea that the just war doctrine, as it is presently conceived of as a coherent and unified body of inherited propositions, has a more or less well-defined and largely linear history of development. In turn, this view of the development of the just war idea tends to retroject upon its supposed originators a greater uniformity and cohesiveness of conception than can be derived from the sources. In the particular case of Ambrose, the result is an overstatement of his conscious development of just war principles and the coherence of his supposed theory.[80]

---

75. Russell, 15.

76. Louis J. Swift, "St. Ambrose on Violence and War," *Transactions and Proceedings of the American Philological Association* 101 (1970): 533–43; idem, *The Early Fathers on War and Military Service* (Wilmington, DE: Michael Glazier, 1983), 96–110.

77. Swift, "St. Ambrose," 533, 534; *The Early Fathers*, 97, 99–100.

78. "St. Ambrose," 538; *The Early Fathers*, 100.

79. "St. Ambrose," 538–43.

80. A noteworthy recent restatement of the interpretation that assigns Ambrose a place in the development of a Christian just war theory is in John von Heyking, "Taming Warriors in Classical and Early Medieval Political Theory," in *Ethics, Nationalism, and Just War: Medieval and Contemporary Perspectives*, ed. Henrik Syse and Gregory M. Reichberg (Washington, DC: Catholic University of America Press, 2007), esp. 23–34. But see the devastating critique in the same volume by Gerson Moreno-Riaño, "Reflections on Medieval Just War Theories," esp. 125–30. Moreno-Riaño correctly notes that "[t]he first question that needs to be addressed is whether Ambrose *actually* [emphasis his] composed anything resembling a theory of just war" (125). He notes that "even when Ambrose does take up the theme of war, his comments are sporadic at best and should not, it can be argued, be construed as aspects of a theory or of a distinctive Christian treatment of armed political conflict," and that his remarks on war in *De officiis* "may be of minimal importance in an attempt to unearth some semblance of an Ambrosian theory of a just war" (129). He concludes that "Ambrose's comments on just war appear to be

Regarding his own words on the matter, it is noteworthy that Ambrose mentions the term only once, in a sort of "throwaway" line that in no way justifies the ink spilled on its behalf as an indicator of his view of the just war. An accurate interpretation of the passage involved has been largely lacking due to an overly narrow concentration on the one sentence at the expense of the broader context, too great a reliance upon the layout of the printed text, and Ambrose's "staccato" style here, which features abrupt swings in the objects of his attention and the insertion of parenthetical material.

I give below an interpretation/translation of the relevant text from the recent *Corpus Christianorum* edition, absent the paragraph division and numbering, artifacts of the modern editions.

> Let us at this point deal with courage, which, being as it were a loftier virtue than the rest, is divided into military and domestic spheres. But the study of military matters seems foreign to our business at hand, given that our focus is more on the duty of the soul than on that of the body, and that our need at present is not to look to arms, but to the business of peace. (Nonetheless, our ancestors, men such as Joshua son of Nun, Jerubbaal, Samson, and David, also attained the highest glory in war.) And so courage, loftier, as it were, than the rest, is yet never a virtue unaccompanied. Indeed, it never depends on itself alone, for in the case where courage is without justice, it is the cause of wickedness. For the stronger it is, the readier it is to crush a lesser party, granted that in the military sphere proper it is thought to be more a matter of looking at whether wars are just or unjust.[81]

nothing more than that—Christian aphorisms on the subject of war not reflective of a theoretical scheme on the subject" (125).

81. *De officiis* I 35, 175–76 (*CCL* 15, 64–65): "Nunc de fortitudine tractemus quae velut excelsior ceteris dividitur in res bellicas et domesticas. Sed bellicarum rerum studium a nostro officio iam alienum videtur quia animi magis quam corporis officio intendimus nec ad arma iam spectat usus noster sed ad pacis negotia. Maiores autem nostri ut Iesus Nave, Ierobaal, Samson, David summam rebus quoque bellicis retulere gloriam. Est itaque fortitudo velut excelsior ceteris sed numquam incomitata virtus; non enim ipsam committit sibi, alioquin fortitudo sine iustitia iniquitatis materia est. Quo enim validior est, eo promptior ut inferiorem opprimat, cum in ipsis rebus bellicis iusta bella an iniusta sint spectandum putetur." I have at times here used both the English translation of *De officiis* by H. De Romestin in *A Select Library of Nicene and Post-Nicene Fathers*, 2nd series, vol. 10, 30 and that by Davidson, vol. 1, 219/ 222.

In this passage Ambrose has turned to a discussion of the cardinal virtue of courage (*fortitudo*). Paralleling Cicero's treatment of that virtue in his own *De officiis*, in which he had spoken of courage in the *res bellicae* and *res urbanae*,[82] Ambrose divides his own discussion of courage between the *res bellicae* and the *res domesticae*, that is, between courage as it is manifested in war and as it appears in the struggles of the civilian lives of individuals. His cycling back and forth here between a focus on *res domesticae* and *res bellicae* reflects an acknowledgment of the difficulty in any treatment of courage as a virtue, since that quality, as both Cicero and Ambrose agree, is commonly though incorrectly associated exclusively with war.[83] Parallel to the bipartite division of courage here is the twofold division of Ambrose's intended audience into Christian and educated non-Christian. On the one hand, Ambrose is assuring his Christian readers that their particular type of courage is not to be despised, at the same time reminding them that they, too, have their own warrior heroes. On the other hand, he is addressing his pagan readers, who know that when Ambrose's model Cicero criticized courage without justice that he was speaking not to war but to *res domesticae*, having especially Caesar in mind. Ambrose is signaling to pagan readers his recognition that while justice has a place in war, it ought not in the heat of battle act so as to moderate courage, the utmost exercise of which is essential for victory. The last sentence of this passage thereby forestalls the charge that he was here advocating a half-hearted prosecution of war, due to the supposed lack of martial courage among Christians.[84] In fact, Ambrose specifically denies that it would be an injustice per se in the *res bellicae* to fight against an opponent inferior in strength, since the justice or injustice of any particular war is independent of the relative strength of the combatants. He is here certainly not interested in propounding any just war doctrine per se, for the true *officium* of Christians is the *pacis negotia*. Both Christian and non-Christian educated readers would have recognized in the counsel of the necessity for determining the justice of wars a reference back, if they so desired to pursue it, to his model Cicero's treatment of the *iura belli*.

Only at one point does Ambrose indicate a specific criterion for engaging in a just war, when he immediately follows up the passage being discussed with the comment that "David never waged war unless provoked."[85] It is interesting

---

82. Cicero, *De officiis* I 22, 74 (30).

83. Cicero, *De officiis* I 22, 78 (32): "Sunt igitur domesticae fortitudines non inferiores militaribus" and Ambrose, *De officiis* I 40, 196 (73).

84. A charge he later directly addresses in *De officiis* I 196 (*CCL* 15, 73).

85. *De officiis* I 177 (*CCL* 15, 65): "Numquam David nisi lacessitus bellum intulit."

that Ambrose here seems to be allowing for political leadership that which he denied to be licit for the individual, with specific reference to the Ciceronian dictum that justice's first duty is to prevent someone from harming another "unless provoked by some wrong."[86] His use of David in *De officiis* to exemplify true Christian leadership can sustain a reading of this passage as being praise for the emperor Theodosius's reluctance to fight until pushed to extremities, a claim that was a tenet of contemporary Theodosian propaganda, and also as being admonitory for succeeding Christian emperors. Other than for this one, somewhat vague condition, however, Ambrose "never asks how we might establish the overall justice of a particular war."[87]

Ambrose had earlier in *De officiis* touched on the matter of justice during war itself, the modern ethical and legal category of *ius in bello*, in the course of his discussion of the cardinal virtue of justice. Ambrose's comments regarding *ius in bello* are difficult to recognize as such because they are introduced casually as almost a parenthetical aside, and difficult to comprehend and evaluate because of the compression and abruptness of his style here,[88] because he is continually in his own *De officiis* glancing back at his Tullian model, and explicitly or (as here) implicitly contrasting unfavorably Cicero's *exempla* with Christian.

What follows is a translation of the relevant text that takes into account the abrupt transitions and references to Cicero:

> How great justice is can be understood from the fact that it makes no exception for place, person, or time. Even opponents in war observe justice, as in the case of it being considered contrary to justice to arrive earlier at the place or to anticipate the time for a battle when either the place or the day has already been pre-arranged with the enemy. Of course, regarding prisoners it makes a difference as to how they were captured, whether it was in a hard-fought battle, or as a result of divine favor or some other happenstance. For when dealing with fiercer foes, the faithless, and those who have done worse harm, a fiercer vengeance is exacted, as in the case of the Midianites, who through their women had caused most of the Jewish people to sin, leading to the wrath of God being poured out upon the people of our forefathers. What happened as a consequence was that when Moses defeated them, he allowed none of them to survive.

---

86. Cicero, I 7, 20 (9); Davidson (commentary), vol. 2, 607.

87. Davidson, vol. 2, 607.

88. Cf. Davidson's comments on Ambrose's "slightly bumpy" style in *De officiis* I 140 in his commentary, vol. 2, 579–80.

In the case of the Gibeonites, however, who had tested the people of our forefathers more by guile than open warfare, Joshua, instead of fighting them, inflicted upon them the punishment of the state [of servitude]. Then there is the case of the Syrians who were besieging a city and whom Elisha had brought into the city after striking them with a temporary blindness so that they could not see where they were going. When the king of Israel wanted to kill them, Elisha did not acquiesce. Rather, he said "thou shalt not kill those whom thou hast not taken captive by thy sword and spear; set bread and water before them, that they may eat and drink, and return and go to their master," so that they would be so inspired by such humane treatment as to return the favor. The end result was that Syrian raiders forthwith stopped coming into the land of Israel.[89]

This passage reflects Cicero's discussion of justice in war, especially in *De officiis* I 34–40.[90] As does Cicero, Ambrose contends that even warring parties must maintain between themselves justice and good faith.[91] Ambrose goes on to adduce as an example of injustice in war the failure to respect the conditions for the time and place of a battle when those have been prearranged by the combatants.[92] Then, without any signal of transition other than the weak

89. *De officiis* I 29, 139 (*CCL* 15, 49–50): "Quanta autem iustitia sit ex hoc intellegi potest quod nec locis nec personis nec temporibus excipitur, quae etiam hostibus reservatur; ut si constitutus sit cum hoste aut locus aut dies proelio, adversus iustitiam putetur aut loco praevenire aut tempore. Interest enim utrum aliqui pugna aliqua et conflictu gravi capiatur an superiore gratia vel aliquo eventu, siquidem vehementioribus hostibus et infidis et his qui amplius laeserint, vehementior refertur ultio; ut de Madianitis qui per mulieres suas plerosque peccare fecerant ex plebe Iudaeorum, unde et Dei in populum patrum iracundia effusa est; et ideo factum est ut nullum Moyses victor superesse pateretur, Gabaonitas autem qui fraude magis quam bello temptaverant plebem patrum, non expugnaret Iesus, sed conditionis impositae adficeret iniuria; Syros vero Eliseus, quos obsidentes in civitatem induxerat, momentaria caecitate percussos cum quo ingrederentur videre non possent, volenti regi Israel percutere non acquiesceret dicens: 'Non percuties quos non captivasti in gladio et lancea tua: pone eis panem et aquam, et manducent et bibant et remittantur et eant ad dominum suum,' ut humanitate provocati gratiam repraesentarent. Denique postea in terram Israel venire piratae Syriae destiterunt."

90. Note the verbal parallel between Cicero, I 11, 36 (15) ("Ex quo intellegi potest nullum bellum esse iustum . . .") and Ambrose here ("ex hoc intellegi potest quod nec locis nec personis nec temporibus excipitur").

91. Cicero, III 29, 107 (154): "Est autem ius etiam bellicum fidesque iuris iurandi saepe cum hoste servanda." Cf. *De officiis* I 29, 139 (49) ("quae [viz. iustitia] etiam hostibus reservatur") and I 140 (50–51): "Liquet igitur etiam in bello fidem et iustitiam servari oportere."

92. Ambrose seems to be referring here to an archaic practice of ritual battle ascribed to the Romans of the early Republic in Livy 42.47.5 (*Titi Livi ab urbe condita*, ed. John Briscoe [Stuttgart: Teubner, 1986],

enim, he turns to the treatment of prisoners taken during war, a discussion that occupies the rest of the passage. Ambrose is responding here to Cicero's discussion of the treatment of defeated enemies, and the abrupt transition seems to take for granted a reader's familiarity with the earlier *De officiis*. Cicero had written that Romans should spare defeated foes who had not acted barbarously or committed atrocities, and even those who had delayed surrender until the battering-ram was actually hammering at their walls.[93] As is his practice, Ambrose replaces the pagan with biblical *exempla*, but here does not make explicit the superiority of the latter over the former. The first example given is, in fact, crueler than any cited by Cicero, who had spoken at most of the destruction of cities, whereas Ambrose speaks of Moses wiping out the Midianites.

What did Ambrose intend for his original audience to take away from this discussion of the justice due enemies in war, especially with its example of Elisha's treatment of the captured Syrian raiders? Ambrose is letting his Christian readers, clerical and lay, know that as leaders in an increasingly Christianized empire they were expected not simply to equal traditional pagan standards in the treatment of defeated enemies, but to exceed the pagans in their *humanitas* toward the foe.

More than previous Christian writers, then, Ambrose deliberately devoted some attention to issues related to war. But besides the fact that such reflections amount to a relatively minuscule proportion of Ambrose's total output, such statements have to be seen in the context of his continual polemical combat

119–20), a passage in turn perhaps derived from a now lost section in Book 27 of Polybius (F. W. Walbank, *A Historical Commentary on Polybius* [Oxford: Clarendon, 1967], vol. 2, 416). In a surviving passage Polybius also ascribes to the archaic Greeks the practice of announcing beforehand the time and place for a battle (13.3.5). On this passage see Hans Van Wees, *Greek Warfare: Myths and Realities* (London: Duckworth, 2004), 134: "Full-scale pitched battles knew some 'agonal' restraints, especially in the classical period, but they were never the formal engagements of Polybius' imagination, fought by arrangement at a stipulated time and place." A link with Ciceronian discussions of the *iura belli* is suggested by the fact that both Polybius and Livy here mention as a laudable usage the formal declaration of war (Polybius, loc. cit. and 13.3.7 [in the case of the Romans] and Livy, loc. cit.), as does Cicero (*De officiis* I 11, 36 (15); *De republica* II 17, 31 (67), III 25, 33 (107), as well as by the fact that both Livy (42.47.8; op. cit., 120) and Cicero (*De republica* II 17, 31) make the formal declaration a requirement for a war to be *iustum et pium*. Perhaps Ambrose derived this description of ritual battle from a now lost portion of *De republica*.

93. Cicero, *De officiis* I 11, 35 (14–15). He seems here to argue for a softening of the traditional Roman practice, as for instance seen in Caesar, *BG* II 32 (*Bellum Gallicum*, ed. O. Seel [Leipzig: Teubner, 1961], 72), that only spared enemies who surrendered before the battering-ram touched their walls (Griffin and Atkins, 15, n. 3).

in *De officiis* with Cicero. This is true whether he is speaking of the need to preserve a place for justice in war, of the dispositive role of political leadership in determining whether to go to war in the first place, or his mentioning, if only briefly and allusively, the just war. And since Cicero's relevant statements were such an accepted point of comparison, Ambrose clearly had no desire to craft a specifically Christian concept of just war or Christian laws of war, and did not do so. His larger point on this subject within the broader polemical thrust of *De officiis* is that Christians in positions of leadership should aspire not only to equal but to exceed the admittedly humane standards of the Roman *iura belli*, the same point he had made regarding capital punishment in his letter to Studius.[94] As we will see, Augustine likewise took for granted a Ciceronian conception of the laws of war, and likewise used that conception for polemic contrasting pagan values, to their detriment, with Christian.

94. See chapter three above, notes 150 to 153.

PART II

5

Interpreting Augustine

In retrospect it is understandable that there would eventually emerge an interpretation of St. Augustine that would make him an authority on the Christian view of war. To begin with, more of his writings survive than is the case for any other Christian writer of the first millennium. In the small-print Migne edition of the *Patrologia Latina*, they fill fourteen quarto volumes. The survival of so much material is in itself a testament not only to how much he wrote during his lifetime, but also to the authority with which his works were regarded in subsequent centuries, since succeeding generations were motivated to the laborious task of repeatedly copying works of his that were often quite lengthy and involved. Furthermore, since Augustine wrote in the late fourth and early fifth century, the very time when Christian writers were grappling with issues presented by the rise to prominence and dominance of their fellow believers in the Roman empire, it is only to be expected that in the vast bulk of his writings one can find instances where issues of war and military service were addressed. Yet there is actually relatively little to be found in his works on these issues in comparison to the amount of material devoted to other subjects.

In evaluating both the place that Augustine's thoughts on war and military service occupied in the context of his time and how his views were regarded by succeeding generations, there arises for a modern interpreter the question of how common or unique his ideas were in comparison with those of his Christian contemporaries. Nowadays we tend to prize originality in a writer, and consequently a modern interpreter of Augustine might tend to emphasize his distinctiveness among contemporaries. Such was not the way his ideas were viewed during, for example, the medieval period. In becoming one of the premier Latin Fathers, what became valued in his work was evidence of its congruence with the *consensus doctorum*. By that reading, Augustine's difference with his contemporaries would be minimized, and anything that fell outside that consensus marginalized or ignored. This consideration sets up a conceptual filter, so to speak, which in succeeding centuries tended to constrict the content of his original views on war and military service. One must seek to set aside the constraints placed on that material by especially his medieval interpreters, the canonists and theologians who helped to construct him as an authority on war.

It is true that at this date it is arguably impossible to free oneself entirely from the accumulated weight of the intervening centuries of scholarship on Augustine that has often been shaped by the conceptual filters of his medieval interpreters. But even a cursory attempt to do so reveals that much of what has been written on Augustine's views on war and military service in especially twentieth-century scholarship is at best misconceived, and at worst simply wrong. It would not be very productive to engage in an unenlightening "ordeal by footnotes" whenever anything in what follows contradicts one writer or another. Although arguably there is at least something new in what follows, it is also true that there is much that is familiar here to those who have looked at Augustine's views on war. In particular, there is marked congruence with the path laid out in Herbert Deane's classic work *The Political and Social Ideas of St. Augustine.*[1] One could argue that that work presented an Augustine that was overly schematized and inadequately historicized, but the same could be said to some extent of any interpretation of Augustine, including the present one.[2]

---

1. Herbert Deane, *The Political and Social Ideas of St. Augustine* (New York: Columbia University Press, 1963). The following works have been especially useful for the next three chapters: On Augustine's biography, Peter Brown's *Augustine of Hippo: A Biography*, 2nd ed. (Berkeley and Los Angeles: University of California Press, 2000); hereafter Brown, remains fundamental. On the Donatist conflict in particular, and more generally on the state of the African church in Augustine's day, there is now the excellent book of Brent D. Shaw, *Sacred Violence: African Christians and Sectarian Hatred in the Age of Augustine* (Cambridge: Cambridge University Press, 2011); hereafter Shaw. On Augustine's works in general, and *The City of God* in particular, *Augustine through the Ages: An Encyclopedia*, ed. Allan D. Fitzgerald (Grand Rapids: Eerdmans, 1999); hereafter Fitzgerald; and Gerard O'Daly, *Augustine's City of God: A Reader's Guide* (Oxford: Oxford University Press, 1999); hereafter O'Daly, which incorporates much of the important earlier as well as recent scholarship on that daunting work. On Augustine's views on providential history, and the possibility of just war within that history, R. A. Markus, *Saeculum: History and Society in the Theology of St. Augustine* (Cambridge: Cambridge University Press, 1970); hereafter Markus, *Saeculum*; and idem, "Saint Augustine's Views on the 'Just War,'" *Studies in Church History* 20 (1983); hereafter Markus, "Saint Augustine's Views on the 'Just War.'" On the theological underpinnings of "Augustine's" just war, Josef Rief, *"Bellum" im Denken und in den Gedanken Augustins* (Barsbüttel: Institüt für Theologie und Frieden, 1990); hereafter Rief. On the supposed philosophical coherence of an Augustinian just war theory, John Mark Mattox, *Saint Augustine and the Theory of Just War* (London and New York: Continuum, 2006); hereafter Mattox.

2. A pitfall noted by Mattox, 8, before dismissing it.

This investigation of Augustine's views on war and military service has been guided by at least three overriding interpretive considerations. First, due to the often protean nature of what we can recover of his views, as well as the variety of genres he employed over a literary career spanning more than four decades, it can be argued that not only did Augustine seemingly contradict himself at times, but that he also changed his mind on certain things. Particularly pertinent in this regard is the argument of Robert Markus that Augustine reacted against his earlier embrace of Christian "triumphalism" at the end of the fourth century and moved to a more jaundiced view of the possibilities of a Christian empire.[3] To the extent such an interpretation is valid, it would also imply a change in Augustine's view of war.[4] But I hope to show that Augustine's views on war and military service were actually fairly consistent over the span of his literary career. The following investigation is therefore largely organized topically rather than chronologically. Besides, any attempt to chart the development of Augustine's thinking on war and military service is rendered difficult by the impossibility of dating many of his works, particularly his sermons. Therefore, unless an argument for the dating of a particular sermon appears in a note, the dates I give for his sermons are quite provisional.

Another, related consideration has to do with evaluating Augustine's statements on war and military service in the original contexts in which they appeared. But this is easier said than done. Augustine wrote no treatise *De bello* or *De militia*. All his statements relevant to our inquiry appear in works whose purpose was other than our current focus. And since the underlying ideas for much of what Augustine did write on war and military service are common to much of his work entire, it cannot be denied that in fact the only proper context for such statements is his entire oeuvre![5] Realistic choices, then, have to be made, and I have striven for what I judge to be a usable level of context, while recognizing that by so doing I necessarily perpetuate to some degree the misleading view of Augustine as a self-conscious authority on war.

Finally, it is understandable given Augustine's genius and energy that his ideas have often been treated as though sui generis, without sufficient attention to framing them within the context of contemporary Christian writers and ideas. Augustine was nothing if not argumentative, and it is the case with much of what he wrote on war and military service that he cast it originally in opposition to the views not only of pagans and heretics, but also to

3. Markus, *Saeculum*, esp. 29–44, 51–71.

4. As argued by Markus, "Saint Augustine's Views on the 'Just War,'" 4–11.

5. Mattox speaks to this, 5–6.

those of more "orthodox" Christian contemporaries. A difficulty in recognizing this practice arises from the fact that Augustine often did not expressly name his Christian interlocutors or explicitly detail their views.[6] Augustine himself provides probably the best clue as to why he avoided naming his Christian opponents in his *De gestis Pelagii*, written as a brief history of his involvement with Pelagius and his followers. At one point early in the controversy he wrote concerning the Pelagians that "we thought it would be of greater benefit in acting against them if the errors themselves were refuted and disproved while not mentioning their names."[7] When he did come to write a work against a book written by Pelagius himself

> still, I did not introduce the name of Pelagius in my work in which I refuted the same book, thinking that it would be more useful if by still preserving a friendly relationship with him I could keep him from losing face ("eius verecundiae parcerem").[8]

But later, when it became clear that Pelagius could not be convinced of the error of his ways, Augustine did not hesitate to name him expressly in his works.[9]

Aurelius Augustinus was born in 354 at Thagaste in the province of Numidia in Roman North Africa, the son of Patricius, a modest burger of the town, and Monica, who imparted something of her Christianity and strong personality to her son.[10] After receiving a classical education and moving to

---

6. I have not been able to find any good discussion of this practice by Augustine in the secondary literature. Bengt Alexanderson, "Après la conférence de Carthage (411): Augustin et les réactions des Donatistes," *Comunicazione e ricezione del documento cristiano in epoca tardoantica: XXXII Incontro di studiosi dell'antichita cristiana* (Rome: Institutum patristicum Augustinianum, 2004), 197, does note the vagueness of the references, none by name, to Augustine's opponents in his anti-Donatist polemics immediately after the conference of 411, but his argument that this is intended to signal his disdain for his opponents does not apply to the practice mentioned here. The same is true for Hagendahl's observation of Augustine's practice of occasionally suppressing the names of his pagan opponents ("Methods of citation in post-classical Latin prose," *Eranos* 45 [1947]: 114–28). Obviously the practice noted here oftentimes makes it difficult to determine that Augustine was at times in his writings reacting against particular opponents, and the vagaries of source survival make it likely that he was oftentimes so doing in cases where the subsequent textual disappearance of his interlocutors render it now impossible to realize that this was going on in particular instances.

7. *De gestis Pelagii* 46 (*CSEL* 42, 100): "Salubrius sane adversus eos agi putabamus, si hominum nominibus tacitis ipsi refutarentur et redarguerentur."

8. *De gestis Pelagii* 47 (*CSEL* 42, 101): "Nec sic tamen operi meo, quo eundem librum refelli, Pelagii nomen inserui, facilius me existimans profuturum, si servata amicitia adhuc eius verecundiae parcerem."

9. *De gestis Pelagii* 50 (*CSEL* 42, 103–4).

Carthage, Augustine, who was put off by what he regarded as the coarse and vulgar language of the Christian Bible, became briefly a follower of Manichaeism. That religion, considered a Christian heresy by some, posited a radically dualistic cosmology, in which the good God was engaged in a cosmic struggle against an equally potent god of evil. We know from Augustine's works later written against them that Manichaeans were highly critical of what they considered the vengeful, violent God of the Old Testament, and contrasted that with the pacific principles of the New Testament.

In coming to Milan in 384, a city then the de facto capital of the Western empire, Augustine was looking to advance his worldly career. But in the summer of 386 he experienced a spiritual crisis, from which he emerged a convert to Christianity. In the months before his baptism he retired with a group of young men and his mother to the country estate of Cassiciacum, where the group engaged in a series of philosophical dialogues that were written up into books he later had published. He returned to Africa in 388, Monica having died in Italy.

In the spring of 391 during a visit to the Mediterranean port city of Hippo Regius, Augustine was "drafted" into the priesthood by the local congregation, over which he was consecrated as bishop in 395. During the same years Augustine began regularly preaching sermons to the congregation at Hippo Regius and occasionally in other towns in the area, and especially at Carthage. His sermons, hundreds of which survive, even in his day came to be recognized for their forceful, simple eloquence, and along with his numerous writings helped to establish him as one of the leading figures of the Catholic Church in North Africa. His early years as bishop were dominated by religious conflict with the Donatist schismatics.

The last of Augustine's writings were largely taken up in combat with the Pelagians. His last years were darkened by the revolt of the general Boniface, with whom Augustine had engaged in friendly correspondence but who seems to have disappointed the aged bishop in the end. Augustine died in Hippo Regius in 430 while it was being besieged by the Vandals, who had taken advantage of the chaos engendered by Boniface's revolt to invade Roman North Africa.

Most of Augustine's statements on war and military service are found in two treatises. Sometime in the period between 400 and 404/5, and probably closer to the earlier than the later date,[11] there appeared the work *Contra Faustum*

---

10. Most of the biography here from Brown.

11. *Contra Fausto*, trans. Pio de Luis, *Obras completas de San Agustín* 31 (Madrid: Biblioteca de Autores Cristianos, 1993), 20–21, gives a good recent summary discussion of the dating for *Contra Faustum*.

Manicheum, written as a reply to the work of the prominent African Manichaean Faustus, a man known personally to Augustine and who makes a noteworthy appearance in the *Confessions*.[12] Faustus's work, the *Capitula*, was organized in a question-and-answer format as the reply to the objections of an orthodox Christian to certain Manichaean tenets, particularly those concerning their rejection of the Old Testament and their criticism of what they regarded as the immoral behavior of the Old Testament patriarchs. Augustine organized his own reply to Faustus's work as a point-by-point rebuttal of the Manichaean's arguments. In the course of so doing, especially in Book 22, Augustine laid out certain aspects of his theology more clearly and succinctly than he does in other, more celebrated treatises, and his *Contra Faustum* deserves to be included in any short list of the half-dozen or so major works of the African Father.[13]

There is little disputing that *The City of God* deserves inclusion in such a list. This massive treatise can be considered as the final, culminating monument of the Latin apologetic tradition. As Augustine himself made clear in his *Retractationes*, written not long after the completion of *The City of God* in 426 or 427,[14] the work was begun as a reply to those pagans who blamed the rise of Christianity for the sack of Rome by the Goths in 410.[15] *The City of God*, however, had broader aims than the narrowly apologetic. It became in some respects a more or less comprehensive compendium of Augustine's theological views, and a sustained attack on a pagan culture that seemed visibly in the process of disappearing. In the course of its twenty-two books he engaged classical pagan literature, history, philosophy, religion, and science, and countered at every point the pagan values and attitudes revealed in those areas with the values of Christianity. He organized his polemic around the image of two cities: the earthly city, where mortal human beings seek to enjoy for their own sakes things either wicked or at best transitory; and the eternal city of God, where the immortal faithful enjoy that which is eternal. In addition to his primary pagan opponents, Augustine also occasionally in *The City of God* countered the views of other Christians, and it is often in the course of refuting such adversaries that we find statements relevant to the present inquiry as to his views on war and military service.

12. *Confess.* 5.6–7.

13. *Contra Faustum* receives its due in Paula Fredriksen, *Augustine and the Jews: A Christian Defense of Jews and Judaism* (New York: Doubleday, 2008), for its evidence of Augustine's views on Jews and Judaism, past and present.

14. For the date of the *Retractationes*, Fitzgerald, 723, and for *The City of God* having been completed not long before, O'Daly, 35.

15. *Retract.* II 69 (*CSEL* 36, 180–81; *CCL* 57, 124).

In order more fully to understand Augustine's attitudes toward military service, it will be helpful to look not only at the intellectual, but also the material and institutional context for his views. I have therefore addressed the following questions, among others:

- What was the nature of the Roman military establishment in North Africa with which Augustine was most familiar?
- What do incidental references to *militia* in Augustine's works reveal, both about his attitudes toward the Roman army in particular and state service in general?
- What in his material circumstances might help account for what seems at times Augustine's favorable view of careers in the military or civil service?
- Did Augustine, like many of his contemporary Christian prelates, believe that Christians who had done such service needed to do penance upon retirement, especially if they were considering a career in the church?
- In addition to the role that material circumstances played in the formation of Augustine's views, what were the intellectual and theological bases for Augustine's attitudes toward service to the state?
- How did Augustine's conception of order inform his view of society in general, and in particular his understanding of the maintenance of societal order through obedience to legitimate authorities and the exercise of lawful coercion?
- As to the military itself, how does Augustine's conception of societal order and the mechanisms that maintain it explain the lawfulness of soldiers killing other human beings? How does he justify the participation of *Christian* soldiers in such legitimate killing?
- How did Augustine view war? How could he justify the participation of Christians in it, whether as commanders or soldiers serving in the ranks?
- What role did divine providence play in war? Could war be an instrument of divine justice? How could Christians know whether wars were being waged for providential or just ends, and what was the relationship of such wars to the Roman just war?
- What was Augustine's view of such ideologically charged terms as *pax* and *victoria* in the realm of Roman ideas about war? What did Augustine understand by the word "peace," in both its peculiarly Roman and Christian meanings?

•

6

Augustine on *Militia*

THE ROMAN MILITARY IN AUGUSTINE'S AFRICA

Like his Christian contemporaries who touched on similar matters, Augustine often framed his discussion of military service under the broader rubric of *militia*, service to the state. It is under this broader rubric that Augustine discussed issues of punishment and coercion, and especially the issue of capital punishment, the last being of particular relevance for our purposes as he is often seen to conflate judicial killing with the killing done by soldiers in war, since both involve the state-sanctioned taking of human life, the exercise of the state's *ius gladii*. It is also under the broader rubric of *militia* that Augustine discussed the issue of how to conceive of and justify the proper authority that ordered killing, and the obedience owed to that authority by those responsible for carrying out such orders.

To begin with military service in particular, in order best to comprehend his attitude, it is necessary first to outline the contours of the Roman military establishment in Africa with which Augustine was most familiar and that backgrounded his view of such service. In the central North African provinces of Mauretania Sitifensis, Numidia, and Byzacena which fell within Augustine's local horizon, the *comes Africae* was the overall commander of Roman military forces.[1] Thanks to his relative geographical isolation on the other side of the Mediterranean from most of the rest of the empire and his control of a granary vital for Italy and especially Rome, the *comes Africae* headed a regional command of greater military weight in imperial affairs than numbers alone could tell, and his loyalty to the central government was correspondingly of greater concern than the size of his establishment might suggest. Unlike the case of the huge military complements of the Rhine and Danube armies in the late empire, the *comes Africae* commanded a relatively modest-sized field army—the so-called

---

1. On the *comes Africae*, see now Shaw, 36–37.

comitatenses—that has been estimated to have totaled about 22,000 men in the early fifth century, a force almost equally divided between infantry and cavalry. The relatively high proportion of cavalry in the African field army as compared with that in armies outside Africa reflects the need to have an effective mobile force to deal with raids from nomadic tribesmen across the frontier.[2]

In addition to the main field army, the Roman military establishment in Augustine's Africa also included a few thousand *limitanei*, who functioned as a sort of border police to monitor and control movement through the frontier zone, particularly of transhumant groups who annually migrated north into Roman territory for summer pasturage.[3] For such purposes the border troops were divided into a series of sector commands, each headed by an officer designated as a *praepositus limitis*.[4] We have a letter from Augustine to a local landowner in which the bishop alludes to the activities of such regional commanders.[5]

INCIDENTAL REFERENCES ON *MILITIA*

There is sufficient evidence in Augustine's works to enable us to assess with a fair degree of confidence and with some considerable depth and range his view of the military, and to what extent that attitude evolved over time, or remained constant. Besides what it might tell us directly, such evidence is also at points indirectly eloquent in its silences and emphases in comparison with other Christian views of the military, whether those be of contemporaries and compatriots or of predecessors and foreigners. In reviewing this evidence, it should be noted that there are, of course, certain Augustinian passages long known to scholarship that speak explicitly to the issue of Christian attitudes toward military service. More broadly, there is other evidence in his works consisting of casual representations or illustrative examples drawn from military life, evidence that because of its very casualness has its own eloquence in illuminating Augustine's view of the military, or at least that reflects a broad familiarity with military life, a familiarity he likely shared with the audience for his writings and sermons. In this last category falls, for example, Augustine's writing in *De doctrina Christiana* that soldiers communicate in battle using trumpets or banners,[6] and his mentioning in a sermon on Psalm 131 that

---

2. Alan Rushworth, "Soldiers and Tribesmen: The Roman Army and Tribal Society in Late Imperial Africa," Ph.D. dissertation, University of Newcastle upon Tyne, November 1992.

3. Rushworth, 138–40.

4. Rushworth, 14–48.

5. *Epist.* 46 (*CSEL* 34, 123).

messmates are called *contubernales* because they share the same tent, a *tabernaculum*, while on active campaign.[7]

In various passages Augustine reveals his familiarity with the stages of a military career and uses this familiarity and that of his audience to draw apposite comparisons with contemporary issues of Christian life. Beginning in the fourth century, recruits were tattooed on the hand upon induction into the service, a procedure that helped in identifying deserters.[8] Augustine regarded this procedure and its rationale as an excellent analogy in the controversy over baptism with the Donatists, who insisted on rebaptizing converts from the Catholics, who for their part not only did not rebaptize converts from the Donatists but also acknowledged the validity of Donatist baptism. For whereas baptism is like the military tattoo, the *character*, which is an adornment to the soldier serving in the army, it convicts the soldier who has deserted.[9] Just as those discovered outside the army bearing the military tattoo are to be dragged back to the service and punished, so those outside the Catholic church bearing the *character* of baptism are to be recognized as deserters, brought back into the fold, and corrected.[10] Specifically as to Donatist baptism, it is likened to a deserter branding with the military tattoo someone who has never even been in the service. Not only is the mark of the latter recognized as valid, but he is positively welcomed into the service as a full-fledged member, while the deserter receives punishment.[11] At first glance these passages seem only to refer to a particularly apposite analogy drawn from a familiar aspect of military life, but they also reveal a certain antipathy toward deserters from the army and a desire to see them apprehended and punished, an attitude potentially at odds with the anti-military sentiments seen earlier in the *Vita Martini* and in the letters of Paulinus of Nola.[12]

A more telling analogy drawn from military life is Augustine's comparison of the toils and rewards of service in the army with the sufferings and rewards

6. *De doctrina Christiana* II, 1 (1); III. 4 (5) (*CSEL* 80, 33, 35).

7. *Enarr. in Ps. 131*.10 (*CSEL* 95:3, 299).

8. Pat Southern and Karen R. Dixon, *The Late Roman Army* (New Haven: Yale University Press, 1996), 75.

9. *Enarr. in Ps. 39*.1 (*CCL* 38, 424): "Baptismus ille tamquam character infixus est, ornabat militem, convincit desertorem"; also, *Tract. in Ioh.* 6.15, 16 (*CCL* 36, 6).

10. *Serm.* 359.5 (*PL* 39:1594).

11. *Serm.* 260A (*Denis* 8; *Sermones M. Denis, Miscellanea Agostiniana* I:37); *Epist.* 185.23 (*CSEL* 57, 22). See also *In Iohann. Evang.* 13.17 (*CCL* 36, 140) and *Epist.* 87.9 (*CSEL* 34, 405), where instead of the military tattoo Donatist baptism is likened to military standards carried off by deserters.

12. Chapter 3, notes 187 to 196.

of the martyrs. He used this analogy at least three times in sermons, most extensively in a sermon dated to 397. In the following passage Augustine refers to the benefits a soldier might expect upon retirement after long service (twenty-four years to receive full benefits), which included immunity from certain taxes and especially from compulsory curial duties. In addition, veterans upon retirement received a cash grant, or an allotment of land.[13] Such rewards might seem to have made military service an attractive option, especially for a poor peasant, yet they were rewards attained, if at all, by someone who joined as a youth but left the service as an old man.[14]

> Contemplate, brethren, the day of the martyr. It's good that we take encouragement from his suffering. Contemplate the toils of soldiers who bear arms, what perils they undergo, what harsh difficulties they endure, in cold, in heat, hunger, thirst, wounds, deaths. They are in peril every day, yet they don't have before their eyes the toils of a soldier, but the retirement of the veteran. "Look," they say, "the toils are finished, followed after a few years by retirement, we'll do well, we won't lack for our expenses, we'll be exempt from public service, we won't be called up for any civic duties, no one will impose his own burdens on us after our military service." With this reward held before them, they still toil away in uncertainty. For when a soldier in the service says, "the toils are finished," how does he know that *he* won't be finished before his toils are finished? Maybe even when his toils are finished, he suddenly dies as soon as he retires. He who had toiled a little longer for the sake of the retirement promised him is not allowed to enjoy for very long that very retirement he'd attained with his toils. They toil in uncertainties, and yet for the sake of an uncertain retirement they undertake certain toils.

Surely Christians, inspired by the example of the martyrs, should be willing to endure even worse toils than soldiers, not for the sake of an uncertain and brief reward, but for the sake of the certain reward of life everlasting.[15] Just

---

13. A. H. M. Jones, *The Later Roman Empire, 284-602* (Norman: University of Oklahoma Press, 1964), vol. I, 635–36.

14. *Enarr. in Ps. 36, s.* 2, 23, 16 (*CCL* 38, 357–58): "incipiunt militare in iuventute, exeunt senes."

15. *Serm.* 283 (Dolbeau 15), dated to July 22, 397. Text in *Augustin d'Hippone, Vingt-Six Sermons au peuple d'Afrique*, ed. François Dolbeau (Paris: Brepols, 1996); hereafter Dolbeau, 198–99. See also *Serm.* 70.2 (*PL* 38:443), where Augustine notes that a soldier "is probably at his toils without rest for more years than he will be resting in retirement ("pluribus fortasse annis in laboribus inquietus, quam in otio

as surely, in making this comparison between the soldier and the martyr one detects in Augustine some sympathy and even admiration for the former and the sufferings he undergoes in fulfilling his duty.

Not surprisingly, then, there are only a couple of remarks in Augustine's works indicating anywhere near the same reflexive and generalized abhorrence of the military found in his contemporaries Sulpicius Severus, Paulinus of Nola, and Maximus of Turin.[16] To be sure, there are some such statements to be found on the evils that *certain* soldiers do. In *quaestio* 79 of his *De diversis quaestionibus*, a passage written about 394 or 395,[17] Augustine explains how evil men are able to secure the help of malign spirits to perform miracles by invoking the name of Christ.

> For it is one thing for an owner to be compelled to give his horse to a soldier, it is another thing for him to hand it over to a buyer, or to give or lend it to someone. And just as a great many evil soldiers, whom imperial discipline condemns, terrify some owners with the ensigns of their commander and extort from them something which is not in accord with public law, so evil Christians, or schismatics, or heretics sometimes exact through the name of Christ or Christian words or sacraments something from the powers who have been enjoined to defer to the honor of Christ.[18]

In a sermon of uncertain date, Augustine gives a real-life example of soldierly misconduct, in a situation where the soldier's oppressive actions—perhaps related to the collection of customs duties at the port—had been so extreme that they had led to his death at the hands of a mob at Hippo Regius itself.[19] It should be emphasized that in both these cases Augustine was quick to point out that such misconduct was prohibited by Roman law and the perpetrators liable to legal punishments.[20]

---

quieturus").” Translation of Edmund Hill, *The Works of Saint Augustine: A Translation for the 21st Century* (New York: New City Press, 1994); hereafter Hill.

16. Chapter 3, notes 187 to 196 above.

17. I here adopt the chronology suggested by David L. Mosher in his translation, *Saint Augustine: Eighty-Three Different Questions*, Fathers of the Church (Washington, DC: Catholic University of America Press, 1982), 20.

18. *De diversis quaestionibus* 79.4 (*CCL* 44A, 229); translation in Mosher, 21.

19. *Serm.* 302 (*Stromata Patristica et Mediaevalia* I, *S. Aurelii Augustini Sermones Selecti Duodeviginti* (Utrecht/Brussels, 1950), 100–111). For a reconstruction that may exceed the data, Shaw, 28–30.

20. *De diversis quaestionibus* 79.4 (*CCL* 44A, 229): “quos imperialis disciplina condemnat”; *Serm.* 302.11,13 (previous note, 106–7).

These depictions of hypothetical or vague injustices Augustine balanced with assurances of due punishment for soldierly misconduct, and there are early writings in which the military almost comes across as a desirable career choice. In a sermon dated to 397,[21] Augustine discussed the nature and possibility of happiness in this lifetime, the *beata vita*, remarking that some think that such happiness correlates with one's occupation. At one point he notes that some think "beati qui militant."[22] Later on he further explores the meaning of *beata vita*, arguing that true happiness transcends one's occupation, and involves at a more basic level one's life and health.

> If someone's asked, "Do you want to go on living?" the question is hardly heard, is it, in the same way as if it were, "Do you want to join the army?" I mean, with that question, "Do you want to join the army?" some would answer me, "I do," and rather more people, in all probability, "I don't." But if I asked, "Do you want to go on living?" I don't think there's anyone who would say, "No, I don't."[23]

Although it is arguable that *militare* here bears the broader definition of any government service, including the military, the remark that more might not want to serve than would likely points to the more specific meaning. The foregoing passage is very similar to something Augustine wrote at about the same time in the *Confessions*:

> How could it be that if two men were asked whether they would serve as soldiers, one might reply that he would, the other that he would not; whereas if they were asked whether they would want to be happy, both would immediately and without hesitation say that they would; and that one would serve, and the other would not, for no other reason than to be happy?[24]

In both passages Augustine acknowledges that military service is not everyone's cup of tea, and that those who would prefer not to serve probably outnumber those who would. But it is equally clear that for some a career in the military was not only a conceivable option, but one that could contribute to happiness in this lifetime.

21. Fitzgerald, 785.
22. *Serm.* 306.3 (*PL* 38:1491).
23. *Serm.* 306.4 (*PL* 38:1492) (Hill translation).
24. *Confessions* 10.21.31 (*CCL* 27, 172).

The notion that some of Augustine's compatriots might have found military service to be an attractive career choice seems to contradict a widespread view on this matter in the scholarship on the late empire, a view exemplified by A. H. M. Jones's remark that "[t]here is a good deal of evidence which suggests *prima facie* that . . . military service was very unpopular." Jones went on, however, to concede that "[t]here were regional variations in the popular attitude to military service."[25] Did popular attitudes to military service in Roman Africa constitute such a regional exception? The question is worth pursuing here, since it would have been specifically the African attitudes to military service and not some hypothesized, general antipathy to the army that would have informed Augustine's own view of the matter. To begin with, unlike the case with the large military establishments along the Rhine and Danube, the late Roman army in Africa did not heavily rely on levies drawn from the so-called barbarians in and beyond the frontier zone, but was largely composed of indigenous recruits and conscripts.[26] The indigenous manpower pool in Roman North Africa, in fact, was sufficient to sustain an expansion in the size of the field army at the end of the fourth century and the beginning of the fifth.[27] Not until after about 410 was there a significant presence of northern, especially Gothic, troops to be found in Roman Africa. "Nevertheless, the regular units of the field army will have retained a predominantly local character for as long as they continued to exist."[28]

The reasons why the late Roman army in Africa seems to have had little difficulty in filling its ranks from the native populace seem at least partially to lie in geopolitical and historical factors particular to the region. Up to the very eve of the Vandal invasion, there is not much evidence for any serious external threat to Roman Africa, and certainly nothing like the titanic struggles along the northern and eastern frontiers of the empire.[29] It was along those same frontiers that troops could be transferred, sometimes thousands of miles, in order

25. Jones (n. 13 above), I, 617–18.

26. Rushworth, 86–90, 236, who states, against the evidence of Augustine noted here and also, for example, evidence from Tertullian (ch. 2, notes 18, 19 above), that the Roman army in Africa was recruited from the population living close to the frontier. Not that military service in Africa was idyllic: recruiting/conscription *was* resisted, Shaw, 32, noting that many Catholic African bishops were absent from the Council of Carthage in 403, unable to leave their sees due to the violence engendered by one such manpower sweep.

27. Rushworth, 76, 78.

28. Rushworth, 90.

29. Shaw, 32: "At no point until the early 430s did Africans face large-scale violence as it was experienced on the war frontiers of the empire, to the north along the Rhine and Danube and to the east along the frontiers with Sassanid Persia."

to counter an external threat, or in support of one or another contender for the purple in the periodic civil wars that characterized Augustine's time. Small wonder, then, that in such regions the peasants who would have constituted the manpower pool for the army would have avoided military service as much as possible not only because of its inherent dangers, but also because of "the prospect of being torn from their homes and sentenced to life exile in some remote province." Small wonder, too, that once having joined the army there was resistance in the ranks to such long-distance transfers, the most notable example of which is probably that of the Germans in Julian's army in Gaul who stipulated as a condition of their enlistment that they would not have to serve south of the Alps.[30] In contrast, an African enlistee, who would have been posted relatively close to where he had grown up, faced little to no possibility of such a long-distance transfer. The geographical isolation of Roman Africa from the rest of the empire, the longer period of time it would consequently take to shift troops from Africa elsewhere as compared to the situation along the northern and eastern frontiers with their river and road networks, and finally the relatively small size of the military establishment in Africa, which made it at best a minor piece in the great game of imperial warfare, all these factors combined with the relative quiet of the African frontier to help ensure that in Africa at least a soldier would have served out his term close to home, having to face fewer dangers and hardships than his fellow soldiers across the Mediterranean.

It is certainly true that the Roman army in Africa was not quite a null factor in imperial politics, since it was situated in one of the most important grain-growing regions of the empire, the primary granary for the city of Rome itself. It was this circumstance and not the power of his legions that rendered the *comes Africae* a major player in imperial politics, given his ability to cut off African grain shipments, an action tantamount to a declaration of war. A measure of his power is seen in the fact that the *comes Africae* Gildo was able for a time to defy Stilicho's supremacy in the Western empire with the support of the Eastern court.[31] Given the power of the *comites Africae*, it is unsurprising that a couple of them were tempted to revolt, and even to aim for the purple itself.[32] But here the relatively small size of the African military establishment comes into play. With the exception of the revolt of Firmus, who was able to draw on reinforcements from the native Berbers, for most of Augustine's lifetime

30. Jones (n. 13 above), I, 618, 619–20.

31. John Matthews, *Western Aristocracies and Imperial Court, AD 364-425* (Oxford: Clarendon, 1975), 272–73.

32. Heraclian, in 413. See Matthews (previous note), 354.

African revolts were put down by outside intervention with apparent ease.[33] The point is that rather than any forces being sent out of Africa in support of foreign or domestic wars, it was more likely at this period that forces would be sent *into* Africa, some of them to stay. In sum, there were reasons particular to African conditions that rendered military service a not unattractive option for an African peasant, especially given that in the army the "standard of living should have been substantially higher than that of the peasantry from whom most of them were drawn."[34] That Augustine for his part regarded military service as being on a par with other career options is indicated in a sermon where he lists *militia* alongside other occupations in law, education, business, and agriculture.[35]

In fact, there are passages in Augustine's works, some of which will be investigated later in more detail, that indicate or at least imply that his attitude toward serving soldiers was not merely concessive in its acknowledgment of military service and all that it entailed, but at times positively laudatory. In his commentary on the Sermon on the Mount, written about 394, Augustine admits that some who preach the gospel do so for the material benefits they receive, just as there are some in state service who likewise selfishly do so for material gain. But there are also those who serve for the good of the church, just as there are those selfless individuals who "are in state service [or, 'military service'] for the sake of the state's well-being" ("propter salutem rei publicae militant").[36] We know from other evidence that supplies from designated estates were earmarked for the victualing of military units stationed close by,[37] and this, according to Augustine, is as it should be in the greater scheme of things, the provincial thereby demonstrating his loyalty while the soldier displays his bravery.[38] In a letter written about 409, Augustine again indicates a certain admiration for the bravery of a soldier, in this case giving the hypothetical example of a soldier who wants to leave on his body traces of the wounds he had received, fighting *pro patria*, as visible badges of honor.[39]

---

33. Matthews, 273, 354.

34. Jones (n. 13 above), I, 647.

35. *Enarr. in Ps.* 72.32 (*CCL* 39, 1002): "Inveniamus divitias nostras; eligat sibi partes genus homanum. Videamus homines cupiditatum diversitate laniari; eligant alii militiam, alii advocationem, alii diversas variasque doctrinas, alii negotiationem, alii agriculturam; istas partes sibi faciant de rebus humanis."

36. *De serm. Dom. in monte* II, 17, 56 (*CCL* 35, 148).

37. Rushworth (n. 2 above), 21.

38. *Enarr. in Ps.* 90, *s.* 1.10 (*CCL* 39, 1263). See also *In Iohann. Evang.* 122.3 (*CCL* 36, 670).

39. *Epist.* 102.7 (*CSEL* 34, 550–51).

One could by a selective citation of evidence from Augustine and other sources easily paint too idyllic a picture of attitudes toward the late Roman military among both soldiers and civilians in the African provinces. One of the same conditions that made military service in Africa attractive to Africans themselves, the likelihood that they would end up stationed not far from their homes, also seems to have facilitated desertion, in that, unlike the case of soldiers posted far from their homes somewhere along the northern or eastern frontiers, a deserter in Africa did not have far to go to find friendly people potentially inclined to hide and shelter him. Thus in 412 we find an imperial constitution related to the roundup of deserters in Africa.[40] We have already cited passages showing how Augustine speaks of deserters as though they were not an uncommon phenomenon, and in another passage he notes that occasionally deserters strike fear into provincials, whose recourse is to recognize on their oppressors the military tattoo and, presumably, turn them in to the authorities.[41]

It is also undeniable that there was among some African Christians a longstanding rigorist tradition, stretching back to Tertullian if not beyond, that regarded military service as inherently contaminating, a tradition with which, as we will see, Augustine had to contend. But as we have also already seen, it is from that very rigorist tradition, as well as other evidence, that one can determine that alongside it ran an equally longstanding tradition of Christians serving in the ranks even under pagan emperors, a pragmatic accommodation to the world's realities occasioned by the promise of material benefits and by the relative absence in Africa of the factors that made military service unattractive in much of the rest of the empire.[42] The particularities of military service in Augustine's Africa and how they backgrounded both his views and those of his contemporaries toward such service provide a useful reminder of the nonintellectual determinative elements involved in the history of ideas. Antecedent to a consideration of any detached intellectual justifications for Augustine's view of the military is a recognition of the extent to which he and his contemporaries were conditioned in their specific attitudes by the larger historical and geopolitical factors noted above, factors that in Augustine's case and that of others could act to override the scruples arising from the rigorist tradition.

Although such contingent factors peculiar to his time and place arguably influenced Augustine's somewhat positive view of military service in particular,

---

40. *Cod. Theod.* VII.18.17, ed. T. Mommsen (Berlin, 1962 [reprint]), 349; Rushworth, 88.

41. *In Iohann. Evang.* 13.17 (*CCL* 36, 140).

42. Notes 25 to 34 above.

such factors cannot as readily be invoked to explain what seems a similarly positive view of state service in general, the broader definition of *militia*. There is evidence for at least a neutral if not explicitly positive view of state service from virtually the earliest of Augustine's works. In the first of the Cassiciacum dialogues, *Contra Academicos*, Augustine mentions that a certain Trygetius, one of the young men gathered at the estate to pursue their studies and engage in philosophical disputations under Augustine's direction, had come there from the *militia*.[43] That Trygetius had been not in the military but the civil service is indicated by the unlikelihood of a young man's being able to leave the military to pursue philosophical studies.[44] Insofar as can be determined from such brief remarks, Augustine here viewed *militia* somewhat casually and was certainly not overtly condemnatory of it.

A fuller example of Augustine's early attitude to state service is provided by his longtime friend Alypius. Alypius had gone to Rome to pursue legal studies, and while there had sat three times as *assessor*, that is, as an expert legal adviser for an untrained judicial magistrate. At Rome he also later served as *assessor* for the *comes largitionum Italicianarum*, the head of the imperial treasury for Italy.[45] Again, although especially while serving in the former position Alypius likely sat in on sessions involving judicial torture and even execution, Augustine gives no hint of censure in his description of Alypius's career in the civil service.

It is certainly conceivable that Augustine's social origins and education, perhaps combined with particularities of his mentality largely irrecoverable by us now, predisposed him toward a generally positive view of state service from very early on. It seems more certain that, especially while in Italy during the mid-380s, his social intercourse with individuals involved in state service motivated at least in part early statements on the honor associated with such service and on its being something it was worthwhile to aspire to. In *De ordine*, Augustine takes it as a matter of course that young students of the liberal arts might aspire to the civil service, but "they should not serve in state administration unless they have finished [their studies], although they should hurry to be finished at least while they are still of senatorial age, or at any rate before middle-age."[46] The importance of state service was such that it

43. *Contra Academicos* I. 1 (4) (*CCL* 29, 5).

44. *De ordine* II. 2 (5) (*CCL* 29, 91): "Trygetium item nobis militia reddiderat, qui tamquam veteranus adamavit historiam." *Militia* also seems to indicate civil rather than military service in the later case of Augustine's deacon Faustinus, who "had been converted to the monastery from the *militia* of the world (*Serm.* 356.4, *PL* 39:1576: 'de militia saeculi ad monasterium conversus est')," and for much the same reasons that apply in the case of Trygetius.

45. *Conf.* VI 10, 16 (*CCL* 27, 84–85).

should not be considered as merely a way station in one's career before moving on to better things—as perhaps had been the case with Trygetius and even Alypius—but as the culmination of a worldly career, only to be aspired to after much preparation. Accordingly, Pythagoras was praiseworthy

> in that he gave his teachings on ruling the state last of all to his pupils, who were by that point learned, finished with their studies, wise, and happy. For he saw that the roiling tides of the state were such that he would only put into them a man who in his rule could avoid the rocks almost like a god, and one who, if all else failed, would himself be like a rock against the tide.[47]

In his *De quantitate animae*, written a year or so after the Cassiciacum dialogues in 387 or 388,[48] Augustine at one point describes each successively higher *gradus* or level of the soul. In writing of the third *gradus*, he speaks of certain rational powers, to be considered both "great and altogether human," which characterize "the ranked levels (*ordines*) of duties, authority, honors and dignities, whether [they be] in families, or in the commonwealth in both the domestic and the public spheres [or here, perhaps, 'the military sphere (*militiae*)'], or in tasks both sacred and profane."[49]

High praise for Augustine, that state service is worthy to be mentioned, alongside rhetoric, poetry, and music, as being among the highest products of the rational part of the human soul. Yet such things are not necessarily a good of human life, for they are common to learned and unlearned, good and evil alike.[50] Especially before about 400, Augustine's positive appreciation of state service is seasoned by an acknowledgment of the pitfalls inherent to it. In his *De catechizandis rudibus*, written soon after he had become bishop of Hippo as an outline or guide for catechetical instruction, Augustine writes of "the honors of this world—what are they but empty pride and vanity and the danger of downfall?"[51] At least in this period it seems manifest to Augustine that it were better for someone seeking to serve God to forsake service to the state, no

---

46. *De ordine* II 8 (25) (*CCL* 29, 121): "Rem publicam nolint administrare nisi perfecti, perfici autem vel intra aetatem senatoriam festinent vel certe intra iuventutem."

47. *De ordine* II 20 (54) (*CCL* 29, 136).

48. *Augustinus-Lexikon*, ed. Cornelius Mayer et al. (Basel: Schwabe & Co., 1986–94), col. 351.

49. *De quantitate animae* 33.72 (*CSEL* 89, 220): ". . . officiorum, potestatum, honorum, dignitatumque ordines, sive in familiis sive domi militiaeque in republica sive in profanis sive in sacris adparatibus . . . magna haec et omnino humana."

50. *De quantitate animae* 33.72 (*CSEL* 89, 220): "Sed est adhuc ista partim doctis atque indoctis, partim bonis ac malis animis copia communis."

matter how honorable and worthwhile such service was generally considered to be, even by Augustine himself. Thus Evodius, a compatriot of Augustine's, was baptized while still serving as an *agens in rebus*, but thereafter left *militia saecularis* to enlist in the Lord's *militia*,[52] and Alypius likewise had to retire from his duties as *assessor* to free up time for his studies with Augustine.[53] What was particularly distressing about *militia* is revealed in a conversation between a certain Ponticianus and a companion, both *agentes in rebus*, later retold to Augustine on the eve of the famous conversion in the garden. One of them, feeling shame after reading the life of Anthony, turned to the other and said:

> Tell me, I ask you, what are we trying to gain with all these labors of ours? What are we looking for? What is our motive for serving the state? Can there be a greater hope in the palace than for us to be the friends of the emperor? And what there is not precarious and full of dangers? And through how many dangers does one attain to a greater danger? And when will we get there?[54]

Service to the state, then, was imbued with anxieties and perils. Was it also for Augustine, then, as it had been for Tertullian and others of the rigorist tradition, tainted with blood pollution? With only one possible and early exception,[55] there is not a trace of such an attitude visible anywhere in Augustine, nor any evidence for his sharing the idea that those who had served the state—or the military in particular—were required as a consequence specifically of that service to leave it and to do penance as expiation for blood pollution, whether that be as a precondition for entering or reentering the church, or for entering the clergy. Augustine certainly approved of penance, and penance was certainly practiced in his church at Hippo.[56] As had Ambrose, Augustine recognized that many were ashamed to do penance,[57] but nonetheless extolled the value of confession.[58] As had also been Ambrose's

51. *De catechizandis rudibus* 16.24.5 (*CCL* 46, 149): "Sic et honores huius saeculi, quid sunt nisi typhus et inanitas et ruinae periculum?" Also, 16.25.7 (149): "vanas honorum pompas."

52. *Conf.* IX 8. 17 (*CCL* 27, 143): ". . . Evodium iuvenem ex nostro municipio. Qui cum agens in rebus militaret, prior nobis ad te conversus est et baptizatus et relicta militia saeculari accinctus in tua."

53. *Conf.* VII, 6, 13 (*CCL* 27, 121).

54. *Conf.* VIII, 6, 15 (*CCL* 27, 122–23).

55. See below, note 154.

56. A.-M. La Bonnardière, "Pénitence et réconciliation des Pénitents d'après Saint Augustin," *Revue des Études Augustiniennes* 13 (1967a): 31–53; (1967b): 249–83; 14 (1968): 181–204 gives the best account of penance in Augustine.

57. Chapter 3, note 169 above; *Enarr. in Ps. 33, s.* II.11 (*CCL* 38, 289–90).

experience,[59] some on their own abstained from the Eucharist out of a consciousness of sin, while others thought it wrong to deprive oneself of sin's very remedy; unlike Ambrose, Augustine took no stand on the question, counseling everyone to decide what it was best to do for themselves according to their own faith understanding.[60] In addition to such individuals who, in Ambrose's Milan and Augustine's Hippo Regius, subjected themselves to a sort of informal penance, there were those who had committed more serious sins than those of daily life, sins such as murder (*homicidium*), who were subjected to a correspondingly more severe penance.[61] It seems it was the bishop himself who, after the sinner had confessed, imposed the penitential state on an individual.[62] There appears to have been a place reserved for the penitents in Augustine's church—the *locus paenitentium*—and there they would line up for the bishop to lay his hand on them.[63] And again as at Ambrose's church, and at many another church around the Roman world, penitents would display their inner contrition by outward signs of humility such as tears, groans, and the giving of alms.[64]

Yet despite the visibility and prevalence of penance in Augustine's church, and despite a tradition in Africa itself, propagated by luminaries such as Tertullian and Lactantius, which held that service to the state necessarily involved sinful complicity in bloodshed, there seems in Augustine's works no connection visible between the need for penance and state service per se. As we saw in chapter three with Ambrose and Studius, Augustine at least once confronted a public official whose behavior revealed his deep consciousness of the sins inherent to public life. In early 414 Augustine wrote a letter to the imperial official Caecilian, in which he closed by lamenting that

> there is one thing in you of which I thoroughly disapprove, and that is that a man of your age and uprightness should still wish to be a catechumen, as if it were not possible for the faithful to be in public administration more devotedly and faithfully in proportion as they are themselves more devoted and more faithful.[65]

58. *Enarr. in Ps.* 74.
59. Chapter 3, notes 157 to 159 above.
60. *Epist.* 54, 3 (4), (*CSEL* 34, 162–63).
61. *Serm.* 352.3, 8 (*PL* 39:1558).
62. *Epist.* 153.6 (*CSEL* 44, 401).
63. *Serm.* 232.8 (*SC* 116, 274/276).
64. *Serm.* 351.7, 12 (*PL* 39:1542–43, 1549); *Enarr. in Ps.* 67.3 (*CCL* 39, 870).

Augustine's wording shows that Caecilian likely thought it *not* possible for a baptized Christian to act in faith while in state administration, and was therefore, as had most famously Constantine before him, postponing his baptism until he was no longer in public life and thus no longer in a position to commit a mortal sin. But in the century since the battle of the Milvian Bridge, Christians or would-be Christians had come to serve at all levels of the imperial administration; a new type of imperial official, Christian born and bred, had begun to appear in Augustine's Africa; and the scrupulousness of a Caecilian was coming to seem not so much old-fashioned as rendered obsolete by a shift in culture. At any rate, Augustine for his part would have none of it. In his *De catechizandis rudibus*, the bishop included among the *accedentes* receiving catechetical instruction people of authority in public office ("honoratum, in potestate aliqua constitutum"), without a hint that such individuals had to do penance before baptism, let alone resign their office.[66] It is true that during the interview of his imprisoned friend and imperial official Marcellinus, who was in prison awaiting trial for treason, Augustine had asked him whether he had committed some major sin that would require penance. But Augustine was wondering whether Marcellinus had committed fornication or adultery,[67] not the shedding of blood in torture or execution in the performance of his public duties, which actions Augustine expressly allowed in Marcellinus's case as legitimate exercises of his authority, only counseling leniency not out of a concern for the soul of the judge, but that of the condemned.[68] It was not the state-sanctioned taking of life in general that was sinful in itself, but the justice or injustice of a particular exercise of that power which rendered the official potentially culpable of a major sin. So Augustine in speaking of the imperial official Marinus, a baptized Christian, who had had Marcellinus and his brother Apringius executed, wrote that Marinus's soul would suffer in the afterlife "if he does not amend his life by repentance and by availing himself of the patience of God" not because Marinus had executed the brothers, but because they had been executed unjustly.[69]

---

65. *Epist.* 151.14 (*CSEL* 44, 392). Translation by Wilfrid Parsons in *Fathers of the Church* 20 (New York, 1953), modified.

66. *De catechizandis rudibus* 15, 23.4 (*CCL* 46, 148).

67. *Epist.* 151.9 (*CSEL* 44, 389).

68. *Epist.* 133 and 139; notes 225 and 226 below.

69. *Epist.* 151.6 (*CSEL* 44, 387).

ORDO AND THE SOCIAL ORDER

Augustine, then, although he was well aware of the negative aspects of public life, in general evidenced a positive attitude toward service to the state. We have seen that historical and geopolitical factors peculiar to his time and place helped to condition his view of military service in particular. His social origins and education may have combined with his own short-lived experience in Italy in the mid-380s as a man aspiring to public service, at the time socially interacting with friends and acquaintances already in such service, to help foster at least a neutral attitude toward service to the state. There may also be something peculiar to Augustine as an individual, now irrecoverable, that also played a role in developing his attitude. What still seems recoverable, though, are the intellectual and theological considerations that Augustine himself explicitly adduced to support his perception of that realm of human activities which included state service in general, and military service in particular. A fundamental constituent of those considerations was Augustine's conception of order. Certainly few principles appear more often in his works throughout or seem more fundamental to his thinking than that of order. One of his first books was devoted to that very subject. Since scholars have already thoroughly investigated several aspects of Augustine's idea of order, the discussion here, largely based on earlier scholarship, will be brief.

It is almost typical of Augustine that his cognizance of how imperative it is to define such a significant term as *ordo* is not matched in the definition's execution. In *De ordine*, written in late 386, Augustine first wrote that "the order in reality is that by which this world [in its entirety] is held together and ruled."[70] Later, he defined order as "that by which all things that God has constituted are moved."[71] Yet again, he elsewhere emphasizes the ethical aspect, stating that "order is that which, if we hold to it during life, will lead us to God, and which unless we hold to it during life, we shall not attain to God."[72] One could easily find instances where Augustine seems to define order in terms of order. Such seems the case in his most famous definition of order in *The City of God*: "Order is the arrangement of things similar and dissimilar that assigns to each its own place."[73] For what determines anything's "own place" other than

70. *De ordine* I.1.1 (*CCL* 29, 89): "ordinem rerum . . . quo cohercetur hic mundus et regitur."

71. *De ordine* I.10.28 (103): "Ordo est per quem aguntur omnia, quae deus constituit." Also, II.4.11 (113): "ordo est, quo deus agit omnia, quae sunt."

72. *De ordine* I.9.27 (102): "Ordo est, quem si tenuerimus in vita, perducet ad deum, et quem nisi tenuerimus in vita, non perveniemus ad deum."

73. *De civitate Dei* 19.13 (*CCL* 48, 679): "Ordo est parium dispariumque rerum sua cuique loca tribuens dispositio."

order?[74] Rather than stressing Augustine's inadequacies in defining a term none find easy to define, we would do better by looking at particular ways in which Augustine framed the concept. Simply put, order is universal, and occurs at all levels of reality, from the motions of the stars[75] to the members of a flea.[76] Order is so closely bound up with being itself as to be virtually identical with it, and there is good reason for that. For the universe in which being is constituted has been created by God, who is himself ordered, and thus Creation necessarily reflects the order of its Creator.[77]

Closely related to the idea of a divine order recognizable in reality is that of the eternal law, oftentimes termed by Augustine the *lex aeterna*, though his terminology is not rigorous or consistent.[78] This eternal law, for Augustine, seems to represent the principle of divine governance in Creation, by which, ultimately, the ends of providence are served. The eternal law is also the supreme reason,[79] and thus identifiable with "the reason from above which rules all things."[80] This law is eternal, immutable, and all-encompassing.[81] It is binding on all creatures in Creation, and is recognizable not only in the laws of nature, but in those of human beings.[82] It is thus this eternal law which acts to bring about the order visible in reality.[83]

Josef Rief has argued that Augustine in his anthropology did not conceptualize a sharp distinction between intellect and will, as had earlier Aristotle and as did later Thomas Aquinas. For Augustine, the intellect—again expressed by an imprecise terminology—bears with it the volitional. Since for Augustine man's *mens*, the seat of his *ratio*, his intellect, is in its nature ordered but fundamentally simple, the same must be true of God, in whose image man

---

74. On Augustine's difficulty in defining order, see Josef Rief, *Der Ordobegriff des jungen Augustinus* (Paderborn: F. Schöningh, 1962), 355–56. That difficulty persists. The relevant definition in the 1966 edition of *The American College Dictionary* (New York: Random House, 1966) defines order as "a condition in which everything is in its proper place with reference to other things and to its purpose," a definition that resembles Augustine's not only in its content but in its circularity, since it begs the definition of what determines a thing's "proper place."

75. *De ordine* II.5.14 (*CCL* 29, 115).

76. *De ordine* I.1.2 (89–90).

77. See the concluding definition in Rief (n. 74 above), 360–62.

78. On this see Rief (previous note), 184.

79. *De libero arbitrio* I. 6. 15 (48) (*CSEL* 29, 220).

80. *De ordine* I.8.25 (*CSEL* 29, 101): "ratio desuper omnia moderans."

81. Alois Schubert, *Augustins Lex-aeterna-Lehre nach Inhalt und Quellen. Beiträge zur Geschichte der Philosophie des Mittelalters, Texte und Untersuchungen* 24:2 (Münster, 1924), 5–7.

82. Schubert, 9–17; Rief (n. 74 above), 185, 186.

83. Rief, 185.

was created. As with His creature, made in His image, God is ordered, and His will is less an activity separable from intellect than an integral characteristic of the divine reason. The eternal law, like the divine order, is bound up with being itself. It was not created separately by God, was not, so to speak, issued by God standing apart from Creation. Rather, because the universe reflects the order of its Creator, the eternal law exists as a consequence of Creation itself. It is, one might say, the law of existence, and this fact has significant implications for the capacity of human beings to recognize the eternal law in themselves and the world and their attempts to enact it in the human reality.[84]

At first glance, there seems little difference between Augustine's conception of the eternal law and that of the order visible in reality. When speaking of the operation of the eternal law visible in the universe, what could be justly termed the law of nature, he emphasizes the aspect of the constraints placed on all things to prevent their falling into disorder. In the *Soliloquies* such language appears as part of Augustine's opening contemplation on God, "by whose laws the heavens rotate, the stars traverse their courses, [and] the sun is busy with the day."[85] It would seem that, so conceived, the law of nature operates to direct the activity of every creature in a way conformable to its being, an activity particular to each creature.[86] When Augustine speaks in the same period of the order actually visible in nature, the context is in attempting thereby to account for the seeming *disorder* sometimes seen in reality, especially in human affairs. While it is true that the minute examination of one of God's tiniest visible creatures, a flea, reveals a marvelous and succinct arrangement of its members, upon lifting one's gaze one is struck by the apparent disorder and disturbance in the reality of human life.[87] Humans often appear the sport of mindless cruelty, whether that be the cruelty of chance that makes some women fertile and others infertile, or the intentional cruelty of the rich, who can afford to be generous to the poor but are not, while the poor, who cannot afford to be generous, often are.[88] Any order or design in human affairs seems well hidden away; at best it is an *occultissimus ordo*, or an *occultissima ratio*.[89] Still, even this apparent disorder is part of the overall order of nature. This is true even in cases where creatures other than man seem to exhibit disorder. For not every creature is as well put together as a flea.

---

84. Rief, 186–88.

85. *Sol.* I.1.4 (*CSEL* 89, 8).

86. Rief (n. 74 above), 188–89.

87. *De ordine* I.1.2 (*CCL* 29, 89–90).

88. *De ordine* II.5.14 (115).

89. *De ordine* I.11.33 (106); II.7.24 (120).

Are there not certain members in the bodies of animals which you could not [bear to] gaze upon if you were only looking at them? Yet the order of nature (*naturae ordo*) would not have them lacking because they are necessary, nor does it let them stand out because they are unsightly. And yet those very misshapen members by keeping their proper places yield a better place to the better members.[90]

In a striking image, Augustine compares the inability of those who cannot perceive the hidden order of the universe to someone too focused on the apparent irregularity and disorder of the individual *tessellae* that comprise a mosaic floor to be able to discern the mosaic's overall pattern and design.[91] Just as it is necessary for such an observer to step back from a too-narrow focus on its individual elements to be able to make out the greater design, so one must be able to raise and extend the gaze of "the eyes of the mind" to survey reality as a whole and thereby discern the universal and eternal order, within which is comprised the apparent disorder of human life, and even that which human beings call evil.[92] When he wrote *De ordine*, Augustine emphasized how an education in the liberal arts enables one to surmount appearances and see the order in reality, since owing to its dominance in music, geometry, astronomy, and mathematics, "one could see in them, so to speak, the source and very shrine of order, or be led to it through them."[93] Later, Augustine was not so sure of the necessity for training in the liberal arts,[94] and, as we will see, he also within a few years of writing *De ordine* began to speak more of an order visible and not so hidden in the human reality.[95]

The concern with order evident in Augustine's writings at the very least bespeaks the continuity of his thought with a theme prominent in other, earlier ancient writers, the same idea expressed by *kosmos* in Greek philosophy.[96] But the fact that he not only devoted one of his earliest works to the concept, but also reverted to order time and again, throughout his entire writing career and in every genre he employed, whether that be sermon, letter, or treatise, as a way of comprehending the various conditions and dynamics visible and active

90. *De ordine* II.4.12 (114).
91. *De ordine* I.1.2 (90).
92. *De ordine* II.4.11 (113).
93. *De ordine* II.5.14 (115).
94. *Retract.* I.3.2 (*CCL* 57, 12).
95. Notes 97, 98 below.
96. Rief (n. 74 above), 40–60.

at all levels of reality, probably indicates something more about the man himself than merely his repeated usage of a philosophical commonplace. Augustine, one presumes, was a man who personally valued order. Though his society was rife with disorder, and though during his lifetime the order of the Roman empire began to break apart, not in spite of such circumstances, but perhaps in fact because of them, Augustine clung steadfastly to the value of order.

As we have seen, in his earliest writings Augustine emphasized the disturbances in human affairs and the difficulty of discerning in them anything but disorder. But later, especially after his assumption of the responsibilities of the episcopate at Hippo in the mid-390s, where he had to deal increasingly with both ecclesiastical and secular authorities, particularly in connection with the Donatist conflict, Augustine came to appreciate more the *ordo rerum humanarum*. This aspect of the universal order was no longer conceived of as remote and hidden, to be fitfully discerned by a select few of liberal education, but was rather a phenomenon readily visible to all. Augustine referred to this conception of the order of the human reality in a sermon preached in the summer of 404 in a country church on a return journey home from Carthage to Hippo.[97] Augustine is making the point that although the human soul, the *anima*, is invisible and incorporeal, nonetheless actions proceeding from it have very powerful and concrete results in the world around us, or at least in a certain privileged part of that world.

> What delights you about the human reality? Look round at the order in the human reality, at the beauty of cultivated fields, of whole forests torn up by the roots and the productive crops planted in their place, and all we see and love in such fields; look round at the order in the commonwealth itself, at the mass of buildings, at the variety of arts and crafts, at the multitude of languages, at the vast depths of memory, at the richness of eloquence. All these things are the works of the soul.[98]

97. Augustine, *Sermo* 360B (Dolbeau, 248–67).

98. *Sermo* 360B.9 (Dolbeau, 253): "Veni ad ipsam animam, quia et ipsa non videtur. Non videtur anima, et magna vis est naturae incorporeae. Non enim corpus est anima, invisibile quiddam est, et magnum quiddam est: videri non potest, sed ex operibus mirare quod non vides. Quid te delectat in rebus humanis? Circumspice ordinem rerum, pulchritudinem cultorum agrorum, exstirpatarum silvarum, insitorum fructuosorum, quaeque in agris videmus et amamus, ordinem ipsum reipublicae, moles aedificiorum, varietates artium, copiam linguarum, profunditatem memoriae, eloquentiae ubertatem. Haec omnia animae opera sunt. Quanta vides opera animae, et ipsam non vides!" Hill translation, modified. Compare similar remarks on the power of the unseen human soul in a sermon delivered in 406/7 (*In Iohann. Evang.* 8.2 [*CCL* 36, 82–83]): "How many things it [the soul] does through the body!

The order of the human reality here seems to refer to the tangible and visible effects of human activity in the world. The *res humanae* largely correspond to our modern "civilization," as in that part of our world to which we refer wryly and often with feigned regret as returning to after a long camping trip (Augustine, like most premodern intellectuals, was no lover of the wilderness).

In seeking a basis for the proper Christian attitude toward the worldly authority within this human reality, Augustine had recourse to the Pauline text in Rom. 13:1-7, which as we have already seen from the same text's use by Ambrose and Pope Innocent I[99] speaks not so much to Augustine's intensive rereading of Paul in the mid-390s[100] but rather to his participation in a broader conversation in Christian circles in the late fourth century regarding how Christians should view the secular authorities, an issue then made acute by Christianity's newfound prominence in the Roman empire. In one of his *expositiones* on certain passages in the epistle to the Romans, delivered in 394 or 395, Augustine commented on Rom. 13:1: "Let every soul (*anima*) be subject to higher authorities: for there is no authority but from God." Augustine noted that the constitution of human society has established a rank (*ordo*) in it for every Christian in this lifetime, in which that individual is subject

> to higher authorities, to whom for a time the governance of temporal affairs has been entrusted. . . . Given that we are constituted both of soul (*anima*) and of body, for so long as we are in this temporal life we should also use temporal things in support of living this life. It behooves us to be subject to the authorities in the part which pertains to this life, i.e., to men in any office administering human affairs.

Observe the whole world organized in the human republic itself. With what administrations, with what ranks of authorities, constitutions of cities, laws, customs, arts! All this is accomplished by the soul and this power of the soul is not seen." (Translation by John W. Rettig in *The Fathers of the Church, St. Augustine: Tractates on the Gospel of John 1-10* [Washington, DC: Catholic University of America Press, 1988], 181) ("quanta agit per corpus! Adtendite universum orbem terrarum ordinatum in ipsa humana republica; quibus administrationibus, quibus ordinibus potestatum, condicionibus civitatum, legibus, moribus, artibus! Hoc totum per animam geritur, et haec vis animae non videtur").

99. Chapter 3, notes 150, 154 above. The same passage in Romans, of course, became a *locus classicus* in the construction of Christian political ideology for well into the medieval period, and beyond.

100. *Pace* R. A. Markus, "Saint Augustine's Views on the 'Just War,'" *Studies in Church History* 20 (1983): 7, who does not there note that Augustine's use of Romans 13 in a "political" context is not unique from a contemporary perspective. On Augustine's rereading of Paul at this period see Brown, 144–48.

It is therefore incumbent on all Christians by virtue of their rank in society to be obedient to higher authorities by paying their taxes and showing due deference to their superiors, save any infringement by those authorities "as to that part whereby we believe we are called to God and into His kingdom." But during this lifetime and up to the point when Christians attain God's kingdom, "we should put up with our condition for the sake of the order of the human reality itself ('pro ipso rerum humanarum ordine'), doing nothing insincerely and conforming to that very [order] not so much for men as for God, who commands these things."[101]

Although Augustine criticized here those who presume upon their freedom in Christ to defy their superiors, he also wrote that the temporal authority which maintains the order in human affairs is not an end in itself. Whereas Paul had gone on to state that the higher powers are ordained of God, and that therefore those who resisted those powers also resisted God's ordinance (Rom. 13:1b-2a), Augustine here stresses more the temporal order's temporality than its divine origin, looking forward instead to the ultimate disappearance of all earthly authority. Rather than justifying obedience to temporal authority solely on the grounds of its being divinely ordained, Augustine adds that the soul's dependence on the body requires submission to the powers of this world for the sake of bodily needs. While Paul seems almost positive in his appreciation of authority, Augustine somewhat reluctantly concedes that in this life we Christians "had to put up with" ("toleremus") a less-than-ideal situation in being subject to earthly power. Nonetheless, Augustine closes by reaffirming Paul's contention that subjection to earthly power is decreed by God.

In speaking in his commentary on Romans 13 on the order in human society, Augustine had placed great stress on the obedience owed authority. Augustine's understanding of the virtue of obedience and how it should be realized vis-à-vis both God and man is basic to our comprehension of how he viewed the legitimation of state-sanctioned violence. His mentioning of it in a number of works written around the year 400 shows that obedience was much on his mind then; one indication, to be sure, that its converse disobedience was more than theoretical in his own experience. In understanding his view of it, though, we are little helped by his own definition, typically circular, of obedience: "I say obedience [is] that whereby commands are complied with."[102] In the same work where this definition appears, Augustine writes that an obedient married woman is better than a disobedient maiden, an example that

---

101. *Expositio quarundam propositionum ex epistola ad Romanos* 64 (72), (*CSEL* 84, 44–45).

102. *De bono coniugali* 30 (*CSEL* 41, 225): "oboedientiam vero illam dico, qua praeceptis obtemperatur."

in its domestic familiarity tells us more about a common understanding and estimation of obedience to which Augustine was appealing than any formal definition.[103] Viewed from a more elevated perspective, obedience was in a way the mother of all the virtues, and was herself the daughter of love.[104] From the individual perspective, obedience almost always points two ways. For almost any individual, there are superiors—ultimately God—to whom obedience is owed, and inferiors who owe their obedience. So, by and large, kings are obeyed in human society. Such obedience in human society of the lesser authority for the greater is a model for the obedience owed God, the greatest authority of all.[105] For "authorities have been ordained in this world, and over all authorities is divine authority." And just as all are to obey God, on earth "the one to be listened to more is he who has the greater, the legitimate authority."[106]

The necessity for obedience, its theological ramifications, and its operation in maintaining divine and human order are all themes prominent in a sermon Augustine delivered at Carthage in early 404, a sermon titled in the manuscript, *Sermo eiusdem* [sc. Augustine] *de oboedientia*.[107] Bishop Aurelius of Carthage, who had invited the bishop of Hippo to his cathedral-basilica to preach, had worked for years with like-minded clergy such as Augustine to reform certain practices prevalent among the Christians of North Africa, including inappropriate behavior such as drinking and dancing at the tombs of the martyrs, and a mingling of the sexes in crowded churches which sometimes led to romantic liaisons, a sin of which the young Augustine himself had been guilty. On 22 January 404, the feast day of St. Vincent of Tarragona, when Augustine stood up to speak, the disgruntlement among some of the congregants at the reforms foisted upon them manifested itself with a certain disorder and jostling in the crowd standing to hear him speak, and shouts to Augustine to come down among the crowd to preach so as to be better heard. When Augustine, angered by the disorder, turned his back on the congregation, refused to speak, and resumed his place among the other seated bishops, the shouts only grew louder. In his sermon the next day, Augustine reminded the congregation that, whether they liked the reforms or not, they had been successfully implemented by Bishop Aurelius, which would not have

103. *De bono coniugali* 29 (*CSEL* 41, 224).

104. *De bono coniugali* 30 (*CSEL* 41, 225): "omnium virtutum quodam modo matrem esse oboedientia" (an estimation repeated years later in *DCD* 14.12 [*CCL* 48, 434]); *Serm.* 359B.12 (see n. 106 below; 337): "Quid est enim oboedientia? Amatis caritatem: filia eius est, filia caritatis oboedientia est."

105. *Conf.* 3. 8 (15) (*CCL* 27, 35).

106. *Serm.* 359B.13 (Dolbeau, 337–38).

107. A good discussion is in Brown, 455–57.

happened "had he not had an obedient people."[108] The centrality of obedience in God's eyes was shown by the fact that his command to the first humans not to eat of the one tree in paradise, that of the knowledge of good and evil, was intended as a test of obedience. The fruit of disobedience was nothing other than death. But whereas Adam was the author and model of disobedience, Christ was the model for obedience. For "he humbled himself, becoming obedient unto death, even to the death of the cross." [Phil. 2:8][109] Elsewhere, Augustine ascribed the original crime of disobedience to Eve, and noted that while death was the result of disobedience, eternal life was justly given to the obedient.[110]

For our purposes here it is of great interest to look at Augustine's conception of how the authorities of the state acted so as to preserve the divinely legitimated societal order by way of punishment and coercion, and of how such punishment or coercion was effected by the state's agents, whether they be judges, executioners, or soldiers. As he did in defining the virtue of obedience, Augustine continually reverted to a domestic model in discussing this topic, here that of the role of the head of the household, the *paterfamilias*, in enforcing familial discipline and harmony, sometimes through harsh punishments. This particular domestic model was more than merely theoretical in the case of Augustine himself, who tells the story in the *Confessions* of how his father had beaten the malicious maidservants who had traduced Augustine's mother Monica to her mother-in-law, a punishment reported as though it were only just and proper.[111] In using the domestic sphere to provide a model, Augustine most commonly cites the instance of a father disciplining his son in order to correct or improve his behavior, thus showing that "there can be love in punishment."[112] This example is repeated throughout Augustine's works.[113] In a sermon delivered in 418, decades after first mentioning it, Augustine goes at length into how paternal correction can inflict pain for good ends.

> You instruct your own son, don't you? First, you use shame and leniency as much as possible in his instruction, so that he will not so much be afraid of his father as a harsh judge as to be ashamed to offend him. You rejoice in such a son. But in case he remains defiant,

---

108. *Serm.* 359B (Dolbeau, 331).

109. *Serm.* 359B.7–8 (Dolbeau, 332–34).

110. *De bono coniugali* 30 (CSEL 41, 225); *Contra Faustum* 22.21 (CSEL 25, 610).

111. *Conf.* 9. 9 (20) (CCL 27, 145–46).

112. *Contra Adimantum* 17.3 (CSEL 25, 167): "Potest ergo esse dilectio in vindicante."

113. In addition to the examples cited, see also *De Genesi ad litteram* 11.11 (CSEL 28:1, 343–44).

you apply the rod, you impose punishment, you inflict pain, but you also look to his welfare. Many by love, many by fear are corrected, but what they arrive at through fear and trembling is love. . . . Look, the father is devoted in his beating, by beating his son he is merciful. Now give me a man who is cruel by sparing [the rod]. I keep the same cast of characters and put them before your eyes. But now the boy goes unpunished and is undisciplined, and if he goes on living thus to his ruin, and the father pretends not to notice, the father spares him, the father is afraid of offending his wastrel son with the harshness of discipline, isn't he cruel by sparing him?[114]

According to Augustine, the rod is so useful for enforcing discipline that it is "a method of coercion used not only by teachers but also by parents and even sometimes by bishops in the episcopal courts."[115] And the veritable duty to chastise those under his charge is proper not only for bishops and heads of household, but also "for the governor ruling his province, [and] for the king ruling his people. All these, when they are good men, surely want the best for those whom they rule."[116]

But just as the *paterfamilias* is the only one in the household competent to inflict punishment for the sake of preserving familial harmony, so not just anyone has the authority to inflict punishment for the sake of preserving order in society. Already in 394 in his commentary on the Sermon on the Mount, Augustine argued that

the only one fit to exact such a punishment is he who by the magnitude of his love has overcome the hatred which usually inflames those who burn to avenge themselves. . . . He should punish who in the natural order of things has been granted the power to do so, and he should punish with the disposition of a father punishing his little boy, whom he is simply incapable of hating yet owing to his age. This last certainly provides the most pertinent example, where it is quite clear that, rather than let wrongdoing go unpunished, it is better when it can be punished with love, where the desired result for the one punished is not sadness from the penalty but happiness from the correction.[117]

114. *Serm.* 13.9 (*CCL* 41, 182–83).
115. *Epist.* 133 (*CSEL* 44, 82).
116. *Serm.* 164A, *Revue Bénédictine* 66 (1956): 157.
117. *De sermone Domini in monte* I, 20 (63) (*CCL* 35, 72, 73).

In a sermon delivered in 418, Augustine said that for anyone in authority to be able to punish justly it was not sufficient merely that he had been granted the power to do so.

> In order not to be unjust in your authority, all you human beings who wish to have authority over human beings, *be instructed* [Ps. 2:10], lest you judge wrongly and lose your own soul even before you destroy anyone else's flesh. . . . First, for your own sake, be the judge of yourself. First judge yourself, so that as one untroubled to the depths of your conscience you may proceed to judge someone else. Return to yourself, observe yourself, examine yourself, listen to yourself. It is there I want you to prove yourself an honest judge, where you require no witness.[118]

Those in human society who had the divinely legitimated power to punish, therefore, bore a great burden of responsibility to act with "tough love" and a clear conscience. This is especially the case inasmuch as such individuals not only acted to maintain the secular order, but were also in Augustine's Africa increasingly called upon to enforce Catholic orthodoxy. In 408 the bishop wrote a well-known letter to the sectarian Vincent detailing the shift in his thinking regarding the physical coercion of the Donatists. Now Augustine thought that "it does not seem to me unprofitable for them [the Donatists] to be restrained and corrected by the authorities ordained by God."

> Do you think that no one should be forced to justice, when you read that the master of the house said to his servants: "Whomever you find, compel them to come in"; when you read also that Saul himself, afterward Paul, was forced by the great violence of Christ's compulsion to acknowledge and hold the truth. . . . Surely, in whatever the true and legitimate mother [church] does, even if it is felt to be harsh and stern, she is not returning evil for evil, but is applying the good of discipline to drive out the evil of wickedness.

At first Augustine had resisted using the secular authorities to coerce the Donatists. He had ended up changing his mind, though, due to the intransigence and violence of the schismatics, and the undeniable success the enforcement of imperial edicts had had in convincing many of them to become orthodox.

118. *Serm.* 13.7 (*CCL* 41, 181–82).

I have, then, yielded to the facts suggested to me by my colleagues, although my first feeling about it was that no one was to be forced into the unity of Christ, but that we should act by speaking, fight by debating, and prevail by our reasoning, for fear of making pretended Catholics out of those whom we knew as open heretics. But this opinion of mine was overcome not by the words of those who controverted it, but by conclusive examples.[119]

The preservation of societal order could at times require severe measures. The church could for its part appear as a stern parent, motivating her children to change through their fear of harsh punishment.[120] But how far should such punishments go?

In 394 in his anti-Manichaean work *Contra Adimantum*, Augustine had expatiated on the model of paternal correction, and on how even the harshest punishments in such a situation can be motivated by love. In fact, the more a father loves his son and thinks he can be weaned from his bad habits by coercion, the more he punishes him. Of course, human fathers in their loving punishment do not go so far as to kill their children, and neither will wise men go so far in correcting those who need correction, since with death there is no further hope of amendment. But God, on the other hand, certainly does go so far as to kill whomever he wishes. "It is manifest that God corrects with love . . . even with temporal death, those He would not condemn with the world."[121] In about the same year Augustine reminds us in his commentary on the Sermon on the Mount that in Old Testament times certain human beings also used the punishment of death.

It is true that great and holy men, who knew full well that that death which separates the soul from the body is not to be feared, nonetheless in recognition of the sentiment of those who did fear it punished some sins with death. A salutary fear was thereby instilled in the living, and as for those who were punished with death, what

---

119. *Epist.* 93.2 (5, 6); 5 (16, 17) (*CSEL* 34, 449–50, 461–62). Translation by Wilfrid Parsons in *The Fathers of the Church* 18 (New York, 1953).

120. On *Epist.* 93 and the change in Augustine's attitude on coercing the Donatists, see P. R. L. Brown, "St. Augustine's Attitude to Religious Coercion," *JRS* 54 (1964): 107–16, especially on how Augustine conceptualized and justified the role of external pressures in bringing about internal conversion.

121. *Contra Adimantum* 17.3 (*CSEL* 25, 167–68).

was harmful was not really death but sin, which could have become worse had they lived.

Augustine goes on to adduce the example of Elijah calling down fire from heaven against the followers of Baal (1 Kings 18:36-40), and notes that even Christ in reproving his disciples for asking him to do the same did not blame the example itself, but the vengeful spirit of the disciples in asking for it (Luke 9:54-55). According to the Manichaean heretics, Christ's injunction to "turn the other cheek" was antithetical to the picture of the vengeful, violent God of the ancient Israelites, but Augustine points out that mortal punishments, such as the slaying of Ananias and his wife (Acts 5:1-11), were not absent in the early church, "though they were much rarer than in the Old Testament." In any case the Manichaeans, who rejected the Old Testament, could find even in the apocryphal *Acts of Thomas*, which they regarded as canonical, the account of a man who struck the apostle being killed by a lion, and his dismembered hand being carried by a dog to Thomas while the apostle was dining.[122]

Peter Brown has noted how the relations of prophet and king in the Old Testament had come to represent the ecclesiastical and political realities of Augustine's Africa better than anything to be found in the actions of the apostles, and how at this very period "the events of the Old Testament had become the true *gesta maiorum* of a large body of the Roman governing class."[123] Augustine points out in this new reality how the obligation to enforce religious discipline is now incumbent upon secular Christian rulers, for whom it is no longer sufficient that they themselves are Christian, in a letter to the general Boniface in 417.

> How, then, do kings serve the Lord in fear except by forbidding and punishing with religious severity those things which are done against the Lord's commandments? For he serves in one way because he is a human being, and in another way because he is a king. As a human being, he serves by living faithfully; but because he is also a king he serves by sanctioning with suitable vigor laws that enjoin just behavior and prohibit its opposite.

---

122. *De sermone Domini in monte* I, 20 (64–65) (*CCL* 35, 73–75): "Magni autem et sancti viri, qui iam optime scirent mortem istam, quae animam dissoluit a corpore, non esse formidandam, secundum eorum tamen animum qui illam timerent nonnulla peccata morte puniuerunt, quo et uiuentibus utilis metus incuteretur, et illis qui morte puniebantur non ipsa mors noceret sed peccatum, quod augeri posset si uiuerent," etc.

123. Brown (n. 120 above), 114.

Augustine went on to cite the biblical examples of the Judean kings Hezekiah and Josiah, and of the pagan kings Darius and Nebuchadnezzar, to exemplify pious rulers destroying idols and reverencing God.[124]

Christian rulers, then, are obligated to use the powers attendant to their office to enforce a standard of righteousness in human society. What instruments and methods they had at their disposal to accomplish this are listed in a letter Augustine wrote in 413 or 414 to Macedonius, vicar of Africa.

> Doubtless it is not without purpose that there have been established such things as the authority of the king, the death penalty of the judge, the hooks of the executioner, the weapons of the soldier, the master's right to punish his slave, even the strictness of the good father. All these things have their own methods, causes, rationales, and benefits. Whenever these things are feared, evil men are restrained and good men live quite peacefully among evil ones. Not that any are to be called good because they do not sin out of fear of such things—for someone is good not out of fear of punishment but out of love for justice—but yet the fear of the law has also not acted uselessly in restraining human recklessness, so that innocence may be safe among the wicked, and also for the wicked themselves, that as long as their power to act is reined in by the fear of punishment their will could be healed by their calling upon God.[125]

Merely the fear itself of punishment, Augustine thought, helped to maintain societal order, in that it deterred the wicked from their crimes and simultaneously enabled the innocent to live at peace in the midst of evil men. Again in this letter he turns to the model of paternal correction, giving the example this time of a little boy who insists on playing with snakes. Would it not be merciful for someone to use the rod against such a child who refused to be corrected by words alone? "Just as it is sometimes mercy to punish, so it may be cruelty to forbear."[126]

124. *Epist.* 185.19 (*CSEL* 57, 17–18). Parsons translation in *The Fathers of the Church* 30 (New York, 1955), modified.

125. *Epist.* 153.16 (*CSEL* 44, 413–14).

126. *Epist.* 153.17 (*CSEL* 44, 415). Augustine gives the same example of a little boy careless with snakes to illustrate the same point in *Serm.* 114A.6 (*Miscellanea Agostiniana* I, Frangipane 9.6, 236–37). On the evolution in Augustine's thinking regarding the religious coercion of the Donatists, Mattox, 66–68, especially on the ideological resonance of using in this context the example of the pagan king Nebuchadnezzar (67).

Augustine in this letter associated with the soldier as an agent of state violence the somewhat mysterious figure of the *carnifex*, the executioner.[127] This individual had an integral, and frightening, role in the administration of justice. He was responsible not only for executing criminals, but for carrying out the *quaestio*, the questioning of witnesses and of the accused under judicial torture.[128] His instruments of torture could be prominently displayed before the judge's tribunal, a powerful inducement on its own for the accused to confess, and he practiced his trade not in the depths of a dungeon but in full public view. The repeated staging of this dramatic, public spectacle of judicial violence throughout the Roman world made the *carnifex* into a universal figure of dread. In a sermon delivered in 397, Augustine acknowledges that Christians are reluctant to confess their sins because in their minds confession is linked to judicial torture, where "whips and scourges, hooks and fire are used to elicit an oral confession," and where sometimes the *carnifices* go so far as to torture the accused to death before they can confess.[129] And even for those Christians who had never witnessed such tortures themselves, or preferred not to think about it, there were repeated reminders of the scenes typical of trials, tortures, and executions in the *passiones* of Christian martyrs read out annually on the anniversaries of their martyrdoms, and in the sermons often preached on those days. Thus in or shortly after 410 on the feast day of St. Vincent, a Spanish martyr of the Diocletianic persecution, Augustine detailed the cruel work of the *carnifex* in a sermon preached after the reading of the *passio*:

> Who would want to see the violence of the *carnifex*, a human being who has lost his humanity in raging against a human body? Who is pleased to look upon limbs stretched by the machinery of torture? The natural shape of a human being seized up into such a mechanism, the very bones pulled apart and laid bare with deep gashes, who would not be opposed to that? Who would not shudder at that?[130]

127. On the *carnifex*, Gillian Clark, "Desires of the Hangman: Augustine on Legitimized Violence," in *Violence in Late Antiquity: Perceptions and Practices*, ed. H. A. Drake et al. (Aldershot, UK: Ashgate, 2006), 137–46.

128. On the *quaestio*, Jill Harries, *Law and Empire in Late Antiquity* (Cambridge: Cambridge University Press, 1999), 122–34.

129. *Serm.* 29A.3 (*CCL* 41, 379–80).

130. *Serm.* 277A (Caillau I, 47; *Miscellanea Agostiniana* I, 243): "Quis enim velit saevientem videre carnificem, et hominem in corpus humanum humanitate amissa furentem? Quem cernere libeat

The bishop's consistent use of the historical present in this passage shows his intent and ability to vitalize the memory of an event in the past via a horrific shared experience of the present. The picture that emerges of the *carnifex* is of a type with that of the faceless and remorseless killer in modern horror movies, made all the more hideous by his sadistic love of inflicting pain on his victims.[131] Small wonder, then, that the *carnifex* and his deeds haunted the dreams of men and women in the ancient world.[132] Small wonder, too, that Augustine as a schoolboy conceived of himself as praying no less fervently to be spared the schoolmaster's rod as he imagined people generally praying to avoid falling into the *carnifex*'s power, and likened his parents' amusement at his schoolboy torments to a devout Christian's composure in the face of the rack and the hook.[133]

And yet, as bestial and even evil as he might seem, the *carnifex* had his place in the order of human society, a proposition Augustine set forth in one of his earliest works, *De ordine*. There the executioner heads the list of occupations that seem evil and disordered when viewed "close up," but which when viewed properly resolve into the overall goodness of divine providence.

> For what is more repulsive than the *carnifex*? Whose disposition is more grim and ominous than his? Yet he has a necessary place within the law itself, and is part of the order of a well-governed state. By his own disposition harmful, in accordance with the ranked order of someone else [in society] he nonetheless is the punishment for those who cause harm.[134]

This someone else who holds a ranked position in society apart from that of the *carnifex* is the judge, unqualified by law or temperament himself to carry out a capital sentence, who exploits the innate cruelty of the *carnifex*, and of him only, to serve the ends of the law.[135] In a sermon of uncertain date, Augustine chastises the recent actions of certain citizens of Hippo Regius in lynching an

---

divaricatos artus machinatione tormenti? Naturae figuram arte humanitatis arreptam, ossa extendendo separata, exarando nudata, quis non adversetur? Quis non exhorreat?"

131. *De diversis quaestionibus* 53.2 (*CCL* 44A, 88–89).

132. Brent D. Shaw, "Judicial Nightmares and Christian Memory," *Journal of Early Christian Studies* 11 (2003): 533–63.

133. *Conf.* 1. 9 (15) (*CCL* 27, 8).

134. *De ordine* II. 4 (12) (*CCL* 29, 114).

135. *De diversis quaestionibus* 53.2 (*CCL* 44A, 88–89). See Clark (n. 127 above), 141–42.

oppressive *miles*. The bishop insisted that the rioters in so acting had usurped a judicial privilege not their own. He reminds them that

> the state is well ordered, *for the authorities that exist have been ordained by God* (Romans 13:1). Why are you furious? What authority have you received? except that this isn't a case of public execution, but of blatant murder! Well then? Consider a man destined for execution, and condemned, the sword already hanging over him; it is not permissible for him to be struck down by just anyone among the various ranks of the authorities, but only by the one who serves that public function ("qui ad hoc militat"); the executioner so serves ("militat quaestionarius carnifex"); it's by him that the condemned man is to be struck down. If the judicial clerk (*exceptor*) strikes down the condemned man, already destined for execution, isn't he both killing a condemned man, and also condemning himself as a murderer? Certainly the one he kills had already been condemned, already destined for execution, but to strike him down irregularly is murder.[136]

Morality and the Military

The *carnifex*, then, serves a useful function in society in that, acting under the lawful commands of those in a superior rank, he has a license to kill those who threaten the order of the state. Much the same could be said of those who served in the military proper, and many of the same considerations that justified the role of the *carnifex* in human society also applied to soldiers. Of the agents of state power for whom it was permissible to kill other human beings, Augustine may have mentioned the *carnifex* earliest in his writings, but he has much more to say about those who served in the army, both as commander and as subordinate. His comments on the military also often engage a contemporary conversation in Christian circles on the stance Christianity ought to take vis-

---

136. *Serm.* 302.13 (*Stromata Patristica et Mediaevalia*, 106): "Ordinata est respublica. *Quae enim sunt, a Deo ordinatae sunt. Tu quare saevis? Quam potestatem accepisti, nisi quia sunt ista non publica supplicia, sed aperta latrocinia! Quid enim? Considerate in ipsis ordinibus potestatum, destinatum supplicio et damnatum, cui gladius imminet, non licere feriri, nisi ab illo qui ad hoc militat. Militat quaestionarius carnifex: ab illo percutitur damnatus. Si damnatum, iam supplicio destinatum, percutiat exceptor, nonne et damnatum occidit, et tamquam homicida damnatur? Certe quem occidit, iam damnatus erat, iam supplicio destinatus: sed inordinate ferire, homicidium est.*" On this incident, Shaw, 28–30.

à-vis the military, though without ever naming those to whom his views were deliberately opposed.

Augustine first discussed the morality of soldiers killing in Book I of his dialogue *De libero arbitrio*, written during his stay in Rome during the winter of 387/388.[137] In that book Augustine and his interlocutor Evodius were discussing what makes certain actions evil. Augustine proposes that an act is evil if it is motivated by lust, *libido*, for someone or something,[138] and Evodius later further defines *libido* as a type of bad desire originating in the love of those things that can be lost against one's will, things that evil men seek to enjoy for their own sakes and struggle to hold onto.[139] Earlier Evodius in order to facilitate their investigation of what constitutes an evil act had listed three that were incontrovertibly evil: adultery, murder, and sacrilege.[140] He concedes, though, that there may be instances when killing is not motivated by a bad desire and is consequently not sinful.[141]

> If any killing of a human being is considered murder, it can sometimes occur without its being a sin. For in the case of a soldier and the enemy, that of a judge or his agent and a criminal, as well as in the instance when a weapon unintentionally or in ignorance accidentally slips out of someone's hand, in these cases when they kill a human being it does not seem to me to be a sin.[142]

Thus far Augustine is seen seamlessly assimilating the role of the soldier as an agent of the state to that of the executor of its laws, as well as emphasizing the role of intent in determining whether an act is sinful. Although Augustine and Evodius are agreed that an act is against even the human law because it is evil, a sin, and that acts are not judged sinful merely because they are illegal,[143] to this point the distinction has been moot because there has been equivalence between sinful and illegal acts.

---

137. *Retract.* I.9 (*CCL* 57, 23). I accept the conclusions of Simon Harrison that the dialogue did not originally feature Evodius as Augustine's interlocutor by name, and further accept his convention of nonetheless using his name for convenience's sake. See Simon Harrison, *Augustine's Way into the Will: The Theological and Philosophical Significance of* De Libero Arbitrio (New York: Oxford University Press, 2006), esp. 31–50.

138. *De lib. arb.* I.iii.8, 20 (*CCL* 29, 215).

139. *De lib. arb.* I.iv.10, 31 (217).

140. *De lib. arb.* I.iii.6, 14 (214).

141. *De lib. arb.* I.iv.9, 24 (215–16).

142. *De lib. arb.* I.iv.9, 25 (216).

143. *De lib. arb.* I.iii.6, 15 (214).

But now Augustine attempts to throw a monkey wrench into the discussion. He asks Evodius whether an attacking enemy or a would-be rapist or murderer can be killed, as the law permits, for the sake of defending one's life, liberty, or chastity. When Evodius replies that since to use the sword in their defense is an act proceeding from *libido* and is therefore evil, Augustine counters that the laws that permit such actions are consequently unjust. In the case of a soldier he is actually legally required to kill the enemy, and is even liable to punishment by his commander if he refuses to do so.[144] The reply put into the speech of his interlocutor speaks to Augustine's early conception of the relationship between the earthly, human law and the higher law that is manifested in the workings of divine providence, and also provides an incidental insight, particularly germane for our purposes, into something of the debate contemporary Christians were having over how to accommodate themselves to the realities of a state where theirs was now the dominant religion, and particularly to the realities of military service.

To begin with, one can presume from Evodius's reported words that in the late 380s Augustine thought that ideally earthly law should be, in good Platonic fashion, the image of its original, the eternal law.[145] If that be the case, then the promulgator of the law did so at the prompting of God, a good man making good law. Good law can even issue from bad men with bad motivations. Human law is necessarily inferior to the eternal law, a stopgap that allows lesser evils to prevent greater ones from being committed. In this earthly realm of necessary compromises, it is better that a would-be murderer or rapist be killed than that he be allowed to kill or violate his victim, and therefore on balance the law that permits such actions is not unjust. Specifically, "in killing an enemy the soldier is an agent of the law, and has thereby readily carried out his duty without any *libido*." And in general, the law of a state that allows force to be met with force for the sake of defending the state's citizens can be followed without any *libido*. This is true not only for soldiers, but for all those who lawfully and by their rank in society are the duly subordinate agents of the legitimate authorities ("de omnibus ministris, qui iure atque ordine potestatibus quibusque subiecti sunt").[146]

"But," Evodius goes on to say, "I still do not see how such human beings, though blameless as to the law ('lege inculpata'), can actually be without blame ('inculpati'). For the law does not force them to kill, but merely leaves that

---

144. *De lib. arb.* I.v.11, 32–33 (217).

145. John M. Rist, *Augustine: Ancient Thought Baptized* (Cambridge: Cambridge University Press, 1994), 209. On the eternal law, notes 78 to 83 above.

146. *De lib. arb.* I.v.12, 34–36 (217–18).

in their power." At this point Augustine's argument has become somewhat murky and even contradictory, and we shall presently see why this should be so. Without explicitly differentiating the cases, Augustine seems to be arguing here that while duly authorized agents of the state *can* kill would-be assailants without *libido* being involved, the ordinary private citizen—who from Augustine's perspective had few powers or rights as an autonomous political actor[147]—in exercising self-defense *would* be seeking thereby to preserve things that can be lost against one's will, things such as chastity and even life,[148] and therefore *would* be motivated in that action by *libido*. "Accordingly, I certainly am not blaming the law which permits such assailants to be slain, yet I can find no way to defend those who kill them." For although there is nothing to be read in any human law book that renders such deeds blameworthy and those who commit them criminal or sinful, "I am not sure that they are not bound by some more compelling and entirely unseen law" ('aliqua vehementiore ac secretissima lege') that holds human beings to a higher standard than the human law. This is certainly not to say that the human law is to be despised or rejected, on the specious grounds that "because it does not do everything, what it does do should consequently be condemned." Human law reflects the best possible human attempt to regulate the political community, and must necessarily make many concessions to human weakness. What it leaves unpunished will be reckoned with by divine providence.[149]

In this part of *De libero arbitrio* Augustine's larger argument was that the origins of evil are not external to human beings, but proceed from an internal inclination of the human will, the immoderate, passionate desire, *libido*, for temporal things that ought not to be loved and desired as an end in themselves. There seems at first glance nothing in such an argument per se that would require him to get at the nature of evil by way of giving concrete examples of evil acts. And even if one concedes that for no reason other than clarity it was productive, in the tradition of philosophical dialogues, to get at the nature of evil by uncovering what it is that particular evil acts have in common, there

---

147. Rist (n. 145 above), 232: "In such statements we notice that the powers of ordinary citizens are almost non-existent. Plato and Aristotle, despite their similar fears of violence, would have shuddered at such an empty concept of citizenship, but in this Augustine speaks from his own late Imperial background, far from the virtues of the classical *polis*."

148. Augustine puts into Evodius's mouth the consideration that, first, the soul is either destroyed upon death and is inconsequential, or is immortal and thus beyond an attacker's power; and second, chastity is a virtue that ultimately resides in the soul and is likewise unable to be taken by an outsider (I.v.12, 37–38 [218]).

149. *De lib. arb.* I.v.12, 37–13, 41 (218–19).

seems no necessary reason why Evodius should have given as examples the acts that he does, nor why, although adultery is listed and treated first, most of the discussion is given over to killing, even though the motivation common to all the evil acts listed, *libido*, is oftentimes more naturally associated with sexual desire, in somewhat the same fashion as its nearest English equivalent, "lust." Clearly discussions of the moral issues attendant to killing were "in the air" at the time Augustine wrote Book I of the *De libero arbitrio*. A concern with the morality of killing could also be expected to occur with someone writing a treatise against Manichaeism, which by Augustine's lights took the seeming pacifistic and nonviolent injunctions of Christ far too literally. But it is also clear that in this part of *De libero arbitrio* Augustine knew that by virtue of its subject matter he had to deal with the views of more "orthodox" Christians on the morality of killing, Christian views that were part of a late fourth-century debate on such matters taking place throughout the Roman empire.

A number of details found in this portion of *De libero arbitrio* point to such a conclusion. It cannot be coincidental that Evodius's list of examples of evil acts—adultery, murder, and sacrilege—correspond exactly, in the same order, to the three worst mortal sins, weighted according to the frequency of their being cited, that are mentioned in the New Testament and the post-apostolic literature, there classified in terms of sexual delicts, murder, and idolatry. These were the "top three" mortal sins that would require ecclesiastical intervention in the form of penance to enable the sinner to be reconciled to God and once again receive the Eucharist.[150] Evodius's list is thus seen to reflect the moral viewpoint of a more-or-less mainstream ecclesiastical community of Christians. This observation also explains why Augustine in *De libero arbitrio* passed on determining whether the sacrilege associated with paganism partakes of *libido* as in the cases of adultery and murder.[151] For such a determination would be superfluous for his intended Christian audience, who would of course acknowledge the rejection of paganism to be a basic tenet of the faith itself, and would at the same time for any non-Christian audience require an extended *apologia* that would constitute a separate work, something like his first ten books of *The City of God*.

We have already seen that in the very same years when Augustine was writing *De libero arbitrio*, Ambrose of Milan in his *De officiis* had also addressed the question of whether an ordinary Christian citizen was entitled to exercise

---

150. C. Vogel, "Le péché et la pénitence," in *Pastorale du péché*, ed. Ph. Delhaye et al. (Tournai: Desclée, 1961), 151–52.

151. *De lib. arb.* I. 31 (217).

the right of self-defense. Ambrose categorically rejected the notion, writing that Christians cannot defend themselves even against the attacks of an armed attacker seeking to rob and kill them. For Christ had come "to confer grace, not to inflict misery." To kill another human being, even in this situation, would cause a Christian to become contaminated. "For all who hath struck with the sword shall be slain by the sword."[152] That Augustine rejected the notion of a Christian killing in self-defense on grounds other than those of Ambrose actually proves the contemporary currency of this question in Christian circles in the late fourth century. Augustine, who almost certainly did not know of Ambrose's work at the time he wrote Book I of De libero arbitrio, would seem to be responding to yet one more issue engendered by Christianity's newfound prominence in the Roman empire, an issue that could no longer be finessed by Lactantius's serene confidence of almost a century earlier—now seeming rather smug in retrospect—that Christians, members of a minority religion, would because of their avoidance of greed not be likely to venture abroad in search of wealth and hence put themselves at risk of being attacked by highway robbers in the first place.[153] Both Ambrose and Augustine seem to be responding to a relatively recent contention by some Christians that it *was* permissible to defend one's life against an attacker, as well as in their replies to be tapping into a more pacifistic tradition. After all, if the holy martyrs had been willing to sacrifice their lives, why could not contemporary Christians likewise trust to the promise of the immortality of their souls in the face of death? Both Ambrose and Augustine rejected the right of self-defense, but whereas the former had based his argument on Scripture, Augustine, aware of and sympathetic to the pacifistic tradition but unacquainted with Ambrose's work, disallowed killing in self-defense via a philosophical argument that ended up defining it as an evil act.

There is one explicit allusion to the ancient Christian pacifistic position on the killing of human beings in Augustine's take on the matter in De libero arbitrio. In arguing that although someone's killing of a would-be attacker is legal by human law but culpable according to a higher law, Evodius had asked "how in the face of that [higher law] are those people free from sin who are polluted by human bloodshed ('humana caede polluti') for the sake of things which should be despised?"[154] To my knowledge, this is the only instance in Augustine's works where he alludes to the early Christian sensibility,

152. De officiis I 131; III 27 (CSEL 15, 47, 163); ch. 3, notes 117, 119 above.

153. Chapter 2, note 70 above.

154. De lib. arb. I.v.13, 39 (218): "Quomodo enim apud eam sunt isti peccato liberi, qui pro his rebus, quas contemni oportet, humana caede polluti sint?"

traceable as far back as Tertullian in Africa almost two centuries earlier,[155] that associated blood pollution with the killing of human beings. The mention of blood pollution here in Book I of *De libero arbitrio* in the late 380s is yet another indication of the persistence of that ancient Christian sensibility, and of its continued vitality in underlying the ongoing resistance among some Christians to contaminating entanglements with the world.

Tertullian, though, followed by Lactantius, had held that pollution was the consequence of involvement in any human bloodshed, whether it be sanctioned by law or not. At first glance Augustine in *De libero arbitrio* took exception to this uncompromising rejection of killing in the case of agents of the state. But a closer look reveals an apparent contradiction in Augustine's argument on this point. When Evodius had said that a soldier could kill an enemy without its being a sin,[156] Augustine had explicitly agreed, and had even gone on to point out that such men are not usually called murderers.[157] Later, Evodius had contended that in killing an enemy, a soldier acts without *libido* as an agent of the law and is therefore not committing an evil act,[158] and this contention goes unchallenged by Augustine. But when Evodius makes the distinction between the human and the higher law in the course of arguing that some acts are legal under the former while *culpae* under the latter, he is dealing with the cases introduced by Augustine, which involve not only the law regarding self-defense, but also specifically the case of a soldier legally ordered to kill an enemy.[159] And when Evodius goes on to speak of "illi homines"—who in the context of his argument just earlier seems plainly to include agents of the state acting under superior authority—who are not *inculpati* in terms of the higher law,[160] it would seem he is saying that even the soldier commits a sin when he kills an enemy, which contradicts what both had agreed on earlier. This contradiction is not resolved by Augustine's observation that a soldier who refuses to kill an enemy is liable to military punishment, since both have concluded that killing in order to avoid harm to oneself involves sin. Certainly Augustine's primary aim in this portion of the dialogue is to establish the operations of a higher law that is the ultimate source of the human law. The unchecked, passionate pursuit of matters temporal to the neglect of those

155. Chapter 2, notes 37 to 49 above.

156. *De lib. arb.* I.iv.9, 25 (216).

157. *De lib. arb.* I.iv.9, 25 (216): "Adsentior, sed homicidae isti appellari non solent."

158. *De lib. arb.* I.v.12, 34 (217).

159. *De lib. arb.* I.v.11, 33 (217).

160. *De lib. arb.* I.v.12, 37 (218): "Sed illi homines lege inculpata quomodo inculpati queant esse non video."

eternal contravenes that higher law and the moral absolutes derived from it, contraventions that include the killing of other human beings.[161] But just as certainly, Augustine at the same time seemed to carve out an exception for those who kill in the course of executing the human law of the state. The contradiction is real, and the apparent ambivalence of the dialogue at this point reflects a real ambivalence in contemporary late fourth-century Christianity over the issue of the Christian stance to be taken vis-à-vis state violence, and the involvement of Christians in it.

No such ambivalence is visible in Augustine's next recorded words on the killing done by soldiers, penned about a decade after he first wrote on the subject in *De libero arbitrio*.[162] A certain Publicola, a grandee among the Arzuges, a people who inhabited areas in the pre-Saharan zone on the Roman frontier that correspond to today's southern Tunisia along the Libyan border,[163] had written a letter to Augustine with questions regarding the attitude it was proper for Christians to take in situations where they had to deal with the pagan barbarian peoples who were often hired in that region for jobs such as guarding the crops. In the relatively lawless conditions of a frontier area, it was perhaps natural that the issue of killing in self-defense would arise. So among his other questions, Publicola asked: "If a Christian should see a barbarian or a Roman wanting to kill him, ought the Christian kill them himself so as not to be killed by them?"[164] Augustine answered most of Publicola's questions in some detail, but his response to the question of self-defense was short and to the point.

> As for killing human beings so that one be not killed by them, I do not approve of such a course, except in the case of a soldier or someone performing his public duties, since then he is acting not on his own behalf but on behalf of others or the state where he himself resides, having there received the legitimate authority to do so insofar as it accords with his public role.[165]

---

161. *De lib. arb.* I.xvi.34, 115 (234–35). See also Rist (n. 145 above), 193–94.

162. The correspondence with Publicola is dated to 396–99 in Fitzgerald, 300.

163. *Barrington Atlas of the Greek and Roman World* (Princeton: Princeton University Press, 2000), Map 35. On the Arzuges, Alan Rushworth, "From Arzuges to Rustamids: State Formation and Regional Identity in the Pre-Saharan Zone," in *Vandals, Romans and Berbers: New Perspectives on Late Antique North Africa* (Aldershot, UK: Ashgate, 2004), 95–96.

164. *Epist.* 46 (*CSEL* 34, 127). Parsons translation in *The Fathers of the Church* 12 (New York, 1951), modified.

165. *Epist.* 47.5 (*CSEL* 34, 135).

Augustine's paramount consideration in disallowing the right of self-defense here seems to arise from the same consideration seen a decade earlier in Book I of *De libero arbitrio*, that there are certain absolute moral rules of human conduct derived from the eternal law, and that among them is the prohibition against killing other human beings.[166] Only duly authorized agents of the state, including soldiers, are allowed to kill other human beings, and then only while not acting merely as individuals, but as agents with a particular public role (*persona*). Otherwise, as Augustine wrote at about the same time in *Contra Faustum*, anyone who "uses the sword . . . without the order or permission of any higher and legitimate authority" falls under the Lord's condemnation when he said that "all that take the sword shall perish with the sword (Mt 26:52)."[167]

Perhaps Augustine's most definitive statement on the morality of state-sanctioned killing came over a decade later in 412 or 413 in Book 1 of *The City of God*.[168] The statement occurs in what amounts to an aside on the question of whether suicide can ever be justified, since in most cases the killing of a human being, including of oneself, is a mortal sin.[169] Pagan critics had highlighted the failure of the Christian God to protect Christian women, including nuns, from being raped during the recent Gothic sack of Rome. To avoid such a fate, some Christian women had resorted to committing suicide, and their extreme actions posed a problem for Augustine's apologetic aim in the early part of *The City of God* of relativizing the significance of the Gothic sack. Like a scientist who examines a geologic feature from multiple angles in order to provide as exhaustive a description of it as possible, Augustine, applying an argumentative method he will use repeatedly throughout his great and arduous work, investigates the issue of suicide, both in general and specifically to avoid rape, from a number of different perspectives, himself raising and refuting one objection after another to his central contention that suicide, with only the rarest of exceptions, can never be justified. He recognizes that his implied

---

166. Rist (n. 145 above), 191–95.

167. *Contra Faustum* 22.70 (*CSEL* 25, 667).

168. O'Daly, 32–94 on the chronology of composition for Book 1.

169. Augustine's discussion of suicide covers *De civitate Dei* (hereafter *DCD*) 1.16–29 (*CCL* 47, 17–30). See the discussion in O'Daly, 77–79 and in particular Augustine's take here on the rape of Lucretia in Karla Pollmann, "Augustins Transformation der traditionellen römischen Staats- und Geschichtsauffassung," *Augustinus: De civitate Dei*, ed. Christoph Horn (Berlin, 1997), 27–28 and Robert Dodaro, *Christ and the Just Society in the Thought of Augustine* (Cambridge: Cambridge University Press, 2004) (hereafter Dodaro), 37–41. On Augustine and suicide, the historical background of his attitude, and his subsequent influence on the making of suicide a crime, Shaw, 727–70, and the literature cited there.

criticism of Christian women who had killed themselves to avoid rape is an opinion not shared by all of his fellow religionists, and realizes that in his resorting to the Decalogue commandment against killing to justify his position he will either be accused by some Christians of going too far, or by any yielding on that point be accused by other Christians of not going far enough. While sticking in the main to his rejection of suicide, Augustine's solution is to try to steer a rational middle course.

In refuting the potential critics of his stance against suicide, Augustine follows his practice of oftentimes specifying the name or religion of his pagan or (less often) his heretical opponents, but of discreetly suppressing the name or religion of his more "orthodox" Christian ones.[170] Thus in discussing the closest pagan parallel to the suicide of the Christian women at Rome, the suicide of Lucretia, he makes no specific allusion to the fact that a number of Christian writers had both praised Christian women who had killed themselves to avoid rape and Lucretia's suicide as an example worthy of emulation, writers who included Ambrose and Jerome.[171] When Augustine then turns to Scripture in his argument against suicide, he must continue to have a Christian audience in mind, since pagan readers would have rejected scriptural authority. Not only could no passage be found in the Bible specifically supportive of suicide, but the terse commandment "Thou shalt not kill" seems to admit of no exception in its application, including to oneself. But in emphasizing the all-inclusive sweep of the Decalogue commandment, Augustine recognizes that he lays himself open to the charge of siding with those who take the commandment too far, and he realizes he has to confront those potential opponents also. On the one hand, there are those who extend the prohibition against killing to animals. Augustine refutes this argument by a *reductio ad absurdum*, reasoning that if the prohibition is extended to animals it may as well include plants, which, being alive, can likewise be killed. Here he is willing to name the Manichaean heretics who hold the ridiculously crazy notion that it is wrong to pull up shrubbery.[172]

On the other hand, there are those who regard the commandment "Thou shalt not kill" as an absolute, unqualified prohibition of the killing of other human beings. The fact that Augustine does not name such potential opponents

170. On this practice, see chapter 5, notes 6 to 9 above.

171. On the positive Christian appreciation of Lucretia's story, see Ian Donaldson, *The Rapes of Lucretia: A Myth and Its Transformations* (Oxford: Clarendon, 1982), 25–26; Dennis Trout, "Re-Textualizing Lucretia: Cultural Subversion in the *City of God*," *Journal of Early Christian Studies* 2, no. 1 (1994): 61–62. For Augustine's discussion of Lucretia, *DCD* 1.19 (*CCL* 47, 20–21), and Pollmann and Dodaro (n. 169 above).

172. *DCD* 1.20 (*CCL* 47, 22).

is one indication that they are Christian. That they exist at all, despite his failure to specify their position except by implication, is proved by the wording of Augustine's response to them. These are the Christians contemporary to Augustine of the "pacifistic" stripe described in chapter three, Christians associated with the ascetic currents of the late fourth century and early fifth, admirers and would-be emulators of St. Martin and the military martyrs, and of the ideal of nonviolence for which they stood. It would seem that such Christians in Augustine's day prized as a definitive statement on the matter, or could be imagined so to prize, Lactantius's discussion a century earlier in his *Divine Institutes* of the commandment "Thou shalt not kill." After arguing that the commandment prohibits Christians not only from committing outright murder, but even from any participation in killing at all, whether that be direct or indirect, sanctioned by law or not, he concluded: "Therefore *no exception whatsoever* ("nullam prorsus exceptionem") should be made regarding this commandment of God, in that it is always wrong to kill a human being, who by God's will is a sacrosanct creature."[173] Augustine replies:

But the very same divine authority [viz., Scripture] made *certain exceptions* ("quasdam . . . exceptiones") as to one not being permitted to kill a human being, these exceptions involving those whom God orders to be killed, whether by promulgated law or by express injunction to someone fulfilling a public role in accordance with specific circumstances ("ad personam pro tempore expressa iussione"). Now he does not kill who as a deputy dutifully follows orders, just as a sword acts as an assistant for the one wielding it. This is why there was no contravention whatsoever of that commandment which said "Thou shalt not kill" for those who either waged God-originated wars or who in carrying out a public role of authority in accordance with His laws, that is, rule by the most righteous rational power, punished criminals with death.[174]

173. Lactantius, *Div. Inst.* VI.20.17 (*CSE* 19, 558): "Itaque in hoc Dei praecepto nullam prorsus exceptionem fieri oportet, quin occidere hominem sit semper nefas, quem Deus sacrosanctum animal esse voluit."

174. *DCD* 1.21 (*CCL* 47, 23): "Quasdam vero exceptiones eadem ipsa divina fecit auctoritas, ut non liceat hominem occidi. Sed his exceptis, quos Deus occidi iubet sive data lege sive ad personam pro tempore expressa iussione, non autem ipse occidit, qui ministerium debet iubenti, sicut adminiculum gladius utenti; et ideo nequaquam contra hoc praeceptum fecerunt, quo dictum est: *Non occides*, qui Deo auctore bella gesserunt aut personam gerentes publicae potestatis secundum eius leges, hoc est iustissimae rationis imperium, sceleratos morte punierunt." On Augustine's (usually unacknowledged) use of Lactantius, see Peter Garnsey, "Lactantius and Augustine," in *Representations of Empire: Rome and the*

Augustine is reminding his Christian interlocutors that the Bible itself provides evidence that the Decalogue prohibition is not absolute on the issue of killing. Abraham had exhibited a praiseworthy obedience to God in seeking to slay his son. Jephthah's actual carrying out of the sacrifice of his daughter is more problematic, as it is unclear whether his doing so in fulfillment of a vow to God constitutes obedience to divine command. Samson's action, more pertinent to the issue of suicide since in bringing down the temple upon his enemies he had also brought it down upon himself, was done at the express command of God.[175] As Augustine had written years earlier in his commentary on the Sermon on the Mount, it is true that there are more examples of divinely sanctioned killing to be found in the Old than in the New Testament.[176] Naturally, then, his language here of "God-originated wars" and the infliction of the death penalty in accordance with "the most righteous reason" of God's law looks back to the wars of the ancient Israelites and the Old Testament law, and his subsequent choice of scriptural examples points in the same direction. But if it is uncertain whether by this passage Augustine meant that God-originated wars could still happen in his time, it seems that he at least here wanted to indicate to his interlocutors that scripturally justified killing *could* occur in the present day in the administration of justice, even as part of the imperfect order of a fallen earthly city. He links the present-day administration of justice to the Old Testament past via an allusion here to Rom. 13:4, where "he who beareth not the sword without cause" acts as God's agent in the administration of justice.[177] As we have seen, Romans 13 was for Augustine, as for his Christian contemporaries, a key scriptural justification for the present temporal order.[178] Its usage here links this passage to Augustine's earlier statements in *De libero arbitrio* and in the letter to Publicola on the exceptions to the prohibition against killing when done by someone acting in the role of a legitimately authorized *persona.*

Certainly it is not the case that killing is sometimes permitted solely because Scripture says so. Augustine rounds off this passage on the exceptions to the Decalogue commandment by reiterating that such justifiable killing can

Mediterranean World, ed. Alan K. Bowman et al., *Proceedings of the British Academy* 114 (Oxford: Oxford University Press, 2002), 153–79.

175. *DCD* 1.21 (*CCL* 47, 23).

176. *De sermone Domini in monte* I, 20 (64) (*CCL* 35, 74).

177. *DCD* 1.21 (*CCL* 47, 23): "ipse occidit, qui ministerium debet iubenti, sicut adminiculum gladius utenti." Cf. Rom. 13:4: "Dei enim minister est tibi in bonum. Si autem male feceris, time, non enim sine causa gladium portat. Dei enim minister est, vindex in iram ei qui malum agit."

178. Chapter 3, notes 150, 154 above.

only occur in obedience either to the general application of the law or to the express command of God in a particular circumstance. Augustine goes on to illustrate both situations in discussing the case of earlier holy women who had drowned themselves to avoid being raped and who had subsequently come to be venerated as martyrs.[179] He concedes that the women, like Samson, could have killed themselves in obedience to a divine command. It is a common weakness of intellectuals, the love of paradox, which leads Augustine then to illustrate the linkage between legitimate killing and obedience by recourse to the same example he had used a quarter century earlier in *De libero arbitrio*.[180]

> But it does not follow [from the necessity to obey divine commands] that just anyone who has decided to sacrifice his son to God does not thereby commit a crime, simply because Abraham did it and was even praised for so doing. It is also true that whenever a soldier has killed a human being in obeying some authority to whom he has been legally subordinated he cannot be charged with murder under any of his state's laws. In fact, if he does not do it he is guilty of dereliction of duty and insubordination. Yet if he had done this of his own accord and on his own authority he would have been charged with shedding human blood. And so that for which he is punished if done without orders is that for which he will be punished if he does not do it when ordered. Now if this is the case when a commander issues an order, how much more so when the Creator gives an order!

In allowing for the possibility, however, that God could order ordinary individuals, not agents of the state, to kill other human beings, or themselves, Augustine sounds a very loud note of caution: anyone who does so must be absolutely certain, without any shred of doubt, that he *has* received a divine command.[181]

Augustine, then, seems to have held to a consistent view for at least a quarter of a century that soldiers who killed in military service did not thereby sin. But did that necessarily mean that it was acceptable for *Christians* to serve as soldiers? And does the Christian commander—or Christian emperor, for that matter—bear any culpability for ordering soldiers to kill in war? Augustine as a rule did not pose and address such questions directly. This is not to say that

179. On the saints to whom Augustine probably referred, see *Bibliothèque augustinienne, Oeuvres de saint Augustin* 33, *La Cité de Dieu, Livres I–V* (Paris: Desclée de Brouwer, 1959), 775–76.

180. *De lib. arb.* I.v.11, 32–33 (*CCL* 29, 217).

181. *DCD* 1.26 (*CSEL* 47, 27).

he did not at times confront these questions. Rather, what seem his oftentimes indirect or allusive responses to the issue result from their being more or less ancillary considerations in a larger argument, or they are the consequence of a polemical tactic. For Augustine in addressing the issue of the licitness of Christians serving as soldiers at times engaged the same contemporary interlocutors—again, without specifying them by name—who were opposed to any Christian participation at all in the business of killing. He adduced in arguments against his Christian interlocutors the same principles of authority and obedience he used to defend the killing that soldiers do, and likewise at times invoked scriptural warrant. There seems to be only one instance in all of his works where Augustine explicitly signaled his intent to address directly the question of the licitness of Christian military service.

Augustine first confronted the stance taken by contemporary Christian "pacifists" in about 400 in his anti-Manichaean treatise *Contra Faustum*.[182] In Book 22 of that work Augustine is addressing the claim by the Manichaean Faustus that Moses had acted evilly in warring against and slaughtering the enemies of the Israelites. He counters that Moses' wars had been undertaken in obedience to God, and asserts that even in ordinary human affairs the dictates of societal order and the rank of individuals within that order sometimes require even good men to fight in wars in obedience to legitimate authority.[183]

> Otherwise, when soldiers came to John to be baptized and asked, *And what should we do?* (Lk 3:14) he would have replied to them, "Throw down your weapons; desert the military; strike, wound, and kill no one." But because he knew that when they did these things as soldiers they were not murderers but agents of the law, not avengers of injuries done to them but defenders of public safety, he replied to them, *Do violence to no one; slander no one; be satisfied with your wages* (Lk 3:14). But because Manichaeans are accustomed to blaspheme John openly, let them listen to the Lord Jesus Christ commanding that this money with which John says a soldier ought to be satisfied should be given to Caesar. He says, *Render unto Caesar what is Caesar's, and unto God what is God's* (Mt 22:21). For taxes are paid so that wages may be given to a soldier who is needed for wars. And of that centurion who said, *I too am a man placed under another's authority and having soldiers under me; and I say to one, Go, and he goes,*

---

182. On the date of *Contra Faustum*, see chapter 5, n. 11 above.

183. *Contra Faustum* 22.74 (*CSEL* 25, 671–72). See also ch. 7, notes 119 to 121 below.

and to another, Come, and he comes, and to my servant, Do this, and he does it (Mt 8:9), He rightly praised his faith; He did not command that he desert the military.[184]

Augustine here uses the same arguments we have seen him use earlier to defend soldiers' killing. They serve not on their own behalf but in defense of all of society, acting as *ministri legis*. The reminiscence of Romans 13 is reinforced by the reference to paying taxes so that soldiers can fight in wars, which in his commentary on the Pauline text Augustine had declared to be the duty of all good Christians.[185] Since he had just been speaking of how it was sometimes necessary for "good men" (*boni*), i.e., Christians, to fight in wars initiated by duly constituted authorities, this passage can certainly be read as a justification for Christians serving in the military. As scriptural warrant for this stance he cited the words of John the Baptist, who had told soldiers coming to him for baptism not to leave military service but to reform their behavior, an attitude that implied approval of such service. Augustine cited this text on John the Baptist at least five times in his works in support of the same argument.[186] For example, in a sermon delivered at about the time of his writing *Contra Faustum*, Augustine had spoken of his desire that (presumably) Christian soldiers listen to the precepts of the gospel. He puns: "One isn't prevented from doing good by the military, but by malice," then went on to cite the text on John the Baptist.[187] To the Manichaeans who spurned the testimony of John for his failure to recognize Jesus as the Christ,[188] he quoted the words of the Lord himself, who had not only said that taxes should be paid to the ruling power—then as now with the understanding that much of that money would go to the military—but had also praised the attitude of the faithful centurion, and had not insisted that

---

184. *Contra Faustum* 22.74 (*CSEL* 25, 672–73). For this work I have sometimes modified (as here) the translation by Roland J. Teske, SJ, *St. Augustine: Answer to Faustus, A Manichean* (*Contra Faustum*) (Hyde Park, NY: New City Press, 2007); hereafter Teske.

185. *Expositio quarundam propositionum ex epist. ad Romanos* 64 (72) (*CSEL* 84, 45).

186. The other examples besides the current one are: *Serm.* 302.15, *Stromata Patristica et Mediaevalia*, 107 (discussed here); *Epist.* 138.15, *CSEL* 44, 141–42 (see note 203 below); *Epist.* 189.4, *CSEL* 57, 134 (discussed below, note 216); and *Enarr. in Ps. 118, s.* 31.1, *CCL* 40, 1770. He cites the same text at *De fide et operibus* 13 (19), *CSEL* 41, 59, but there to a different point.

187. *Serm.* 302.15 (see previous note): "Nec nos volumus talia fieri a militibus ut pauperes affligantur, nolumus: volumus et ipsos audire Evangelium. Non enim benefacere prohibet a militia, sed a malitia. Venientes enim milites ad baptismum Iohannis," etc.

188. For an example of this attitude of the part of the Manichaean Faustus, see *Contra Faustum* 5.1 (*CSEL* 25, 271–72).

he leave the service, another passage that he would also use later to justify Christian soldiers.[189]

Given the Manichaeans' rejection of John the Baptist, that he would even bother to cite his words indicates that Augustine here had in mind fellow religionists who did not share his view of Christians serving in the military. The words he puts into John the Baptist's mouth had he rejected such service read like the pacifistic program urged by some at this time. The call to throw down one's weapons hearkens back to the behavior of Christian conscientious objectors outlawed by the Council of Arles in 314,[190] uses the same expression found in Paulinus of Nola's account of Victricius of Rouen (*arma abicere*),[191] and clearly relates to an action symbolic of the public renunciation of military service. Victricius obviously had, and Sulpicius Severus argues that Martin also had, deserted outright, a course also praised in the contemporary cult of the military martyrs.[192] Not only can the existence of those opposed to Christian participation in the military and something of what they advocated be read as in a mirror, as it were, from Augustine's argument in *Contra Faustum* in favor of such service, but we can even identify a specific text here against which Augustine was reacting. After laying out his scriptural justification for military service, he had gone on to write that even wars waged for base motives cannot harm either God or his "holy ones," i.e., Christians, for such wars are beneficial in schooling them in humility and the patient sufferance of divine discipline.

> For no one has any power over them [viz., Christians] unless it has been given to him from above (cf. Lk 19:11), for there is no power save by God's command or permission. Since, then, a just man, though he may be serving a human king, or even an impious one, can duly wage war at his bidding in conformance to the order of the peace of the state—when he is either sure that what he is ordered to do is not contrary to God's commandment or is even unsure whether it is, in which case the wickedness of ordering it may render the king guilty, while his subordinate rank shows the soldier to be innocent—how much more completely innocent in conducting war is anyone who wages war at the command of God, who, as anyone

189. *Epist.* 189.4, *CSEL* 57, 133–34, discussed below, note 216.

190. *CCL* 148A, 9: "De his qui arma proiciunt in pace, placuit abstineri eos a communione"; ch. 2, notes 106 to 116 above.

191. Paulinus of Nola, *Epist.* 18.7 (*CSEL* 29, 134): "ante pedes sacrilegi tribuni militiae sacramenta permutans arma sanguinis abiecisti ut arma pacis indueres"; ch. 3, note 194 above.

192. Chapter 3, notes 214 to 217 above.

in His service cannot fail to know, does not command anything evil.[193]

Augustine here has been speaking of two types of wars, the one instigated at the direct command of God, and the other initiated by some legitimate human authority.[194] His main argument in this passage is that there can be no question as to the innocence from sin of anyone who wages the former type of war, since it is taken for granted that ordinary Christian soldiers can without sin wage wars at the command of human authority, even at the behest of pagan emperors. Now Augustine realizes that not everyone, including at least some fellow Christians, accepts this last premise. The insertion of a lengthy parenthesis to justify that premise acknowledges the existence of such opponents and the necessity to confront them, and the parenthesis's content reflects in mirror image their stance. A *vir iustus*, a truly virtuous Christian, *cannot*, they argued, engage in war. And that Augustine felt compelled to add in countering that position that Christian soldiers could even fight while serving under a pagan emperor points specifically to an engagement with the famous incident recounted in Sulpicius Severus's *Vita Martini*, where the saint had in the presence of Julian the Apostate renounced military service and refused to fight.[195] Although Augustine does not mention Julian by name, that he had him in mind here is indicated by a passage in a sermon on Psalm 124 the bishop delivered a few years after writing *Contra Faustum* in 406 or 407.[196] In that sermon Augustine had preached that even if unrighteous men attain worldly honors, "the honor due them must be exhibited. For God has so ordained His church, that every authority ordained in this world should be honored, and

---

193. *Contra Faustum* 22.75 (CSEL 25, 673–74): "Bellum autem, quod gerendum deo auctore suscipitur, recte suscipi dubitare fas non est vel ad terrendam vel ad obterendam vel ad subiugandam mortalium superbiam, quando ne illud quidem, quod humana cupiditate geritur, non solum incorruptibili deo, sed nec sanctis eius obesse aliquid potest; quibus potius ad exercendam patientiam et ad humiliandam animam ferendamque paternam disciplinam etiam prodesse invenitur. Neque enim habet in eos quisquam ullam potestatem, nisi cui data fuerit desuper. Non est enim potestas nisi a deo sive iubente sive sinente. Cum ergo vir iustus, si forte sub rege homine etiam sacrilego militet, recte possit illo iubente bellare civicae pacis ordinem servans—cui quod iubetur, vel non esse contra dei praeceptum certum est vel utrum sit, certum non est, ita ut fortasse reum regem faciat iniquitas imperandi, innocentem autem militem ostendat ordo serviendi—quanto magis in administratione bellorum innocentissime deversatur, qui deo iubente belligerat, quem male aliquid iubere non posse nemo, qui ei servit, ignorat."

194. For more on this, see ch. 7, notes 95 to 137 below.

195. *Vita Martini* 4 (CSEL 1, 114–15); ch. 3, note 187 above.

196. A.-M. Bonnardière, *Recherches de chronologie augustinienne* (Paris, 1965), 94–99.

sometimes by their betters." The model for such due obedience is that a slave owes his master, even an unrighteous master.

> Now what I've said of master and slave, understand the same to be true of authorities and kings, of all the lofty powers in this world. For sometimes the authorities are good, and fear God; sometimes they don't fear God. Julian was an unbelieving emperor, was an apostate, wicked, idolatrous. When Christian soldiers who were in the service of this unbelieving emperor came over to the cause of Christ, they acknowledged Him only who was in heaven. If Julian ever wanted them to worship idols or to offer incense, they preferred God to him. But when he said, "Dress the line! Attack those people!" they obeyed immediately. They made a distinction between their eternal and their temporal lord; and yet for the sake of their eternal lord they were also subject to their temporal lord.[197]

Here Augustine stresses the same message made earlier in *Contra Faustum*, both based scripturally on Romans 13, that, excepting any religious infringement on their part, authorities were due obedience from all Christians, including those in the army, because their power ultimately derived from God. In the passage from *Contra Faustum* the appearance of what seems an offhand qualification of the military authority to whom the Christian soldier should be obedient—"serving a human king, *or even an impious one*" ('sub rege homine etiam sacrilego militet')—is explained by the same consideration that had Augustine in the later sermon choose to exemplify the irreligious ruler by Julian the Apostate; in both instances he was reacting against the *Vita Martini*. Nor was Augustine the only Christian luminary of that time to do so. In commenting on Isa. 58:7, "when thou shalt see one naked, cover him," Jerome had linked the verse to Christ's commandment, "he that hath two coats, let him give to him that hath none" (Luke 3:11), then added: "Certainly He did not order the one [coat] to be split

---

197. *Enarr. in Ps. 124.7* (CSEL 95:3, 156, 157–58): ". . . non potest fieri nisi ut exhibeatur illis honor debitus potestati. Ordinavit enim sic Deus ecclesiam suam ut omnis potestas ordinata in saeculo habeat honorem, et aliquando a melioribus. . . . Quod autem dixi de domino et servo, hoc intelligite de potestatibus et regibus, de omnibus culminibus huius saeculi. Aliquando enim potestates bonae sunt, timent Deum. Aliquando non timent Deum. Iulianus exstitit infidelis imperator, exstitit apostata, iniquus, idolatra. Milites Christiani servierunt imperatori infideli. Ubi veniebatur ad causam Christi, non agnoscebant nisi illum qui in caelo erat. Si quando volebat ut idola colerent, ut turificarent, praeponebant illi Deum. Quando autem dicebat: 'Producite aciem, ite contra illam gentem', statim obtemperabant. Distinguebant dominum aeternum a domino temporali, et tamen subditi erant propter dominum aeternum etiam domino temporali."

and divided, which many do for the sake of popular acclaim."[198] This is clearly a criticism, albeit oblique, of the famous incident in the *Vita Martini* where the saint had divided his military cloak with a beggar.[199] Not everyone at the time, it seems, was enamored of the miracle-working bishop of Tours, or at least of the presentation of him by his hagiographer.[200]

In this section of *Contra Faustum* we see Augustine in his argumentation maneuvering as he often does in his more polemical works, especially *The City of God*.[201] While the central thrust of his argument will be directed against a main opponent, in this case the Manichaeans, he also along the way will spin off secondary assaults against other adversaries. Here those adversaries were fellow Christians who, although of pacifistic leanings like the Manichaeans, were arguably neither heretical nor schismatic but merely mistaken, and so he is circumspect in handling them. It would seem that those at this time who believed that military service was incompatible with Christianity publicized via Sulpicius Severus's *Vita* the example of Martin of Tours, who at risk to his life had defied a pagan emperor and rejected participation in war. But Augustine and other Christians believed just as strongly that what Martin had done was wrong. If being a soldier was incompatible with being a Christian, then John the Baptist would have said so to soldiers coming to him to be baptized. As St. Paul had written, the authorities, even pagan ones, had been ordained by God, and should be obeyed, including in matters of war. Of course, if Julian had ordered Martin to worship idols, that was something else entirely. But he had not.

One should not exaggerate Augustine's seeming casual acceptance of the reality of Christians in the military and his disavowal of the pacifistic assertions of some of his co-religionists, for as we will see he was no lover of war. Though he seems to have hated extremes, his polemical zeal often got the better of him, and led him to make statements that were themselves immoderate, or at least inconsistent with what he wrote elsewhere. Such would explain what he wrote in a letter to his friend Marcellinus in 411 or 412.[202] In the section from *Contra*

198. Jerome, *In Esaiam* XVI. 58, 6.7 (*CCL* 73A, 666): "Non enim unam iussit scindi et dividi, quod multi popularis aurae causa faciunt."

199. Boniface Ramsey, "Almsgiving in the Latin Church: The Late Fourth and Early Fifth Centuries," *Theological Studies* 43 (1982): 234. My thanks to Eric Shuler for providing me with this citation.

200. On the relevance of these passages for Augustine's view of the legitimate authority of sovereigns, Christian or pagan, to order soldiers into combat, and the few limitations Augustine placed on that authority, see also Mattox, 56–59.

201. As we have already seen him doing in his discussion of the morality of suicide, notes 169 to 181 above.

Faustum discussed above, Augustine had countered Manichaean pacifism with proof that God had sometimes authorized wars, and took the opportunity as a sort of aside to show the pacifistic error of some fellow Christians. In the later letter to Marcellinus he was countering a pagan's assertion that Christianity itself was pacifist to the core, given what its founder had said about loving one's enemies and turning the other cheek. Surely such an attitude was at odds with the need to fight to defend the empire against dangerous barbarian invaders of the sort who had recently taken and sacked Rome itself. Augustine replied that

> If Christian teaching condemned all wars, then the soldiers in the Gospel who were seeking salvation would have been advised to throw down their arms and withdraw from military service altogether. But instead it was said to them: "Do violence to no one, slander no one, be satisfied with your wages." He advised them that they ought to be satisfied with their wages; he assuredly did not forbid them from military service. Accordingly, they who say that Christ's teachings are opposed to the state, let them give us an army with the sort of soldiers Christ's teachings command them to be; let them give us provincials, husbands, wives, parents, children, masters, slaves, kings, judges, and finally taxpayers and tax-collectors of the sort Christ's teachings command them to be. Then let them dare to say that Christ's teachings are opposed to the state, or, rather, let them even hesitate to admit that if they were to be observed they would actually save the state.[203]

202. For more on the background to *Epist.* 138, see below, ch. 7, notes 39 to 42, 44 to 49, 58 to 67.

203. *Epist.* 138.15 (*CSEL* 44, 141–42): "Nam si Christiana disciplina omnia bella culparet, hoc potius militibus consilium salutis petentibus in evangelio diceretur, ut abicerent arma seque militiae omnino subtraherent. Dictum est eis autem: *Neminem concusseritis, nulli calumniam feceritis, sufficiat vobis stipendium vestrum.* Quibus proprium stipendium sufficere debere praecepit, militare utique non prohibuit. Proinde, qui doctrinam Christi adversam dicunt esse rei publicae, dent exercitum talem, quales doctrina Christi esse milites iussit; dent tales provinciales, tales maritos, tales coniuges, tales parentes, tales filios, tales dominos, tales servos, tales reges, tales iudices, tales denique debitorum ipsius fisci redditores et exactores, quales esse praecepit doctrina Christiana, et audeant eam dicere adversum esse rei publicae, immo vero dubitent confiteri magnam, si ei obtemperetur, salutem esse rei publicae." For another example of this evocation of a Christian army, see *Serm.* 302.15 (*Stromata Patristica et Mediaevalia*, 107): "And truly, brethren, if soldiers were such [as John the Baptist had told them to be], this empire would be fortunate." ('Et vere, fratres, si tales essent milites, felix esset ipsa respublica.') Again, Augustine writes similarly in *DCD* 2.19 (*CCL* 47, 51), but with more restraint.

Augustine would have his pagan adversary know that Christians were the furthest thing from being unreliable pacifists. But since he was even then, and partly in response to pagan criticisms of the effect of Christianity on the Roman empire, beginning to write *The City of God*, with its somber depiction of an ultimately irredeemable earthly city that was at best an inferior good, and its resigned acknowledgment that the church on earth had chaff inextricably mixed with the wheat, it seems impossible to regard his picture here of a Christian army, let alone a Christian society, as a seriously envisioned possibility, but rather an exaggerated counterweight to his pagan opponent's equally unrealistic image of Christians passively sitting on their hands while the barbarians raged.

In *Contra Faustum* Augustine had addressed the question of whether Christians could serve as soldiers incidentally in the course of countering the pacifistic views of his Manichaean opponent. In his letter to Marcellinus he had approached the issue as one item in a more general defense of Christianity against pagan criticisms. In only one instance did Augustine author a work that had as one of its primary and explicit aims the intent to address specifically the issue of the licitness of Christian military service, his Letter 189 to Boniface. If one were to search throughout all of his works for the text that best addresses the questions moderns typically have of Augustine's views on war and military service, Letter 189 provides about the most direct and intentional answers one could find. But for that very reason it is important to keep in mind that Augustine did not write this letter in the disinterested spirit of someone calmly prescribing authoritative precepts, but was instead, in a pastoral spirit, addressing the concerns of a particular individual at a particular time and place.

When Augustine wrote to him in 417,[204] Boniface, who had already gained military renown years earlier in battle at Marseilles against the Visigothic king Athaulf, was serving as commander of a detachment of *foederati*, probably of Gothic cavalry attached to the *comitatenses*, along the African frontier.[205] In another letter written to him about the same time,[206] Augustine had praised

---

204. *Nuova Biblioteca Agostiniana, Opere di sant'Agostino* 23 (Rome: Città Nuova Editrice, 1974), 194/5.

205. On Boniface as a whole, H.-J. Diesner, "Die Laufbahn des comes Africae Bonifatius und seine Beziehungen zu Augustine," in his *Kirche und Staat im spätrömischen Reich. Aufsätze zur Spätantike und zur Geschichte der Alten Kirche* (Berlin: 1964), 100–126; Bonifatius 3: *PLRE* 2.237–40; Robert A. Markus, "Bonifatius comes Africae," in *Augustinus-Lexikon*, ed. Cornelius Mayer (Basel: Schwabe & Co., 1986–94), 1:653–55. On his exploits at Marseilles against Athaulf, Olympiodorus, frag. 22.2, in R. C. Blockley, *The Fragmentary Classicising Historians of the Later Roman Empire: Eunapius, Olympiodorus, Priscus and Malchus* (Liverpool: Francis Cairns, 1983), 2:184–87. On Boniface's command of *foederati* at this period, *Epist.* 220.7 (*CSEL* 57, 436), and on at least their later Gothic composition, Possidius, *Vita*

Boniface's "ardent desire to know the things that are of God while in the midst of the cares of war and arms."[207] Although it is true that that very letter, written to inform Boniface of the details of the Donatist controversy, show him to be somewhat theologically ill-informed and seemingly unaware of the threat to Catholicism posed by the Donatists,[208] there seems little reason to doubt the sincerity of his attachment to the faith. One measure of the authenticity and depth of his Christian sentiment can be seen in the reaction to the death of his wife three or four years later,[209] when such became his trepidation that he resolved to renounce the *vanitas saeculi huius* and enter a monastery. He was only dissuaded from doing so by a personal visit to his frontier headquarters at Tubunae in southern Numidia by Augustine and Alypius, a journey that in itself demonstrates the seriousness of his intent since the urgency to keep at his post such a valiant defender of Africa compelled the bishop of Hippo, then in his late sixties, to undertake one of the longest known journeys of his episcopacy.[210] Clearly, then, at the very least Boniface at this stage of his life wanted to be a good and virtuous Christian. And it appears that already by 417 he had concerns that a life in the military, with the violence and bloodshed attendant to it, was incompatible with that desire. It may be that no single instance of the horrors of war motivated his questionings about military service, but rather the dispiriting dreariness of a frontier posting in the pre-desert high plains of southern Numidia,[211] where war consisted of an endless series of small-scale police actions against nomadic raiders, where no victory was ever final and there was little scope for fame and glory. It is easy to conceive that such a man in such a circumstance, someone who only three or four years later was prepared to cast aside all the panoply of worldly honor to pursue a religious vocation, would have been receptive to the proposition—whether it was conveyed to him by the writings or in person by individuals of the persisting pacifistic "wing"

Augustini 28.12 (*Vite dei Santi* III, ed. and trans. A. A. R. Bastiaensen, Luca Caneli, and Carlo Carena [Milan: Fondazione Lorenzo Valla, 1975], 208).

206. *Epist.* 185 (note 124 above), the so-called *Liber de correctione Donatistarum*. It is unclear whether this is the same letter to Boniface referred to in *Epist.* 189.1.

207. *Epist.* 185.1 (*CSEL* 57, 1): "Laudo et gratulor et admiror, fili dilectissime Bonifati, quod inter curas bellorum et armorum vehementer desideras ea nosse, quae dei sunt." Parsons translation in *The Fathers of the Church* 30 (New York, 1955).

208. Diesner (n. 205 above), 103; Markus (n. 205 above), cols. 653–54.

209. On the date of the death of Boniface's first wife, see the discussion in Serge Lancel, *Saint Augustine*, trans. Antonia Nevill (London: SCM, 2002), 529 and the works cited there.

210. *Epist.* 220.3 (*CSEL* 57, 432–33). On the journey, Othmar Perler, *Les Voyages de saint Augustin* (Paris: Études augustiniennes, 1969), 366–69.

211. For a description of the area, see Lancel (n. 209 above), 470.

of contemporary Christianity, or whether it was simply "in the air"—that one could not be a good soldier and a good Christian at the same time.

Upon learning of Boniface's questionings as to whether it was necessary for him to leave the military in order to grow in the faith, Augustine hurriedly wrote to him a rather brief letter "which might build you up for the eternal salvation for which your hope is in our Lord Jesus Christ."[212] As is appropriate in a brief letter from a cleric to a soldier sincere in his faith but unsophisticated in his theology, Augustine began his pastoral advice with the central, succinct, and unambiguous marching orders issued by the Lord himself, to "love the Lord thy God with all thy heart and with all thy soul and with all thy might," and to "love thy neighbor as thyself."[213] If Boniface followed those orders with daily prayers and good works, Christian love would grow in him "until, being perfected, it may perfect you,"[214] and presumably then his doubts about the compatibility of Christianity with military service would take care of themselves. Though the end of all this striving, the attainment of the vision of God as He truly is, constituted a promise inconceivably great, that was no cause for a Christian caught up in lonely soldierly toils in the wastes of Numidia to despair of ultimately attaining it. For just as it had been through the exercise of such Christian love that "all our holy fathers and patriarchs and prophets and apostles had been pleasing to God . . ."[215]

> [d]o not suppose that no one who serves in the weaponry of war can be pleasing to God. Among such was holy David, to whom the Lord offered such high testimony. Among such were also many just men of that time. Among such also was that centurion who said to the Lord: *I am not worthy that you should enter under my roof, but only say the word and my boy shall be healed. For I too am a man placed under authority and having soldiers under me; and I say to one, Go, and he goes, and to another, Come, and he comes, and to my servant, Do this, and he does it.* Of him the Lord said: *Amen I say to you, I have not found so great a faith in Israel* (Mt 8:8-10). Among such, also, was that Cornelius to whom the angel was sent, who said: *Cornelius, your alms are accepted and your prayers are heard,* when he advised him to send for the blessed apostle Peter and to hear from him what he ought to do. He also sent a religious soldier to the apostle that he might

---

212. *Epist.* 189.1 (*CSEL* 57, 131).
213. Deut. 6:5; Lev. 19:18; Matt. 22:37, 39; Mark 12:30-31; Luke 10:27.
214. *Epist.* 189.2 (131–32).
215. *Epist.* 189.3 (132–33).

come to him (Acts 10:1–8). Among such were also those who when they came to be baptized to John, the holy precursor of the Lord and friend of the bridegroom, of whom the Lord himself said: *Among those born of women there has not arisen a greater one than John the Baptist* (Mt 11:11), and they asked of him what they should do, he answered them: *Do violence to no one; slander no one; be satisfied with your wages* (Lk 3:14). He certainly did not forbid them from military service under arms when he commanded them that they should be satisfied with their wages.[216]

Boniface, of course, should not take this to mean that he could act as a Christian when "off duty" but had a blank check to exercise unrestrained violence when he went into battle. "So think on this first when you are arming for battle, that your power, even that of the body itself, is a gift of God, for in so doing you will not think of using the gift of God against God." Thus a Christian soldier would keep faith even with enemies, go to war only when necessary, and show mercy to the defeated and the captive.[217]

Although Augustine in this letter was seeking to reassure Boniface that a soldier could be a good Christian, perhaps because he realized that Boniface would have known better, he did not want to leave the impression that there was no spiritual downside to military service. One did not have to leave the military to be a good Christian, but one did if one wanted to be a better one. So, "it is true, they have a higher place before God who have forsaken all such worldly activities and serve Him with the utmost continence of chastity. . . .

216. *Epist.* 189.4 (133–34): "Noli existimare neminem deo placere posse, qui in armis bellicis militat. In his erat sanctus David, cui dominus tam magnum perhibuit testimonium, in his etiam plurimi illius temporis iusti. In his erat et ille centurio, qui domino dixit: *Non sum dignus, ut intres sub tectum meum, sed tantum dic verbo et sanabitur puer meus. Nam et ego homo sum sub potestate constitutus habens sub me milites et dico huic: 'Vade' et vadit, et alio: 'Veni' et venit, et servo meo: 'Fac hoc' et facit.* De quo et dominus: *Amen dico vobis; non inveni tantam fidem in Israhel.* In his erat et ille Cornelius, ad quem missus angelus dixit: *Corneli, acceptae sunt elemosynae tuae et exauditae sunt orationes tuae*; ubi eum admonuit, ut ad beatum Petrum apostolum mitteret et ab illo audiret, quae facere deberet; ad quem apostolum, ut ad eum veniret, etiam religiosum militem misit. In his erant et illi, qui baptizandi cum venissent ad Iohannem, sanctum domini praecursorem et amicum sponsi, de quo ipse dominus ait: *In natis mulierum non exsurrexit maior Iohanne Baptista,* et quaesissent ab eo, quid facerent, respondit eis: *Neminem concusseritis, nulli calumniam feceritis, sufficiat vobis stipendium vestrum.* Non eos utique sub armis militare prohibuit, quibus suum stipendium sufficere debere praecepit."

217. *Epist.* 189.6 (135): "Hoc ergo primum cogita, quando armaris ad pugnam, quia virtus tua etiam ipsa corporalis donum dei est; sic enim cogitabis de dono dei non facere contra deum." For more on this portion of the letter, see ch. 7, notes 140 to 145 below.

Some fight for you against invisible enemies by prayer, while you toil for them by fighting against visible barbarians."[218] We are still far from an ideology of the Crusades, when warfare was not merely tolerated within limits, but itself regarded as a religious act.

It is also true that a survey of Augustine's writings that focuses on his justifications for state-sanctioned killing and the licitness of Christian participation in it leaves a misleading impression of a certain bloody-mindedness on his part. On the issue of capital punishment, simply because he argued that legitimate authorities *could* execute criminals due to their having derived their authority ultimately from God does not mean that he thought they *should*. From early on, we see Augustine being sympathetic to the notion of avoiding the exaction of the ultimate penalty whenever possible. In 394 in his treatise *De mendacio* Augustine treated the question of whether a Christian should lie to conceal someone accused of murder, regardless of his innocence or guilt, since "it is part of Christian teaching not to despair of anyone's correction or to shut off to anyone the possibility of repentance." Augustine concluded that it is always wrong to lie. Nevertheless, he counsels a Christian who knows where a fugitive is to reply on being asked where, "I know but I will never reveal it," even on pain of torture.[219] One should go so far to preserve even the slightest possibility of someone's repentance, even in the case of murderers. Augustine's counsel here to go to such lengths to avoid the execution of criminals, regardless of their culpability, is at odds with the picture of him as the apologist for capital punishment.[220]

That the exercise of human justice involved moral conundrums was not only a theoretical consideration in Augustine's case. As bishop of Hippo, he heard cases daily in the episcopal court, and was a party to investigations and apprehensions involving capital crimes.[221] Some of the dilemmas he felt in his role as judge boil over into a letter to Paulinus of Nola in 408.

---

218. *Epist.* 189.5 (134): "Maioris quidem loci sunt apud deum, qui omnibus istis saecularibus actionibus derelictis etiam summa continentia castitatis ei serviunt. *Sed unusquisque*, sicut dicit apostolus, *proprium donum habet a deo alius sic alius autem sic* [1 Cor. 7:7]. Alii ergo pro vobis orando pugnant contra invisibiles inimicos, vos pro eis pugnando laboratis contra visibiles barbaros."

219. *De mendacio* 13,22, 24 (*CSEL* 41, 440–42, 443–44).

220. On Augustine and capital punishment, see also James J. Megivern, *The Death Penalty: An Historical and Theological Survey* (New York: Paulist, 1997), 35–45, and especially the conclusions summarized there of the work of Niceto Fernández Blázquez.

221. On the *episcopalis audientia*, see Jill Harries, *Law and Empire in Late Antiquity* (Cambridge: Cambridge University Press, 1999), 191–211.

What shall I say about punishing or not punishing, when we want it to be completely for their own good, in matters where the decision to punish or not is mine? In addition, what should be the extent of the punishment, not only taking into consideration the nature and degree of the crime, but also the strength of the convicted's spirit, what can each one endure, and what he should avoid, lest he not only not profit from it, but even suffer a relapse, how profound and intricate all these questions are! And as to the fear of impending punishment in the way men fear it, I don't know whether more are corrected by it than go off to something worse. What about when, as often happens, if you were to punish someone he would die, but if you were to leave him unpunished someone else would die? I confess that I sin and don't know what to do about this every day.[222]

Augustine's appreciation of the exquisite dilemmas involved in the exercise of human justice culminates in his bleak portrait of a secular judge in Book 19 of *The City of God*, a man who because of his position can be compelled to torture innocent people, who sometimes die under torture before their innocence is established, or who sometimes, to avoid further torture, confess to a crime they did not commit, and are as a result condemned and executed.[223]

Given the imperfections inextricably associated with human justice, it was incumbent upon human judges to exercise mercy. For

even in the case of those who punish crime, who are not driven by personal anger in the performance of their duties but act as agents of the law, who try and punish crimes not against themselves but others, as judges ought to do, divine judgment has inspired fear even in them, so that they might reflect upon the fact that they themselves have need of God's mercy because of their own sins and not suppose that they have fallen short in their duties if they act at all mercifully toward those over whom they have the lawful power of life and death.[224]

And clearly the greatest act of mercy for a judge is to spare the lives of those who have been sentenced to death, even if they deserve to die. In a sermon in 418 to an audience that apparently included secular judges, Augustine spoke

222. *Epist.* 95.3 (*CSEL* 34, 508).
223. *DCD* 19.6 (*CCL* 48, 670–71).
224. *Epist.* 153.8 (*CSEL* 44, 404).

explicitly against the imposition of the death penalty, urging the judges in his audience not to "go so far as death, that there may be someone left to repent. Don't let a human being be killed, that there may be someone left to be reformed."[225] In late 411 Augustine put his beliefs on this matter to the test in interceding with the authorities for the lives of certain Donatists who were awaiting execution and judicial retaliation for the murder of one Catholic priest and the mutilation of another. He wrote to his friend Marcellinus: "I beg you by your faith which you have in Christ, and through the mercy of our Lord Christ himself, neither to do this nor allow it to be done at all." Augustine is satisfied with the condemned receiving legal punishment, so long as they remain "alive and unmutilated in any part of their body," and thus can potentially receive the "medicine of penance."[226] Augustine repeated his plea for mercy in another letter to Marcellinus's brother Apringius, the *proconsul* of Africa and the man ultimately responsible for the fate of the condemned. "As a bishop I warn a Christian, as a Christian I appeal to a judge not to let this happen." The bishop, citing Rom. 13:4, admits that Apringius has the legitimate authority to apply the death penalty, but adds that the sufferings of the Catholic victims, which should serve as a profitable example to others, should not be defiled by the blood of their enemies.[227]

And yet despite his opposition to the actual exercise of capital punishment in contrast to its theoretical justification, Augustine apparently expressed no similar reservations about the killing that soldiers do as such. There is certainly a significant difference between the two cases. Whereas it was up to his discretion as to whether a judge had to execute a criminal, a soldier, as Augustine points out a number of times, has due to his subordinate position in society no real choice in the matter when acting under the orders of legitimate authority. In this respect his role was similar to that of the *carnifex* in that he acted as the tool of a higher authority, although it is surely significant that Augustine in writing on soldiers if anything at times expressed a certain admiration for them and nothing like the detestation and horror he felt for the executioner. When it comes to the military, the element of choice enters in with the original decision to go to war in the first place, the responsibility of rulers and commanders, and it is to Augustine's views on war that we now turn.

225. *Serm.* 13.8 (*PL* 38:110). On this passage, see *Augustine: Political Writings*, ed. E. M. Atkins and R. J. Dodaro (Cambridge: Cambridge University Press, 2001), 276, n. 12: "This is probably A.'s strongest statement against capital punishment in any of his writings."
226. *Epist.* 133.1 (*CSEL* 44, 81).
227. *Epist.* 134 (*CSEL* 44, 84–88).

7

Augustine on War

War as an Evil

While at Carthage in 419 for a council of African bishops, Augustine took advantage of the release from his onerous pastoral duties to write a work on certain interpretive *cruces* in the first seven books of the Bible, the *Quaestiones in Heptateuchum*.[1] In commenting on the remark in Joshua's farewell address to the Israelites that "they who lived in Jericho waged war against you" (Josh. 24:11), Augustine dealt with the question of how it could be said that the inhabitants of Jericho had waged war when all they had done was to close their city gates against the Israelites. Augustine insisted the statement was correct

> because the closing of gates against an enemy pertains to war, given that they had not sent emissaries to ask for peace. In that case if it had been said, "they fought against you," it would have been false. Keep in mind that war is not an uninterrupted succession of battles, but instead that they are sometimes frequent, sometimes rare, and sometimes there are none at all. To conclude, it is war when there is some kind of armed conflict.[2]

1. W. Rüting, "Untersuchungen über Augustins Quaestiones und Locutiones in Heptateuchum," *Forschungen zur Christlichen Literatur- und Dogmengeschichte* 13 (1916): 1–12; Alessandra Pollastri, *Sant'Agostino, Questioni sull'Ettateuco, Nuova Biblioteca Agostiniana, Opere di Sant'Agostino* 11:1 (Rome: Città Nuova, 1997), 290–97; Fitzgerald, "*Quaestiones in Heptateuchum*," 692–93.

2. *Quaestiones in Heptateuchum* 6.26 (CSEL 28:2, 444; CCL 33, 330): "*Et bellaverunt adversus vos qui habitabant Iericho. Quaeri potest quomodo id verum sit, cum clausis portis se murorum ambitu tantummodo tuerentur. Sed recte dictum est, quia et claudere adversum hostem portas, ad bellum pertinet. Non enim miserunt legatos qui poscerent pacem. Unde si dictum esset: Pugnaverunt adversum vos, falsum esset. Neque enim bellum continuas pugnas habet, sed aliquando crebras, aliquando raras, aliquando nullas. Bellum est tamen quando est quodam modo armata dissensio.*"

Josef Rief has argued that *bellum* for Augustine meant far more than the conflict on the battlefield between opposing armies, but spoke instead to a broader, basic principle of strife inherent in the world—somewhat analogous to the Darwinian struggle for existence—which is manifested also, for example, in the internal human battle between virtue and vice.[3] It is inarguable that Augustine used the word *bellum* to denote struggles other than war per se, just as he used such ideologically loaded words as *pax* and *victoria* in ways removed from their original political sense. But as with *pax* and *victoria*, it is not so much a case of Augustine using an extended conceptualization of *bellum* of which armed conflicts are a subset, but rather his establishment of derivative comparisons that gain force by being likened to their bloody original, war with all of its horrors. As his remark on Josh. 24:11 shows, Augustine knew very well what war was, and for him the meaning of *bellum* as large-scale armed conflict remained primary and largely consistent.

Augustine's attitude toward war, in fact, remained fairly constant, with little or no change discernible, in the almost three decades' worth of written evidence we possess on the matter. Far from his being the stance of a detached theoretician of war, in either the broader or the narrower sense of the word, the constancy in his attitude was one of abhorrence. Even in the few instances when he seemed to approve of war, Augustine felt compelled to defend such statements; ironically, those very statements ultimately motivated by his aversion to war later helped make him into its justifier. His most consistent attitude toward war Augustine expressed a number of times quite simply and straightforwardly: war was one of the evils of this world.

In his anti-Manichaean work *De natura boni*, written about 400 or soon thereafter, Augustine listed among good things (*bona*) peace, and balanced against peace in a list of evil things (*mala*) war, along with other evils such as death, disease, and poverty.[4] A decade later in *The City of God* he added famine to a similar list of evils that included war, and about a decade after that, near the very end of that lengthy work, he cataloged war among other evils that now included grief, fear, fraud, theft, envy, murder, adultery, incest, heresy, and blasphemy.[5] It is in the admittedly polemical context of the latter work, where in its first five books he could be accused of exaggerating the disasters of early Roman history in order to buttress his argument that the pagan gods

3. Josef Rief, *"Bellum" im Denken und in den Gedanken Augustins* (Barsbüttel: Institüt für Theologie und Frieden, 1990), esp. 5–24, 58–68.
4. *De natura boni* 41 (*CSEL* 25, 874–75).
5. *DCD* 3.1, 22.22 (*CCL* 47, 65; 48, 842).

had not helped Rome in its rise, that one finds Augustine's most passionate denunciations of war. In the First Punic War, one of those "rabid wars" (*ipsa rabida bella*) by which Rome had acquired dominion, the tide of success had swung back and forth, with countless soldiers and sailors dying in battles on land and sea, while entire cities and kingdoms were ruined or even wiped out, their lands devastated far and wide.[6] The Second Punic War had been even worse. This time Italy itself became the devastated battleground, with Roman disaster piled on disaster until the bloody massacre at Cannae, when even Hannibal's bloodlust was sated.[7] The period of those wars provided an admittedly extreme example of what is always true. For how can human beings ever be happy amidst the bloodshed and devastation of war, shadowed as they are by fear and bloodlust? Any joy they might feel at such times is "like the brittle sheen of glass, of which one has the terrible fear that it may be shattered at any moment."[8]

Even when years earlier Augustine had argued in another polemical context that, despite its horrors, war is sometimes necessary, his detestation of war threatened to get the better of him, and his argument. We have already seen how in Book 22 of *Contra Faustum* Augustine defended the wars of Moses against the attacks of his Manichaean opponent.[9] Not only had Moses been obedient to divine command in waging such wars, but God had used them to exact punishment upon those who richly deserved it.

> After all, what is it about war that deserves censure? Is it because in the course of pacifying an enemy they are conquering that some die who are going to die someday anyway? To find fault with this is the mark of cowardly, not religious men. The desire to do harm, cruelty in taking vengeance, a belligerent and unforgiving spirit, a savage rebelliousness, the lust to dominate, and anything similar—these are what are justly deserving of censure in war . . .[10]

---

6. *DCD* 3.18 (*CCL* 47, 85–56).

7. *DCD* 3.19 (*CCL* 47, 87).

8. *DCD* 4.3 (*CCL* 47, 100).

9. Chapter 6, notes 183, 184 above.

10. *Contra Faustum* 22.74 (*CSEL* 25, 672): "Quid enim culpatur in bello? An quia moriuntur quandoque morituri, ut domentur in pace victuri? Hoc reprehendere timidorum est non religiosorum. Nocendi cupiditas, ulciscendi crudelitas, inpacatus atque inplacabilis animus, feritas rebellandi, libido dominandi et si qua similia, haec sunt, quae in bellis iure culpantur . . ." For another take on this passage, see Mattox, 46–47.

Although he goes on to state that such evils justify good men in waging their own wars to suppress those very evils,[11] in conceding that there are evils attendant to war and then proceeding to list them, Augustine out of his inherent abhorrence of war appears to have gotten carried away a bit, providing a list constituting such a bald acknowledgment of war's horrors that to an extent it undercuts his case for defending the wars of Moses. Small wonder, then, that when later in *The City of God* Augustine wrote of created human nature as being midway between the angelic and the bestial, he observed that from the beginning God had foreseen "that the wild animals, though lacking a rational will, would live more safely and peaceably with their own kind than would humankind. . . . For never did lions or dragons wage such wars among themselves as have human beings."[12]

It is perhaps unsurprising that a Christian bishop, a follower of the Prince of Peace, would have abhorred war. Until the Vandal invasion at the end of his life brought it to his very doorstep, it is true there is no evidence for Augustine having directly witnessed war. Yet there were times throughout his public career when he confronted and had to deal with its effects,[13] and in a man of his compassion and imagination an animus against war was further enflamed by the mere report of it. Thus in late 409 we find him commiserating with the priest Victorian over the ravages committed by barbarians in Italy and Gaul, and now Spain, where clergy had been slain and nuns taken into captivity. Augustine noted in passing that a few years earlier, closer to home, the niece of the bishop of Setif had likewise been captured by barbarian raiders. In the midst of such tribulations the bishop of Hippo could only advise his correspondent to turn to Scripture for consolation.[14] Of course, the most prominent example in Augustine's lifetime of barbarians taking Christians captive occurred when the Goths took Rome in August 410.[15] All these calamities provided the most recent illustrations of another great evil of this life, slavery, yet another sorrowful consequence of war.[16] Such was war's ubiquity that Augustine noted how one could not help but be anxious for the welfare of one's friends, particularly acute

---

11. Below, notes 119, 120.

12. *DCD* 12.23 (*CCL* 48, 380).

13. As, for example, when he sold church plate to redeem captives, already a practice of commonplace virtue in the biographies of holy bishops. On Augustine's practice and its link to the earlier example set by Ambrose, see Possidius's *Vita Augustini* 24.14–16 (*Vite dei Santi* III, ed. and trans. A. A. R. Bastiaensen, Luca Caneli, and Carlo Carena [Milan: Fondazione Lorenzo Valla, 1975], 194).

14. *Epist.* 111 (*CSEL* 34, 642–57).

15. *DCD* 1.1,14,16 (*CCL* 47, 1–2, 15–16, 17–18).

16. *DCD* 19.15 (*CCL* 48, 682–83).

in his own case considering his farflung network of friends, prey as they were to the ever-present possibility of captivity and slavery.[17]

Although his lifetime saw far-ranging and sometimes spectacular hostilities by non-Roman groups deep within Roman territory, the so-called "barbarian invasions," until the end of his life the provincial Augustine, particularly as he lived at some distance from the frontier, was more likely to witness the effects of war in the series of civil wars that wracked the empire in the late fourth and early fifth centuries. These civil wars, as recent research has reemphasized, were often causally bound with the movements of barbarians—a significant example of this being the Vandal invasion of Roman Africa—and played no small role in the decline of the Western empire.[18] As is historically the case with civil wars, given that the opponents are equivalent in terms of military technology and tend to be more or less evenly matched, these conflicts are often bitterly contested, widespread, and costly in blood and treasure. With the severing of loyalties, the fault lines of society lie exposed. Old grievances are renewed and new ones engendered in an overall atmosphere rife with suspicion, an atmosphere that individuals exploit to settle old scores. Vengeance and violence become the norm, and while innocents are condemned, the guilty prosper.

All these phenomena are visible in the civil wars of Augustine's day. We have already seen how the closely matched struggle between Theodosius and the Western usurper Eugenius was settled at the bloody battle of the Frigidus in 394, a battle that, as we will see, made as profound an impression on Augustine as it did on other Christian contemporaries.[19] Both that war and the earlier contest with Magnus Maximus, involving as they did the Eastern half of the empire matched against the Western half, witnessed an intensive mobilization of resources on both sides that must have had deep and far-reaching economic consequences. Some idea of what must have been involved, and in particular a hint of the economic effects, may be gained from a passage in Eusebius's *Ecclesiastical History* on the early fourth-century civil wars, where he noted the widespread manufacture of armaments and emphasized the construction of ships for naval operations, all of which disrupted ordinary maritime commerce in the Mediterranean.[20] In the late 380s Maximus had employed a fleet in the war against Theodosius,[21] and when that fleet blockaded the harbors of Rome

17. *DCD* 19.8 (*CCL* 48, 672).

18. As can be seen, for example, in Matthew Innes, *Introduction to Early Medieval Western Europe, 300-900* (New York: Routledge, 2007), 82–88.

19. Chapter 3, notes 40 to 59 above; notes 177 to 208 below.

20. *HE* VIII.15 (786/788).

21. Orosius, 7.35.3–5 (*CSEL* 5, 525–26).

in late 387 Augustine witnessed firsthand the effects of civil war when he was forced to postpone his return to Africa and remain at Ostia, where his mother Monica died shortly afterward.[22] Later, situated as he was in the Mediterranean port of Hippo Regius, Augustine was in a good position not only to see the effects of civil war on commerce and the economy in general, but was also well posted to hear reports on the pernicious effects of civil wars in other parts of the empire. In 413 Augustine got a close-up view of how civil war can spread the virus of violence and vengeance beyond the battlefield. In the wake of the suppression of the *comes Africae* Heraclian's revolt that year, the consequent purge of Heraclian's supporters in Carthage caught up Augustine's friend Marcellinus, to whom he had dedicated *The City of God*. Despite his efforts and those of other churchmen, Marcellinus and his brother Apringius, both Roman officials whose involvement with Heraclian was arguably tenuous at best, were eventually executed.[23]

Augustine's personal acquaintance with both the direct and indirect consequences of the civil wars of his day helps to explain why he wrote at such length and with such passion on the civil wars of the Late Republic in *The City of God*, and helps to explain as well a similar attitude toward those wars in the history of his contemporary Orosius.[24] Those wars, as even the pagan historians admitted, had been bitterer than any foreign war.[25] "What fury of foreign nations, what savagery of barbarians can be compared with this victory of citizens over citizens?"[26] When Marius was at first victorious in his war against Sulla, the result was a Rome where the streets, markets, and temples were full of corpses.[27] Sulla's vengeance was if anything worse, and in the consequent purge of Marius's followers, when thousands were slain, torturers were reputed to have mutilated and torn to pieces their victims in a frenzy more violent than that of any wild beast. Of that time it could truly be said that peace was crueler than war, for while armed men died in war, peace slew men who were unarmed and defenseless.[28] Among the series of calamities that had befallen Rome in the centuries before Christ, in terms of their sheer evil the civil wars took first place.[29]

---

22. Brown, 121.

23. Brown, 337.

24. To my knowledge, this aspect of Augustine's and Orosius's discussion of the civil wars of the Late Republic has not received much scholarly attention.

25. *DCD* 3.30 (*CCL* 47, 96).

26. *DCD* 3.29 (95). Loeb translation by George E. McCracken.

27. *DCD* 3.27 (94).

28. *DCD* 3.28 (94–95).

War and Christianity

If war in all its forms is such a manifest evil, productive of so many other human evils such as poverty, slavery, violence, devastation, and death, since Christ had said "Blessed are the peacemakers" and had preached nonresistance to evil and love of one's enemies,[30] should not Christianity be a resolutely pacifist religion? This is a question then asked both by Christians, whether heretics or those of a more "orthodox" stripe, who believed that Christians in their newfound status in the empire had gone too far in accommodating themselves to war and participation in it, and by those outside the Christian fold who thought the religion had gone too far in the opposite direction in instilling a pacifistic spirit that would prove fatal to the state. The same question was asked later in similar terms, and is still asked today by the modern counterparts to the ancient critics, Christian and non-Christian, religious and nonreligious, of Christianity's stance on war. Augustine himself in the span of about a decade had the chance to confront two such attacks, one from the left flank and one from the right, so to speak. Unsurprisingly, his two responses bear significant commonalities, commonalities that demonstrate a noteworthy consistency and continuity in his thinking on war and in their content show how the seemingly straightforward precepts of the gospel actually bear an interpretation that is not so simple.[31]

Augustine spoke most directly and most at length on the phenomenon of war itself in his anti-Manichaean treatise *Contra Faustum*.[32] It is unsurprising that in all of his works, Augustine dealt most explicitly with the issue of war in the context of a polemic against Manichaeism, a religion whose cosmology featured an ongoing war between the forces of good and evil, light and darkness, and a religion as well whose Gnostic roots encouraged among its adherents an antipathy toward the often brutal warrior God of the Old Testament and a doctrinaire pacifism.[33] In Book 22, by Augustine's own acknowledgment the longest book in his work,[34] the bishop is responding to Faustus's criticisms

---

29. *DCD* 3.31 (97): "quod cuncta mala praecedit, bella illa civilia."

30. Matt. 5:9, 38-45.

31. On Augustine's explanation for the apparent changeableness in God regarding war, see also Mattox, 128–38.

32. On the date of *Contra Faustum*, see chapter 5, n. 10 above.

33. On Manichaeism in general, see S. N. C. Lieu, *Manichaeism in the Later Roman Empire and Medieval China* (Tübingen: J. C. B. Mohr, 1992).

34. *Retractationes* II, 7 (33), 1 (*CSEL* 36, 139; *CCL* 57, 95). By my reckoning Book 22 alone accounts for slightly over one-fifth of the text of the *Contra Faustum*.

that the behavior of the Old Testament patriarchs was inconsistent with the teachings of Christ in the New. Germane to our purpose here is Faustus's criticism of the actions of Moses. That patriarch had not only ordered but had personally carried out actions that included murder and the waging of a series of savage wars in which thousands of human beings had died.[35] Faustus, who at another point in his work had spoken of himself as being *pacificus* in conformance with Christ's injunction in the Beatitudes,[36] noted that Christ had retained the Decalogue commandment "Thou shalt not kill" from the old law[37] and that therefore that commandment was incontestably part of "what is truly the law,"[38] a law that Moses had broken, more than once. A Christianity that approved of such behavior, and by extension approved of the contemporary wars waged by supposedly Christian emperors and soldiers, was no real Christianity at all.

About a decade later Augustine found himself defending Christianity on the issue of war against an attack from the opposite end of the spectrum. This time Augustine's interlocutor was not a Christian heretic, but a pagan Roman. In 411 or 412 a certain Rufius Antonius Agrypnius Volusianus, an up-and-coming young man from a prominent and powerful Roman family, came to know Augustine and other leading Christians of North Africa while serving at Carthage as *proconsul Africae*. Although he was himself pagan, his mother, sister, and niece were Christian.[39] From the courteous tone of Augustine's correspondence with Volusianus and other evidence it seems that the bishop was anxious to avoid alienating such a potential convert, even though Volusianus for his part was not above lacing with a trace of gentle mockery his own skeptical inquiries to Augustine regarding the Incarnation and the Virgin Birth.[40]

In addition to such purely theological questions, Volusianus also in a conversation with Marcellinus, Augustine's high-ranking friend to whom the bishop would soon dedicate *The City of God*, had raised other issues having a more "political" edge, questions now given added force by the Gothic sack of Rome in August 410 and the presence in Carthage of aristocratic refugees

35. *Contra Faustum* 22.5 (*CSEL* 25, 595).

36. *Contra Faustum* 5.1 (271).

37. *Contra Faustum* 19.3 (498).

38. *Contra Faustum* 22.2 (591–93).

39. A. Chastagnol, "Le sénateur Volusien et la conversion d'une famille de l'aristocratie romaine au Bas-Empire," *Revue des études anciennes* 58 (1956): 241–53.

40. *Epist.* 135.2 (*CSEL* 44, 91–92); *Enchiridion* 34 (*CCL* 46, 69: "that eminent man Volusianus, whose name I mention with respect and affection"); Brown, 298–301.

from the disasters in Italy, many of whom were pagan.[41] It is to be expected that such individuals would have favored a rather straightforward religious explanation for the recent catastrophes. As long as Rome had maintained the *mos maiorum*, the customs and religious rituals hallowed by antiquity, the empire had prospered. But when Romans abandoned the ancestral religion and embraced this newfangled superstition of Christianity, the gods had withdrawn their divine assistance and disaster soon followed. Although he clearly sympathized with such sentiments, Volusianus in his objections to Christianity was not content with referring the causes for Rome's recent troubles solely to the supernatural plane. Quite apart from any attempted interpretation of the ambiguities of divine will, surely it was evident that the very teachings of the new religion's founder, especially insofar as they were actually realized in practice, were detrimental to the empire.

As reported by Marcellinus in a letter to Augustine, Volusianus had argued that Christ's

> preaching and teaching is incompatible at any point with the usages of the state, to wit (as is said by many), as in the case of his well-known commandment that we ought not to return evil for evil to anyone, and to turn the other cheek when anyone strikes us, and to give up our cloak when anyone takes our tunic, and when anyone forces us to go with him, we should go twice as far; all of which he asserts is contrary to the usages of the state. For who could allow anything to be taken from him by an enemy, or who would not in accordance with the law of war want to return evil upon those who ravage a Roman province?

It is manifest that evils have befallen the empire even though Christian emperors on the whole have been observant of the Christian religion.[42]

Regarding Faustus's objections, Augustine concedes that there is certainly an appearance of inconsistency between the teachings of the Old Testament

---

41. Brown, 298–301.

42. *Epist.* 136.2 (*CSEL* 44, 95): ". . . eius praedicatio atque doctrina rei publicae moribus nulla ex parte conveniat, utpote sicuti a multis dicitur, cuius hoc constat esse praeceptum, ut nulli malum pro malo reddere debeamus et percutienti aliam praebere maxillam et pallium dare tunicam tollere persistenti et cum eo, qui nos angariare voluerit, ire debere spatio itineris duplicato, quae omnia rei publicae moribus adserit esse contraria. Nam quis tolli sibi ab hoste aliquid patiatur vel Romanae provinciae depraedatori non mala velit belli iure reponere? . . . Haec ergo omnia ipsi posse iungi aetimat quaestioni in tantum, ut per Christianos principes Christianum religionem maxima ex parte servantes tanta, etiam si ipse de hac parte taceat, rei publicae mala evenisse manifestum sit."

and the New. As the bishop preferred to express it, whereas the Old Testament patriarchs and prophets had by waging wars taught that God was capable, as was reputed to be the case with the pagan gods, of granting military victories to his people, the martyrs of New Testament times and later had been slain without offering any resistance to show that it was a preferable victory to die for the true faith.[43] Augustine had to answer a similar objection of inconsistency among the later assertions of Volusianus, who had argued that the God of the New Testament had been inconsistent and even fickle in rejecting the sacrifices of the Old, an especially grievous inconsistency since from the viewpoint of veneration for the *mos maiorum* a long-established religious practice was presumed to be correct and should not be changed.[44] In responding to both critics, Augustine stated as a fundamental principle the idea that divine providence, operating according to a rationally thought-out plan (*ratio*), a plan the details of which are hidden from mortal ken, throughout all of time changes what is required of humankind according to what is suitable for any particular time (*pro temporum opportunitate*), effecting those changes while it itself—the divine plan of providential action—remains changeless.[45] This is possible because God, who created time, on account of his eternity is literally timeless, therefore cannot in any sense ever be new, although new things do exist in the created temporality, arranged by God according to the particularities of different times.[46] "God is not changeable because at one period of the entirety of history in an earlier Book [the Old Testament] He ordered one sort of offering to be made to Him and another sort to be offered at a later period."[47] When the reason for something is no longer valid because of changed temporal circumstances, the *vera ratio* requires that the thing be changed.[48] Thus to answer Volusianus's charge of inconsistency in the matter of sacrifice, "the sacrifice which God had commanded was appropriate in those

43. *Contra Faustum* 22.76 (676).

44. *Epist.* 136.2 (*CSEL* 44, 94–95).

45. *Epist.* 138.2 (127, 128): "rerum ipsa natura et opera humana certa ratione pro temporum opportunitate mutentur nec tamen eadem ratio sit mutabilis, qua ista mutantur . . . haec omnia mutantur nec mutatur divinae providentiae ratio, qua fit, ut ista mutentur"; 138.8 (132–33): "quod recte alio tempore constitutum est, itidem recte alio tempore posse mutari mutantis opere non dispositione mutata."

46. *Epist.* 138.7 (132): "quod in tempore novum est, non esse novum apud eum, qui condidit tempora et sine tempore habet omnia, quae suis quibusque temporibus pro eorum varietate distribuit."

47. *Epist.* 138.7 (131): "ita non ideo mutabilis deus, quia universi saeculi priore volumine aliud aliud posteriore sibi iussit offerri."

48. *Epist.* 138.4 (129): "mutata quippe temporis causa, quod recte ante factum fuerat, ita mutari vera ratio plerumque flagitat."

early times, but now it is not so. Therefore, He prescribed another one which is appropriate for these times."[49] As to the charge of inconsistency coming from Faustus and his followers, "Do they now understand how commandments or counsels or permissions are changed without any inconsistency on the part of the one giving the commands but in accord with God's providence for different times?"[50]

Given the underlying consistency of divine purpose throughout time, was it possible for mere mortals to understand what lay behind what seemed the specific contradictions in the times involved? Augustine believed as a matter of faith that God had left clues in Scripture, however faint and difficult to discern, to enable human beings to glimpse a way to reconcile such apparent inconsistencies. In leaving such clues, God for his own purposes intentionally made it difficult for human beings to interpret the Scriptures.[51] The most important interpretive approach among Augustine's contemporary Christians recognized that the Old Testament preserved types, incomplete though signifying precursors of what would eventually be fully realized in the New Testament.[52] But the typological approach was not the only possible means of interpretation. In attempting to reconcile the apparent inconsistencies between Christ's precepts and Christian accommodation to war in *Contra Faustum* and in Letter 138 to Marcellinus, Augustine spoke in both works of the "preparation of the heart" (*praeparatio cordis*). This expression is central to Augustine's efforts to resolve the seeming contradiction between the gospel message of peace and Christian acceptance of war.

Augustine at one point in *Contra Faustum* confronted directly the Manichaean assertion that Christ's injunction to "turn the other cheek" ruled out Christian participation in war.

> If, however, they [the Manichaeans] think that God could not have commanded the waging of war because the Lord Jesus Christ later said, *I tell you not to resist evil, but if anyone strikes you on your right cheek, offer him your left as well* [Matt. 5:39], let them understand that

---

49. *Epist.* 138.5 (130): "Aptum fuit primis temporibus sacrificium, quod praeceperat deus, nunc vero non ita est. Aliud enim praecepit, quod huic tempori aptum esset . . ."

50. *Contra Faustum* 22.77 (Teske trans.; *CSEL* 25, 677): "Iamne intellegunt, quemadmodum nulla inconstantia praecipientis, sed ratione dispensantis pro temporum diversitate praecepta vel consilia vel permissa mutentur?"

51. Dodaro (ch. 6, n. 169 above), 135.

52. The best guide here remains Jean Daniélou, *Sacramentum Futuri* (Paris: Beauchesne, 1950); Eng. trans. *From Shadows to Reality* (London: Burns & Oates, 1960).

this is not preparation in the body, but in the heart. For in the heart is found the holy chamber of the virtue that also dwelled in those righteous men of old, our fathers.[53]

Here the *praeparatio cordis* is to be understood as an aspect of typology.[54] *Praeparatio* refers, as it were, to the potentiality of a seed, at first hidden in the recesses of the earth, which at the appropriate time will come into full bloom. It was the *ordo temporum* which required that this potentiality be originally hidden in the hearts of the Old Testament patriarchs and prophets and not manifested in exterior actions, so that they then were not only not pacifists but waged successful wars against their enemies. For it was first necessary for the minds of human beings in their primitive, childish ignorance to learn that it was the one true God and not any pagan deity who was responsible for providing earthly goods such as human kingdoms and victories over enemies.

For this reason the Old Testament, with its earthly promises, veiled and, in a certain sense, wrapped in deep shadows the secret of the kingdom of heaven, which was to be revealed at the proper time. But when the fullness of time came, so that the New Testament, which was veiled by symbols of the Old, might be revealed, it had now to be shown by clear testimony that there was another life, for whose sake it was necessary to endure most patiently the opposition of all earthly kingdoms.[55]

Those who had "to endure most patiently the opposition of all earthly kingdoms" were the martyrs, who by their righteous sufferings demonstrated that, due to the later differences in the *ordo temporum*, it was for them better to die than to kill for the true faith.[56] Yes, there does *seem* to be a contradiction between the behavior of the patriarchs and that of the martyrs, but after

---

53. *Contra Faustum* 22.76 (*CSEL* 25, 674; Teske trans., modified).

54. Although I accept Dodaro's interpretation of the phrase *praeparatio cordis* in *Epist.* 138 (n. 63 below), he doesn't convince me in interpreting as *not* being an example of moral casuistry Augustine's reply using the same phrase in *Contra Faustum* 22.76 specifically to the Manichaean criticism of Old Testament wars, although such a casuistic interpretation seems to follow naturally from the text. Indeed, I am not sure but that the exact signification of the phrase, in both *Contra Faustum* and *Epist.* 138, continues to be a bit of a mystery. The expression comes from Ps. 9:38, "desiderium pauperum exaudivit Dominus: praeparationem cordis eorum audivit auris tua" ("The Lord hath heard the desire of the poor: thy ear hath heard the preparation of their heart"), a verse that sheds little light on Augustine's use of the phrase.

55. *Contra Faustum* 22.76 (674–75; Teske trans.).

56. *Contra Faustum* 22.76 (675–76).

explaining how this apparent contradiction could be resolved in view of the changes in the times, Augustine asks rhetorically of his Manichaean interlocutors "why do they not admit that for some hidden reason one and the same God then commanded the prophets to wage war and now forbids the apostles to do so?"[57]

In responding to Volusianus's charge that Christ had preached pacifism, Augustine not only argued that such counsels in the Gospels should not always be taken literally, he also accused the pagan Romans of being themselves in their words and actions inconsistent with and positively harmful to their own principles and ideals. As to Christ's exhortation to forgive one's enemies, Augustine pointed out that the ancient Romans had lauded the same disposition in themselves, citing Sallust and Cicero's praise of Caesar in that he never forgot anything except the wrongs done to him.[58] Was it not hypocritical for Romans to praise such conduct in themselves, but criticize the very same precept when it was preached from Christian pulpits?[59] In criticizing Christians for preaching the forgiveness of their enemies, the Romans criticized themselves, and were unfaithful to the very *mos maiorum* that Volusianus had adduced against Christianity. Augustine in defending Christ's injunction to forgive one's enemies aimed, to begin with, to demonstrate that its literal application tends to the preservation of domestic peace, as can be shown even from pagan authorities.[60] When someone is wronged by another person who takes something from him and does not exact vengeance in return, the former by his patient sufferance of his injury instructs the latter by example on the contemptible value of the temporal goods taken, and thereby, hopefully, through the latter's repentance and reform restores *concordia*, the harmonious reconciling of individual desires for the common good that binds together the political community, the *res publica*.[61] Otherwise, if those who are wronged indulge their passion for revenge, breaking the bonds of *concordia*, the Romans end up imitating the discord among the false gods they worship, and the result, both in the Late Republic and in Augustine's own day, is civil war.[62]

---

57. *Contra Faustum* 22.77 (Teske trans.; 677). Since Augustine, as we have already seen, explicitly allowed for Christians to serve as soldiers, it is tempting to regard this statement that apostles are "at present" (*nunc*) forbidden to wage war as at least partially referring to the prohibition of clerical participation in war.

58. *Epist.* 138.9 (*CSEL* 44, 134).

59. *Epist.* 138.10 (134–35).

60. Augustine's application of Christ's pacific precepts to the preservation of domestic peace occupies *Epist.* 138.9–12 (133–38).

61. *Epist.* 138.10–11 (135–37).

But, as Volusianus had argued, surely the literal application of Christian forbearance in the face of foreign invasion would be injurious, not beneficial, to the *concordia* of the state. In addressing this concern Augustine played on another shade of meaning of *praeparatio cordis*. For not only were there seeming inconsistencies between the Old Testament and the New, but even within the New Testament itself there were apparent inconsistencies between Christ's bald injunction to turn the other cheek, and both his own behavior and that of Paul when they were struck on the face during interrogation. It was the very act of a Christian wrestling to reconcile these apparent inconsistencies that constituted a *praeparatio cordis*, a preparation or training of the heart in learning to harmonize what seemed at first discordant notes into the melodious song of divine justice, which could not be expressed directly and transparently but only indirectly discerned, and that only in part. It was this *praeparatio cordis* as interpretative exercise that provided the internal moral guide for external acts in conformance with divine justice.[63]

So, when Augustine at last turned to consider how to preserve foreign as opposed to domestic peace in light of "turn the other cheek," he wrote:

> In the final analysis, these precepts refer more to the internal preparation of the heart than to the external act; consequently, forbearance in conjunction with goodness should be kept hidden in the mind, but be acted out openly whenever it seems possible it would benefit those for whom we ought to wish well.[64]

Augustine goes on to adduce the example of Christ himself, who when struck on the face during his questioning before the high priest had not literally turned the other cheek, but had in fact rebuked the one who had struck him lest he compound his already grievous offense (John 18:22-23). Though Christ in this instance had not followed his own precept in terms of the external act, that he held to the injunction internally was proved later by his readiness to forgive those who crucified him (Luke 23:34). Likewise, when Paul during his own interrogation before the high priest had been struck on the face, he not only did not turn the other cheek, but rounded on his tormentors with words that, according to Augustine, dripped with insult and mockery from beginning to end (Acts 23:3-5).[65]

62. *Epist.* 138.10 (135–36).

63. Dodaro (ch. 6, note 169 above), 133–39.

64. *Epist.* 138.13 (*CSEL* 44, 138).

65. *Epist.* 138.13 (138–39).

Having established that "turn the other cheek" should not always be followed literally, while it should always be preserved as the internal mainspring of external acts, Augustine then turns to show how the injunction could be applied in the case of war.

> So those precepts of forbearance should always be retained in the preparation of the heart, and the same goes for kindness, which, lest evil be returned for evil, should always be perfected in the will. In point of fact, many things even have to be done with a sort of kind harshness in punishing some against their will, out of consideration for what is their own good rather than what they want.

Once again, Augustine in this context invokes the image of a father who harshly punishes his son out of love. If only the empire would truly take Christ's precepts to heart, then "even wars themselves would not be waged without kindness," and those vanquished by the empire would end up living peacefully in a pious and just society.[66] Clearly, then, Christian teaching did not condemn all wars, just as John the Baptist had not condemned soldiers for their military service per se.[67]

War and Providence

It is easy to see what especially Manichaeans would have made of such arguments. For if war, as Augustine believed and wrote, was one of the great evils of this world, how could God, whom Augustine himself frequently identified with the highest good, the *summum bonum*,[68] or those who worshiped him in truth have anything to do with it? Augustine's response to this question takes us further into his understanding, such as it was, of the workings of divine providence in this world, and ultimately to a consideration of how some wars could even partake of divine justice.[69]

That God decides the fates of kingdoms and the outcome of the wars that often determine those fates is apparent from Scripture. The specific language Augustine used to express this aspect of the workings of providence, however,

---

66. *Epist.* 138.14 (139–40).

67. *Epist.* 138.15 (141): "Nam si Christiana disciplina omnia bella culparet, hoc potius militibus consilium salutis petentibus in evangelio diceretur, ut abicerent arma seque militiae, omnino subtraherent," etc. On this passage, ch. 6, notes 186, 187, 203 above.

68. E.g., *Conf.* 7.4 (6) (*CSEL* 33, 145; *CCL* 27, 95).

69. On war and providence in Augustine, see also Mattox, 32–36.

and even something of the conceptual framework behind such language can be seen earlier in the Latin apologetic tradition. In his own great apologetic work *The City of God*, Augustine in particular reaches back two centuries to Tertullian's *Apologeticum*,[70] understandably so in the instances where both writers were arguing that it was God and not some pagan deity or deities who controlled the course of history. Did the pagans really think that it was their gods who were in charge?

> Look out, then, that it is not He who doles out kingdoms, whose is both the world which is ruled and the human beings themselves who rule; that it is not He who set in order the succession of empires in every period of history, who before there was even any time created the structure of time that is history.[71]

At one point in *The City of God*, Augustine lists some of the things God bestows upon both good and evil people in this life and in this world, "which also include empires of every size, which He doles out in accordance with His control of time."[72] The use of the verb *dispensare* by both writers calls to mind its original setting in the actions of the money managers of the household who would weigh out varying sums at different times, perhaps according to a predetermined plan, in order to meet various expenses as they occurred;[73] likewise, God at different points in history disburses the fates of kingdoms, a disbursement that would vary according to the *ordo temporum* which he himself had created. A similar notion and vocabulary had earlier appeared in *Contra Faustum* when Augustine sought to explain against his Manichaean opponents the apparent inconsistency between the wars of the Old Testament and the pacific spirit of the New. Although God had not changed, the circumstances of the temporal order had, and thus "the order of the times demanded that arrangement and distribution of events."[74]

---

70. O'Daly, 40–52, tends to minimize Tertullian's direct influence on *The City of God*, but as in the case of Lactantius (ch. 6, notes 173, 174 above) this conclusion may need some revision.

71. Tertullian, *Apologeticum* 26.1 (*CSEL* 69, 74): "Videte igitur, ne ille regna dispenset, cuius est et orbis qui regnatur et homo ipse qui regnat; ne ille vices dominantium ipsis temporibus in saeculo ordinarit, qui ante omne tempus fuit et saeculum corpus temporum fecit."

72. *DCD* 5.26 (*CCL* 47, 162–63): ". . . in quibus est etiam quaelibet imperii magnitudo, quam pro temporum gubernatione dispensat."

73. Lewis and Short, *s.v. dispensare* and *dispensatio*.

74. *Contra Faustum* 22.76 (*CSEL* 25 [Teske trans.]; 674): "eam rerum dispensationem ac distributionem temporum ordo poscebat."

But if God as the helmsman of history is indeed the highest good, the *summum bonum*, how does one explain the fact that throughout history he has at times doled out success to evil empires such as that of the Assyrians? Could it be that there really is no direction of history's course, that it is merely the product of random chance, "one damned thing after another"?

> God, therefore, the author and giver of happiness, because He is the only true God, himself gives earthly kingdoms to the good and the bad. This is not done rashly or at random, for He is God, not Fortuna, the goddess of chance. He does this in accordance with an order of things and of times which is hidden from us but very well known to Him. Yet He is not in subjection, to be a slave to this order of times, but He rules it as Lord, and dispenses it as Master. But as for happiness, He gives it only to the good. Those who are servants may gain it or fail to gain it, just as those who are rulers may gain it or fail to gain it, but it will be complete only in that life where no one will any longer be a servant. And so earthly kingdoms are granted by Him both to the good and to the evil, in order that His worshippers, who are still as little children in the growth of their minds, may not covet these gifts from Him as if they were something great.[75]

Echoing a sentiment he had voiced a decade earlier in *Contra Faustum*, where he had explained the secreting away internally of God's pacific counsels among the Old Testament patriarchs as a necessary concession to the immature conceptions of primitive human beings,[76] but now extending that human immaturity to the present, Augustine would have us know that political power is not, as many think, something to be desired, but is simply one more perishable thing of this world, the possession of which cannot yield true happiness. In the end, as to why evil empires occasionally appear, human beings are too close to history to be able with confidence to discern the overall pattern of events, the *ordo temporum*, and are in any case incapable even of accurately assessing whether a particular polity is truly good or bad, a mortal incapacity Augustine explicitly confesses to sharing.

> Although I have discussed some points that God has chosen to make clear to me, still it is too great a task, and one far surpassing my

---

75. *DCD* 4.33 (*CCL* 47, 126 [William M. Greene trans. in Loeb, slightly modified]).
76. Note 55 above.

strength, to search into the secrets of human affairs and by a clear test to pass judgment on the merits of kingdoms.[77]

Still, one thing is clear about the role of providence in history. The fate of kingdoms is "not outside God's providence, in whose power exists the possibility of anyone to conquer or to be conquered in war."[78]

In fact, Augustine believed that it was precisely in war and its effects, even its evil effects, that one could determine some of the rationale behind the workings of providence. In a passage that has been dated to as early as 391, he wrote that "every tribulation is either a punishment of the impious or a testing of the just"—an interpretation supported by his derivation of *tribulatio* from *tribula*, a threshing sledge—and Augustine repeatedly reverted to this idea in subsequent writings to explain the providential role of war in human history.[79] About a decade later in *Contra Faustum* he invoked the idea to account for the slaughter of thousands of human beings in the wars of the Old Testament, wars that were necessarily effected by divine providence since it is sovereign throughout the universe, as even pagans acknowledged.[80] God was conceived of using war like a farmer's pruning knife in tending to his vines:[81]

> For that sovereign cultivator of the vine readies the pruning knife in one way for fruitful branches and in another way for barren branches. Yet He does not spare either the good or the evil, in order to purify the former and to cut away the latter. For no human being is endowed with such great righteousness that he does not need the test of tribulation either to make his virtue perfect or to strengthen it and to test it.[82]

In going on to cite the "thorn in my flesh" of Paul as an example of tribulation testing the righteous, Augustine sought to refute the Manichaean assertion

---

77. *DCD* 5.21 (*CCL* 47, 157 [Greene trans.]). See also *Contra Faustum* 22.72 and 78 (*CSEL* 25, 670, 679) on the ultimately hidden nature of divine justice.

78. *DCD* 18.2 (*CCL* 48, 593).

79. *De diversis quaestionibus LXXXIII* 27 (*CCL* 44A, 33): "Sed cum omnis tribulatio aut poena impiorum sit aut exercitatio iustorum, quia eadem tribula et paleas concidit et frumenta a paleis exuit, unde tribulatio nomen accepit." Translation by David L. Mosher, *Saint Augustine: Eighty-Three Different Questions, The Fathers of the Church* (Washington, DC: Catholic University of America Press, 1982), 52; chronology, intro., 20.

80. *Contra Faustum* 22.19, 78 (*CSEL* 25, 607, 678).

81. The figure is derived from John 15:1-2.

82. *Contra Faustum* 22.20 (608; Teske translation).

that an all-good God could not be responsible for anything evil. Given that Paul wrote that he had been afflicted to prevent him from taking pride in his revelations, since "virtue is made perfect in weakness" (2 Cor. 12:7-9), how could the Manichaeans say that the god responsible for evil had afflicted the apostle for what was in the end a good purpose?[83] If God had imposed such tribulation upon a holy apostle, it was understandable that he would employ even war to test Christians of lesser virtue, as well as to punish the wicked.

> He does not slay thousands of persons for no sins at all or only for slight ones that they have committed, but in His most just judgment He imposes upon peoples through the temporal deaths of mortals a beneficial fear of himself. He does not in blind confusion punish indiscriminately the just and the sinners, but He distributes to the just a salutary rebuke for the sake of their perfection and to sinners a due severity for the sake of equity.[84]

In *The City of God* Augustine also argued that not only the time in history when wars occurred but also their severity and duration revealed something of their providential purpose, such varying characteristics of war thereby providing various lessons to humankind, the most important being that it was God and not any pagan deity or deities who was ultimately in charge.

> The periods of warfare also are fixed in accordance with His will and just judgment and mercy, either to chasten or to comfort the human race; thus some wars are finished more quickly, others more slowly.[85]

Having previously argued that the disastrous wars of Roman history before Christ had demonstrated the impotence of the pagan gods in bringing success in war,[86] Augustine now showed that there was no correlation between the supposedly greater virtue of the early Romans—owing to their superior piety then vis-à-vis the gods—and the duration of wars. For the further back in time, the longer and more disastrous the wars had been. The Second Punic War had lasted eighteen years, outdone by the First Punic War that had lasted twenty-three. Further back, the Samnite war had lasted almost fifty years, and had featured a catastrophe without parallel before or since of a Roman

83. *Contra Faustum* 22.20 (608–9).
84. *Contra Faustum* 22.21 (611).
85. *DCD* 5.22 (*CSEL* 47, 158; Green trans.). The same sentiment occurs at *DCD* 7.30 (211).
86. *DCD* 3.13–30 (*CCL* 47, 74–96).

army passing under the yoke.[87] By contrast, in 405/6, only a few years before Augustine wrote this section in *The City of God* and well within the *tempora Christiana* lamented by pagans as the period of Christian supremacy fraught with peril because of the desertion of the traditional gods,[88] the invasion of Italy by the king of the Goths Radagaisus had been crushed so swiftly and in such a miraculous manner as not only to betray the workings of providence in that defeat but also forcibly to convey certain lessons to those willing to pay attention.[89] Radagaisus, whose army was huge, was said to sacrifice daily to the gods, and the pagans of Italy reportedly thought he could therefore not be defeated by men, viz., the Christian regime of the Western empire, who neither worshiped the gods nor allowed their worship. But in the space of one day Radagaisus was defeated so thoroughly that not a single Roman was killed or wounded, while over one hundred thousand of his followers were slain.[90] The lesson that divine providence sought to teach by this was clear, both to those being chastened and those being tested.

> In this way the true master and helmsman of reality both scourged the Romans mercifully and at the same time showed to the worshippers of demons by such an unparalleled defeat that their sacrifices were not indispensable for present-day security, with the result that those who do not stubbornly contend with the facts but rather prudently attend to them will not desert the true religion because of present-day crises, and will hold onto it all the more in the most trustworthy expectation of eternal life.[91]

Unquestionably Augustine's most striking example of God using war as both punishment and test is his providential interpretation of the sack of Rome by the Goths in August 410. In sermons delivered shortly after the event, the bishop urged the faithful to regard the sack as constituting for them a "training through tribulations" (*exercitatio tribulationum*),[92] and yet again reverted to his figure of a loving father punishing and thereby correcting his son.[93] When a

87. *DCD* 5.22 (158).

88. *DCD* 5.22 (158–59).

89. On Radagaisus's invasion, Zosimus 5.26.3–5, in *Zosime: Histoire Nouvelle* III1, ed. François Paschoud (Paris, 1986), 39–40 and n. 57, 202–4. On the chronology, Matthews (ch. 6, n. 31 above), 274 and n. 5.

90. *DCD* 5.23 (159). Radagaisus's invasion is also treated at *Serm.* 105.13 (*PL* 38:624–25), again as punishment for the pagans and purification for Christians.

91. *DCD* 5.23 (160).

92. *Serm.* 105.13 (*PL* 38:625).

year or so later he commenced the composition of *The City of God*, Augustine turned more explicitly and summarily to the discernible role of providence in the recent disaster, writing that the sufferings of the Romans should

> be attributed to that divine providence which is wont to chastise and pulverize corrupted human morals through wars, and at the same time by such afflictions to test those of humanity leading just and praiseworthy lives, and to transfer those who have passed the test to a better world or to keep them still on this earth for other uses.[94]

Just War

The fundamental part played by God in regulating the occurrence and duration of wars for providential ends colors Augustine's view of the just war. Here it must be noted that judging by the number of times the term *iustum* or *iniustum bellum* occurs in the Augustinian corpus, it was a relatively minor matter of interest to the African Father even within the narrower scope of the material in his works on war and military service.[95] The situation is further complicated by the fact that at times Augustine meant different things by the term, depending on the context. At times he did with just war what he did similarly with other terms such as *gloria*, *victoria*, and *pax* that were also basic elements of Roman political ideology, that is, he transposed the term from a Roman into a Christian key. In a Christian guise, just war could denote a war waged for justice or righteousness, a war that by that fact necessarily involved divine activity. Understandably so in light of the fact that the term almost always appears in a polemical context, Augustine by such an act of rhetorical

93. *De excidio urbis Romae* (PL 40:716–24).

94. *DCD* 1.1 (*CCL* 47, 2).

95. Well assessed in David A. Lenihan, "The Just War Theory in the Work of Saint Augustine," *Augustinian Studies* 19 (1988): 55: "Any analysis of Augustine must acknowledge that the corpus of Augustine's written work is immense. Migne's *Patrologiae Latinae* devotes twelve large tomes to Augustine, more than any other writer, the close second being Jerome with eleven volumes. In this ocean of words the just war is mentioned in but a few scattered references. . . . The just war theory is clearly a minor aspect of Augustine's work. He did not perceive it as a major problem worthy of the fuller treatment he gave to issues of doctrine such as the Trinity, Grace, Original Sin, Predestination and Free Will." By my count, in those small-print Migne tomes, forms of *iustum bellum* occur sixteen times (*Contra Faustum* 22.74; *DCD* 2.17, 4.15 [three times], 19.7 [three times], 19.15; *Quaestiones in Heptateuchum* I.167, IV.44, VI.10 [five times]) and forms of *iniustum bellum* twice (*Contra Faustum* 22.74; *DCD* 2.17).

transposition was criticizing—sometimes implicitly, sometimes explicitly—the original Roman just war idea, which was at best an inferior good of the earthly city.

Augustine, in fact, ultimately came to argue explicitly that there were two types of just war, the one waged at the instigation and under the direction of God—these being primarily though not exclusively the wars of the Old Testament—and wars fought at the behest of human beings. Having never written a treatise specifically on just war, it is understandable that though he explicitly differentiates these two types, the distinction is not systematic and clearcut, especially given the human agency involved in even divinely instigated wars. There is hence occasionally some terminological confusion between the use of just war to denote conflicts fought for the ends of divine justice and its use to mean the more "secular" Roman just war. In what follows, it is good to keep in mind that this lack of terminological rigor means that although at times one can read Augustine as giving a divine imprimatur to the Roman just war, any such statements are always subservient to polemical ends, one of which is a criticism of the very Roman just war concept. Perhaps a better way to reframe the terminological and interpretative issues involved is to place at the center Augustine's sphere of wars waged for justice—a sphere that can be conceptualized without sharp distinctions between them as consisting of wars instigated by God and man respectively—and to place at the side the Roman just war, which has some overlap with the human-instigated wars of justice. But although such a scheme might help in visualizing the interpretive issues involved, it does so by imposing a scheme where none is visible in Augustine's works themselves.

Augustine explicitly linked God-originated wars to just wars in 419 in a passage in *Quaestiones in Heptateuchum*. Centuries later this passage was cited by Gratian to define just wars, and a sentence from it by Thomas Aquinas for the requirement that a just war must have a just cause.[96] From its medieval beginnings until today, the interpretation of this text within the framework of the Christian just war idea evidences little interest in Augustine's original intent of distinguishing God-originated wars as a special category, or in the text's polemical context. For the passage under consideration, as is true throughout the *Quaestiones in Heptateuchum* but in this passage more explicitly than is often the case, reflects a polemical debate with one of Augustine's opponents, here the Manichaeans.[97] As we have seen before, the position he is arguing against has to

---

96. *Corpus iuris canonici* I, *Decretum magistri Gratiani*, ed. Emil Friedberg (Leipzig, 1879), II c.23 q.2 c.2 (col. 894–95); *S. Thomae de Aquino Summae Theologiae Secunda Secundae* (Ottawa: Commissio Piana, 1953), II-II q.40 a.1 (1633a).

be read in a mirror in Augustine's response. In line with their rejection of the Old Testament, its patriarchs, and its bloodthirsty God, the Manichaeans could point to Joshua's destruction of Ai and the wholesale slaughter of its inhabitants, a crime made worse by the subterfuge and deception employed by the Israelites in accomplishing it, they having secretly placed a force beyond the city that took it from the rear when its defenders were drawn out by a feigned retreat of the main body of the Israelites in front (Josh. 8:1-29). How could the deeds of such a God, imbued as they were with blood and deceit, possibly be defended, and how could Augustine, who had written treatises arguing that lying was always wrong under any circumstance, possibly defend the deception involved?

Augustine begins his response with the assertion—betraying thereby an affinity but not identity with the so-called realist ethical stance that "all's fair in love and war"[98]—that the justice of a war is not affected by the employment of a stratagem such as an ambush.

> When God in speaking to Joshua commands him to lay an ambush in the rear, that is, ambushing warriors to ambush the enemy, let us keep in mind that this is not unjustly done by those who are waging a just war, and that a just man in particular, for whom it is right to wage war (for it is not right for everyone), should think on nothing other than the undertaking of a just war. But once he has undertaken a just war, it makes no difference as to its justice whether he prevails in open battle or by ambush.[99]

Note that here Augustine states his consistently held position on military service that we saw in the previous chapter, that not just anyone is legitimately empowered to engage in war. For a just man (*homo iustus*), a category that we will see Augustine developed more fully elsewhere, the presence or lack of stratagem in battle is immaterial as long as it occurs in a just war.

It seems that with such a position Augustine is appealing with approval to a contemporary understanding of the just war. At first it is unclear how it helps his case to do so here, since the Manichaeans he was arguing against held no brief for *any* war, just or otherwise. Using the term *iustum bellum* with

---

97. Pollastri (n. 1 above), 355–73.

98. Well discussed in Michael Walzer, *Just and Unjust Wars* (New York: Basic Books, 1977), 3–20.

99. *Quaest. in Hept.* 6.10 (*CSEL* 28:2, 428; *CCL* 33, 318–19): "Quod deus iubet loquens ad Iesum, ut constituat sibi retrorsus insidias, id est insidiantes bellatores ad insidiandum hostibus, hinc admonemur non iniuste fieri ab his qui iustum bellum gerunt, ut nihil homo iustus praecipue cogitare debeat in his rebus, nisi ut iustum bellum suscipiat, cui bellare fas est; non enim omnibus fas est. Cum autem iustum bellum susceperit, utrum aperta pugna, utrum insidiis vincat, nihil ad iustitiam interest."

deliberate ambiguity, Augustine here in an argumentative strategy seeks to elide the category of wars fought under divine auspices with that of the just war as it was commonly understood, in order in the end to privilege God-originated wars as a special case of just war.

> Now just wars are usually defined as those that avenge wrongs, when the nation or the city-state that is going to be attacked in war has either failed to make right what was done wrongly by its people or to restore what had been taken by such wrongful acts. But especially this kind of war is undoubtedly just, the kind of war in which the commander is God, in whom there is no injustice and who knows what ought to be done and to whom. In this kind of war the leader of the army and the common soldiery itself should be considered not so much the instigator of war but rather a deputized agent.[100]

The sentence defining just war has been cited since the Middle Ages as Augustine's definition for what was, in the words of Frederick Russell, "Augustine's just war."[101] However, the definition is almost certainly Cicero's, echoing as it does his statement in *De officiis* that no war can be just unless first the offending party has been asked to make restitution, and his remark in *De republica*, preserved by Isidore, that a war to avenge wrongs is just.[102] The Ciceronian origin of the definition is clinched in light of Augustine's frequent use of him, significantly seen in certain passages on war.[103] Rather than wanting to give his own authoritative definition, Augustine in speaking of the term as it was *usually defined* ("definiri solent") wished to compare the ordinary just war—to its detriment—with the undeniably just war commanded by God. The ordinary just war, as the definition shows, was fought to avenge injury, whereas "*this* kind of war" ("hoc genus belli")—meaning the wars of the Old Testament such as the one being discussed in this passage—partakes of divine

---

100. *Quaest. in Hept.* 6.10 (*CSEL* 28:2, 428–29; *CCL* 33, 319): "Iusta autem bella ea definiri solent quae ulciscuntur iniurias, si qua gens vel civitas, quae bello petenda est, vel vindicare neglexerit quod a suis inprobe factum est vel reddere quod per iniurias ablatum est. Sed etiam hoc genus belli sine dubitatione iustum est, quod deus imperat, apud quem non est iniquitas et novit quid cuique fieri debeat. In quo bello ductor exercitus vel ipse populus non tam auctor belli quam minister iudicandus est."

101. Frederick H. Russell, *The Just War in the Middle Ages* (Cambridge: Cambridge University Press, 1975), 18–19.

102. *De officiis* 1.36 (*M. Tulli Ciceronis de officiis*, ed. M. Winterbottom [Oxford: Clarendon, 1994], 15); *De republica* 3.25 (35) (*M. Tulli Ciceronis de re publica*, ed. J. G. F. Powell [Oxford: Clarendon, 2006], 107).

103. On Augustine's use of Cicero, Harald Hagendahl, *Augustine and the Latin Classics* 2 (Göteborg: Elanders, 1967), 479–588, and see notes 139 to 145 below.

justice. Augustine must to some extent be speaking past putative Manichaean opponents to Christians who were similarly embarrassed by some aspects of the Old Testament God. His point is that if even wars fought over property are generally considered to be just by society, how much more just must be wars fought under divine aegis. In such wars the real instigator is God, not man, and any human being participating in it, as we saw in the previous chapter, acted as a deputized agent of God, a *minister*, and could not be held morally accountable for any deception involved in its prosecution. The justice of such God-directed wars was manifest because there can be nothing but justice in God, "who knows what ought to be done and to whom."

Augustine similarly appeals to the common understanding of the term while simultaneously privileging the role of providential justice in war in another passage in *Quaestiones in Heptateuchum* that mentions the just war. Here the question does touch on the general Manichaean objection to Old Testament war, but has more to do with resolving apparent contradictions in the biblical text. When Sihon king of the Amorites had refused permission to the Israelites to pass through his kingdom, they defeated and killed him in battle and settled in his kingdom's cities, even though in the earlier defeat of the Canaanite king of Arad his cities had been utterly destroyed (Num. 21:1-3, 21-31). Also, the Edomites had earlier refused passage through their lands to the Israelites, who did nothing in response except go another way (Num. 20:14-21). Augustine's answer to the first objection is that the Israelites had not placed the Amorite cities under anathema as they had the cities of Arad.[104] Augustine then remarks: "It should be noted at any rate how the wars waged were just." They were just because the Israelites, who had promised to stick to the road and take nothing from the countryside, had been denied passage, "which should have been extended to them by the fairest right of human society," an appeal to another secular conception, here probably the *ius gentium*.[105] But in dealing with the apparent contradiction between the treatment of the Edomites and the Amorites for the same offense, an offense that would have warranted a just war in both instances, Augustine folded all the actions of the Israelites under the overarching primacy of divine governance. God did not have the Israelites conquer Edom because it did not, as did the cities of Sihon, form part of the Promised Land. The playing out of that divine promise trumped any justification of war on the purely human plane.[106]

104. On the harsher aspects of the wars of the ancient Israelites as presented in the Old Testament, see Gerhard von Rad, *Holy War in Ancient Israel* (Grand Rapids: Eerdmans, 1991), 49–50; Eng. trans. of *Der Heilige Krieg im alten Israel* (Göttingen: Vandenhoeck & Ruprecht, 1958).

105. Russell (n. 101 above), 21.

Augustine's characterization in the passage on Ai of the justice of God, "who knows what ought to be done and to whom," is another example of his transposing classical into Christian terminology.[107] In *The City of God* Augustine's definition of justice, "that virtue which assigns to each his due,"[108] as in the case of his definition of just war was probably taken from a now-lost portion of *De republica*, although the definition itself goes as far back as Plato and Aristotle.[109] If this describes human justice at its (alas, unattainable) best, how much better must it apply to the actions of divine providence, even in war! Already when writing *Contra Faustum*, Augustine had concluded that the perfect justice in God necessarily comprehended divinely directed wars. In Book 22 of that work in defending the actions of Moses he repeatedly deployed the transposed definition like a refrain. Only God knows what it is appropriate for each person to experience, and only God knows who should suffer what, when it should happen, and by whom it should be commanded or allowed to happen.[110] Augustine applied this view of providential justice specifically to justify the wars of Moses.

> Hence, if the hardness of the human heart and a wicked and disordered will at long last understand that in correct actions there is a big difference whether something is done out of human greed or rashness and whether it is done in obedience to the command of God, who knows what He should permit or command, and when, and to whom, and who knows what is right for each person to do or to suffer, it should not be surprised at or horrified by the wars that Moses waged. For, in following the commands of God in them, Moses was not cruel but obedient, nor was God cruel when He commanded these things. Rather, He was giving punishments that they deserved to those who deserved them and was striking terror into those who deserved it.[111]

---

106. *Quaest. in Hept.* 4.44 (*CSEL* 28:2, 352–53; *CCL* 33, 263).

107. For another example of Augustine's transposition of justice to a Christian key see Robert Dodaro, "Justice," Fitzgerald, 481.

108. *DCD* 19.21 (*CCL* 48, 688): "Iustitia porro ea virtus est, quae sua cuique distribuit."

109. Hagendahl (n. 103 above), vol. 2, 543–45.

110. *Contra Faustum* 22.71, 72bis.

111. *Contra Faustum* 22.74 (*CSEL* 25, 671–72; Teske trans.).

And Augustine goes on later to ascribe to such divinely directed wars, whose justice was beyond reproach, the same providential ends he elsewhere associated with war.

> But it is wrong to have doubts about the righteous undertaking of a war to be waged at the instigation of God, whether it is intended to strike terror into, wear down, or subdue the pride of mortals, considering that even war which is waged out of human acquisitiveness cannot do any harm either to the incorruptible God or to His saints. Rather, it profits them in practicing patience and in humbling the soul and in bearing the Father's discipline. For no one has any power over them unless it has been given to him from above [cf. Luke 19:11], for there is no power save by God's command or permission.[112]

Although Augustine in his transposed conception of just war allowed for God-directed wars, fought for the ends of divine justice, it is surely significant that the only wars he specifically denoted as just were those of the Old Testament. The question then arises as to whether Augustine thought such God-directed just wars to be a present possibility, or were relegated entirely to a privileged, cut-off part of the sacred past. There had been progression in the *ordo temporum*, and without the imprimatur of Scripture no Christian, though still convinced that providence ruled in the end, could be certain of any providential interpretation of contemporary wars. There is much to be said for this reading of Augustine. It would help had he been clearer. That he in general terms envisioned the possibility of good contemporary Christians fighting in wars somehow associated with divine instigation and direction is certainly in the texts as well, and there were in Augustine's mind at least a couple of instances of contemporary wars that revealed, more or less directly, the hand of providence. Unfortunately, in the one text where he comes closest to saying specifically that divinely directed war could occur in the present, a passage from *The City of God* discussed in the previous chapter, his language is, perhaps intentionally, ambiguous.[113] Augustine had written that the exceptions to the Decalogue commandment "Thou shalt not kill" included:

> those whom God orders to be killed, whether by promulgated law or by express injunction to someone fulfilling a public role in

---

112. *Contra Faustum* 22.75 (673).

113. See ch. 6, notes 173 to 177 above.

accordance with specific circumstances. Now he does not kill who as a deputy dutifully follows orders, just as a sword acts as an assistant for the one wielding it. This is why there was no contravention whatsoever of that commandment which said "Thou shalt not kill" for those who either waged God-originated wars or who in carrying out a public role of authority in accordance with His laws, that is, rule by the most righteous rational power, punished criminals with death.[114]

On the one hand, the law under which certain individuals could be legitimately killed could refer to the provisions for capital punishment in the Torah. More telling is the fact that Augustine uses verbs in the perfect tense in speaking of those who did not violate the commandment when they had waged "God-originated wars" and had punished criminals with death, an indication these actions were all relegated to the past. Likewise, all the examples he uses in support come from the Old Testament (Abraham, Jephthah, and Samson). On the other hand, as noted above, his allusion here to Rom. 13:4 especially points to this passage as at least being a justification for present-day capital punishment. As to the possibility of God-originated wars in the present, Augustine seems deliberately vague though suggestive.

THE BONI

It turns out Augustine did think it possible for there to be present-day God-originated wars that somehow were linked with the ends of divine justice. Rather than having a list of requirements that had to be satisfied before a war could be just, however, Augustine had only one: that it be initiated and directed by boni, "good men."[115] As to how such "good men" could be recognized and their actions in war related to the ends of divine providence, Augustine

114. DCD 1.21 (CCL 47, 23).

115. A merit of Josef Rief's book on war in Augustine is that he sees in the bishop's writings and emphasizes clearly the role of the boni in determining whether a war is just, that it is not the exterior causative elements that define which war is just, but the internal moral constituents of the men who initiate and conduct such a war. See "Bellum" im Denken und in den Gedanken Augustins (n. 3 above), 69–77, 88–102, esp. 89: "Diese [the bella gerenda, the wars that are waged out of necessity of Contra Faustum 22.74 (notes 119, 120 below)] können nur von den boni homines als sittliche Pflicht und Sachaufgabe übernommen werden, weil nur sie in der Lage sind, die Sachebene richtig und umfassend genug zu sehen, im Blick auf die sie vor den sittlichen Anspruch gelangen, daß sie den in einem bestimmten Sachzusammenhang erkannten 'Krieg-der-geführt-werden-muß' auf sich zu nehmen haben."

appealed to the operation of the natural order in human society. This natural order in turn was regulated by the eternal law, "the divine reason or will of God which commands that the natural order be preserved and forbids that it be disturbed," a formulation repeated with slight variants like a refrain through Augustine's defense of the patriarchs and their actions in Book 22 of *Contra Faustum*.[116] In discussing this natural order Augustine the philosopher played on the correlation between the internal human microcosm and the external human macrocosm. In the natural constitution of a human being consisting of body and *anima*—the latter in this context seeming to mean the vital principle exteriorized in movement and purposeful action, a characteristic humans shared with animals though lacking in plants—the *anima* has precedence. Further, within the human *anima* is *ratio*, a reasoning faculty not present in animals, to which the body should be subservient, just as in the exterior world a ruler should be obeyed.[117] In this exterior world, the natural order in the human sphere can be seen in human institutions such as marriage that act in conformance with the eternal law to preserve society in an ordered peace.[118]

Now human society is held together by bonds of obedience, an obedience that plays a central role in the participation of the *boni* in just wars. After listing what is deserving of censure in war, Augustine noted:

> For the just punishment of these very things wars themselves are also quite often undertaken as having to be fought by good men against the violence of their opponents, whether at the bidding of God or of some legitimate high command [*imperium*], whenever good men are found in that rank of the human sphere where the rank itself justly constrains them either to command such a thing or to be obedient in such matters.

Augustine goes on to illustrate the necessity of obedience for soldiers with the story of John the Baptist and the soldiers coming to him for baptism.[119] He is

116. *Contra Faustum* 22.27, 28, 30, 43, 61, 73, 78 (622, 624, 635, 657–58, 670, 678). On this see F. Edward Cranz, "The Development of Augustine's Ideas on Society before the Donatist Controversy," *Harvard Theological Review* 47 (1954): 255–316; reprinted in *Augustine: A Collection of Critical Essays*, ed. R. A. Markus (New York: Anchor Books, 1972), 336–403 (cited here), 371 and 399, n. 164. See also the remarks on this formulation by Markus, *Saeculum*, 90. I would argue that Markus there overstates the separation in Augustine's conception between the eternal law and the natural order. The same formulation appears over twenty years later in *The City of God* (*De civitate Dei* 19.15 [*CCL* 48, 682]): "ea lege ordinatur quae naturalem ordinem conservari iubet perturbari vetat."

117. *Contra Faustum* 22.27–28 (*CSEL* 25, 621–23).

118. *Contra Faustum* 22.61 (656).

still dealing with issues of societal order, authority, and obedience when he then goes on to mention just and unjust wars, in a passage best understood in context absent the intrusive paragraph division of the printed editions.

> A discussion of just and unjust wars would at this time take too long and is not really necessary. Certainly it does make a difference for what reasons and at whose instigation human beings undertake the wars which should be waged. Yet the natural order adapted to the peace of mortals requires that the authority and the decision to undertake war be the prerogative of a prince, while the duty of following orders in war for the common peace and security falls to soldiers.[120]

In this passage Augustine is more concerned with the proper authority and dutiful obedience attendant to war than with its justice or injustice. That is why a discussion here of just and unjust wars would constitute a time-consuming and irrelevant digression. He briefly concedes that the causes for which wars are fought do matter. But he is more interested here in, first, the proper locus for the authority to initiate war, and second, the role of soldiers in carrying out orders in war. The "natural order adapted to the peace of mortals" can only be the *ordo rerum humanarum*, which allots to the rulers in human society the power to decide whether to wage war, and to their subordinates and soldiers the duty to prosecute war in conformance with legitimate commands. This hierarchy of authority and obedience ensures the well-being of all. The fact that Augustine even mentions the just war here does reveal, to be sure, his awareness that there were those in his audience who might wonder why in defending some wars he did not adduce the idea of just cause, an indication of the enduring topicality of the Roman just war idea in contemporary discourse. But Augustine is here saying that any consideration of whether a war is just or unjust is superseded by the requirement of obedience to the ruler whose authority is divinely legitimated, and that any consideration of a war's justice

119. *Contra Faustum* 22.74 (CSEL 25, 672): ". . . quae plerumque ut etiam iure puniantur, adversus violentiam resistentium sive deo sive aliquo legitimo imperio iubente gerenda ipsa bella suscipiuntur a bonis, cum in eo rerum humanarum ordine inveniuntur, ubi eos vel iubere tale aliquid vel in talibus oboedire iuste ordo ipse constringit. Alioquin Iohannes, cum ad eum baptizandi milites venirent," etc.

120. *Contra Faustum* 22.74–75 (673; Teske trans., modified): "Et de iustis quidem iniustisque bellis nunc disputare longum est et non necessarium. Interest enim, quibus causis quibusque auctoribus homines gerenda bella suscipiant; ordo tamen ille naturalis mortalium paci adcommodatus hoc poscit, ut suscipiendi belli auctoritas atque consilium penes principem sit, exequendi autem iussa bellica ministerium milites debeant paci salutique communi."

or injustice is especially irrelevant in the case of a ruler "who wages war at the command of God, who, as anyone in His service cannot fail to know, does not command anything evil."[121]

This *bonus* who could undertake just wars at the command of God was certainly no ordinary Christian. He was someone burdened with authority and responsibility, who had to carry out public duties that were often sorrowful, violent, and bloody; in other words, the type of Christian official or military commander we saw Augustine speak to in the previous chapter. Undoubtedly it was partly his own appreciation gleaned from the *episcopalis audientia* of the dilemmas inherent to the exercise of public authority that elicited from him in *Contra Faustum* the observation that the civil and military authorities, whether of the past or of the present, often in seeking to preserve societal order had to do terrible things.

> For the eternal law which commands that the natural order be preserved and forbids that it be disturbed has so placed certain deeds in a sort of middle position for human beings, that it deservedly blames the effrontery involved in doing them while at the same time it rightfully praises the obedience involved in accomplishing them. There is a great difference in the natural order in terms of who does what and at whose bidding someone acts.[122]

Augustine's examples here of the despoiling of the Egyptians and Abraham's willingness to sacrifice his son Isaac show that this "middle position" of human deeds is occupied by acts that conform to the divine will but seem reprehensible on their surface.

Because the actions attendant to war were especially grievous, the dynamic of divine instigation of war needed to be radically straightforward: God issued the orders, and the good man obeyed.[123] By contrast, no truly good man would initiate war solely on his own initiative, for to do so would be to sin and to fall under Christ's condemnation that "he who uses the sword shall fall by the sword."[124] Such decisions belong solely to the judgment of God. Who else could know enough to be able to make such decisions?

---

121. *Contra Faustum* 22.75 (674).
122. *Contra Faustum* 22.73 (670).
123. *Contra Faustum* 22.71, 73, 74, 75, 77 fin., 78 init.
124. *Contra Faustum* 22.70, 72, 73, 78 init.

> Who is there of humanity who knows whom it benefits and whom
> it harms to rule or to serve or to be at ease or to die in peacetime, or,
> on the contrary, to be in command or to fight or to conquer or to be
> killed in wartime?[125]

Those who usurp such a divine privilege for themselves love for their own sakes
temporal goods that should only be used toward attainment of eternal goods. As
Augustine would put it in *The City of God*, such men start wars out of a lust for
power, *libido dominandi*, for power's sake. With good men, on the other hand,
since their wills conform to God's law, the good order of that law sets bounds
to their desires. "Thus a good man does not desire anything other than what he
is commanded."[126]

But what about the pagan Romans of old? They had not worshiped the
one true God and hence could not be considered good men. Yet they had by
their success in war created a huge, powerful empire. Why, then, should good
men be leaders in war? How could the Romans' success be reconciled with the
providence of God, about whom it was impossible to conceive "that He would
have excluded from the laws of His providence the kingdoms of men and their
dominations and servitudes"?[127] Augustine's response to these questions leads
into a consideration of what qualities were constitutive of a good Christian ruler
and to what end. Our own consideration of Augustine on this point is justified
not only by its description of the good ruler empowered to initiate war, but also
by the discussion culminating in an Augustinian "mirror of princes," a passage
that would heavily influence later medieval *Fürstenspiegel* and other literature.[128]

The secret of the success of the ancient Romans had lain in their passion
for high reputation and renown, *gloria*, an attainment acknowledged by the
praise of other men, and kept from infamy by that and glory's tight association
with honor and honorable conduct, an honor also assessed and acknowledged
publicly by other men.[129] Ancient Roman noblemen had lived for glory and
had not hesitated to die for it. "So it was this eagerness for praise and passion
for glory that performed so many marvellous deeds, which were no doubt
praiseworthy and glorious as men judge things."

---

125. *Contra Faustum* 22.78 (679–80; Teske trans., modified).

126. *Contra Faustum* 22.78 (678).

127. *DCD* 5.11 (*CCL* 47, 142; Greene trans.).

128. See Hans Hubert Anton, *Fürstenspiegel und Herrscherethos in der Karolingerzeit* (Bonn: Ludwig Röhrscheid, 1968), 47–48 on the influence of the passage on later *Fürstenspiegel*.

129. On the Roman *gloria* and Augustine's critique and Christian transposition of the term, see Louis J. Swift, "Pagan and Christian Heroes in Augustine's *City of God*," *Augustinianum* 27, no. 3 (1987): 509–22.

Since to be in subjection is dishonorable and autonomy glorious, the Romans first fought for independence. "But once they had freedom, so great was the passion for glory which arose that liberty seemed too little by itself unless they were also seeking dominion over others." As the Roman state grew, the passion for the attainment of *gloria* remained so strong that the Romans would place the greater good before their private interests, an instance of vice engendering virtue. "For one vice, that is, love of praise, they overcame the love of money and many other vices." They would restrain their desires and keep to the law for the sake of the fatherland, the *patria*, the country where they sought their glory, whose security they put before their own. God had willed the preeminence of such a state, driven to success by a dominant vice though it be, as an imperfect instrument to subdue the worse vices of other nations. In the end, the Romans attained more honor than any other nation, were able to impose their laws on others, and still in Augustine's day were widely considered a nation of glory.[130] And having given his explanation for Rome's rise, Augustine confessed himself unable finally to comprehend all the workings of providence.

> Thus I have sufficiently explained, as best I could, for what reason the one true and just God helped the Romans—good men by the standards of the earthly city—to obtain the glory of so great an empire. Yet there can also be another, more hidden reason, the result of the various merits of humankind, better known to God than to us.[131]

Augustine was well aware from both historical examples and his contemporary experience that the naked desire for power as an end in itself, *libido dominandi*, can override any restraints imposed by the desire to be seen and praised as a glorious though honorable man. His acute dissection of the dilemmas involved in the pursuit of power leads to a subversive conclusion.

> Of course, there is a difference between the desire for human glory and the desire for power. For although it is easy for someone who enjoys human glory too much also to aspire to power, still those who covet true glory, though it be the praise of men, take pains not to offend good judges. There are many good traits of character of which many are good judges, though not many have such traits. It

---

130. *DCD* 5.12, 15 (142–44, 149 [Greene trans.]).
131. *DCD* 5.19 (155 [Greene trans., mod.]).

is by means of these good traits that men climb to glory and power and rule. . . . Whereas anyone desirous of rule and power without the desire for glory that makes him fearful of displeasing those good judges, he also usually seeks to obtain whatever he loves by the most blatant crimes.

The ancient Romans of virtue had used virtuous means to attain glory,[132] but tyrants fight for glory with plots and lies, trying to seem good when they're not. Since the praise of glorious men is insufficient to stave off tyranny, it is better to dispense with valuing praise, together with the glory that called it forth. "And so for those who have virtue it is a great virtue to despise glory."

And with the pursuit of glory removed, Augustine begins to frame the virtuous disposition of a good Christian ruler, subject as he was still to the praise of others:

> He who disregards the opinions of those who praise him also disregards the rashness of those who suspect him, though if he is truly good he does not disregard their salvation. For so great is the justice of him who has his virtues from the spirit of God that he even loves his enemies. . . . But as for those who praise him, however little he thinks of their praising him, he nonetheless does not think little of their loving him, not wanting to disappoint them in their praise by deceiving them in their love; and so he ardently insists that they praise more Him from whom humankind has whatever is rightly praised.

This ruler was not only Christian but was no lover of glory, and for that very reason deserved power.

> Only let it be agreed among all the truly religious that no one can have true virtue absent true religion, that is, the true worship of the true God, and that there is no true virtue where virtue is subordinate to human glory. However, those who are not citizens of the eternal city which in our sacred literature is called the city of God are more useful to the earthly city when they have their own kind of virtue than if they did not have even that. But if those who are endowed with true religion and live good lives have the knowledge for ruling

132. *DCD* 5.12 (144).

peoples, there is nothing better for human affairs than that, by God's mercy, they have the power.[133]

In an earlier passage Augustine had expounded on the advantages to ruler and ruled alike when good men were in power, and the disadvantages to both when evil men ruled.

> Wherefore if the true God is revered and served with true worship and good morals, it is advantageous for good men to rule far and wide and long; nor is it advantageous for them so much as it is for those whom they rule. For as far as they themselves are concerned, their piety and probity, which are God's great gifts, are sufficient for their true happiness, whereby this life may be well spent, and eternal life attained hereafter. Thus on this earth the kingdom of good men is advantageous not so much for them as for human affairs in general, but the kingdom of evil men harms more the rulers, who lay waste their own spiritual side from a greater license for crime, while those who are subjected to their service are not harmed except by their own iniquity. For whatever evils are imposed upon the just by unjust masters are not the punishment of crime, but a testing of virtue. Hence even if a good man is in service, he is free; whereas if an evil man is ruling, he is a slave, not of one man, but, what is worse, to as many masters as he has vices. When treating of these vices divine Scripture says: "For whatever overcomes a man, to that he is enslaved." (2 Pet 2:19)[134]

Of course, there had already been Christian emperors by Augustine's time. Their varying fortunes provided both support for the bishop's contention that it was best for virtuous Christians to rule and ammunition for Christianity's critics. Constantine's accession showed that it was not required for one to worship the pagan gods in order to become emperor. He had defeated enemies both foreign and domestic, reigned for a long time, and died peacefully, leaving the rule to his sons. By contrast, the Christian emperor Jovian had died after an even shorter reign than his immediate predecessor, the pagan apostate Julian, and Gratian had been killed by a usurper.[135] Being a Christian, it seems, provided no guarantee of success. But this was to judge as humans judge

---

133. *DCD* 5.19 (154–56 [Greene trans., mod.]).

134. *DCD* 4.3 (101 [Greene trans., mod.]).

135. *DCD* 5.25 (160–61).

worldly things, and Augustine reframed the issue of a ruler's success according to whether he actually possessed divine favor, *felicitas*.

> We do not say that certain Christian emperors are divinely-favored either because they had a somewhat lengthy reign, or left the empire to their sons after a peaceful death, or because they subdued the state's enemies or were able both to be on the lookout for hostile citizens and to crush them when they revolted against their rule. Even some worshippers of demons, who do not belong to the kingdom of God as do the Christian emperors, obtained those and other rewards or consolations in this wretched life. This occurred by His mercy, that those who believed in Him might not be desirous of such things from Him as though they were the highest good. Rather, we say they are divinely-favored if they rule justly; if amid the voices of those loftily honoring them and the lowly, abject fawning of those paying them court, they do not get puffed up, and remember that they are but human beings; if they make their power a servant to His Majesty for the spreading of God's worship as far as possible; if they fear, love, and worship God; if they love more that kingdom where they are not afraid to have partners; if they are slow to punish, prompt to pardon; if they inflict punishment as necessary for the rule and protection of the state, not to satisfy grudges against personal enemies; if they grant pardons not to let wrongdoing go unpunished, but in the hope of reform; if as often as they are forced to make harsh decrees they compensate with the gentleness of mercy and an abundance of kindness; if the more they could be unrestrained in self-indulgence they are all the more restrained; if they prefer mastery over their base desires than that over any nations, and if they do all this not out of a passion for vainglory, but out of a longing for eternal happiness; if for their sins they do not neglect to offer to their true God the sacrifice of humility and mercy and prayer. We say that such Christian emperors are divinely-favored—now in hope, later in reality, when that for which we hope has arrived.[136]

Augustine's brief "mirror of princes" here reflects many of the same values such as humility, justice, and mercy that were traditional to the classical genre of advice for rulers, but to these traditional values he adds the requirement that a good Christian ruler be personally pious and work to spread the faith.[137]

---

136. *DCD* 5.24 (160 [Greene trans. mod.]).

THE ROMAN JUST WAR

Could such a paragon of virtue exist in reality? And were the only wars that were just commanded by such rare men? What about the just war as that was ordinarily understood, initiated, and fought by ordinary men? As to the last, Augustine actually has relatively little to say on the Roman just war per se, other than what we have already seen. What he does convey is often borrowed wisdom, or else is, in fact, a criticism of the whole idea. Since Thomas Aquinas, writers on the just war have often focused on the conditions that have to be met for a war to be just, the *ius ad bellum*. On this, Augustine is relatively unenlightening. When in *Contra Faustum* he had listed the evils associated with war and then noted that good men initiated wars to punish those very evils, one could deduce from this that the justification of wars depended on what the enemy had done, whether he had acted the barbarian, was in revolt, or was an aggressor.[138] In Book 22 of *The City of God* he cites from a lost section of Book 3 of Cicero's *De republica* that had argued the best state went to war only out of loyalty to allies or interests of national security.[139] In his letter to Boniface urging him to remain at his post, Augustine had counseled him to wage war only out of necessity, not choice, in a combat with peace as its aim.[140] Whatever else of the conditions for a just war that has been ascribed to Augustine is a later construct.

Considering that arguably only the emperors were subordinate to no human authority in war-making decisions, but that for most Christian commanders and soldiers it was not a matter of deciding whether to fight but of obeying legitimate orders, it is understandable that Augustine was more specific on the *ius in bello*, the parameters of just conduct in war.[141] Here again Cicero was an important source, both directly and via Ambrose, who as we have already seen used Cicero especially on the *iura belli*.[142] So when Augustine in writing to Boniface urged him to show mercy to the defeated and the captive, he was echoing both Cicero and Ambrose on the humane treatment of enemy

137. O'Daly, 99.

138. *Contra Faustum* 22.74 (*CSEL* 25, 672); note 10 above.

139. *DCD* 22.6 (*CCL* 48, 814): "Scio in libro Ciceronis tertio, nisi fallor, de re publica disputari nullum bellum suscipi a civitate optima, nisi aut pro fide aut pro salute."

140. *Epist.* 189.6 (*CSEL* 57, 135): "Pacem habere debet voluntas, bellum necessitas, ut liberet deus a necessitate et conservet in pace. Non enim pax quaeritur, ut bellum excitetur, sed bellum geritur, ut pax adquiratur. . . . Itaque hostem pugnantem necessitas perimat, non voluntas." On all this, see also Mattox, 15, 45–46.

141. *Pace* Mattox, 60. See also idem, 61–65 on *ius in bello* in Augustine.

142. Chapter 4, notes 84 to 93 above; Mattox, 14.

prisoners.[143] In the same letter Augustine had written: "When your word is given it is to be kept even with an enemy against whom war is being waged . . ."[144] This reflects Cicero in *De officiis* saying that promises made even to an enemy must be honored.[145]

But Augustine also in Letter 126 in early 411 seems to be lessening the praiseworthy honor due those who made and kept such promises, "for what else made them take the oath in the first place except that each side feared being killed or captured by the other?" Such men were more concerned with the stigma of committing perjury than they were about the killing of other human beings.[146] Easily most of what Augustine wrote about the Roman just war devalued it relative to the ideals of the city of God. He considered the Roman just war at best a necessary evil, at worst a pretext for crime. For did not the very need to fight just wars in the first place depend on there being evil in the world? And because Rome had grown as a result of such wars, did not the empire's very existence depend on the injustice of others?

> To be sure, the injustice of those against whom they waged just wars helped their realm to grow, a realm that would surely have been small had peaceful and just neighbors not provoked them by any wrongdoing into waging war against them. In such a happier human history all realms would be small and would enjoy harmony with their neighbors, and thus there would be many national realms in the world, just as there are many homes of citizens in a city. Hence waging war and extending one's sway over conquered nations seems a good thing to the wicked, but a necessity to the good. But since it would be worse for the unjust to rule over the just, so this is also not inappropriately termed a good thing. Yet undoubtedly it is more of a good thing to have harmony with a good neighbor than to subjugate a bad neighbor in war.[147]

143. Cicero, *De officiis* I 34–40; Ambrose, *De officiis* I 29, 139.

144. *Epist.* 189.6 (*CSEL* 57, 135): "Fides enim quando promittitur, etiam hosti servanda est, contra quem bellum geritur . . ."

145. *De officiis* I 39–40.

146. *Epist.* 126.11 (*CSEL* 44, 16): "Hostiles inter se acies et armatae certe apertissima mortis intentione confligunt et tamen, cum invicem iurant, laudamus fidem servantes, fallentes autem merito detestamur. Ut autem iurarent, quid utraeque ab alterutris nisi occidi vel capi timuerunt? Ac per hoc vel mortis vel captivitatis metu extortae iurationi nisi parcatur, nisi fides, quae ibi data est, custodiatur, sacrilegii, periurii crimine detinentur etiam tales homines, qui magis metuunt peierare quam hominem occidere . . ."

147. *DCD* 4.15 (*CCL* 47, 111): "Iniquitas enim eorum, cum quibus iusta bella gesta sunt, regnum adiuvit ut cresceret, quod utique parvum esset, si quies et iustitia finitimorum contra se bellum geri nulla

It has been noticed that this passage gives us a glimpse of Augustine's political ideal, an ideal hinted at in a couple of other passages as well,[148] of the human world being divided into a number of relatively small states living in harmonious peace with one another, the model being the peaceful concord existing among the citizens of a city.[149] In such a world no realm would wrong its neighbor, and thus there would be no need for just wars. But Rome had not grown into an empire in such a world, a fact the Romans seemed to have taken insufficient account of in constructing their pantheon.

> So if it was by waging just wars, not unholy and not unjust, that the Romans were able to acquire such a large empire, should they not also worship the injustice of foreigners (*iniquitas aliena*) as a goddess? Assuredly we see that she did much to extend the empire, she who caused some to be unjust so there would be those against whom just wars could be waged and the empire enlarged.[150]

In the end, what does it matter that a leader of good breeding and education, a wise man (*sapiens*) by classical standards, restricts himself to fighting only just wars?

> But the wise man, they say, will only wage just wars. As if he would not, if he remembers his humanity, grieve all the more that there exists the necessity of just wars in the first place; for unless they were just, he would not have to wage them, and then for a wise man there would be no wars at all. For it is the injustice of the opposing side that imposes on the wise man the necessity of waging just wars; and this injustice, even if no necessity of waging war were to arise from it, must still be deplored by a human being, since human beings perpetrate it. (W. C. Greene trans., mod.)[151]

provocaret iniuria ac sic felicioribus rebus humanis omnia regna parva essent concordii vicinitate laetantia et ita essent in mundo regna plurima gentium, ut sunt in urbe domus plurimae civium. Proinde belligerare et perdomitis gentibus dilatare regnum malis videtur felicitas, bonis necessitas. Sed quia peius esset, ut iniuriosi iustioribus dominarentur, ideo non incongrue dicitur etiam ista felicitas. Sed procul dubio felicitas maior est vicinum bonum habere concordem quam vicinum malum subiugare bellantem."

148. *DCD* 4.3 (100–101) and *Contra Faustum* 10.3 (*CSEL* 25, 312–13), on which see n. 154 below.

149. O'Daly, 91–92.

150. *DCD* 4.15 (*CCL* 47, 111): "Si ergo iusta gerendo bella, non impia, non iniqua, Romani imperium tam magnum adquirere potuerunt, numquid tamquam aliqua dea colenda est eis etiam iniquitas aliena? Multum enim ad istam latitudinem imperii eam cooperatam videmus, quae faciebat iniuriosos, ut essent cum quibus iusta bella gererentur et augeretur imperium."

Because the only reason for there being just war in the first place was as a consequence of the existence of evil in a fallen world, it along with much else the Romans valued was nothing for them to be proud of, and at times could even be associated with the evil it was supposed to suppress. Twice early in *The City of God* Augustine treated the story of the Sabine women as an example of the most ancient Romans failing to live up to their own ideals. At Rome's very beginning there were no women, and Romulus had asked for the right to marry the daughters of the surrounding peoples, a request that had been refused. Now this refusal was grounds for a just war. But instead, the neighboring peoples were invited to a feast by the Romans, who then kidnapped the daughters they wanted for their wives. Even Livy, our main source for the story, admitted that the Romans had thereby violated the sacred right of hospitality. And when the parents of the kidnapped women, understandably enraged, launched a war against the Romans, the Romans were then—as opposed to the just war they never fought in response to the initial refusal—clearly fighting an *unjust* war, since they had committed the initial violence and were now fighting their own fathers-in-law, a violation of the Roman's own value of *pietas*, here the dutiful and reverent behavior due one's relatives. Only the anguished intervention of the Roman brides, fearful of becoming a widow or an orphan or both, stopped the carnage. Since at its very beginning the continued existence of Rome had depended on the violent and impious acquisition of women, the Roman state that fought just wars had actually been founded on injustice.[152]

Given his devaluation of the idea, it is not surprising to find Augustine at times looking askance at claims to be fighting a just war. In Book 10 of *Contra Faustum* in mocking Faustus's claim that the ethical prescription against desiring the property of others had caused him to reject the Old Testament, given the rampant acquisitiveness among the ancient Israelites seen in it, Augustine countered that the God of light in Manichaean cosmology was no positive role model in that respect. For Mani had taught that the God of light had in a grand counterattack extended his kingdom into that of his adversary, the realm of darkness. Even if this had been in response to an earlier assault from

151. *DCD* 19.7 (*CCL* 48, 672): "Sed sapiens, inquiunt, iusta bella gesturus est. Quasi non, si se hominem meminit, multo magis dolebit iustorum necessitatem sibi extitisse bellorum, quia nisi iusta essent, ei gerenda essent, ac per hoc sapienti nulla bella essent. Iniquitas enim partis adversae iusta bella ingerit gerenda sapienti; quae iniquitas utique homini est dolenda, quia hominum est, etsi nulla ex ea bellandi necessitas nasceretur."

152. *DCD* 2.17; 3.13 (*CCL* 47, 47–48, 74–75); Karla Pollmann, "Augustins Transformation der traditionellen römischen Staats- und Geschichtsauffassung (Buch I-V)," in *Augustinus: De civitate dei*, ed. C. Horn (Berlin: Akademie Verlag, 1997), 28–31.

the realm of darkness, did not the seizure of his attacker's property bespeak covetousness, and an aggressive desire to expand his realm of light—perhaps previously considered too small—at the expense of his opponent? Furthermore, if invading the realm of darkness and thereby expanding the realm of light did not indicate covetousness but was rather ipso facto a good thing, why then did the God of light feel the need to wait to do so until he was first attacked by his enemy? Would it be so that when the enemy was conquered it would seem "as though [it were] more just"? In thus concretizing this thread from Manichaean mythology, Augustine allows us a fleeting glimpse of his feelings, feelings undoubtedly shared by many of his contemporaries, on the wars of states. There is a presumption here against wars undertaken solely for the sake of conquest. In speaking here of the God of light's realm before its expansion, when "he was content with his own boundaries and lived in complete happiness," Augustine again hints at his political preference for relatively small states living at peace with one another.[153] There is also, finally, a hint of a certain cynical mistrust of the just war rhetoric of the state and its use of pretexts to justify the unjustifiable, since it is clear that in this passage Augustine is deriding the Manichaean God of light's cold, calculating forethought in waiting on and exploiting an attack as an excuse for expansionism.[154]

There is one instance of Augustine's doubts about claims to be fighting in a just cause related to a "real world" example of a phenomenon we have seen earlier, the use of just war rhetoric by one of the parties in a Roman civil war. When Augustine wrote Letter 220 to the general Boniface in 428, much had happened to the latter in the several years since Augustine had visited him at Tubunae to persuade him not to become a monk and to remain at his post.[155] He had risen to the position of *comes Africae*, and for his support of the queen-mother Galla Placidia and the child emperor Valentinian III against the usurpation of John in 423–425 he was rewarded with the full title *comes domesticorum et Africae*.[156] Boniface had become one of the most powerful men

153. Notes 148, 149 above.

154. *Contra Faustum* 10.3 (*CSEL* 25, 312): "Et tamen confessus est Faustus non concupiscere aliena non solum se ex novo testamento, sed etiam ex vetere didicisse: quod certe a suo deo non posset discere. Ille quippe, si non concupivit aliena, quare super terram tenebrarum, ubi numquam fuerunt, nova saecula construxit? An dicturus est: prior ipsa gens tenebrarum regnum meum concupivit, quod ab illa erat alienum? Ergo imitatus est gentem tenebrarum, ut et ipse concupisceret aliena? An angustum antea fuerat regnum lucis? Optandum igitur erat bellum, ut adquireretur de victoria latitudo regnandi. Quod si bonum est, et ante potuit concupisci, sed expectabatur, ut gens hostilis in bellum prior erumperet, quo *quasi iustius* [italics mine] expugnaretur. Si autem non est bonum, quare inimico victo super alienam terram crescere voluit regnum suum, cum prius contentus suis finibus plena felicitate vixisset?"

155. *Epist.* 220.3 (*CSEL* 57, 432–33); ch. 5, notes 209, 210 above.

in the Western empire, one of the "last of the Romans" in the estimation of posterity;[157] from contemplating retirement to a monastery, he was now caught up in the pursuit of *gloria*, and protective of the high honor he had obtained. Aspects of his personal life were now questionable. At one point a widower considering a chaste retirement, he had since not only remarried but was reported to have a number of girlfriends on the side.[158] As bad as his private life was, his public life was worse, with worse effects because felt by more people. When he had been summoned to the Italian court by the machinations of his rivals there in 427, Boniface had refused to come, whereupon he was declared a public enemy and armies dispatched to Africa against him.[159] Perhaps partly because of the expansion of the Roman field army at the end of the fourth century and the beginning of the fifth,[160] Boniface outperformed earlier African rebels in defeating the first forces sent against him.[161] But he did so by attracting many greedy and ruthless men to his banner with promises of money and loot, and at the expense of defending the frontiers, which denuded of troops now lay open to barbarian attack.[162]

Augustine had meant to communicate with Boniface for some time, but first the infirmities of his age (he was seventy-four in 428) and then the disorder and intrigue accompanying the civil war had made it difficult to find a messenger willing to risk the danger and well known enough to Boniface to be trusted.[163] The bishop wrote out of concern not for Boniface's powerful position and height of honor, "which you hold in this wicked age," but for the state of his immortal soul.[164] Augustine feared the advice Boniface was getting from the men who surrounded him, who were devoted to him "according to the life of this world," but whose advice was necessarily of doubtful utility because human.[165] Worse, the core of Boniface's forces was a body of retainers

156. Diesner (ch. 6, n. 205 above), 107–13, and *PLRE* 2:238–39.

157. Procopius III.iii.15 (*Procopii Caesariensis opera omnia*, ed. J. Haury [Leipzig: Teubner, 1962], I, 321).

158. *Epist.* 220.4 (433–34).

159. Prosper *a.* 427 (*MGH:aa* 9, 471–72): "Bonifatio, cuius intra Africam potentia gloriaque augebatur, bellum ad arbitrium Felicis, quia ad Italiam venire abnuerat, publico nomine inlatum est . . ." On the difficulties that Boniface or indeed any *comes Africae* faced vis-à-vis the Italian court, see now Shaw, 37. On Boniface's revolt in particular, idem, 772–73.

160. Chapter 6, n. 27 above.

161. Prosper (n. 159 above) *a.* 427.

162. *Epist.* 220.6–7 (435–36).

163. 220.1, 2 (431, 432).

164. 220.1 (431–32).

165. 220.2 (432).

bound to him by a loyalty reinforced by the promise and provision of material rewards. "To do this, many things have to be done which displease God." Such things seemed to include a certain license for disorder and pillage allowed his barbarian supporters.[166] When there was added to that the widespread devastation wrought by African barbarians, now able to traverse unopposed a frontier stripped of troops to reinforce Boniface's central army,[167] it is understandable that Augustine would speak of "those evils, so many and so great," perpetrated by Boniface or in his name, evils well known to all. If Boniface paused to reflect, he would realize that he had been responsible for such evils as obligated him to do penance,[168] a remark incidentally showing that for Augustine it was not the holding of public office per se that necessitated penance, but any sinful acts committed in the exercise of such office.

What had driven such an outstanding individual, who had once contemplated taking up the religious life, to do such things? By his own lights, Boniface had rendered years of loyal and dutiful service to the imperial court in Italy, only in the end to be betrayed by his enemies there.[169] After being declared a public enemy and having armies sent against him, what choice did he have but to take up arms? Because he had done nothing wrong but had instead been wronged, Boniface, like centuries of contenders in Roman civil wars before him, claimed to be fighting in a "just cause," and this claim doubtless was part of the propaganda he spread in Africa to rally supporters and sway waverers.

"You say that you have a just cause," wrote Augustine to him. "Of that I am no judge, since I can't give a hearing to both sides." But that does not matter. For "can you deny before God that you would not be in such a crisis if you had not loved the goods of this world, which, like the servant of God we knew you formerly to be, you should have despised entirely and have counted as nothing?" (Parsons trans., mod.).[170] Augustine did not accept that Boniface had had no choice. He would not be in his present predicament in the first place had he not become caught up in the pursuit of *gloria*, and anxious to defend against any affront the high honor that accompanied power. But all that was transitory. As to his "just cause," Boniface in the course of his worldly career had received many benefits from the imperial government that had enabled him ultimately to attain high office. Even if that government had now turned against him, was

166. 220.6 (435–36).
167. 220.7 (436).
168. 220.5 (434).
169. 220.8 (436–37).
170. 220.5 (434–35).

it not incumbent upon a Christian not to return evil for evil, or, considering his past benefits, evil for good?[171]

In the end, the things for which Boniface is fighting—personal safety, victory over his enemies, honor and worldly power—are earthly things given to good and evil men alike. But the safety of the soul, the victory over the inner passions that are our true enemy, and eternal glory, honor, and peace are granted only to a good man, a *bonus*.[172] Augustine went all out in arguing that Boniface should renounce his worldly ambitions and do penance for the evil done in his name,[173] but the resigned tone of the letter bespeaks little hope that such a course would be followed. In Augustine's eyes, and surely in those of many contemporaries, the general's evocation of a just cause was merely a tawdry pretext justifying his pursuit of power. Sadly, Boniface was no *bonus*.

AUGUSTINE AND THE BATTLE OF THE FRIGIDUS

The example of Boniface shows how difficult it was to find in the present-day political reality, with all of its moral compromises and ambiguities, a truly good man who could in obedience to divine will wage a God-directed war. Although almost all such wars mentioned by him were in the Old Testament, however, Augustine did think there to be rare instances of contemporary wars where the workings of divine providence could be discerned and even something of their providential purpose discovered. As noted earlier, Augustine saw the divine hand at work in the swift and crushing defeat of the pagan Gothic king Radagaisus, and a providential purpose in thereby demonstrating the impotence of the pagan gods.[174] But it is in the bishop's appraisal of the emperor Theodosius's victory at the battle of the Frigidus in 394 that one finds a clear contemporary example of a *bonus* waging war under divine auspices.

Augustine first alludes to the battle a decade or so after it occurred in *Contra Faustum*.[175] He had been discussing how the differences in the *ordo temporum* between Old Testament times and New required temporally variant understandings of Christ's injunction to turn the other cheek.[176] A theme of this chapter in *Contra Faustum* is the varying status of earthly political powers,

171. 220.8 (437–38).

172. 220.11 (439).

173. 220.9–10 (438–39).

174. Notes 88 to 91 above.

175. To my knowledge, Augustine's allusion to the battle of the Frigidus in *Contra Faustum* 22.76 has hitherto gone unnoticed.

176. See notes 45 to 50, 53 to 65 above.

regna, throughout time, and the consequently varying position of the saints vis-à-vis such powers. In the childish ignorance of primitive times humankind had supposed that earthly goods such as kingdoms and victories over enemies were obtained by supplicating idols and demons. The wars of the Old Testament showed instead that such goods fell under the sovereignty and will of the one true God.[177] In a later time the martyrs had had to endure for the sake of the kingdom of heaven the opposition of all the kingdoms of the earth.[178] At the present time the position of the saints vis-à-vis earthly political power had changed yet again, for now with the era of Christian emperors there was fulfilled the prophecy of the psalm, "and the kings of the earth shall worship him, all the nations shall serve him" (Ps. 71[72]:11).[179] In such a time

> Christian emperors also, relying fully on their faith in Christ, gained a most glorious victory over their impious enemies, who had placed their hope in the rites of idols and demons. The prophecies of the demons deceived the latter with proofs that were quite unambiguous and well-known, some of which were at that time committed to written record; while the predictions of the saints were an encouragement to the former.[180]

The victory of the Christian emperors is here obviously meant to be associated with the wars of the Old Testament, wars in which God had granted victory to his people and thereby demonstrated the uselessness of pagan worship. In this one instance present-day political power in its relationship to God had reverted to that of ancient Israel, the point being in the context of *Contra Faustum* to prove to Augustine's Manichaean opponents that such a clear contemporary

---

177. *Contra Faustum* 22.76 (*CSEL* 25, 674, 676): "Sed eam rerum dispensationem ac distributionem temporum ordo poscebat, ut prius adpareret etiam ipsa bona terrena, quibus et humana regna et ex hostibus victoriae deputantur, propter quae maxime civitas inpiorum diffusa per mundum supplicare idolis et daemonibus solet, non nisi ad unius dei veri potestatem atque arbitrium pertinere. . . . Illi regia bella gesserunt, ut tales quoque victorias adpareret dei voluntate praestari."

178. *Contra Faustum* 22.76 (674–75): "Ubi autem venit plenitudo temporis, ut Novum Testamentum revelaretur, quod figuris veteris velabatur, evidenti testificatione iam demonstrandum erat esse aliam vitam, pro qua debet haec vita contemni, et aliud regnum, pro quo oportet omnium terrenorum regnorum adversitatem patientissime sustineri."

179. *Contra Faustum* 22.76 (676).

180. *Contra Faustum* 22.76 (676): "Christiani quoque imperatores, plenam gerentes fiduciam pietatis in Christo de inimicis sacrilegis, qui spem suam in sacramentis idolorum daemonumque posuerant, gloriosissimam victoriam perceperunt, cum apertissimis notissimisque documentis, de quibus nonnulli iam scriptum memoriae commendarunt, illos fallerent vaticinia daemoniorum, hos firmarent praedicta sanctorum."

example of God using war to defeat his enemies showed that he could have done the same in Old Testament times.

The "most glorious victory" of which Augustine here speaks has to be the battle of the Frigidus. As noted in chapter 3, Rufinus of Aquileia had staged the battle as a conflict between paganism and Christianity, with Theodosius fighting "in the name of Christ." The Christian emperor had relied on the intercession of the saints, while the pagan supporters of the usurper Eugenius had divined from the inspection of entrails certain victory for their imperial patron.[181] Eugenius's pagan adherents took added encouragement from a prophecy—perhaps the one alluded to here—saying that Christianity would come to an end after a year of years, i.e., 365 years after its beginning, in the year 395.[182] Meanwhile, Theodosius had received his own assurances of victory from the holy monk John of Lycopolis.[183] The victory is here ascribed to "imperatores," meaning Theodosius and his sons, as it was customary to assign victories to all members of the imperial college,[184] and as it was especially politic of Augustine for him so to honor his own, current sovereign, Theodosius's son Honorius.

Augustine returned to the battle about a decade later in a chapter in *The City of God* largely devoted to an account of the emperor Theodosius that emphasizes his exercise of Christian virtues. When the boy Valentinian II fled to the East after the usurper Maximus had killed his older brother Gratian, Theodosius had taken him under his protection and treated him like a son.

181. Rufinus, *HE* XI.11.33.

182. Augustine details the pagan prophecy some twenty-odd years after *Contra Faustum*, in *DCD* 18.53–54 (*CCL* 48, 652–55). The mention of the battle of the Frigidus in *Contra Faustum* and the more detailed later account in *DCD* 5.26 go to the question of the extent to which Augustine relied for his knowledge of the battle upon Rufinus's account. Yves-Marie Duval argued that Augustine derived most of his account of the battle in *DCD* 5.26 from Rufinus, while acknowledging he also used other sources ("L'éloge de Théodose dans la *Cité de Dieu* (V, 26, 1): Sa place, sons sens et ses sources," *Recherches augustiniennes* 4 [1966]: 144ff.). If Rufinus was also Augustine's source in *Contra Faustum*, that would incidentally provide a *terminus a quo* for *Contra Faustum* of 402 or 403, the date of the composition of Rufinus's history (on the circumstances of Rufinus's translation and continuation of Eusebius's church history, see F. X. Murphy, *Rufinus of Aquileia (345-411): His Life and Works* [Washington, DC: Catholic University of America Press, 1945], 158–85). However, there is really no reason to suppose that Augustine could not have learned at least some of the details of the battle on his own, which would also explain his knowledge of the prophecy, a prophecy not detailed by him until years later in *DCD*. On doubts as to whether Rufinus's account of Theodosius influenced that in *DCD* 5.26, see O'Daly, 263–64.

183. Chapter 3 above, notes 2 to 4.

184. Michael McCormick, *Eternal Victory: Triumphal Rulership in Late Antiquity, Byzantium, and the Early Medieval West* (Cambridge: Cambridge University Press, 1986), 111–19.

Augustine repeats the story also seen in Rufinus and other writers of Theodosius consulting the hermit John in Egypt before embarking on his campaigns against the Western usurpers. In his account of the defeat of Eugenius at the battle of the Frigidus, Augustine as with other Christian authors makes great play of the wind during the battle that blew in the faces of Eugenius's soldiers, turning their cast spears back upon them, even quoting (selectively) from the pagan poet Claudian's account of the occurrence. Augustine's own account of Theodosius's reign culminates with the emperor's penance after the massacre at Thessalonica.[185]

Certain aspects of this Book 5, chapter 26 on Theodosius in *The City of God* have proved troubling for some modern scholars. The connection of the chapter's contents with the previous chapters betrays to some a logical incoherence and therefore a jarring abruptness in the transition between chapters 25 and 26.[186] Some have regarded Augustine's portrait of Theodosius here as inappropriate given the writer's otherwise generally pessimistic take on *homo politicus*, and certainly see the chapter as inconsistent with Augustine's measured assessment just earlier in Book 5 of what could be realistically expected of a Christian ruler. In this regard, Peter Brown at one point went so far as to characterize this chapter as being among "some of the most shoddy passages of the *City of God*," terming this chapter in particular a "sketchy and superficial panegyric," and he was followed more or less in this judgment by others.[187]

Yves-Marie Duval, on the other hand, has argued that this chapter does bear a logical connection with what precedes it, and forms a fitting conclusion to the entire unit of the first five books of *The City of God*. Elements of Augustine's portrait of Theodosius correspond to characteristics of the ideal Christian ruler outlined in previous chapters of Book 5, and in particular to

185. *DCD* 5.26 (*CCL* 47, 161–63). I agree with Dodaro's contention that this chapter is rhetorically structured to emphasize at the conclusion the account of Theodosius's penance, and that one aim of the chapter is to present an alternative Christian heroic ideal to that of the Roman heroes treated earlier in Book 5. See Robert Dodaro, "Language and Justice in Political Anthropology in Augustine's *De civitate dei*" (Ph.D. dissertation, Oxford, 1992), 199–200, and on Augustine's discussion of Christian heroism at the end of Book 5 see also Louis J. Swift, "St. Ambrose on Violence and War," *Transactions and Proceedings of the American Philological Association* 101 (1970): 520–22.

186. Duval (n. 182 above), 134 and n. 2.

187. P. R. L. Brown, "Saint Augustine," in *Trends in Medieval Political Thought*, ed. Beryl Smalley (Oxford: Basil Blackwell, 1965), 8 and 19, n. 28; R. A. Markus, *Saeculum: History and Society in the Theology of St. Augustine* (Cambridge: Cambridge University Press, 1970), 57 and n. 1, and "Saint Augustine's Views on the 'Just War,'" *Studies in Church History* 20 (1983): 12; Swift (n. 183 above), 520–21.

the sketch of such a ruler found in Augustine's summary "mirror of princes" in chapter 24, to the extent that Theodosius could be regarded as the realization of that ideal.[188] For instance, his merciful treatment of the children of the defeated usurpers, who lost neither life nor property, is in line with the compassionate conduct expected of a Christian prince in chapter 24, as is his use of the law to suppress paganism and heresy, since Christian rulers should "make their power a servant to His Majesty for the spreading of God's worship as far as possible."[189] But it is especially Theodosius's penance that establishes him as the real-life embodiment of Augustine's ideal Christian ruler.[190]

Why did Augustine make Theodosius and not Constantine his ideal prince? Quite apart from whether Augustine was disenchanted with Constantine because of his having had his wife and son executed,[191] the first Christian emperor was an inappropriate model because the "successes" of his reign were of a sort indistinguishable from those of pagan princes and bore no distinctive Christian stamp, as did many of Theodosius's. We can see Augustine more or less explicitly making this very point. In his brief "mirror of princes" in chapter 24 Augustine had written that Christian emperors who defeat enemies foreign and domestic, have a long reign, and leave the empire to their sons after a peaceful death are not for those things alone considered to be divinely favored, since "even some worshippers of demons, who do not belong to the kingdom of God as do the Christian emperors, obtained those and other rewards or consolations in this wretched life."[192] That Augustine had Constantine in mind here is proved by his listing of these very aspects of Constantine's reign in his brief account of the emperor in the next chapter.[193] God's favor, in a ruler as

188. Duval (n. 182 above), 136–43.

189. *DCD* 5.24 (*CCL* 47, 160): ". . . felices eos [viz. the Christian emperors] dicimus . . . si suam potestatem ad Dei cultum maxime dilatandum maiestati eius famulam faciunt . . . si eandem vindictam pro necessitate regendae tuendaeque rei publicae, non pro saturandis inimicitiarum odiis exerunt . . ." Cf. *DCD* 5.26 (162): "Inimicorum suorum filios, quos, non ipsius iussu, belli abstulerat impetus, etiam nondum Christianos ad ecclesiam confugientes, Christianos hac occasione fieri voluit et Christiana caritate dilexit, nec privavit rebus et auxit honoribus. In neminem post victoriam privatas inimicitias valere permisit. . . . Inter haec omnia ex ipso initio imperii sui non quievit iustissimis et misericordissimis legibus adversus impios laboranti ecclesiae subvenire, quam Valens haereticus favens Arrianis vehementer adflixerat; cuius ecclesiae se membrum esse magis quam in terris regnare gaudebat. Simulacra gentilium ubique evertenda praecepit, satis intellegens nec terrena munera in daemoniorum, sed in Dei veri esse posita potestate."

190. Dodaro (n. 185 above), 199–202.

191. On the executions of Constantine's son Crispus and wife Fausta, see T. D. Barnes, *Constantine and Eusebius* (Cambridge, MA: Harvard University Press, 1981), 220–21.

192. *DCD* 5.24 (*CCL* 47, 160).

193. *DCD* 5.25 (161).

for anyone, is not earthbound, since God "makes his sun rise on the evil and on the good, and sends rain on the just and on the unjust" (Matt. 5:45),[194] but is rather exemplified by the good works Theodosius carried with him into eternity from the fleeting smoke of this earthly existence.[195] It is probably the case that, in addition to forestalling pagan arguments that Constantine was not distinguishable in his successes from their emperors, Augustine was here undercutting the Christian "triumphalism" of writers like Eusebius and Rufinus, who uncritically linked causally the Christianity of rulers like Constantine and Theodosius to their earthly success.[196]

But even though Augustine emphasized as part of his catalog of the emperor's good works Theodosius's clemency in the aftermath of his victories over the Western usurpers, is not his inclusion of a relatively lengthy narrative of the battle of the Frigidus, situated as if for added emphasis in the center of his account of the emperor, inconsistent with his aim of devaluing the merely earthly success of Christian rulers? That may be, but in any case it is evident that here we have a real-life, contemporary example of a *bonus*, a truly virtuous Christian ruler, fighting a war that serves the ends of divine justice. It is true that when he had written of the battle a decade earlier in *Contra Faustum*, Augustine had explicitly associated it with the God-directed wars of the Old Testament.[197] Perhaps because in the decade since he had become more circumspect in making any secure providential interpretations of contemporary events,[198] Augustine's presentation of the battle in *The City of God* is less straightforward in linking the battle to the exercise of divine will, but the association is nonetheless present. Before both of his campaigns against the Western usurpers, Theodosius had received divine imprimatur for his campaigns from the hermit John, who had assured the emperor that his victory was fixed and determined, as though foreordained in the plan of providence.[199] And there is no mistaking the divine intervention during the battle itself in the form of the providential wind that seems to have followed upon the emperor's prayers.[200] At first glance it is admittedly curious that, unlike

194. On this verse as a leitmotiv in Augustine's apologetic in Books 1–5 of *The City of God*, see Duval (n. 182 above), 138 and n. 13.

195. *DCD* 5.26 (162). As Duval noted, this last sentence is yet another reminiscence of the leitmotiv verse from Matthew.

196. Swift (n. 185 above), 521.

197. Notes 177 to 180 above.

198. This change in Augustine's outlook is one of the main points stressed by Markus in his book *Saeculum*, esp. 33–44, 52–57.

199. *DCD* 5.26 (CCL 47, 161).

in Rufinus's account, Augustine does not explicitly from the outset stage the contest between Theodosius and Eugenius as one between Christianity and paganism. That such was the case appears only in the battle's aftermath, when the victorious emperor had taken down statues of Jupiter that his opponents had set up in the Alps as talismans against him, presenting the god's golden thunderbolts as gifts to his followers amidst the gaiety of their victory celebration.[201] Coming as it does in a scene of joyous repose after the storm of battle, the placement of this episode, an episode unique to Augustine's account,[202] can only be a narrative strategy designed to emphasize the war's religious character and the ridiculous impotence of the gods in the face of the providential purposes of the one true God.

Augustine also both implicitly and explicitly contrasts the battle of the Frigidus with conflicts in earlier Roman history mentioned previously in *The City of God*, doubtlessly in order to counter pagan objections that Theodosius's victories in civil wars were no different in kind from those won in similar circumstances by pagan emperors. When Augustine wrote that Theodosius, although oppressed by anxiety on the eve of marching against the hitherto invincible usurper Maximus, "did not lapse into sacrilegious and forbidden inquiries" but had instead consulted the Christian hermit John,[203] he is referring to acts such as Sulla's consultation of the haruspices in his civil war against Marius, an activity Augustine had alluded to on the part of Theodosius's opponents in his earlier account in *Contra Faustum* and mentioned outright by Rufinus in his account.[204] Theodosius's clemency toward his defeated opponents is contrasted explicitly with the vengeance taken by Cinna, Marius, Sulla, and others in the aftermath of their civil wars.[205]

It may be that the seemingly militant Christian "triumphalism" evident in Augustine's view of the battle of the Frigidus, especially that seen in his later account in *The City of God*, is by some reckoning inconsistent with the stance more commonly visible in his later writings of a reluctance to

---

200. *DCD* 5.26 (161).

201. *DCD* 5.26 (162).

202. Duval (n. 182 above), 158–59.

203. *DCD* 5.26 (161): "Deinde cum Maximum terribilem faceret ille successus, hic in angustiis curarum suarum non est lapsus ad curiositates sacrilegas atque inlicitas," etc.

204. *DCD* 2.24 (*CCL* 47, 58-9); *Contra Faustum* 22.76 (*CSEL* 25, 676): ". . . inimicis sacrilegis, qui spem suam in sacramentis idolorum daemonumque posuerant . . ."; Rufinus *HE* XI. 33 (*GCS* 9.2, 1037).

205. *DCD* 3.27–30 (*CCL* 47, 93–96). Cf. *DCD* 5.26 (*CCL* 47, 162): "Bella civilia non sicut Cinna et Marius et Sulla et alii tales nec finita finire voluerunt, sed magis doluit exorta quam cuiquam nocere voluit terminata."

include recent events within the ongoing progress of salvation history, events that a Eusebius or a Rufinus, by contrast, readily interpreted in scriptural categories within the serenely confident embrace of a Christian empire. But no overarching interpretation of his writings, early or late, can grind Augustine the man down to a dead consistency; for it is often a man's inconsistencies that make him come most alive. In his response to the battle of the Frigidus one catches a distant echo of Augustine in his lived present, of the exciting reports conveyed to his Mediterranean port city within weeks of the battle concerning its extraordinary climax, and of his own eagerness in succeeding years to glean eyewitness accounts of the battle's amazing occurrences.[206] There had swiftly emerged an "official" Christian interpretation of the battle, sanctioned by no less an authority than that champion of orthodoxy and confessor of emperors Ambrose of Milan, that saw it as equivalent to the battles of the Old Testament, a contest like those between a pious ruler of God's people and God's enemies that was decided by an act of direct divine intervention.[207] It would be more surprising had Augustine *not* followed the prevailing consensus in Christian circles that in this one instance God had plainly showed his hand in a contemporary event, and had Augustine *not* deployed that interpretation when it suited his polemical purposes in countering the claims of Manichaeans and pagans. In this one instance the mystique of *victoria*, a prop in the theater of Roman imperial politics, could be legitimately associated with the unfolding of the predetermined providential plan, as had been announced beforehand to Theodosius by a prophet of God.[208] It is here that the true anomaly in Augustine's view of the battle lies, since he otherwise not only saw the *victoria* of Roman politics as devoid of any tincture of the divine, but even regarded it as a sham, a fig leaf used to cover up the horrors of war.

206. Cameron (ch. 3, n. 32 above), 93 and n. 3, citing Duval and Courcelle, wants to see the following in Rufinus *HE* XI 33 (1038): [Theodosius's generals are encouraged to the battle by their pious prince's prayer (ch. 3, n. 17 above)] "quam supplicationem pii principis certi a deo esse susceptam hi qui aderant duces animantur ad caedam" echoed in Augustine *DCD* 5.26 (161): "Milites nobis qui aderant rettulerunt extorta sibi esse de manibus quaecumque iaculabantur, cum a Theodosii partibus in adversarios vehemens ventus iret," etc. But *duces* are not *milites, adesse* is a common enough verb, and in Rufinus it's about the generals present at Theodosius's battlefield prayer, while in Augustine it's witnesses to the miraculous wind.

207. Ambrose, *Extra collectionem* 2.3, 3.4 (*CSEL* 82, 178–79, 181); *Explanatio Psalmorum XII*.25 (*CSEL* 64, 91); chapter 3, notes 46 to 50 above.

208. *DCD* 5.26 (161): ". . . ad Iohannem in Aegypti heremo constitutum, quem Dei servum prophetandi spiritu praeditum fama crebrescente didicerat, misit atque ab eo nuntium victoriae certissimum accepit."

8

Final Victory and Perfect Peace

VICTORIA

We have seen how Augustine "baptized" the Roman just war, which in its Christian translation denoted God-authorized wars fought to further the ends of divine justice and providence, wars that were restricted in the main to those of the Old Testament. Augustine also transposed into a Christian key the Roman political terminology of *pax* and *victoria*. But even more so than in the case of just war, the bishop of Hippo derided *victoria* as it was usually manifested in the terrestrial sphere. At its best it could only bring about an earthly peace that was transitory and incomplete. And although it was possible to have a Christian version of *victoria*, that usually referred to the Christian victory over death, and in particular it had an eschatological reference to the final attainment of the full and complete peace of eternal life.

The word *victoria* appears about four hundred times in Augustine's extant works.[1] Of those occurrences, over eighty, about one-fifth of the total, come from his citation of 1 Cor. 15:54: "Death is swallowed up in victory." This verse and that which follows—"O death, where is thy victory? O death, where is thy sting?" (1 Cor. 15:55)—provide for Augustine his predominant signification for the term, the victory over death attained by Christians through Christ. The original such victory, of course, was that of Christ himself.[2] Almost as significant for Augustine was the victory of the martyrs over death.[3] In a language already long-hallowed by centuries of usage in Augustine's day, the struggle of the martyrs in their agony was likened to an athletic contest, and their deaths

---

1. This number is based on my word search in the *Patrologia Latina* database of vols. 32–47, excluding *victoria* when it occurs as the proper name of a person or a place, and when it occurs in works not by Augustine or in works falsely attributed to him. This count, of course, leaves out of consideration Augustinian works discovered since the nineteenth century, particularly in the way of sermons and the Divjak letters, but such material cannot add appreciably to the total.

2. E.g., *Enarr. in Ps. 60.3* (*CCL* 39, 766); *Serm.* 97.4, 263.1bis; 284.5 (*PL* 38:591, 1209, 1210, 1292); *DCD* 13.7 (*CCL* 48, 390).

likened to the winning athlete being crowned with the laurels of victory. In a sermon preached on his feast-day on January 22 in the early 410s,[4] Augustine referred to St. Vincent, a martyr of the Diocletianic persecution, as a soldier of Christ, who had in a great battle attained a glory that was not human or temporal, but divine and eternal.[5] In the battles of the martyrs and saints, far more important in the end than any temporal battle fought on earth, the saints were the soldiers, Christ was their general, and the devil was the enemy.

> Now, brethren, you see saints armed; consider their slaughters, consider their glorious battles. For if there's a commander, there's also soldiers; if soldiers, then an enemy; if war, then a victory.[6]

This battle against the devil was to some extent fought by all Christians. It was a conflict not to be conceived of as being solely against external satanic power, however, but also and especially referred to the internal battle against the propensity to sin, a battle that for Augustine was far more significant in its consequences for a Christian than any merely human war.[7] He made this point the most clearly in a sermon probably preached during the time he was writing the first books of *The City of God* in the early 410s.[8]

> For you continue to have a war against yourself. War is declared upon you, not only against the suggestions of the devil, against the prince of the power of this air, who works "upon the children of unbelief" (Eph. 5:6), against the devil and his angels, the spiritual powers of wickedness; not only against them is war declared upon you, but [war is declared] against you yourself. How against you yourself? Against your bad habits, against the long continuance of

3. E.g., *Contra Faustum* 22.76 (*CSEL* 25, 676); *Serm.* 280.2, 284.5bis, 296.5, 309.1, 311.1, 313.2, 5, 319.2 (*PL* 38:1281, 1291, 1292, 1355, 1410, 1414, 1423, 1424, 1440); *DCD* 8.27, 13.4 (*CCL* 47, 248; 48, 388).

4. Fitzgerald, 784.

5. *Serm.* 274 (*PL* 38:1252–53).

6. *Enarr. in Ps.* 149.12 (*CCL* 40, 2186).

7. On this internal war of man against himself, see Rief (ch. 7, n. 3 above), 58–68.

8. S. M. Zarb, *Chronologia Enarrationum s. Augustini in Psalmos* (Valetta-Malta, 1948), 186–87, 231 dates this sermon to 411 or 412 based on its seeming to postdate the great Donatist-Catholic confrontation at the conference at Carthage in 411, and the presence of anti-Pelagian sentiments. A date in the early 410s is also suggested by his reflections on *pax* in section 6 (*CCL* 39, 1041): "In illa pace aeterna, in illa pace perfecta," the last formulation appearing also in the preface to *The City of God*, written between 411 and 413, on which see note 91 below.

your evil life, which draws you back to old habits, and holds you back from new ones.[9]

In another sermon perhaps preached about the same time on Psalm 143 (144),[10] a psalm according to its superscription referring to the battle between David and Goliath, Augustine argued that the psalm's deeper meaning referred to this spiritual warfare waged by Christians. One such war was waged, according to St. Paul, "not against flesh and blood, but against principalities, and the powers and rulers of the world" (Eph. 6:13). These rulers, according to the bishop, were the devil and his angels.[11]

> This is one kind of battle. But each one of us has another in himself. There was read out this kind of war in the apostle's epistle: "Flesh lusts against the spirit, and the spirit against the flesh, so that you do not do that which you wish" (Gal. 5:17). And this kind of war is serious, and what is more troubling, internal. If anyone is victorious in this war, he will at that moment overcome enemies he does not see. For the devil and his angels have no power to attack us except for that part in us in which the flesh is dominant. In fact, how can we be victorious over those enemies which we do not see unless we're able to sense the internal impulses of our flesh? In our combatting these impulses, we strike down those enemies.[12]

In this internal warfare against the lusts of the flesh, which comprised not only illicit sexual desires but also greed and the lust to power, *libido dominandi*, victory could not be obtained by our own efforts, as the Pelagians thought, but only with the aid of divine grace. In any case, a final victory over the internal vices was only possible at the resurrection.[13]

---

9. *Enarr. in Ps.* 75.4 (*CCL* 39, 1039). On this passage, see Rief (ch. 7, n. 3 above), 60–62.

10. Zarb (n. 8 above), 154–56 argues for a date in December 412, and that in any case the sermon postdates the sack of Rome. A date in the early 410s is also argued by H. Rondet, "Le thème du Cantique Nouveau dans l'oeuvre de saint Augustin," *L'homme devant Dieu: Mélanges offerts au Père Henri de Lubac* (Lyon: Éditions Montaigne, 1963), 350–51. But see the arguments of P.-M. Hombert, *Nouvelles recherches de chronologie augustinienne* (Paris: Institut d'Études Augustiniennes, 2000), 558, n. 18 for 406, and the discussion by H. Müller, *Augustinus-Lexikon*, ed. Cornelius Mayer (Basel: Schwabe & Co., 1986–94), "Enarrationes in Psalmos," 824.

11. *Enarr. in Ps.* 143.4 (*CCL* 40, 2075).

12. *Enarr. in Ps.* 143.5 (*CCL* 40, 2075).

13. E.g., *De libero arbitrio* 3.19 53 (180) (*CCL* 29, 306); *De peccatorum meritis et remissione et de baptismo parvulorum* I.22 (31) (*CSEL* 60, 30); *Contra Iulianum* II.8.27, IV.2.6, VI.23.70 (*PL* 44:692, 739, 866); *Enarr.*

268 | Augustine on War and Military Service

Augustine explicitly contrasted this internal war and its particular sort of battles and victories with the external war in the world in his letter to Boniface in 428.[14] In that letter the bishop admitted he could only offer prayer insofar as helping Boniface to prevail in his civil war. Besides, even if he won that war, any such victory was at best transitory, and said nothing about the justice of his cause. No, it was better for Boniface instead to try, with God's help, to master the internal passions that had led him to strive for power in the first place.[15]

> Let this show whether you are a strong man; conquer the impulses which make you love the world; do penance for your past misdeeds when you were overcome by your impulses and taken captive by vain passions. . . . Pray earnestly and speak to God in the words of the psalm: "Deliver me from my necessities" (Ps. 24:17). For those necessities are brought to an end when the passions are overcome. He who has heard your prayers as we prayed for you that you might be delivered from so many great perils of visible and corporeal wars, where the sole danger is to this life doomed to end sometime—but the soul does not perish unless it is held captive by malign passions—will Himself hear your prayer that you may win an invisible and spiritual victory over your interior and invisible enemies, that is, those same passions.[16]

Augustine spoke most to what was for him the lesser *victoria* in *The City of God*, especially in its early books. As part of his polemic there against pagans who blamed the dominance of Christianity for recent disasters, Augustine in those early books sought to devalue a series of terms that were traditionally considered significant in the pagan Romans' inflated self-image. In the concluding chapter to Book 2 alone he argued that *pietas, gloria, patria, libertas, societas,* and *dignitas* had never really existed in pagan Rome, or had existed in a debased or incomplete form. Augustine argued in each case that the true manifestation of these values could only be found in the city of the one, true God.[17] Among those revalued terms were those of *pax* and *victoria*.

---

in Ps. 118, s. 26.2 (*CCL* 40, 1754); *Serm.* 57.13, 58.3 (4), 128.8 (10), 151.3, 7, 154.6 (8), 163 *passim,* 210.2 (3) (*PL* 38:392, 393, 718, 816, 818, 836, 889–95, 1049), 335A (*Miscellanea Agostiniana* I [Rome, 1930], 221).

14. For the circumstances of this letter, see ch. 7, notes 153 to 167 above.

15. *Epist.* 220.9–12 (*CSEL* 57, 438–41).

16. *Epist.* 220.9, 10 (*CSEL* 57, 438, 439). Parsons trans., *The Fathers of the Church* 32 (New York, 1956).

"Lofty beyond compare is that brighter city where victory is truth, where dignity is holiness, where peace is happiness, where life is eternal."[18] As its very title demonstrates, Augustine's massive work constituted a head-on assault against the validity of traditional Roman civic values, values that could only be completely realized in the society of the faithful. As we will see, the author placed *pax* and *victoria* at the core of this critique, and in translating the values of the earthly to the heavenly city retained peace and victory as central values in the city of God.

What explains Augustine's focus on earthly *victoria* in *The City of God*? As we earlier saw in the case of Volusianus, pagan critics had charged that the gods had withheld their favor because of the predominance of Christianity and the abandonment of the *mos maiorum*.[19] The sack of Rome made it manifest that emperor and empire could no longer claim to possess the numinous mystique of *victoria*. Unable to deny that victory had of late apparently departed, Augustine aimed to counter with the argument that much worse disasters had befallen Rome in the past when it supposedly had enjoyed the gods' favor, and therefore sought to strip *victoria* of its numinous quality. But it is also clear, as we saw earlier in his discussion of the Decalogue commandment against killing in Book 1,[20] that Augustine in *The City of God* also deployed arguments against certain of his fellow believers. From the time of Constantine on, there had been those who believed that Christian emperors now possessed the mystique of *victoria*. Indeed, in the same years in which Augustine was writing the first books of *The City of God*, Christian emperors in both East and West had engaged in a veritable frenzy of victory celebrations and proclamations as though to compensate through propaganda for their lack of military success in reality.[21] In looking at Augustine's critique of *victoria* in *The City of God* one must always keep in mind that he was speaking to a Christian as well as to a pagan audience.

Augustine frequently criticizes earthly *victoria* in his survey of Roman history in Book 3, portraying it as an uncertain and melancholy aspect of that history that is often purchased at the cost of terribly destructive and even monstrous violence. The pattern is set at the very beginning of Roman history with the sad and shameful victories over the Romans' Sabine fathers-

---

17. *DCD* 2.29 (*CCL* 47, 64–65).

18. *DCD* 2.29 (*CCL* 47, 65).

19. Chapter 7, notes 41, 42 above.

20. Chapter 6, notes 173 to 177 above.

21. Michael McCormick, *Eternal Victory: Triumphal Rulership in Late Antiquity, Byzantium, and the Early Medieval West* (Cambridge: Cambridge University Press, 1986), 59.

in-law.[22] Obviously virtue is no prerequisite for obtaining *victoria*, nor are its results guaranteed to be worthwhile. For although the last king of Rome, Tarquinius Superbus, was a parricide, and although the gods, seemingly blind to his crimes, favored him with many victories in war, the end result of all those bloody victories was that Rome's borders advanced a mere twenty miles from the city. Augustine sarcastically wonders whether the gods in so favoring the Romans had actually been punishing them, "seducing them with empty victories and grinding them down with wars most harsh."[23] And the times of the early Republic that succeeded were no better, for its history up to the Second Punic War was plagued with foreign wars and domestic discord. "Accordingly their victories were not the solid and enduring joys of the truly happy, but empty consolations for the wretched."[24] Nor could the pagans claim any improvement in imperial times, as the example of their hero Julian the Apostate attested. Julian had been a devotee of oracles, and relying on their assurances of *victoria* had during his invasion of Persia burned his fleet and along with it his army's provisions, leaving him ultimately stranded in enemy territory without supplies.[25] *Victoria*, then, could be deceptive as well as barren.

The monstrousness of Rome's civil wars illustrated most clearly how valueless was *victoria*. Although Augustine in his critique of victory in civil wars concentrated on those of the late Republic, thereby underscoring the impotence or malice of the pagan gods then worshiped at Rome, as we saw earlier he also by so doing revealed a certain dismay at the destructive civil wars of his own day,[26] and we must therefore likewise understand in these passages an implied criticism of those individuals, pagans as well as Christians, who regarded favorably and even celebrated victories in the contemporary civil wars. Again, the pattern was set at the outset with the Roman war against the Sabines who had been wronged by the kidnapping of their daughters, a war that Augustine characterized with a quote from Lucan's *Pharsalia* on the civil war between Caesar and Pompey, "wars . . . worse than civil" ("bella . . . plus quam civilia").[27] Especially horrific had been the civil wars of Marius and Sulla. Here again the gods had acted maliciously, promising victory to Sulla through messengers and the haruspices, a victory that in the end harmed more than benefited both Rome and the victor's reputation.[28] Marius's victory

22. *DCD* 3.13 (*CCL* 47, 74).
23. *DCD* 3.15 (*CCL* 47, 79, 80).
24. *DCD* 3.17 (*CCL* 47, 82).
25. *DCD* 5.21 (*CCL* 47, 157–58).
26. Chapter 7, notes 18 to 29 above.
27. *DCD* 3.13 (*CCL* 47, 74).

in turn had been bloody, unworthy of a citizen, and more barbarous than that of a foreign enemy.[29] The "victories" of both Marius and Sulla witnessed the wholesale slaughter of Roman citizens in a cycle of bloody vengeance, filling the streets and temples of Rome with corpses.[30] "What fury of foreign nations, what savagery of barbarians, can be compared with this victory of citizens over citizens?"[31]

In Book 4 Augustine's aim shifts to an attempt "to demythologize the imperial ideology."[32] *Victoria*, of course, was a prominent fixture in that imperial ideology. Its association with a pagan goddess had led Ambrose in 384, as we saw in chapter 3, to fight to keep the goddess's image out of the senate house at Rome.[33] Augustine, who arrived in Milan while still a teacher of rhetoric in the summer of the same year,[34] had to have known of the controversy and something of the arguments on both sides. He, too, had ultimately felt it necessary to counter the notion that *victoria* was an independent divine power, a vital and efficacious member of the pagan pantheon. But rather than attempting to rationalize it as had Ambrose, Augustine, who unlike the bishop of Milan regarded earthly victory as a dubious good at best, mounted a full-bore assault on the pagan goddess herself. She seemed useless and her role superfluous, and unlike other gods and goddesses that were regarded by Christians as having at least a demonic reality, she did not even exist.

Augustine's attack on the goddess Victoria is part of a torrent of withering sarcasm he directs in Book 4 against the traditional gods and their roles, in which he portrays them as fussy busybodies operating in a bloated, complicated, quasi-imperial bureaucracy. Even though any one of a number of the various divinities had at times a jurisdiction that was identical to or overlapped another's, not only did the Romans seem to have more gods and goddesses than they actually needed, they also apparently lacked divinities for things they did need and that were of benefit to the republic. As we saw earlier, Rome would not have been able to expand by fighting just wars but for the injustice of its foreign enemies (*iniquitas aliena*).[35] Should we not believe, then, that it was with the help of these two, Foreign Injustice and the goddess Victoria, that

---

28. *DCD* 2.24 (*CCL* 47, 58, 59).

29. *DCD* 2.23 (*CCL* 47, 58).

30. *DCD* 3.27; 28 (*CCL* 47, 94).

31. *DCD* 3.29 (*CCL* 47, 95; George E. McCracken Loeb trans.).

32. O'Daly, 89.

33. See chapter 3 above, notes 193 to 195.

34. Brown, 69.

35. Chapter 7, notes 145, 148, 149 above.

the empire grew?[36] And why stop there? "If Victoria is a goddess, why is not Triumph also a god, and joined to Victoria either as husband or brother or son?"[37] In fact, "why is not the Empire itself a god? Why not, if Victoria is a goddess?"[38]

Augustine with evident relish points out that Jupiter's role as king of the gods and the bestower of Rome's empire would be diminished to the extent that Victoria has independent authority in providing the military success that ensured the growth and preservation of that empire. Which of the two, then, was responsible for Rome's greatness? Did Victoria bring success only while Jupiter was on vacation?[39] Why is Jupiter even necessary

> if Victoria is favorable and propitious and always goes to those whom she wants to be the victors? If she were favorable and propitious, even if Jupiter were idle, or doing something else, what nations could remain unsubdued? What kingdoms would not yield? (Greene trans., modified)[40]

And "if empire is the gift of Jupiter, why isn't victory also regarded as his gift?"[41]

> Do they perhaps say that Jupiter sends the goddess Victoria and that she, in obedience as to the king of the gods, comes to some as she is bidden and takes her place at their side? This is truly said not of that Jupiter whom they fashion to match their fancy as king of the gods, but of that true King of the ages: that He sends not Victoria, who has no real substance, but His angel, and causes whomever He has chosen to be victorious. (Greene trans., modified)[42]

And even for those who did not believe in the Christian God, surely rather than invoking Victoria for military success

36. DCD 4.15 (CCL 47, 111; William M. Greene Loeb trans., modified).

37. DCD 4.17 (CCL 47, 112; Greene trans.).

38. DCD 4.14 (CCL 47, 110; Greene trans.).

39. DCD 4.15 (CCL 47, 111).

40. DCD 4.14 (CCL 47, 110).

41. DCD 4.15 (CCL 47, 111; Greene trans.).

42. DCD 4.17 (CCL 47, 112): "An forte dicunt, quod deam Victoriam Iuppiter mittat atque illa tamquam regi deorum obtemperans ad quos iusserit veniat et in eorum parte considat? Hoc vere dicitur non de illo Iove, quem deorum regem pro sua opinione confingunt, sed de illo vero rege saeculorum, quod mittat non Victoriam, quae nulla substantia est, sed angelum suum et faciat vincere quem voluerit; cuius consilium occultum esse potest, iniquum non potest."

they ought to have prayed to Jupiter for everything, and made supplication to him alone. For wherever he had sent Victoria, if she was a goddess and subject to him as king, she could not possibly venture to oppose him and act by her own volition instead.[43]

It is obvious that, as with other things personified by the Romans, Victoria as a goddess does not exist, but as victory is a gift of God.[44]

Even as a gift of God, earthly victory is at best a doubtful good. The earthly city in its finite existence embraces goods that are themselves the source of anguish, and so "this city is often divided against itself by litigations, wars, battles, and such victories as are either life-destroying or short-lived." For every victory is purchased with death, and since the rule it secures is but temporary, so too is earthly victory.[45] The case was really no better for the Romans of the Republic who had fought, not out of lust for power, *libido dominandi*, but for personal glory.

> As far as security and morality are concerned, those true values of human life, I am quite unable to see what difference it makes that some men are victors and others vanquished, except for the utterly empty pride in human glory. In that pride those men [the Romans] received their reward, burning with intense desire for glory and spreading the flames of war.[46]

Whether regarded as a goddess with independent authority or as a divine gift that exalted and legitimized the rule of emperors and empires, the word *victoria* was invoked to veil with a screen of mystification deeds that were rife with bloodshed and horror, such as those that characterized early Rome's war with her mother city Alba Longa.

> What is this word "fame," what is this word "victory" offered up to me? Once the impediments of such irrational beliefs have been removed, let us look at the naked deeds, weigh them naked, judge them naked.

43. *DCD* 4.17 (*CCL* 47, 112; Greene trans.).
44. *DCD* 4.21, 24 (*CCL* 47, 114, 118–19).
45. *DCD* 15.4 (*CCL* 48, 456–57).
46. *DCD* 5.17 (*CCL* 47, 150).

Those who confront the reality of the thing with their cultural blinders removed cannot fail to see that "victory" is most often the result of the naked lust for power.[47]

Despite *victoria*'s inevitably tragic association with human bloodshed and horror, and despite its contaminating association with pagan religion, Augustine was well aware that long after the sack of Rome in 410, when one would think the empire's leaders would at least have been humbled in their pride and cured of their passion for power and glory, even Christian emperors and generals continued their futile pursuit of *victoria*'s bright illusion. As late as 424 or 425, when he was writing or about to begin Book 19 of *The City of God*,[48] Augustine noted that those who resort to war seek victory not just for the sake of any peace, but for one that redounded to their fame and glory.[49] It was not only true that supposedly Christian rulers and commanders vied with their pagan counterparts in terms of their heedless pursuit of power, but they even went so far as to beseech God in prayer to satisfy that desire. For it was characteristic of the earthly city, whether ruled by pagans or Christians, that it

> pays reverence to God or to gods who help it to rule by means of victories for the sake of an earthly peace, not out of concern for the common good, but out of a lust for mastery.[50]

47. *DCD* 3.14 (*CCL* 47, 76, 77).

48. O'Daly, 35 and Appendix D, 279–80.

49. *DCD* 19.12 (*CCL* 48, 675): "Quod mecum quisquis res humanas naturamque communem utcumque intuetur agnoscit; sicut enim nemo est qui gaudere nolit, ita nemo est qui pacem habere nolit. Quando quidem et ipsi, qui bella volunt, nihil aliud quam vincere volunt; ad gloriosam ergo pacem bellando cupiunt pervenire."

50. *DCD* 15.7 (*CCL* 48, 460–61): "Et hoc est terrenae proprium civitatis, Deum vel deos colere, quibus adiuvantibus regnet in victoriis et pace terrena, non caritate consulendi, sed dominandi cupiditate." The translations by Henry Bettenson (*St. Augustine: Concerning The City of God against the Pagans* [London: Penguin, 1972], 604), Philip Levine in the Loeb edition (*Saint Augustine: The City of God against the Pagans* [Cambridge, MA: Harvard University Press, 1966], vol. 4, 441), and R. W. Dyson in the Cambridge history of political thought series (*Augustine: The City of God against the Pagans* [Cambridge: Cambridge University Press, 1998], 644), all render "Deum vel deos colere" as "to worship a god or gods." I think it fairly clear—given that Augustine had just been discussing how Cain's offering had displeased God, in that he had been thereby trying to bribe God to satisfy a selfish desire (460: ". . . Deum non respexisse in munus eius, quia hoc ipso male dividebat, dans Deo aliquid suum, sibi autem se ipsum. Quod omnes faciunt, qui non Dei, sed suam sectantes voluntatem, id est non recto, sed perverso corde viventes, offerunt tamen Deo munus, quo putant eum redimi, ut eorum non opituletur sanandis pravis cupiditatibus, sed explendis."), leading the author then to his remark on how such prayers for selfish ends were characteristic of those in the earthly city—that by "Deum" in this passage Augustine is referring to the Christian deity, and I therefore concur with the editorial choice by Dombart and Kalb to capitalize

And we have a sermon in which Augustine specifically chides a Christian for praying for such a fleeting triviality as victory in war. In the course of Sermon 145 he counsels his audience on what it is appropriate to ask for in prayer. The bishop knows that many often pray for temporal things (*temporalia*) that are of no value in comparison with what they should ask for.

> One person asks for good health if he's sick; another asks to be set free if he's been put in prison; one person prays for a safe port if he's storm-tossed in a boat; another prays for victory if he's battling with an enemy; and a person prays for all this in Christ's name, and what he prays for is nothing.[51]

It is not surprising, then, that like Lactantius a century earlier, Augustine could not see how the merely temporal good of victory in war could be connected in any way with the justice or injustice of one's cause.[52] He made that point directly in his letter to Boniface in 428.

> Who does not know, who is so foolish as not to see, that the health of this mortal body and its perishable parts, strength and victory over men who are our enemies, and honor and temporal power and all such earthly goods are given equally to the good and the evil, and taken away equally from the good and the evil?[53]

Like Lactantius, Augustine therefore recognized that having a just cause did not guarantee divine support and hence success, and that at times the unjust party to a conflict could prevail. In discussing the origin of slavery in Book 19 of *The City of God*, Augustine argued that sin and its punishment were inextricably linked with even just wars and their outcomes.

> When a just war is waged, the side in the wrong fights to defend its sin; and every victory, even those when the wicked are successful, humbles the vanquished through a divine judgment, correcting or punishing their sins.[54]

the word in their *Corpus Christianorum* edition, and the choice by Marcus Dods so to render it in his translation (*The City of God by Saint Augustine* [New York: Random House, 1950], 485).

51. *Serm.* 145.6 (*PL* 38:795).
52. Lactantius, *Div. Inst.* VI.6.15–17 (*CSEL* 19, 501–2); ch. 2, n. 133 above.
53. *Epist.* 220.11 (*CSEL* 57, 439) Parsons trans. in *The Fathers of the Church* 32 (New York, 1956).
54. *DCD* 19.15 (*CCL* 48, 682).

Of course, this does not mean that the victory of the unjust side is preferable.

> When, however, they win who fought with a more just cause, who can doubt that the victory should be celebrated and that the resulting peace is desirable? These are good things and are undoubtedly gifts of God.[55]

Was victory in war, therefore, simply a matter of which side had the bigger battalions? Was it true that justice, whether human or divine, had little or nothing to do with war's outcome? Augustine's remark that even the defeat of the just side in war can benefit the losers by humbling their pride and punishing their sins reveals his thinking that victory in war, though usually at best an uncertain good, can sometimes partake of divine justice, and can be seen to do so especially at those times when its providential aspect is most apparent. The most evident instances of such victories tinged with divine justice, as in the case of just wars, occurred in the Old Testament. The lesson to be taken from these wars was that an earthly good such as victory in war was not in the power of some pagan deity or deities, but in that of the one, true God. After thoroughly debunking the Roman imperial pantheon in Book 4 of *The City of God*, paying particular attention to the false goddess Victoria, Augustine placed significantly in the last chapter of that book, as though to provide by way of conclusion the proper Christian alternative to the Roman martial deities, a reference to God's helping the ancient Hebrews to grow and prosper through wars stamped with the divine imprimatur of victory.

> Without the mad rites of Mars and Bellona they waged wars. While they did not conquer without victory, yet they regarded victory not as a goddess, but as the gift of their God.[56]

In the long course of writing *The City of God*, Augustine eventually went on to adapt his view of the Old Testament victories in the light of his evolving theological preoccupations. So in Book 16, written no earlier than 419[57] and years after he had become immersed in the Pelagian controversy, he wrote that the Hebrews had gained their victories under Joshua not so much because of

---

55. *DCD* 15.4 (*CCL* 48, 457).

56. *DCD* 4.34 (*CCL* 47, 127; Greene trans.). See also *Contra Faustum* 22.76 (*CSEL* 25, 674) and *Epist.* 140.7 (*CSEL* 44, 170–71) on God supporting the Israelites of the Old Testament through wars.

57. O'Daly, 35.

their merits but because of the sins of the nations they had defeated, once again emphasizing the providential role of God-assisted victory in punishing sin.[58]

We have seen how Augustine had gone out of his way, especially in Books 3 and 4 of *The City of God*, to criticize and denounce with passion and contempt the Roman ideological fixture of imperial *victoria*, which implied divine sanction for the rule of particular emperors. How could he then turn round at the end of Book 5 and apply what looks very much like the traditional Roman conception of *victoria* to Christian emperors, especially Theodosius? Already about a decade earlier in *Contra Faustum* he had written that Christian emperors (viz. Theodosius and his sons) had "gained a most glorious victory ('gloriossimam victoriam perceperunt')" at the battle of the Frigidus,[59] using language that would not have been out of place in a pagan author. He strikes only a slightly less panegyrical tone in Book 5 of *The City of God* when he notes, again using a term pregnant with ideological ramifications, that Constantine in his wars had been "victoriossimus,"[60] and goes on in the next chapter to emphasize the providential aspect of Theodosius's *victoria*.[61] To be sure, Augustine had in the chapter just previous to that in discussing Constantine argued that divine favor in war was not assured for Christian emperors.[62] But unlike the case with Constantine's victories, which as earthly goods were liable to be bestowed upon Christian and pagan emperors alike, it is obvious that Augustine regarded Theodosius's victory at the Frigidus as something special. As was argued above, undoubtedly at least some of the reason for this apparent inconsistency on Augustine's part was due to the fact that he, along with his Christian contemporaries, regarded the battle with its providential wind as a modern-day example of the miracle-tinged battles of the Old Testament.[63] In line with that interpretation, it may be that Augustine regarded Theodosius's success at the Frigidus not so much as the Christian equivalent of the Roman *victoria*, a divine legitimation of one man's rule due to his personal qualities, but as in the case of the Old Testament victories an instance of God using the event of war to defend his people as a group against godless enemies.

58. *DCD* 16.43 (*CCL* 48, 549).
59. *Contra Faustum* 22.76 (*CSEL* 25, 676); ch. 7, notes 178 to 182 above.
60. *DCD* 5.25 (*CCL* 47, 161).
61. *DCD* 5.26 (*CCL* 47, 161).
62. *DCD* 5.24 (*CCL* 47, 160).
63. Chapter 7, notes 195, 198 above.

PEACE

No survey of Augustine's view of the war in the external world can be complete without a look, however brief, at his view of earthly peace, war's opposite. Such a look must be brief because, as Donald Burt noted in his article on peace in *Augustine through the Ages*, "[p]eace is one of the central concepts in Augustine's thought. The word *pax* in one of its various forms appears more than 2,500 times in Augustine's writings."[64] Unlike the case with his view of *victoria*, the secondary literature on Augustine's view of peace is extensive.[65] So pervasive and significant in his writings are Augustine's references to peace that Frederick Russell in his article on war in the same encyclopedia was moved to state that "[i]t is ironic that he is often seen as a theologian of war, for he was more a theologian of peace."[66] This statement is much in need of qualification, however, since arguably Augustine could mean at least one of a half-dozen or so different sorts of peace by the use of the word *pax*. Especially when thinking of Augustine's earthly peace, one must also remember that, unlike the other temporal terms we have seen him dress in Christian robes, peace as a more general theological concept acquired such a prominence in Augustine's writings as to overshadow its specifically terrestrial manifestation. It is thus necessary to address briefly the contours of this more general concept that informed Augustine's understanding of the earthly peace that is war's opposite, especially in *The City of God* where, as we have seen him do with other secular terms, he was at pains to counterpoise that lesser peace with the perfect peace enjoyed by the citizens of the heavenly city.

Augustine's idea of peace has both Christian and classical roots. Christ in the Sermon on the Mount had said, "Blessed are the peacemakers, for they shall be called the children of God" (Matt. 5:9). In his letter to the Philippians, Paul had enjoined upon them "the peace of God, which surpasseth all understanding," that they might keep their "hearts and minds in Christ Jesus" (Phil. 4:7), a verse Augustine used to justify regarding the Christian peace, even that mentioned in the Beatitudes, as referring to internal rather than external

---

64. Donald Burt, "Peace," in Fitzgerald, 629.

65. Rather than attempting a necessarily incomplete listing of works, I list here those most important and list literature especially relevant to Augustine's view of earthly peace. See Harald Fuchs, *Augustin und der antike Friedensgedanke: Untersuchungen zum neunzehnten Buch der civitas Dei*, 2nd ed. (Berlin/Zürich: Weidmann, 1965); Joachim Laufs, *Der Friedensgedanke bei Augustinus: Untersuchungen zum XIX. Buch des Werkes de civitate Dei*, Hermes 27 (Wiesbaden: Franz Steiner, 1973), esp. bibliography, 145–46; Wilhelm Geerlings, "*De civitate dei* XIX als Buch der Augustinischen Friedenslehre," in *Augustinus: De civitate dei*, ed. Christoph Horn (Berlin: Akademie Verlag, 1997), 211–33, esp. bibliography, 232–33.

66. Frederick Russell, "War," Fitzgerald, 875.

human peace. Such an understanding of peace was also congruent with the ancient philosophical virtue of the "peace of the soul," the calming of the turbulence of internal passions.[67]

Augustine first wrote at length on peace in his work *De vera religione*, probably composed sometime in late 390.[68] There he argued that they are better off who want in this life what they should, including a certain "repose of the body" to be obtained "in living this life by abstaining from those things which one can do without." For such individuals, in the life to come what is now only partially known will be fully known "when that which is perfect is come" (1 Cor. 13:10).

> And peace entire will be at hand, for now "another law in my members fights against the law of my mind," but "the grace of God through Jesus Christ our Lord shall deliver us from the body of this death" (Rom. 7:23-25).[69]

He dealt with the subject at greater length a few years later in his commentary on the Sermon on the Mount when he wrote on the Beatitude, "Blessed are the peacemakers" (Matt. 5:9).

> "Blessed are the peacemakers, for they shall be called the children of God." Where there is no contention, there is perfect peace. . . . Those who calm their passions and subject them to reason, that is, subject them to mind and spirit, and who keep their carnal lusts under control, they are peacemakers within themselves, and become a kingdom of God, in which all things are so well ordered that that which is pre-eminent and excellent in human beings rules without opposition over that which is common to us and the beasts; and that very thing which excels in a human being, that is, mind and reason, is subject to something more powerful, which is Truth Itself, the only begotten Son of God. . . . And this is the peace which is given "on earth to men of good will" (Luke 2:14). This is the life of a man of consummate and perfect wisdom. The prince of this world, who rules over the perverse and disordered, has been cast out of such a kingdom that is completely at peace and in perfect order. (Denis J. Kavanagh trans. in the *Fathers of the Church* series, modified)[70]

67. Geerlings (n. 65 above), 213.
68. Fitzgerald, 864.
69. *De vera religione* 53.103 (284, 285) (*CSEL* 77, 73, 74; *CCL* 32, 253–54).

Augustine in this commentary regarded the eight maxims of the Beatitudes as corresponding to eight steps in the believer's progress to perfection, and thought that by ascending those steps some could actually attain perfection in this life.

> And for a fact these very things [viz. the promises of the Beatitudes] can be fulfilled in this lifetime, just as we believe they were fulfilled for the apostles.[71]

We can see already in these early works features of Augustine's view of peace that will remain constant in his thought. For him, peace referred primarily to a state internal to human beings. It was there that an internal war was fought, one conceived of by the early Augustine as that between unruly and rebellious passions, abetted by the devil, and the rational human mind that sought to quell those passions and impose a state of inner peace. This inner peace could be conceptualized as an internal ordering of the human constitution such that, as he put it a decade later in *Contra Faustum*, the rational soul exerted mastery over the irrational soul that human beings had in common with the animals, mirroring internally the same ordered subjection of fleshly impulses to spirit that existed externally between human beings and the Son of God. Other than the inclusion of Christ in the cosmic hierarchy, such a summary description of his view of internal peace in the early 390s does not strikingly differ from positions held by contemporary neo-Platonists, including especially the notion that the perfection of this internal peace was achievable on earth.

By the late 390s Augustine was not so sure of the last. As he reached his forties he was faced as bishop of Hippo not only with the seemingly intractable and never-ending external conflicts with the Donatists, but also had to acknowledge, as he painfully did in Book 10 of the *Confessions*, an ongoing internal struggle in himself against the same old fleshly impulses from which he had once thought he could escape. In wrestling with what could have become "the dangerous disillusionment of a perfectionist,"[72] Augustine reread Paul with new eyes, now seeing the apostle not as someone who like a philosopher had transcended passion, but as someone who frankly acknowledged that the tension between flesh and spirit could not be resolved this side of the grave. This sense of the limits of human perfectibility in this lifetime, and hence the limits of the possibility of attaining perfect internal peace, became a lasting

---

70. *De sermone Domini in monte* I. 2,9 (*CCL* 35, 6).

71. *De sermone Domini in monte* I. 4,12 (*CCL* 35, 12).

72. Brown, 141.

feature of Augustine's thinking.[73] When Augustine more than thirty years after writing his commentary on the Sermon on the Mount reviewed that work in his *Retractationes*,[74] he now expressed discomfort at some of his earlier easy assumptions. He referred specifically to his sentence that perfection "can be fulfilled in this lifetime, just as we believe [it was] fulfilled for the apostles," now writing of that statement that it

> should be understood not as though we think that there were no fleshly impulses fighting against the spirit in the case of the apostles while they were living this life, but rather that these things [again, the promises of the Beatitudes] can be fulfilled in this lifetime to the extent that we believe them to have been fulfilled for the apostles, that is, to that degree of human perfection insofar as perfection is possible in this lifetime.[75]

Augustine's perception from the late 390s on that a perfect internal peace was unachievable on earth does bear an important implication for how he viewed earthly peace. It is certainly true that Augustine spoke little if at all on the earthly peace that is war's opposite before writing *The City of God*. Early on he had even viewed the "peacemakers" of the Beatitudes as those who made peace within themselves.[76] Now even that internal peace seemed impossible in this lifetime. The implication seems inescapable that to the extent that heaven had now become more distant for Augustine, so too had the possibility and solidity of any earthly peace that ended war.

Augustine addressed more specifically and at length the various forms of earthly peace, including that which is war's opposite, in *The City of God*, especially in Book 19, written in the mid-420s.[77] As we have seen him do with other terms prominent in Roman ideology, Augustine both criticized the Roman idea of peace and redefined it as a Christian term. Seeing that *pax* and *victoria* were linked in Roman ideology, the former seen as the consequence

---

73. For this shift in Augustine, see especially Brown, in the chapter titled, "The Lost Future (139–50)," and his revisiting of that interpretation in the second edition of the biography, 490.

74. For the date of the *Retractationes* in 426 or 427, see Fitzgerald, 723.

75. *Retractationes* I.19 (CSEL 36, 88–89; CCL 57, 56).

76. As I have been informed by Professor John Meier of the University of Notre Dame, it seems likely that the "peacemakers" of Matt. 5:9 originally referred to disciples of Jesus who sought to settle grievances not only among the brethren but also those arising in the broader peasant society of Galilee, and hence the original reference of this Beatitude *is* to an external peace, though not perhaps that peace which is war's opposite.

77. On the chronology, O'Daly, 35.

of the latter and as the ultimate justification for the carnage that inevitably accompanied victory in war, he also sought to replicate in Christian guise—and in so doing underscored by implication his criticism of the "original"—that same causal relationship between peace and victory.

From the very beginning of Roman imperial ideology, *pax* had been inseparable from war. Originally the term *pax* itself had meant nothing other than an agreement or treaty to end or prevent war.[78] Its association with war continued under Augustus, and both official propaganda and contemporary literary sources testify to the ongoing linkage in Roman thought between peace and war.[79] Peace is the product of force. It "depends on victory, conquest, and subjugation," "is obtained through war—and manifested through the obeisance paid by defeated or dependent peoples."[80] Given that wars continued on the frontiers, and unrest to a greater or lesser degree persisted in many interior provinces, the greatest achievement that could be claimed for the *pax Romana* was the cessation, or near cessation, of the terrible civil wars that had plagued the Late Republic, wars that had led to the very imperial regime that proclaimed its maintenance of the Roman peace as one of the main props of its legitimation. Peace became an especially prominent theme in official propaganda in periods of civil war, or in civil war's immediate aftermath. At such times *pax* became associated with *concordia*, and was seen as dependent on it. Thus on the frontiers peace was regarded as the product of military force, while in the interior it resulted from the civil harmony existing among the constituent elements of the Roman political community.[81]

It was this Roman peace, the product of violence and subjugation, at which Augustine took aim from the very beginning of *The City of God*. The sack of Rome in 410 might for some have called into question the reality of the *pax Romana*, but certainly for many the loss of peace enkindled rather a heightened compensatory desire to see it restored. The proud Roman tradition of eternal victory over barbarian foes had to be reasserted through war, and certainly the imperial regime in Italy continued after 410 to try to reestablish the proper order of the Roman peace, where defeated enemies lay at the mercy of their imperial lords. Augustine in the preface to *The City of God*

78. Greg Woolf, "Roman Peace," in *War and Society in the Roman World*, ed. John Rich and Graham Shipley (London and New York: Routledge, 1993), 176.

79. E. S. Gruen, "Augustus and the Ideology of War and Peace," in *The Age of Augustus: Interdisciplinary Conference held at Brown University April 30–May 2, 1982*, ed. Rolf Winkes (Louvain-la-Neuve, Belgium: Art and Archaeology Publications Collège Érasme, 1985), 51–72.

80. Gruen, 56, 57.

81. Woolf, 176–77, 186.

quoted Vergil's summation of this imperial mission: "to spare the defeated and subdue the proud."[82] His point in so doing is to show that the claim that the imposition of the Roman peace acts to check human arrogance is itself an arrogant appropriation of what is properly left to God. He juxtaposes Vergil's boast with a quote from Scripture: "God resists the proud, but gives grace to the humble" (James 4:6).[83] In contrast to the Roman peace, the Christian peace is won by the Christian victory of the humble faithful.

Although the composition of *The City of God* took about a decade and a half, Augustine's conception of peace seems to have shifted little during that period. Having mentioned the "perfect peace" of the city of God in the preface to the entire work, it is not until Book 19 that he reflects upon the Christian use of the word "peace" and its relationship both to secular peace and to the traditional terminology of Christian doctrine.

> Since the word "peace" is often used even in these our mortal affairs, where there is no question of there being eternal life, for that reason we have preferred to call the end of this city [of God], where will be its highest good, eternal life rather than peace. Of this end the apostle says, "But now, being freed from sin, and become servants to God, you have your fruit unto holiness, and the end of eternal life" (Rom. 6:22). On the other hand, because those unfamiliar with Holy Scripture could understand by eternal life even the life of the wicked—either owing to the immortality of the soul as taught by certain philosophers, or even in accordance with our own belief as to the endless punishments of the godless, who obviously cannot be tormented forever unless they also live forever—so as to make it possible for everyone easily to understand what is actually the end of this city, where it shall have its highest good, that end should be termed either peace in eternal life or eternal life in peace.[84]

This perfect or complete peace of which Augustine spoke in *The City of God* and elsewhere[85] is certainly therefore not to be found amidst the torments

---

82. *Aeneid* 6.853: "Parcere subiectis et debellare superbos."

83. *DCD praef.* (*CCL* 47, 1): "Rex enim et conditor civitatis huius, de qua loqui instituimus, in scriptura populi sui sententiam divinae legis aperuit, qua dictum est: *Deus superbis resistit, humilibus autem dat gratiam.* Hoc vero, quod Dei est, superbae quoque animae spiritus inflatus adfectat amatque sibi in laudibus dici: *Parcere*," etc.

84. *DCD* 19.11 (*CCL* 48, 675).

85. E.g., *Enarr. in Ps. 143.9* (*CCL* 40, 2079): "plena victoria plena pax."

of the damned, and it is their eternal torment that for Augustine justifies distinguishing the faithful's form of eternal life with the concept of peace. His continued reflections on the nature of the internal strife among both the faithful and the damned that is ended for the former by this perfect peace illuminate something fundamental about the general idea of peace itself, and hence something as well about peace as it was commonly understood in relationship to war. For at its core,

> [w]hat is peace? Where there is no war. Where is it that there is no war? Where there is not any contradiction, where there is nothing resisting, nothing opposing. Look to whether we are there yet; look to whether there is not still a conflict with the devil, look to whether all the saints and the faithful are not still wrestling with the prince of demons. And how do they wrestle with him whom they do not see? They wrestle with their desires, through which he prompts them to sins; and by not consenting to his promptings, even if they are not conquered, they are still nonetheless engaged in a battle. So there is not yet peace where there is still a battle.[86]

Augustine in going on in *The City of God* to describe how internal strife continues after death in the case of the damned also reflects incidentally on the fundamental nature of war.

> But since war seems to be the opposite of peace, just as wretchedness is the opposite of blessedness and death the opposite of life, it can be legitimately asked what or what sort of war can be understood as the final state of the wicked that corresponds to the peace proclaimed and praised as the final state of the good. Whoever asks this should take note of what is actually harmful and destructive in war, and he will see that it is nothing other than the mutual opposition and conflict of things. So then what war can be thought of as being more serious and bitter than one where the will is so opposed to passion and passion so opposed to the will that such hostility cannot be ended by the victory of either of them, and where the violence of pain is in such conflict with the very nature of the body that neither yields to the other?[87]

---

86. *Enarr. in Ps. 84*.10 (*CCL* 39, 1169).
87. *DCD* 19.28 (*CCL* 48, 698).

As for the faithful, their temptations on earth only cause them to long all the more for the final peace,

> where the virtues are not at strife in any way with any vices or evils, but possess eternal peace, the reward of victory, a peace that no adversary can disturb.[88]

The faithful on earth are still as soldiers fighting with an enemy, battling against vices "until that kingdom of total peace is attained, where He shall reign without an enemy."[89] It is to this heavenly realm that Augustine wishes to shift a Christian's understanding of the true meaning of *pax* and *victoria*, away from their bloody association in the merely earthly wars of the Roman empire, a redirection of allegiance and focus that is such a fundamental aim of *The City of God* that he bookends the entire work with statements of this reinterpretation. So in Book 22, the very last of the work, he writes about "this our conflict [on earth], in which we are put to the test and from which we wish to be freed by a final victory."[90] And in the preface to the entire work, only a few lines in he writes that in the end the city of God will attain its eternal seat "in final victory and perfect peace."[91]

If there is such internal strife in human beings, including the good ones, and no true peace attainable in this lifetime, how could we mortals even imagine the possibility of perfect peace? And why do human beings, despite the impossibility of the quest, persist in trying to attain in this world even an imperfect peace? Augustine, especially in Book 19 of *The City of God*, answers these questions by arguing that the human striving for peace, even the imperfect peace, is a consequence of the created order. It is a law of human nature itself that causes humanity to search for peace. For before the Fall, Adam and Eve had been bound by the ties of affection into the smallest atomic unit of human *societas*, the family, and had passed on this desire for community to their descendants. A human community is only possible when its members exhibit a "oneness of heart," *concordia*, and it is the maintenance of this *concordia* among its members that ensures peace within the community.

---

88. *DCD* 19.10 (*CCL* 48, 674).

89. *DCD* 20.9 (*CCL* 48, 716–77).

90. *DCD* 22.23 (*CCL* 48, 846): ". . . noster iste conflictus, in quo periclitamur et de quo nos victoria novissima cupimus liberari . . ."

91. *DCD* 1 *praef.* (*CCL* 47, 1): ". . . victoria ultima et pace perfecta . . ." See also *Enarr. in Ps. 84*.10 (*CCL* 39, 1170): "et erit pax plena et aeterna."

But the first humans had been disobedient to God out of pride, *superbia*, the root of all other sins. Consequently the desire for peace had become perverted in the postlapsarian human community. Now, rather than achieving peace through a harmony between and among human beings, individuals sought to impose their own peace upon others by subjecting them to their power. Such individuals were not motivated to do so out of a love for God, or out of a love for what is eternal, but were driven by a desire for transitory earthly things, and were especially driven by a lust to dominate others, *libido dominandi*. Nonetheless, there remain imprinted in human nature *vestigia*, traces, of the original longing for the perfect peace. What causes humanity to continue to strive for an imperfect peace in this world, perverted and limited as such a peace may be by human weakness and sin, and including the peace that is the opposite of war, is this remnant of the original aspect of the created human nature.[92]

It is unsurprising, given his estimation of the concept, that Augustine links this peace and harmony to a ranked order that is maintained in human society by command and obedience, or that he actually defines peace itself in terms of order. The linking of peace and order appears at a number of points in Augustine's works, but is outlined explicitly in the so-called "peace-table" of chapter 13 in Book 19 of *The City of God*. There the author lists eight types of peace in an ascending hierarchy, in which each step builds upon that below it, beginning with the peace of the human body.[93] Each type of peace is ordered (*ordinata*), and with the level of the "peace between mortal humanity and God" ("pax hominis mortalis et Dei") there is added the characteristic of obedience. In the upper levels of this hierarchy are found the types of external human peace that relate to that peace connected with the absence of war, and each of these levels also involves *concordia*. Thus,

> peace among human beings is an ordered harmony (*concordia*), the peace of the household is an ordered harmony of command and obedience among those dwelling together, the peace of the [earthly] city is an ordered harmony of command and obedience among its citizens.

The highest form of peace is that of the heavenly city of God itself, a "perfectly ordered and harmonious society enjoying God and enjoying one another in God. The peace of all things is the tranquility of order."[94] Even those who are

---

92. Laufs (n. 65 above), 3–7; Geerlings (n. 65 above), 225–26.

93. On the peace-table, see Geerlings, 228–31.

94. *DCD* 19.13 (*CCL* 48, 678–79).

outside the city of God in its temporal manifestation, the *miseri*, have some tranquility of order insomuch as they are by the dictates of order adjusted to their mortal condition, however wretched it may be, and hence even they have some peace. But it is not that perfect peace of the inhabitants of the city of God.[95]

WAR AND PEACE

For Augustine, that perfect peace to be found in the city of God, to be fully realized only at the end of times, was so primary to his thinking about peace that he devalued in comparison its merely earthly equivalent, so much so that he has been criticized for his relative disparagement of the only external peace that humans can encounter in this lifetime, and consequently belittling the human benefits of the peace that at least suspends strife and war.[96] Clearly he did regard the eternal peace of heaven as the highest good. But he also could not help but recognize the depth of the human longing for external, earthly peace, transitory and uncertain though it may be. He recognized that longing in himself, and saw and heard it expressed in others. Earthly peace was not the highest good, but it was a great good, though ultimately impossible of attainment in any complete sense. Earthly peace was also oftentimes purchased at the terrible price of war. But though the bishop of Hippo saw earthly peace as merely a temporal good, he was no detached theoretician on the matter, and if the possibility of attaining it even for a time were ever to present itself, he would not hesitate for his part to grasp for it.

Before the outbreak of civil war and the Vandal invasion in the late 420s, the most serious challenge to the domestic peace of Augustine's North Africa had been posed by the Donatist conflict. Though the extent and severity of it could be exaggerated for propagandistic purposes, and although Donatist-Catholic relationships were not always and everywhere antagonistic, the controversy did at times engender acts of violence. Individuals could be attacked, tortured, and even killed.[97] Roving bands of Donatist fanatics, the somewhat mysterious circumcellions, could sometimes be found in the countryside.[98] Besides the acts of overt violence, there was the ever-present

95. *DCD* 19.13 (*CCL* 48, 679).

96. See Geerlings (n. 65 above), 231–32, commenting on the remarks of Eberhard Jüngel in his *Zum Wesen des Friedens: Frieden als Kategorie theologischer Anthropologie* (Munich: Chr. Kaiser, 1983), 25–36. There are valuable remarks on Augustine's conception of the peace that is war's opposite and of the relationship between the peace and war so conceived in John Mark Mattox, *Saint Augustine and the Theory of Just War* (London and New York: Continuum, 2006), 36–38, 114–15.

undertone of religious division, the sustained background note of a religious civil war that, like any civil war, divided families and friends.

A number of Augustine's sermons allude to the Donatist conflict, especially at its height during the last years of the fourth century and the first decade of the fifth, before the controversy was more or less laid to rest (if only in Augustine's opinion!) by the great conference at Carthage in early June 411.[99] At some point during those years the bishop referred to the conflict in a sermon on Psalm 147.[100] Now his congregation at Hippo might strike some moderns as a somewhat colorful and excitable lot. The stenographers (*notarii*) to whom we owe the preservation of Augustine's sermons have not rubbed out all traces of his congregation's animation, and the bishop's sermons at times probably resembled more the passionate call-and-response often seen in modern African American churches than the staid and largely silent church experience many are today familiar with. Shouts of acclamation, or applause, were not uncommon.[101]

Such was the case when Augustine in his exposition reached verses 13 and 14 of the psalm. He read out:

"He hath blessed thy children within thee." Who? "Who hath placed peace in thy borders."

At the mention of the word "peace" the congregation erupted in shouts. Augustine, who was usually quick to catch the moment and run with it in his sermons, did not miss the chance now.

---

97. On the violence, see W. H. C. Frend, *The Donatist Church* (Oxford: Clarendon, 1952), 257–61, 270, and especially the recent work of Brent D. Shaw, *Sacred Violence: African Christians and Sectarian Hatred in the Age of Augustine* (Cambridge: Cambridge University Press, 2011), *passim*.

98. On the circumcellions, see now Shaw (previous note), 630–720.

99. Good accounts are in Frend (n. 97 above), 275–89, and Shaw, 544–86. For Augustine's appraisal of the results of this conference, Frend, 228–29.

100. François Dolbeau, *Vingt-six sermons au peuple d'Afrique* (Paris: Institut d'Études Augustiniennes, 1996), 426–31 gives a good résumé of the scholarship on this *enarratio* as being one of a block of sermons datable to the first decade of the fifth century. The longing for peace evident in this sermon as well as the mention of "haeretici"—almost certainly the Donatists—in *Enarr. in Ps.* 147.16 (*CCL* 40, 2150) would also be congruent with such a time frame during a period of heightened religious violence.

101. On the interaction between Augustine and his audience during his sermons, see F. Van der Meer, *Augustine the Bishop: The Life and Work of a Father of the Church*, trans. Brian Battershaw and G. R. Lamb (London and New York: Sheed & Ward, 1961), 140, 427–32; and André Mandouze, *Saint Augustin: L'aventure de la raison et de la grâce* (Paris, 1968), 635–43, who emphasizes the dialogic quality of many sermons involving Augustine's "Mediterranean" audience.

How you all exult! Love it, my brothers. We are greatly delighted when love of peace cries out from your hearts. How did it delight you? I had said nothing, explained nothing. I merely uttered the verse, and you cried out. What is it that cried out from you? Love of peace. What did I put before your eyes? Why cry out if you don't love it? Why love it if you don't see it? Peace is invisible. What is the eye that has seen it to love it? For there wouldn't be shouting unless it were loved. These are the shows that God gives of invisible things. An understanding of peace has pierced your hearts with such great beauty! Why should I say any more about peace, or about praise of peace? Your emotions have anticipated all my words. I'm done for, I can't, I'm weak. Let's put off to the country of peace any praise of it. We will praise it more fully there where we will have it more fully. If we love it so much when it has only begun in us, how much shall we love it when in us it has been perfected![102]

It is true that Augustine used the opportunity afforded him by his congregation's response to move them ultimately to reflect on the perfect peace to come.

Now we long for peace, which in this world we only have in hope. For up till now what sort of peace is in us? "The flesh lusts against the spirit, and the spirit against the flesh" (Gal. 5:17). Where is there full peace even in one human being? When it shall be full in even one human being, there will then be full peace in all the citizens of Jerusalem. When will there be full peace? "When this corruptible shall have put on incorruption, and this mortal shall have put on immortality" (1 Cor. 15:54). Then there shall be full peace, then a firm peace. . . . Peace is not yet full and perfect. What you cried out a while back when I mentioned "peace," you cried out from your longing, your shouts came from your thirst, not from your being full. For there will be perfect justice where there is perfect peace.[103]

But it is equally true that Augustine could excite his congregation's feelings for the perfect peace to come only by invoking an analogous connection between it and earthly peace. It was the mere mention of earthly peace that had elicited a deep, emotional response from his audience, born of a heartfelt longing and

102. *Enarr. in Ps.* 147.15 (*CCL* 40, 2149–50).
103. *Enarr. in Ps.* 147.20 (*CCL* 40, 2156–57).

love for it.[104] It was the same yearning for an end to what must have seemed an endless religious civil war that Augustine had tried to exploit years earlier, in 393, when he wrote a popular anti-Donatist song with the refrain, "All you who rejoice at peace, now decide [for yourselves] the truth" ("Omnes qui gaudetis de pace, modo verum iudicate").[105] And as for the peace that ended, not religious strife, but war, the same heartfelt desire for it is revealed in a sermon in the early 410s, when Augustine averred that "[people] don't want war, they want peace. And who doesn't?"[106] Peace, whether earthly or heavenly, was a word the usage of which Augustine could only exploit, not control. Such was its power, even over him, that perhaps as much as two decades after his congregation's passionate outburst at its mere mention, he wrote of peace in *The City of God*:

> For so great a good is peace that even in the earthly and mortal sphere no other word is heard with more pleasure, nothing else is desired with greater longing, and finally nothing better can be found.[107]

The power earthly peace held over the human imagination, including his own, was such that Augustine granted it a special significance in his doctrine of the two cities.

> No more than these two types of human society exist, which in accordance with our Scriptures we may correctly term two cities. For one is the human city living according to the flesh, the other living according to the spirit, each wanting its own kind of peace, and when they attain what they are seeking, they each live in their own kind of peace.[108]

104. On the desire and love for the earthly peace, see also *Enarr. in Ps. 84.12* (*CCL* 39, 1172); *Serm.* 357 (*PL* 39:1582–86).

105. *Psalmus contra partem Donati*, *CSEL* 51, 3–15. On the date, Fitzgerald, 688. On the use of "peace" as a watchword by both Catholics and Donatists, see Frend (n. 97 above), 237–38. On this song, see now Shaw, 475–89, and the literature cited there.

106. *Serm.* 25.4 (*CCL* 41, 337). On the date, Fitzgerald, 774.

107. *DCD* 19.11 (*CCL* 48, 675). (W. C. Greene trans., modified)

108. *DCD* 14.1 (*CCL* 48, 414).

Earthly peace was certainly a great good, but among men it was unstable, treacherous, and uncertain.[109] There is really no peace to be had in this lifetime, so there was no use in hoping for it.[110] For

> [earthly] peace is but a doubtful good, since we do not know the hearts of those with whom we choose to be at peace, and even if we could know them today, in any case we know not what they may be like tomorrow. (W. C. Greene trans.)[111]

And so as good as it is, earthly peace inevitably suffers by comparison with that now enjoyed by the faithful in part, later to be enjoyed by them in full.

> The peace that is ours we even now enjoy with God by faith, and we shall enjoy it with Him forever by sight. But peace in this life, whether that common to all men or our own special possession, is such as must be called rather a solace for our wretchedness than a positive enjoyment of blessedness.[112]

In the "good old days" (as the pagans saw it) of the Roman Republic and the pre-Christian empire, worship of the gods had secured the Roman peace through glorious victories.[113] Augustine agreed that the Roman peace was a benefit, but it was a benefit granted by the one, true God, bestowed like the sun and the rain even on the undeserving.[114] The earthly city sought to obtain this earthly peace through war. If it was successful in war, there was peace, which could not exist earlier when the opposing parties contended for the same earthly goods that were insufficient to satisfy both. "Such is the peace that the toilsome wars are waged to gain; such is the peace that the reputedly glorious victory achieves" (Philip Levine trans.).[115] In the end, though, even the earthly peace was not achievable by human efforts.

---

109. *Enarr. in Ps. 127*.16 (*CCL* 40, 1880): "non pax qualem inter se habent homines infidam, instabilem, mutabilem, incertam."

110. *Enarr. in Ps. 48, s.2*.6 (*CCL* 38, 570).

111. *DCD* 19.5 (*CCL* 48, 669). For another similar passage on the consequences for peace of not knowing the hearts of others, see *In Ioann. Evang.* 77.4 (*CCL* 36, 522).

112. *DCD* 19.27 (*CCL* 48, 697).

113. *DCD* 2.20 (*CCL* 47, 51).

114. *DCD* 3.9 (*CCL* 47, 71).

115. *DCD* 15.4 (*CCL* 48, 457). Besides the evident sour note, it is significant from the context that there seems to be a reference to the contemporary civil wars.

God, then, the most wise creator and most just ordainer of all natures, who has set upon the earth as its greatest achievement the mortal human race, has bestowed on human beings certain good things that befit this life; to wit, temporal peace, so far as it can be enjoyed in the little span of a mortal life in terms of personal health and preservation and fellowship with one's kind, and all things necessary to safeguard or recover this peace. (W. C. Greene trans.)

These things that helped to keep or recover earthly peace included light, speech, air to breathe and water to drink, food, and clothing. Mortals who used these good things rather than enjoy them for their own sake would ultimately receive the better good of the peace of immortality spent in the enjoyment of God, while those who enjoyed temporal goods for their own sake would lose them in the end and not gain eternal life.[116] Therefore, the earthly peace was used by both cities, the earthly city for earthly purposes and the city of God for the sake of ultimately enjoying eternal life.

The earthly city, which does not live by faith, is intent on seeking an earthly peace in the harmony of command and obedience among its citizens so that they may have a sort of combination of human wills for the things pertaining to this mortal life.

But the heavenly city in its pilgrimage on earth also uses the earthly peace.[117] "We also make use of the peace of Babylon."[118]

Twentieth-century scholars who regarded Augustine as an originator of the just war idea included in it the requirement that a just war should have only the securing of peace as its ultimate goal.[119] For Augustine, however, it was self-evident, to pagans and Christians alike, that peace was the aim of all wars, just or not. This circumstance was a consequence not of any rationally determined policy, but of the striving for peace inherent in human nature, a nature that itself could not exist were there not an ordered, harmonious peace binding together its constituent elements of body and soul.

Just as there can be life, then, without pain, while there can be no pain without life, so, too, there can be peace without any war, but no war without some sort of peace. This does not follow from the

116. DCD 19.13 (CCL 48, 680).
117. DCD 19.17 (CCL 48, 684).
118. DCD 19.26 (CCL 48, 696–97).
119. E.g., Russell, 16.

nature of war, but because war is waged by or within persons who have some natural being, for they could not exist to begin with if they did not subsist with some sort of peace.[120]

Furthermore, even pagans had recognized that peace was the desirable end of war. In his *De officiis* Cicero had written that "war should be undertaken in such a way that it is clear that nothing other than peace is the goal."[121] But when he had written on peace as the end of war in *The City of God*, what mattered to Augustine was *what kind* of peace the earthly city sought, and how it went about obtaining it. Playing off Cicero's dictum, Augustine argued that the earthly city—here almost certainly meaning the Roman empire[122]—did not seek peace via the creation of harmony among human beings, but by the violent subjugation of others through military force. In other words, the Romans had not fought for peace, but for *victoria*.

> Whoever is paying even the slightest attention comes to understand along with me that, given the human reality and our common human nature, just as there is no one who does not wish to have joy, so there is no one who does not wish to have peace. Indeed, since even those who decide on wars *want nothing other than to be victorious* ["nihil aliud quam vincere volunt"; cf. the quote from Cicero], it follows that by waging war they want to attain peace with glory. For what else is victory but the subjugation of our opponents? For when this has happened, there will be peace. Even wars, then, are waged with peace as the goal, even by those whose only intention in issuing orders and fighting is to exercise their warrior virtues. Accordingly, it is clear that peace is the desirable end of war. For every man even in waging war is seeking peace, but no one seeks war by making peace. For even those who want to disturb the existing peace do not hate peace, but want to replace it with a peace they prefer. So they do not wish that there be no peace, but that it be the peace they want. . . . Therefore, everyone wants peace with those whom they wish to live under their authority. For, if they can, they even wish to make their own those against whom they wage war, and to impose on them after subjugating them the laws of their own peace.

120. *DCD* 19.13 (*CCL* 48, 679). (W. C. Greene trans., modified)

121. Cicero, *De officiis* I 80, ed. M. Winterbottom (Oxford: Clarendon, 1994), 32: "Bellum autem ita suscipiatur ut nihil aliud nisi pax quaesita videatur."

122. Laufs (n. 65 above), 8–9.

Rather than lauding peace as the proper end of war, Augustine is pointing out that the peace that results from the arrogant and militaristic lust to dominate others, *libido dominandi*, can only result in an earthly peace that is unjust and disordered, scarcely deserving of the name.[123]

Yet despite what seems persistent criticism of earthly peace in Augustine's writings, it must be remembered that by far the majority of such statements appear in *The City of God*, a major polemical purpose of which was to denigrate the values of the earthly as opposed to those of the heavenly city, where all those goods that were uncertain and transitory on earth became certain and eternal. In two "real-world" instances where Augustine dealt with the issue of peace versus war, there appears no qualification of the good of earthly peace. One such instance is seen in his letter to Boniface in 417 urging him not to leave the military,[124] where the bishop's advice seems positively Ciceronian not only in urging the general to keep faith even with enemies, but also in its sententious affirmation of peace as the proper end of war, in a letter written years before his detailed discussion of earthly peace in Book 19 of *The City of God*.[125]

> Your choice ought to be for peace, necessity [only] for war, that God may free you from necessity and preserve you in peace. For peace is not sought in order to stir up war, but war is waged in order to obtain peace. Be, then, a peacemaker, so that by conquering you may lead those whom you subdue to the benefits of peace, for the Lord says: "Blessed are the peacemakers, for they shall be called the children of God."[126]

Here Augustine even adduces the Beatitudes in support of *external* peace, a passage that twenty-odd years earlier he had related solely to the peace *internal* to human beings.[127]

In the winter of 428/429 Augustine wrote a letter to the imperial official Darius, who had been sent to Africa to make peace with the rebel Boniface.[128]

---

123. *DCD* 19.12 (*CCL* 48, 675, 676, 677–78).

124. On the circumstances of *Epist.* 189, see ch. 6, notes 204 to 211 above.

125. On the idea that faith should be kept with enemies in Cicero's *De officiis*, ch. 7, notes 140 to 143 above.

126. *Epist.* 189.6 (*CSEL* 57, 135).

127. See notes 70, 71, 75, 76 above.

128. On the chronology of *Epist.* 229, see Hans-Joachim Diesner, "Zur Datierung der Augustinbriefe 228-231," *Forschungen und Fortschritte* 35 (1961): 184–85. On Darius, see also *PLRE* 2, 347–48 (Darius 2) and *Prosopographie chrétienne du Bas-Empire* 1 (Paris: Éditions du CNRS, 1982), 264–65.

In that letter the seventy-four-year-old bishop, too old to travel especially in the cold of winter, apologized for being unable to see Darius in person, though he expressed confidence that he could read the "countenance of his heart" in the words of the Gospel, "Blessed are the peacemakers."

> Men who are truly great and have their own special glory are not only the bravest warriors but also those who are—which is a source of truer praise—the most faithful. It is by their labors and perils that an unrestrained enemy is vanquished with the help of God's protection and assistance, and tranquillity procured for the empire and its pacified provinces. But it is a greater glory to slay war itself with a word than human beings with a sword, and to acquire or obtain peace through peace itself and not war. It is true that even those who make war, if they are good men (*boni*), undoubtedly have peace as their aim, but are seeking it through bloodshed. Yet you have been sent that there be no blood shed, and so what is unavoidable in their case is sheer bliss in yours.[129]

When, not the idea of it, but the reality of war was on his very doorstep, the aged Augustine, who would be dead less than two years later, yielded to none in his praise of peace on earth.

---

129. *Epist.* 229.2 (*CSEL* 57, 497–98).

9

The Medieval Construction of Augustine as an Authority on War and Military Service

In what is today north-central France, near the modern town of Fontenoy (Yonne), at mid-morning of 25 June 841 the forces of Charles the Bald and Louis the German, allies against their brother Lothar in a civil war for rule over the Frankish realm bequeathed to them by their father Louis the Pious, crested a rise that had for the last three days separated the two opposing armies. After a number of fruitless embassies had passed between the two sides, Charles and Louis had decided to force the issue. When Lothar saw his brothers' army approach his own at points less than two kilometers distant, the West Frankish cavalry fanning out to attack his left flank, the emperor realized the gauntlet was well and truly thrown: to retreat in the very face of the enemy was foolhardy, but to retreat at all was dishonorable.[1] The ensuing battle was long remembered as a catastrophe for the Franks, Regino of Prüm two generations later writing that:

> In this battle Frankish power was so diminished and its famous virtue so enfeebled that not only was it forced to stop expansion, but it was even incapable of handing down to posterity what it already had.[2]

Although Lothar was back on the attack within months after the battle, he undoubtedly suffered a reversal at Fontenoy, and his opponents were left in possession of the field.

---

1. *Nithard: Histoire des fils de Louis le Pieux*, ed. Ph. Lauer (Paris, 1926), 2.9–10 (66–78). Some of the details of the circumstances of the battle given here are based on my reconstruction expanding on Nithard's brief account.

2. *Reginonis chronicon a.* 841, *MGH: srg* 50, ed. F. Kurze (Hannover, 1890), 75.

Arguably of more long-term consequence than the battle itself was a statement issued immediately afterwards by bishops in Charles's and Louis's camp justifying the battle of Fontenoy and interpreting its outcome as a *iudicium Dei*, a sort of large-scale judicial ordeal, in which victory showed that God had judged their cause just. The bishops' statement does not survive, though one presumes the eyewitness Nithard gives a fairly accurate account of it. After celebrating Sunday mass on the battlefield the day after the battle, burying the dead and caring for the wounded of both sides,

> the kings and the army, grieving over their brother Lothar and the Christian people, asked the bishops what should be done about this business. Accordingly all the bishops met in council, and it was found in public assembly that they alone had fought for justice and equity, and that this had been manifested by a judgment of God (*iudicium Dei*), and that because of this everyone, both he who issued commands and he who carried them out, was to be considered an instrument of God free of any sin in this business. But whoever in his conscience knew that he had ordered or done something in this campaign either out of rage or hatred or vainglory or any other vice whatsoever should confess in secret his secret offense and be judged according to the measure of his guilt.

The bishops went on to recommend a three-day fast "for the remission of the offenses of their dead brethren," and to ensure continued divine support for the brothers' cause.[3]

The bishops' statement was a salvo in the propaganda war that paralleled that on the battlefield in the *Brüderkrieg*, the civil war between the sons and heirs of Louis the Pious that broke out after his death in 840 and was concluded by a division of the Carolingian empire at the Treaty of Verdun three years later.[4] No direct response to this statement from Lothar's side survives, but we know something of what it was from a brief penitential written a few months after the battle by one of Lothar's supporters, the learned Hrabanus Maurus, abbot of the monastery at Fulda in the eastern (mostly German) part of the Carolingian realm. Hrabanus at one point took direct aim at the two main assertions of the

---

3. Nithard 3.1 (note 1 above, 82).

4. Some of the following as noted is dependent on my forthcoming article, "Justifying the Judgment of God in *Brüderkrieg* Propaganda: The *Capitula diversarum sententiarum pro negociis rei publice consulendis*," hereafter Wynn, "Justifying."

bishops' statement, that the battle had constituted a judgment of God, and that the victors consequently did not have to do penance.

> Some people excuse the homicide perpetrated in the recent civil war and battle of our princes, as though it were unnecessary to do penance for this at all because it had been carried out under the command of our princes and in the end was decided by a judgment of God. Now we know that the judgment of God is ever just, and deserving of no censure. . . . But no one can penetrate all the judgments of God, for it is written: "The judgments of God are a deep abyss" [Ps. 37:5].

He went on to attack those who intentionally killed in battle at the command of their territorial lords.[5]

In response to such assertions in pro-Lothar propaganda, perhaps at the conference of leading lay and ecclesiastical supporters of Charles and Louis held at the imperial capital at Aachen in late March 842 after Lothar had retreated south to his base in Burgundy, a cleric or clerics in a circle close to Charles produced a propaganda *libellus* or pamphlet that happens to have survived. This work, in addition to *Fürstenspiegel*-like matter advisory to the kings, cited patristic authorities, mostly Augustine, to support the assertions that God favored the just cause in battle, and that soldiers who killed in battle did not have to do penance. In the sole manuscript preserving it, the text is titled *Capitula diversarum sententiarum pro negociis rei publice consulendis* (hereafter the *CDS*), translatable as something like, "a brief of various authoritative statements to be consulted in furtherance of affairs of state." This text has a significance transcending the circumstances of its original production. For, in combination with other ninth-century Carolingian texts, all of which evidenced a scholarship eagerly appropriating Augustine, the *CDS* stands at the font of the textual tradition that ultimately made the African Father an authority on war for medieval canonists and theologians.[6]

Since the cleric or clerics who compiled the *CDS* focused on the two issues of penance and of *iudicium Dei*, at the outset Augustine's statements on war and military service passed through a conceptual filter that admitted some, omitted others. This phenomenon would recur more than two centuries later, ensuring that the medieval, and hence to a great extent the modern,

---

5. Hrabanus Maurus, *Poenitentium liber ad Otgarium* (*PL* 112:1411D–1415A).

6. Wynn, "Justifying."

construction of Augustinian authority so conceived would be, in comparison with what Augustine actually thought and wrote, distorted and incomplete.

THE JUST WAR IN THE PRE-CAROLINGIAN EARLY MEDIEVAL WEST

With the disappearance of the Western empire after the fifth century, the rhetoric of just war as political practice likewise largely disappeared from the West. But not entirely. Such rhetoric is still seen in at least two mid-sixth-century Latin works produced in the East Roman or Byzantine cultural zone, Jordanes's history the *Getica* and Corippus's epic poem the *Iohannis*. Visible in both works is the continuing tendency to link unjust cause and unjust war to usurpers and tyrants. At one point Jordanes has the fifth-century Western emperor Valentinian III write regarding Attila the Hun that he is

> a universal tyrant who wants the whole world to be his slave, who doesn't need causes for war, but thinks whatever war he's embarked upon to be legitimate.[7]

Similarly, in Corippus's Africa the rebel Stutzias "wants to have the name of a tyrant by way of an unjust war."[8]

Another work that possibly originated in the Latin-speaking province of late sixth-century Byzantine North Africa provides the only hint of Augustine being invoked as an authority on war in the four centuries separating Augustine himself from the compilation of the *CDS*. The work purports to be a correspondence between Augustine and the general Boniface, but since Gratian in the early twelfth century it has been known to be bogus. Probably the best indication for a *terminus a quo* for the collection is the use in Letter 10 of the word *saraca*, a linen or woolen tunic, not attested before the mid-sixth century.[9] An arguably circumstantial reference to the North African cult of Saint Stephen, added to the reasonable supposition that for some time after their deaths in 430 and 432 both Augustine and Boniface were names to conjure with in North Africa, do perhaps point to an African origin for the collection.

7. Jordanes, *Getica, MGH: aa* 5.1 (107).

8. *Flavii Cresconii Corippi* Iohannidos *seu de bellis Libycis libri VIII*, ed. J. Diggle and F. R. D. Goodyear (Cambridge: Cambridge University Press, 1970), 4:431 (83).

9. Frank M. Clover, "The Pseudo-Boniface and the *Historia Augusta*," *Bonner Historia-Augusta-Colloquium 1977/78, Antiquitas, Reihe 4, Band 14* (Bonn: Rudolf Habelt, 1980) (hereafter Clover), reprinted in *The Late Roman West and the Vandals* (*Variorum*) (Aldershot, UK: Ashgate, 1993 [cited here]), 86 and notes 63–65.

There are other indications for dating the collection's origin to the mid- or late sixth century, in the Byzantine African province. So in Letter 15 Augustine asked Boniface to keep safe the Roman state, and spoke of the "just party" in war in Letter 13, indications the collection originated where the Roman (Byzantine) state still existed, where just war rhetoric, as we just saw, remained a practice of political culture, and naturally in an area of Latinity.[10] Frank Clover argued that the appearance of certain Gothic names points to the collection's origin in early sixth-century Ostrogothic Italy, but Gothic/Vandal names also occur among Byzantine commanders and solders mentioned in the *Iohannis*.[11] Another indication for a date about this time is a letter from Gregory I to Guduin, the Byzantine *dux* of Naples in December 603, in which the pope professed amazement that Guduin had not punished a soldier for raping a nun, a real-life parallel to Letters 1–3 in the collection, which deal with the case of a Gothic soldier who had raped a nun.[12]

In Letter 12 Boniface seems to address a letter to Augustine from the very front-line.

> Our war is serious. The point of our enemy's sword is touching our breasts. Pour forth prayers to God, as is your wont, that your prayer may be our companion.

Boniface asks Augustine to petition God "to guide our javelins against the foe, and have them cut themselves down in mutual slaughter."[13] Augustine replies in Letter 13:

> You complained about serious fighting. I don't want you to have any doubts; I shall give useful counsel to you and yours. Take your weapons in hand; let your prayer beat against the Creator's ears. For

10. Ps. Aug. *Epist. XIII, XV* (PL 33:1098).

11. Ariarith (*Iohannis* V. 285, VI. 535, 543, 649, 670; cf. Ariaric in Jordanes's *Getica* 112 [a fourth-century Gothic king]); E. Förstemann, *Altdeutsches Namenbuch* (Bonn: Hanstein's, 1900), I. 588–90 (Geisirith [*Iohannis* II.188, IV.489, V.326, VI.522, VIII. 372, 475; same as famous Vandal king Gaiseric]); 708 (Guntarith [*Iohannis* III. 428, IV. 222, 240, 369, 426; name of Gothic king in Jordanes's *Getica* 91 and early fifth-century Vandal king]); 1339ff. (Sinduit [*Iohannis* VI. 522, VIII. 374; Sinderith a Gothic leader in Sicily in Jordanes's *Getica* 308]).

12. Gregory, *Epist.* 14.10 (CCL 140A, 1079–80).

13. Ps. Aug. *Epist. XII* (PL 33:1098): "Grave nobis est bellum. Inimici mucro nostra pectora pulsat: Deo funde preces, ut soles, tua sit nobis comes oratio. Rauca buccina, terrifica tuba, puto quod et sidera terreat; hostium clamor immanis est, sed his non terremur: novimus enim ista non hodie. Ergo, venerande Christi sacerdos, pete Deum ut iacula in hostes dirigat nostra, ac se ipsi trucident mutua caede."

when there is fighting, God looks forth from the open heavens, and then gives the palm [of victory] to the side He perceives as just.[14]

No other sentiment in this collection betrays more clearly its being a forgery, since the real Augustine thought prayers for victory unseemly.[15] Here we have not simply a prayer before battle, but a prayer performed while already armed and ready for fighting. Of arguably the greatest significance here is the blatant statement that victory in war reveals a divine judgment as to who has justice on his side, a sentiment of longstanding currency in pagan antiquity, though roundly rejected by the real Augustine.[16]

Over the course of the seventh century Byzantine cultural influence in the West waned somewhat as Constantinople focused on simply surviving; first in an epic war against Sassanid Persia, in which the enemy even besieged the capital in 626, then later in what became a centuries-long struggle against Muslim armies and fleets that captured the empire's most prosperous provinces and erected what was for a time the largest empire on earth. The only mentions of the term "just war" in the early medieval West before the Carolingians and after Corippus, Jordanes, and the Pseudo-Augustinian letters to Boniface come from what many then would have regarded as peripheral areas: Visigothic Spain and Anglo-Saxon England. Interestingly, in the former case Byzantine cultural influence is evidenced in the late sixth century and throughout the seventh in art and architecture, and in features of state symbolism such as coinage, and royal titulature and ceremonial.[17] In both the Visigothic kingdom and that of Northumbria in Anglo-Saxon England, political elites worked to foster a type of early medieval national sentiment, an identity with a *gens Gothorum* or a *gens Nordanhymbrorum*, albeit a national sentiment restricted to the top players of the royal court, of the armed nobility, and of the church.[18] In both these kingdoms

14. Ps. Aug. *Epist. XIII* (loc. cit.): "Gravi de pugna conquereris: dubites nolo, utile tibi tuisque dabo consilium: arripe manibus arma; oratio aures pulset Auctoris: quia quando pugnatur, Deus apertis coelis prospectat, et partem quam inspicit iustam, ibi dat palmam."

15. Chapter 8, notes 50, 51 above.

16. Chapter 8, notes 53, 54 above.

17. On the Byzantine cultural influence on Visigothic Spain, K. F. Stroheker, "Das spanische Westgotenreich und Byzanz," cited from idem, *Germanentum und Spätantike* (Zürich and Stuttgart: Artemis, 1965), 224–33.

18. On the premodern national idea, Anthony D. Smith, *The Antiquity of Nations* (Cambridge: Polity, 2004). On *gens* and *patria* in seventh-century Visigothic Spain, see S. Teillet, *Des Goths à la nation gothique: Les origines de l'idée de nation en Occident du Ve au VIIe siècle* (Paris: Société d'Édition "Les belles lettres," 1984); and Isabel Velázquez, "*Pro patriae gentisque Gothorum statu* (4th Council of Toledo, canon 75, a. 633)," *Regna and Gentes: The Relationship between Late Antique and Early Medieval Peoples and*

the *gens* required a national king, and an affective attachment to a more-or-less clearly demarcated stretch of territory, the *patria* (OE *eþel*).[19]

Our best sources for seventh-century Spain and England, Isidore of Seville and Bede, are also the ones who wrote of just war at this period, Isidore writing a definition of the term that Ivo of Chartres in the late eleventh century cited as *the* definition, not that of Augustine's *Quaestiones in Heptateuchum*. Both Isidore's and Bede's remarks on just war fit into seventh-century narratives of "nation-building"; in Isidore's case, we even seem to have a self-conscious architect of the Gothic national idea.[20]

Isidore's definition appears in his *Etymologies*, an encyclopedic work of enormous subsequent circulation and influence in medieval Europe, left unfinished at his death in 636. At the beginning of Book XVIII, "On war and games," Isidore writes:

> 1. Ninus, king of the Assyrians, was the first to wage war. Not at all content with his own boundaries, this Ninus, breaking the compact of human society, began to lead armies, to destroy other lands, and to massacre or subject free peoples. He completely subjugated the whole of Asia up to the borders of Libya in an unprecedented slavery. From this point on the world strove to grow fat in reciprocal bloodshed with one slaughter after another. 2. Now there are four

Kingdoms in the Transformation of the Roman World, ed. Hans-Werner Goetz, Jörg Jarnut, and Walter Pohl (Leiden and Boston: Brill, 2003), 161–217. On *patria* in early medieval polities, Thomas Eichenberger, *Patria: Studien zur Bedeutung des Wortes im Mittelalter (6.–12. Jahrhundert)* (Sigmaringen: Jan Thorbecke, 1991).

19. On the early medieval conception of a *regnum* as constituted by *rex*, *gens*, and *patria*, see Eichenberger (previous note), 71–89. The word *patria* appears fifty times in Bede's *Ecclesiastical History*, demonstrably at times in a political sense. The Old English *eþel* by my count is used to translate *patria* in thirty of the thirty-seven instances where there exists a passage corresponding to the Latin original in the Old English Bede (*The Old English Version of Bede's Ecclesiastical History of the English People*, ed. and trans. Thomas Miller [London: Early English Text Society, 1890]). Although later than Bede by three centuries, the same political mentality seen in *The Battle of Maldon* in a speech by Byrhtnoth had to have come from somewhere. In the speech, Byrhtnoth tells a Viking emissary just before the battle, who had offered to withdraw if the English paid them off: "say to thy people a more hostile message, that here stands a brave nobleman with his troop, who will defend this homeland, Æthelred's country, my prince's folk and fold" (ll. 50–54a: "sege þinum leodum miccle laþre spell,/ þæt her stynt unforcuð eorl mid his werode,/ þe wile gealgean eþel þysne,/ Æthelredes eard, ealdres mines/ folc and foldan"). Byrhtnoth's speech is notable not only for proving that loyalty to one's lord was complementary and auxiliary to fighting for one's king and country, but also for its vernacular invocation of all three of the elements then conceived of as constitutive of a *regnum*: *rex* (Æthelred), *gens/folc*, and *patria/eþel*.

20. Velázquez (n. 18 above), 188–205.

kinds of war: just, unjust, civil, and more than civil. A just war is that which is waged in accordance with a formal declaration and is waged for the sake of recovering property seized or of driving off the enemy. An unjust war is one that is begun out of rage, and not for a legitimate reason. Cicero speaks of this in the *Republic*: "Those wars are unjust that are taken up without due cause, for except for the cause of avenging or of driving off the enemy no just war can be waged." 3. And he adds this a little further on: "No war is considered just unless it is officially announced or declared, and unless it is fought to recover property seized." Civil war occurs when factions arise among fellow-citizens and hostilities are stirred up, as between Sulla and Marius, who waged civil war against each other within one nation ("in una gente"). 4. A "more than civil" war is where not only fellow-citizens, but also kinfolk fight—this was done by Caesar and Pompey, when father-in-law and son-in-law fought each other. Indeed, in that battle brother struggled against brother, and father bore arms against son (there follows a quote from Lucan's *Civil War* 2.150, 151).[21]

Not only does Isidore derive "his" definition of just war from Cicero, but in *lib.* XVIII.1 he summarizes an account of Ninus's reign in the brief third-century history, itself an epitome of earlier work, of Junianus Justinus.[22] His summary of Justin is revealing. For Isidore is careful to include his source's concern with boundaries (*fines*). Whereas Justin in referring to the primordial political practice of nations defending rather than extending the boundaries of their *regna* had termed it a custom (*mos*), Isidore in his summary elevated this practice to treaty, a *foedus*.

What Isidore chose to include in his summary regarding Ninus and what he chose to emphasize betray some of the political realities of his own day and his own perception of them. By shortly after 600 the successor kingdoms in the West had more or less stabilized their frontiers in relation to one another.[23] The Goths, somewhat shielded from outside interference on the Iberian peninsula,

21. *The* Etymologies *of Isidore of Seville*, trans. Stephen A. Barney et al. (Cambridge: Cambridge University Press, 2006), 359 (modified); *Isidori Hispalensis episcopi Etymologiarum sive Originum libri XX*, ed. W. M. Lindsay (Oxford: Clarendon, 1911), t. II, *lib.* XVIII.1–4 (without page numbers).

22. *M. Iuniani Iustini epitome historiarum Philippicarum Pompei Trogi*, ed. Otto Seel (Stuttgart: Teubner, 1972), I.i, 3–4.

23. Paul S. Barnwell, "War and Peace: Historiography and Seventh-Century Embassies," *Early Medieval Europe* 6, no. 2 (1997): 129, notes this "hardening" of political boundaries in the context of the

had certain geopolitical advantages over the Franks in the matter of boundaries, the Franks continuing to have a fluid and vaguely demarcated frontier east of the Rhine. Isidore's seventh-century political world roughly resembled Justin's political vision of independent *regna* ruled by individual kings, *regna* that bounded in their entirety the *patriae* of the individual nations. But in Isidore's day relations between nations were regulated not by Justin's golden age custom, but by international treaties such as those between the Visigoths and the Franks. In this political context, Isidore's just war in the *Etymologies* was nothing other than the legitimate defense of one's *regnum* against outside attack by those who dared to transgress the boundaries of the *patria*.

As occurred in Isidore and other works of Visigothic Spain, Bede at times wrote of the national *patria*, especially that of his Northumbria. His *Ecclesiastical History* witnesses to seventh-century Northumbrian "nation-building" in the cult of King Oswald, who died in battle fighting for the *patria* against its pagan enemies. Earlier, Oswald had won a great victory over Northumbria's enemies, and in his prayer before the battle the king, according to Bede, stated that "God himself knows that we undertook just wars for the sake of our nation's security (or, 'salvation')."[24] Bede's understanding of the term is similar to Isidore's in referencing defensive wars against invaders of the *patria*. More explicit in Bede is the linkage of divine favor with the prosecution of defensive wars, implicitly contrasted in his narrative with a later incidence of an unjust war, when in 684 the Northumbrian king Ecgfrith invaded Ireland though the Irish had done nothing to provoke the Northumbrians.[25] In writing that Oswald had fought for his people's *salus*, Bede deliberately played on the word's being ambiguous and polysemic. From the religious perspective, his language speaks to the early medieval political conception of identifying the *gens* with Israel *redivivus*, in the political constellation then of Western Europe an identity in one of what Peter Brown has termed "micro-Christendoms," somewhat self-contained and autonomous polities in which a religio-political, "national" metanarrative was no longer based on Rome, but Jerusalem.[26] Northumbria's *salus*, as with that

---

relatively more peaceful conditions on the seventh-century Continent and the resulting decline in recorded diplomatic activity among the various kingdoms.

24. Bede, *HE* III 2 (Colgrave and Mynors, 214): "scit enim ipse [God] quia iusta pro salute gentis nostrae bella suscepimus."

25. Bede, *HE* IV 26 (Colgrave and Mynors, 426, 428).

26. Peter Brown, *The Rise of Western Christendom: Triumph and Diversity, A.D. 200-1000*, 2nd ed. (Malden, MA, Oxford, and Melbourne: Blackwell, 2003), 138–40.

of its Old Testament type, referenced as an inextricable whole both the *gens*'s physical *and* spiritual well-being.

EARLY MEDIEVAL PENITENTIALS AND KILLING IN WAR

We have seen that although Augustine himself did not think *militia* was inherently sinful, some contemporary leading churchmen thought exactly that. Their number included Pope Leo I (440–461), who in replying to queries from Bishop Rusticus of Narbonne addressed the question of whether anyone who had done penance could return to the *militia*.

> It is completely against the rules of the church to return to secular *militia* after doing penance, for as the Apostle says: "No one serving ("militans") God entangles himself in secular business (2 Tim. 2:4)." Hence whoever has wanted to entangle himself in the *militia* of this world is not free from the snares of the devil.

Elsewhere in the same letter Leo addressed another question on *militia*, this time regarding monks who *militare* after taking their monastic vows. Leo wrote that any such monk had to purge himself with a public penance, even if his *militia* had harmed no one.[27]

Taking into consideration these passages and others from earlier papal letters, the *militia* referenced here has to mean civil, not military, service, congruent with a papal stance maintained from as early as the papacy of Damasus (366–384), who wrote that former imperial officials were generally unfit to become bishops.[28] Even then, this almost absolutist stance was not universal throughout the Latin churches. Leo's position seems to reflect a more rigorous tradition at the see of Saint Peter, a position not shared by bishops in other provinces, who according to the very letters espousing the papal viewpoint continued to query successive popes on the subject at least until the middle of the fifth century. Leo's position regarding *militia* and the clergy has a contemporary echo in canon 7 of the Council of Chalcedon in 451, which held that anyone who had entered the clergy or taken monastic vows was prohibited from entering state service, and if they had done so they were required to resign and do penance.[29]

---

27. Leo, *Epist.* 157, 12, 14 (*PL* 54:1206C–1207A, 1207B–1208A).
28. Chapter 3, notes 135 to 137 above.

This linkage between state service and the need to atone for such service appears as late as in a sermon of Caesarius, bishop of Arles from 502 to 542. In speaking on the need for penance, the bishop gave as a typical excuse for not doing so someone saying, "I am posted to the *militia* . . . so how can I do penance?"[30] Apparently, then, *militia* as civil and not military service was still conceivable in early sixth-century Arles, where Roman traditions remained vital even under barbarian kings. But Caesarius's sermon is arguably the last evidence we have for the stance—perhaps never universal in the Latin West—that it was necessary to do penance after service to the state.[31] At some point thereafter even in the more Romanized parts of southern Gaul, and in different places in Western Christendom at different times, as witnessed already in early fifth-century Roman North Africa, the idea that state service was inherently contaminating seems to have disappeared. As his Letter 189 shows, Augustine did not see Christianity and military service as incompatible. Over time this attitude prevailed in the Latin West, generally established there by no later than the seventh century. What does survive from the earlier period is the idea that military service in particular was incompatible with ecclesiastical office.

The first clear evidence for the reappearance in the West of the idea that there could be something inherently morally opprobrious about the usual and expected conduct of soldiers in war is in certain so-called tariffed penitentials from the end of the seventh and beginning of the eighth centuries, which held that anyone who had killed in war had to do penance. The earliest such provision is in the Penitential of Theodore,[32] so called because it was traditionally associated with Theodore of Tarsus, an ecclesiastic originally from the Greek East who was archbishop of Canterbury from 669 to 690. Although the textual history and interrelationships of the early penitentials is complex and firm conclusions on these aspects of them remain elusive, it is demonstrable that Theodore's penitential rules were cited in an Irish context before 725,[33] and that

---

29. *Acta conciliorum oecumenicorum* II.1.2, ed. E. Schwartz (Berlin and Leipzig: Walter de Gruyter, 1933), canon 7 (159).

30. *Sancti Caesarii episcopi Arelatensis opera omnia*, ed. G. Morin (Maretioli, 1937), *serm.* 65.2, 268.

31. Cyrille Vogel, *La discipline pénitentielle en Gaule des origines à la fin du VIIe siècle* (Paris: Letouzey & Ané, 1952), 114, 149–201.

32. Raymund Kottje, *Die Tötung im Kriege: Ein moralisches und rechtliches Problem im frühen Mittelalter*, Beiträge zur Friedensethik 11 (Barsbüttel: Institut für Theologie und Frieden, 1991), 3 and n. 19.

33. Thomas Charles-Edwards, "The Penitential of Theodore and the *Iudicia Theodori*," *Archbishop Theodore: Commemorative Studies on His Life and Influence*, ed. Michael Lapidge (Cambridge: Cambridge University Press, 1995), 142 and n. 5.

the content of the penitential attributed to him dates to the end of the seventh or beginning of the eighth century. The following appears in the work under the heading *De occisione hominum*:

> Whoever by order of his lord has slain a human being, let him stay away from church for forty days, and whoever has slain a human being in a public war ("in publico bello"), let him do penance for forty days.[34]

What is the *publicum bellum* referred to here? One clue to the term's meaning comes from elaborations of this provision in later Continental penitentials of the eighth and ninth centuries that were influenced by the Penitential of Theodore.[35] A couple of these add "cum rege" to the phrase "in publico bello," and more of them replace the term with variants on "cum rege in proelio."[36] It looks as though *publicum bellum* refers to wars fought for king and country, wars that in the first place would certainly have included those fought in defense of the *patria* against outside invaders.[37] The term may be a Latin calque/translation of the Old English *folcgefeoht*, which from its usage especially in the Anglo-Saxon Chronicle does seem to refer to major battles fought under royal auspices, if not outright direct royal command.[38]

Although the Penitential of Theodore and penitentials related to it that included this provision on killing in war did make it to the Continent, Raymund Kottje has shown that the requirement for a forty-day penance was not universally applied on the Continent in the eighth and ninth centuries, but

34. P. W. Finsterwalder, *Die Canones Theodori Cantuariensis und ihre Überlieferungsformen* (Weimar: Hermann Böhlaus, 1929), I.iv.6 (294): "Qui per iussionem domini sui occiderit hominem XL diebus abstineat se ab ecclesia et qui occiderit hominem in publico bello XL dies peniteat."

35. Kottje, *Die Tötung im Krieg* (n. 33 above), 3–5 and his "Anhang," 20f. (nrs. 1–10).

36. Kottje, "Anhang," 20: nr. 6a: "in publico bello cum rege," nr. 8: "in bello publico cum rege"; nr. 2c: "in proelium cum rege," 3: "cum rege in proelio," 4: "cum rege in praelio," 5a: "in prelio cum rege," 5b: "cum rege in proelium," 6c: "in proelium cum rege."

37. See notes 18, 19 above.

38. The two earliest appearances of the word *folcgefeoht* are in the Parker manuscript of the Anglo-Saxon Chronicle (Robin Flower and A. H. Smith, eds., *The Parker Chronicle and Laws (Corpus Christi College, Cambridge MS. 173: A Facsimile*, EETS os 208 [London: Oxford University Press, 1941]), written at the end of the ninth century. For the year 871 (f. 14r) the chronicle mentions "viiii. folcgefeoht" that Alfred of Wessex fought against the large Viking host that had invaded England six years earlier, and for the year 887 (f. 16r) mentions two *folcgefeoht* fought on the Continent between Wido and Berengar of Friuli, rivals for the kingdom of Italy. Although the word may be older, the fact that its first appearance follows that of *publicum bellum* by almost two centuries may equally indicate that the Old English is a calque/translation of the Latin.

that its influence was limited to certain areas.[39] For the attitude lying behind this provision directly affronted Frankish *amour propre*, stigmatizing as sinful that which a militarized aristocracy regarded as its most honorable role, fighting, often in service to king and country.

The appearance of tariffed penitentials is part of a heightened emphasis on the value of penance that was part of the spiritual baggage carried to the Continent by Irish reformers in the seventh and eighth centuries. Around the year 600 the Irish monk Columbanus, the founder of Bobbio, wrote a brief penitential, intending thereby, as Jonas of Bobbio's *vita* put it, to restore "the medicine of penance" to a Frankish realm where it was almost extinct. Jonas also records a story about Columbanus's confrontation with the Frankish warrior ethos. In 612, as Columbanus's patron and protector King Theudebert II was about to march against his brother Theuderic II, the monk went to Theudebert

> and urged him to put aside the arrogant pride he had taken up and become a cleric, and surrender to a holy religious life in the church, lest he lose eternal life along with his temporal kingdom. This idea provoked laughter in the king and in all those standing around him, with them saying that they had never heard of a Merovingian who had been raised to the kingship voluntarily becoming a cleric.[40]

This conflict between the honorable and proud self-perception of a militarized aristocracy and the healing humiliation of penance is largely invisible in eighth- and on into ninth-century Carolingian Francia. Manuscript distribution shows at least a difference of opinion then, perhaps along regional lines.[41] And there is at least one possible instance of an early Carolingian ruler affected by the same mentality seen in penitentials of the Insular tradition. Charles Martel's son Carloman had "opted out" of princely authority, much as had contemporary and earlier Anglo-Saxon and Irish kings and princes, reportedly horrified by his witness of and participation in a bloodbath involving thousands of Alamanni in 746. "Wherefore, stung in conscience, he abandoned the kingship, and went to a monastery at the fortress of Cassino [Italy]."[42]

---

39. Kottje, esp. 3–5, 9–10.

40. *Ionae vitae sanctorum Columbani, Vedastis, Iohannis* (*MGH: Scriptores rerum Germanicarum in usum scholarum* 37), I.28, 217–18.

41. Kottje, 10.

42. *MGH: Script.* I, ed. G. H. Pertz (Hannover, 1826), *Annalium Petavianorum continuatio*, 11, *s.a.* 746. On this phenomenon, see Clare Stancliffe, "Kings Who Opted Out," in *Ideal and Reality in Frankish and Anglo-Saxon Society: Studies Presented to J. M. Wallace-Hadrill*, ed. Patrick Wormald et al. (Oxford: Basil Blackwell, 1983), 154–76.

Carloman's behavior betokened the same remorse at his deeds *militare* and the same repentance seen earlier in late antique Christians who had been in civil service or the military, and as was prescribed in the Penitential of Theodore and works influenced by it.

The lay aristocratic resistance to this Insular tradition was seconded by resistance to penitentials as a whole in the church, which regarded them as works of foreign and dubious origin, "of which the errors are as certain as the authors are uncertain," works lacking in any authority, scriptural or traditional.[43] And yet despite denunciations at early ninth-century Gallic church councils, at which priests were urged not to use penitentials, and bishops enjoined to search their dioceses for such books and consign them to the flames, the advantages for pastoral care of having a list of sins and a penance appropriate to each were too great to forgo the use of penitentials entirely.[44] Soon after the Council of Paris in 829, Archbishop Ebo of Reims commissioned his suffragan Bishop Halitgar of Cambrai to compile a penitential text of the requisite authority. For his provision on killing in war, Halitgar used an earlier work probably produced in northern France, a work that in the relevant provision can be regarded as a Frankish response to the penitential tradition on the subject stemming from the Penitential of Theodore.

> Concerning those who [commit] murder on a campaign. Now if anyone on a campaign kills another man without cause, let him fast for twenty-two weeks. But if he happens to kill someone in the course of defending himself or his parents or his household, he shall not be culpable. If he wishes to fast [anyway], it is in his power [to do so]; for what he did was compelled [by circumstances].[45]

This provision does seem to concede that war is not morally unproblematic. But in the type of killing more commonly associated with combat, in which one kills to avoid being killed, or kills (even conceptually) in defense of hearth and kin, this is not a sin and does not require penance, though the warrior may do penance on his own, according to the dictates of his conscience.

---

43. *Concilium Cabillonense*, c. 38, ed. A. Werminghoff (*MGH: Leg. sect.* III, *Concilia*, t. II, *concilia aevi karolini*, 281): "quorum sunt certi errores, incerti auctores."

44. Allen J. Frantzen, "The Significance of the Frankish Penitentials," *Journal of Ecclesiastical History* 30, no. 4 (1979): 409–21.

45. Kottje, *Die Tötung im Kriege* (n. 32 above), 4–5; text on 21, no. 11: "De his qui homicidium in expeditione. S[i] q[uis] aliquis [sic] in expeditionem occidit hominem sine causa, ieiunet ebdomadas XXII. Si autem forsitan se defendendum aut parentes suos aut familias suas occidit aliquis [sic], ille non est reus. Si voluerit ieiunare, illius est potestatem, quia coactus hoc fecit."

War, Justification, and Repentance from the *CDS* to Gratian's *Decretum*

The earliest compilation of Augustinian texts on war and military service is preserved in one manuscript, Paris Bib. nat. lat. nouv. acq. 1632. The text is found in the second section of this composite codex, a section provisionally dated to the mid-ninth century, perhaps from Fleury.[46] The text in question runs fol. 78ᵛ–89ᵛ, with the uncial heading, *Incipiunt capitula diversarum sententiarum pro negociis rei publice consulendis.* Internal evidence indicates that the text originated in the context of *Brüderkrieg* propaganda, from partisans of the allies Charles the Bald and Louis the German.[47] Judging by the manuscript, the *CDS* was originally written in a *libellus* or pamphlet that ran about twelve folia. The text is divided into twenty-four *capitula*, preceded by a summary "table of contents" that in some instances lists the source for the *sententia*.[48]

In addition to the citation in the *CDS* of mostly Augustinian texts to argue that victory in battle encoded a judgment of God (*iudicium Dei*), and that soldiers who killed in battle did not commit homicide, the two assertions at issue in the opposing interpretations of the battle of Fontenoy, some of the material in the *CDS* of a *Fürstenspiegel*-like nature can be read not only as advisory for someone like Charles the Bald, but also as implied criticism of his enemy Lothar. One example of this is in *CDS* 19, which cites Augustine's statement in *The City of God* on evil men pursuing power and glory through crimes such as treachery and deceit.[49] *CDS* 3 cites Augustine's statement from the same work that only evil men find happiness in war.[50] *CDS* 2 has Augustine's statement from Book 4 on the advantages and disadvantages of the rule of good and evil men.[51] Even the very first line of *CDS* 1, which largely repeats Augustine's "mini-*Fürstenspiegel*" and is largely positive in tone, may feature a backhanded swipe at Lothar's capabilities as a ruler. Augustine had written that it was best if

---

46. I thank David Ganz for his private communications to me regarding the date and possible place of origin for this manuscript.

47. Wynn, "Justifying."

48. Gerhard Laehr/Carl Erdmann, "Ein karolingischer Konzilsbrief und der Fürstenspiegel Hincmars von Reims," *Neues Archiv der Gesellschaft für ältere deutsche Geschichtskunde zur Beförderung einer Gesamtausgabe der Quellenschriften deutscher Geschichten des Mittelalters* 50 (Berlin, 1935), 106–34.

49. *CDS* 19, fol. 85v–86. Cf. Aug. *DCD* 5.19 (*CCL* 47, 155).

50. *CDS* 3, fol. 80. Cf. Aug. *DCD* 4.15 (*CCL* 47, 111).

51. *CDS* 2, fol. 79v–80. Cf. Aug. *DCD* 4.3 (*CCL* 47, 101).

rulers "have the knowledge for ruling peoples" (*scientia regendi populos*).[52] This language may be reflected in a statement issued by prelates allied with Charles and Louis at a council at the imperial capital of Aachen in late March 842, which among crimes and failings found that Lothar "did not have the knowledge of how to govern the state" (*scientia gubernandi rem publicam*).[53]

Passages in the *CDS* related to military service and the culpability of soldiers who killed in battle do arguably convey accurately Augustine's original meaning. *CDS* 6 consists of an extensive excerpt from Augustine's Letter 189 to Boniface, where the bishop of Hippo, citing scriptural examples, argued that soldiers who fought were not by that alone displeasing to God.[54] In *cap.* 4, 7, and 8 the author or authors cited Augustinian texts to the effect that a soldier acting in accordance with his public role, in obedience to legitimate authority, is not liable to the charge of homicide for killing in battle.[55] This is a direct challenge to the argument pressed by supporters of Lothar like Hrabanus Maurus, who as we have seen had insisted that the killing at Fontenoy had, in fact, constituted homicide. Here the stance of someone like Hrabanus, who in his insistence on the culpability of those who kill in battle does seem to reference the ancient aversion to blood pollution manifested in his day in certain penitentials, is close enough to the viewpoint of late antique pacifistic circles obliquely criticized in the relevant passages as to warrant the judgment that at least in this instance the *CDS* provides a fair representation of Augustine's actual views.

Unquestionably the same cannot be said regarding what the *CDS*, based supposedly on Augustinian authority, had to say on war. In sum, the *CDS* enlisted Augustine in the *Brüderkrieg* propaganda campaign to frame victory in battle as a manifestation of divine approval. But as we saw in the previous chapter, Augustine himself thought there was no connection between *victoria* and just cause.[56] The author or authors of the *CDS* could effect such a transformation of Augustine's views by what can only be described as outright forgery. So, *CDS* 9 cites a brief excerpt from Letter 13 of the bogus correspondence between Augustine and Boniface, where Augustine had supposedly advised the general to pray to God, "for when there is fighting,

---

52. *CDS* 1, fol. 79v: "Qui vera pietate prediti bene vivunt, si habeant (*DCD* habent) scientiam regendi populos, nihil (*DCD* insert. est) felicius rebus humanis quam si Deo miserante habeant potestatem." Cf. *DCD* 5.19 (*CCL* 47, 156).

53. Nithard 4.1 (note 1 above, 118): "neque scientiam gubernandi rem publicam illum habere."

54. *CDS* 6, fol. 81–81v. Cf. Aug. *Epist.* 189 (*CSEL* 57, 131–35), and ch. 6, note 216 above.

55. *CDS* 4, 7, 8, fol. 80–80v, 81v–82. Cf. Aug. *DCD* 1.21 (*CCL* 47, 23); *DCD* 1.26 (*CCL* 47, 27); *Epist.* 47 (*CSEL* 34, 135), and ch. 6, notes 165, 174, 175, 177, 179 to 181 above.

56. *Epist.* 220.11 (*CSEL* 57, 439); ch. 8, note 53.

God looks forth from the open heavens, and then gives the palm [of victory] to the side He perceives as just."[57] Even more outrageous is the transformation of Augustine effected in *CDS* 5.

DCD 4.17 (*CCL* 47, p. 112)

An forte dicunt, quod deam Victoriam Iuppiter mittat atque illa tamquam regi deorum obtemperans ad quos iusserit veniat et in eorum parte considat? Hoc vere dicitur non de illo Iove, quem deorum regem pro sua opinione confingunt, sed de illo vero rege saeculorum, quod mittat non Victoriam, quae nulla substantia est, sed angelum suum et faciat vincere quem voluerit . . .

CDS 5, f. 80^V

Victoriam Omnipotens mittit atque illo tamquam regi deorum optemperans ad quos iusserit venit et in eorum parte consedit. Hoc vere de illo vero rege seculorum dicitur quod mittat non victoriam, que nulla substantia est, sed angelum suum et facit vincere quem voluerit . . .

What had been in Augustine a sarcastic questioning of the need for a goddess Victoria if Jupiter were truly sovereign became an affirmative statement that it was God who sends victory, a radical rewriting requiring modifications of the original that included the bald replacement of Jupiter with Jehovah![58]

Thirty years after the compilation of the *CDS* as a piece of *Brüderkrieg* propaganda, Bishop Hincmar of Reims used it as his main source for the treatise *De regis persona et regio ministerio*.[59] In Hincmar's reworking of the *CDS* for the later work one sees already how would-be authoritative Augustinian texts were transmitted across time in a literarily and historically decontextualized fashion, in the same way as was done by later canonists like Anselm of Lucca, Ivo of Chartres, and Gratian. There is other evidence pointing to the era of ninth-century Carolingian patristic scholarship as the time when many passages were extracted from the African Father's massive oeuvre, which later ended up in high medieval collections of canons regarding war and military service. So, through its citation by Gratian and later Thomas Aquinas, Augustine's supposed definition of the just war in his *Quaestiones in Heptateuchum*—a passage not excerpted in the *CDS*—later acquired canonical authority as *the* definition of the Western Christian just war.[60] This very passage was excerpted by none

57. *CDS* 9, fol. 82. Cf. Ps. Aug. *Epist. XIII, XV* (*PL* 33:1098).

58. On the original context of this passage in Augustine, see ch. 8, notes 35 to 44 above.

59. Laehr/Erdmann (n. 48 above), 120–26; Hans Hubert Anton, *Fürstenspiegel und Herrscherethos in der Karolingerzeit* (Bonn: Ludwig Röhrscheid, 1968), 281–355.

other than Hrabanus Maurus in his commentary on the book of Joshua, and Walahfrid Strabo soon afterwards used the passage as a biblical gloss.[61]

The participation of Hrabanus Maurus, however unintentionally on his part, in the medieval construction of Augustine as an authority on just war illustrates the malleability of the developing textual tradition. The continuing reluctance of some Western Christians at this time to fully embrace the accommodation to war and military service evidenced by the bishops' statement after Fontenoy and the *CDS* is visible in the penitential collection authored by Regino of Prüm, who wrote his *Libri duo de synodalibus causis et disciplinis ecclesiasticis* for Archbishop Rathbod of Trier in about 906.[62] When it came to those who had killed in battle for no good reason (*pro nihilo*), Regino simply quoted the passage from the penitential work of Hrabanus Maurus regarding the combatants at Fontenoy, thus maintaining the stance that such men had to do penance. As to the penance itself, Regino merely repeated the provision going back to the Penitential of Theodore that "whoever has slain a human being in a *bellum publicum*, let him do penance for forty days."[63]

What few historical examples we have of early medieval warriors doing penance for having killed in war entitle us to question how effective the extant penitentials were in prescribing the precise provisions to be followed in such cases. As we already saw, the victors at Fontenoy were urged to confess individually and privately any sin they may have committed in the course of the battle, and the entire army fasted for three days as a sort of corporate penance.[64] In 923 after a battle at Soissons between rivals for the West Frankish throne, a penance was prescribed for those who had participated in the battle. During Lent for each of the three years following the battle, all the penitents were to fast on bread, salt, and water on every Monday, Wednesday, and Friday. They had to fast likewise for fifteen days before the nativity of St. John the Baptist (24 June) and before Christmas, and on every Friday throughout the whole year, unless they should commute their fast (probably through almsgiving), or should a major feast day fall on one of those days.[65] The penitential ordinance has also

---

60. *Corpus iuris canonici* I, *Decretum magistri Gratiani*, ed. Emil Friedberg (Leipzig, 1879), II c.23 q.2 c.2 (col. 894–95); *S. Thomae de Aquino Summae Theologiae Secunda Secundae* (Ottawa: Commissio Piana, 1953), II-II q.40 a.1 (1633a). On the original context of Augustine's "definition," see ch. 7, notes 97 to 103 above.

61. *PL* 108:1029 (Hrabanus Maurus); *PL* 113:512 (Walahfrid Strabo).

62. Sarah Hamilton, *The Practice of Penance, 900-1050* (Woodbridge, UK: Boydell, 2001), 27–44.

63. *Das Sendhandbuch des Regino von Prüm*, ed. W. Hartmann (Darmstadt, 2004), 2.50 (274/6), 2.51 (276): "Si quis hominem in bello publico occiderit, XL dies poeniteat."

64. Note 3 above.

survived for those who had fought on the Norman side in the battle of Hastings in October 1066. It detailed specific penances according to whether the warrior had killed in battle or merely struck someone, and according to whether the offense had occurred during the battle itself, or during the brief campaign between Hastings and William the Conqueror's coronation on Christmas Day 1066. The penitential ordinance even dealt with the exceptional case of archers, who because of the nature of their weapons could not know how many they had killed or wounded.[66] None of these provisions finds an exact parallel in any of the extant penitentials. But rather than dismissing the early medieval penitential provisions for warriors as unreal and irrelevant, it is probably better to regard them as providing general guidelines for those administering penance, written in general language appropriate for clerical authors for whom war was not something—ideally—they had intimate acquaintance with.

The Hastings penitential ordinance seems to be the last recorded instance of penance prescribed for warriors more or less according to the early medieval penitential model. From the viewpoint of the late eleventh-century reforming papacy, such penitential provisions appeared as part of the unwieldy tangle of local church traditions and customs that needed to be reformed and regularized according to a Roman pattern.[67] In a development driven by the reforming papacy, the relationship between penance and war in Western Europe changed radically over the thirty years following Hastings. In acting to mobilize the defense of Christendom against its enemies, late eleventh-century popes increasingly employed penance as part of its spiritual armament.[68] The transformation of the relationship between penance and war culminated in the indulgence granted by Urban II in 1095 to those who with pious intent embarked on the First Crusade, an indulgence that strictly speaking only provided for remission of the need to do penance for earlier misdeeds. But as Carl Erdmann pointed out, this fine distinction was little noted, at the time or later, and the idea quickly arose that crusading itself atoned for sin, and promised immediate salvation to those who fell in its prosecution.[69] Thus by the

65. Mansi 18A:345–46.

66. *Councils & Synods, with other documents relating to the English Church*, ed. D. Whitelock et al., I:2 (Oxford: Clarendon, 1981), 583–84. On this ordinance, see H. E. J. Cowdrey, "Bishop Ermenfrid of Sion and the Penitential Ordinance following the Battle of Hastings," *Journal of Ecclesiastical History* 20, no. 2 (1969): 225–42; C. Morton, "Pope Alexander II and the Norman Conquest," *Latomus* 34, no. 2 (1975): 376–82; Hamilton (n. 62 above), 194–96.

67. Ernst-Dieter Hehl, "War, Peace and the Christian Order," *NCMH* 4:1, 188.

68. Hehl (previous note), 195–202.

end of the eleventh century, the older relationship between penance and war was stood on its head; now war itself counted as an act of penance.

This shift had been anticipated by Anselm of Lucca (d. 1086), who in using primarily Augustinian citations to justify the papacy's wars against the German emperor had argued that the need for one to do penance for having killed in a just war depended on one's inner intention.[70] About the time of the First Crusade, Ivo of Chartres in his canonical collections dispensed with the need for warriors to do penance at all for having killed in war, drawing upon Augustine to argue that any who did so were free of sin because they had been exercising a public function.[71]

Both Anselm's and Ivo's collections of canons were the immediate source for the important *causa* 23 in the second part of Gratian's *Decretum*, which became in turn the earliest comprehensive collection of texts for what ultimately evolved into the doctrine of just war.[72] It is surprising, therefore, that not only did Gratian "not arrive at a neat and comprehensive formula" delineating the elements of a just war doctrine,[73] but that his immediate sources Anselm and Ivo actually focused more effort on arguing for the compatibility of Christianity with military service than on any general, theoretical justification of war, a characteristic of their works shared with the ninth-century *CDS*, and arguably true as well for Augustine, the ultimate source for most of their texts.

Besides sharing a greater focus on issues connected with military service, both Anselm's and Ivo's collections of canons also contain some of the same Augustinian texts found in the *CDS*. Is this merely a coincidence, or is the *CDS* at the head of a textual tradition that, with the subsequent accretion of other, mostly Augustinian texts, ultimately ended up in the collections of Anselm and Ivo? Carl Erdmann thought the former. He argued regarding the *CDS* that "[i]n spite of accidental agreements, Anselm did not use them."[74] It is also true that the Augustinian material used by Anselm and Ivo of Chartres in their compilation of canons, both of which were in turn sources for Gratian's foundational material for the just war doctrine in the *Decretum*, included texts of Augustine and of other church fathers not found in the *CDS*, and featured

---

69. Carl Erdmann, *Die Entstehung des Kreuzzugsgedanken* (Stuttgart, 1935). I cite from the English translation, *The Origin of the Idea of Crusade*, trans. Marshall W. Baldwin and Walter Goffart (Princeton, 1977), 343–45; Hehl, 208–9.

70. Hehl, 203.

71. Hehl, 204–5.

72. Chapter 1, notes 1, 2 above; Russell, 55–56.

73. Russell, 64.

74. Erdmann, *The Origin of the Idea of Crusade* (n. 69 above), 243–44 and note 58.

different configurations of the Augustinian texts they do have in common with the earlier work.[75] That said, *pace* Erdmann, it seems a bit too coincidental that the later compilers would have picked some of the very same passages originally used in the *CDS*, for example, to support arguments in favor of Christian military service, including passages and works that arguably at first glance bear a tenuous relationship to that issue. The single best textual indicator of an ultimate dependence on the *CDS* is both Anselm's and Ivo's use of a passage from Augustine's commentary on the Sermon on the Mount to argue that even the punishment of death—in the textual and historical context of their compilations referring both to capital punishment and killing in a justified war—can be exercised with love and kindness.[76] Anselm begins his citation at the same point in the Augustinian original where the *CDS* does, and ends his citation earlier.[77] Ivo in his corresponding canon prefaced this particular passage with other Augustinian material, and ended his citation from the commentary even before Anselm did.[78] As to the original Augustinian text itself, the idea beggars belief that eleventh-century compilers would have independently trawled through the intimidating bulk of Augustine's works—in manuscript, no less, absent the aids of modern scholarly apparatus—and come up with the same text as had the author or authors of the *CDS*, beginning at the very same spot, in an Augustinian work, by the way, which would seem on the face of it an unlikely place to look for material on war and military service.

Both Anselm and Ivo, then, were responsible for transmitting the textual tradition of Augustinian material, including material ultimately traceable to the *CDS*, which made the African Father appear to be an authority on war and military service. As can be seen from the historical context alluded to above, the historical circumstances of late eleventh-century Western Europe, specifically the papacy's wars with the German emperor and the First Crusade, constrained the textual transmission of such material by way of yet another conceptual filter that admitted some texts and omitted others. It was this textual tradition, limited and distorted as it was in its transmission over the centuries, that provided the basis for Gratian's *causa* 23 on the justification for war, and thus ultimately undergirds the Western idea of just war, and Augustine's supposed role in its origination.

---

75. On the textual correspondences among the *CDS*, and the canonical collections of Anselm, Ivo, and Gratian, see the appendix to this chapter.

76. Augustine, *De sermone Domini in monte* I, 20 (64–65) (*CCL* 35, 73–75 = *CDS* 10, fol. 82r–83r).

77. Pásztor (see appendix below), 13.2, 405–6.

78. Ivo, *Decretum* 10.60 (*PL* 161:710A).

APPENDIX

TABLE OF CORRESPONDENCES AMONG THE *CDS*, ANSELM OF LUCCA, IVO OF CHARTRES, AND GRATIAN

The editions of the works cited below are as follows. As there is now no edition of the *CDS*, I cite from the sole manuscript, Paris Bib. nat. lat. nouv. acq. 1632, fol. 78^v–89^v.

Anselm of Lucca: Edith Pásztor, "Lotta per le investiture e 'ius belli': la posizione di Anselmo di Lucca," *Sant' Anselmo, Mantova e la lotta per le investiture. Atti del convegno internazionale di studi (Mantova 23–24–25 maggio 1986)*, ed. Paolo Golinelli (Bologna, 1987), pp. 375–421.

Ivo of Chartres: *Decretum* 10: *De homicidiis* (*PL* 161:689–746).

Gratian: *Corpus iuris canonici* I, *Decretum magistri Gratiani*, ed. Emil Friedberg (Leipzig, 1879).

CDS	Anselm	Ivo	Gratian
4 (fol. 80^{r-v})		10.4 (*PL* 161:692)	II c.23 q.5 c.9 (col. 934)
6 (81^{r-v})	13.4, pp. 407–8	10.107, 125, 126 (*PL* 161:724, 728, 729)	II c.23 q.1 c.3 (col. 892)
7 (81^v–82^r)		10.98 (*PL*161:722)	II c.23 q.5 c.13 (col. 935)
8 (82^r)	13.18, pp. 413–14	10.1 (*PL* 161:689–91)	II c.23 q.5 c.8 (col. 932)
9 (82^r)	13.5, p. 408	10.109 (725)	
10 (82^r–83^r)	13.2, pp. 405–6	10.60 (709–10)	II c.23 q.4 c.51 (col. 927–28)
11 (83^{r-v})		10.121 (727)	II c.23 q.4 c.42 (col. 923)
12 (83^v–84^r)		10.59 (709)	II c.23 q.5 c.48 (col. 945)
13 (84^{r-v})			II c.23 q.4 c.37; q.6 c.3 (col. 917, 948)

20 (86^r–87^r)		10.96, 97 (721)	II c.23 q.5 c.40 (col. 941)

10

Conclusion

Unlike some of his more rigorist contemporaries, and certainly unlike earlier African Christians such as Tertullian and Lactantius, Augustine did not regard with detestation *militia*, service to the state. Though state service had its pitfalls and was imbued with anxieties and perils, a Christian could conceivably hold state office and not by that alone incur mortal sin. For there was a societal order, and in that order higher authorities to whom the governance of human affairs had been entrusted. There were those in that societal order, Christian as well as pagan, to whom obedience was legitimately due, and who could legitimately issue commands to their inferiors that had to be obeyed. These authorities were forced at times to use coercive measures to preserve societal order, even the application of capital punishment.

Unlike contemporaries such as Sulpicius Severus and Paulinus of Nola, Augustine also thought Christians could serve in the military and not by that alone commit a sin. As with executioners in civil society, soldiers could even kill other human beings in obedience to the lawful commands of their superiors. It is true this amounted to an exception to the Decalogue commandment "Thou shalt not kill," but, *pace* Lactantius, it was an exception authorized by Scripture itself. Scripture also provided warrant for Christians serving in the military, since John the Baptist had not told soldiers coming to him to be baptized to throw down their arms and desert the service. Simply put, Christian soldiers were obligated to obey the orders of their superiors, even those of a pagan emperor or commander. Military service could, in fact, be regarded as pleasing to God. Augustine's acceptance of Christian military service is certainly partly due to his belief that participants in society are by virtue of that participation to act in ways preservative of societal order. But the particularities of military service in Roman Africa also seem to have influenced Augustine's generally positive view of it. Although there are early statements by Augustine showing an awareness of the possibility and reality of soldierly misconduct, he went on to point out that such conduct was illegal and punishable, and even shows some admiration for the sufferings of soldiers. He goes so far as to acknowledge that for some, military service was a desirable career choice.

Augustine's generally positive view of Christian military service does not mean, however, that he had a similar view of war. To him, war was one of the evils of this world. Roman history amply illustrated the truth that human beings in fighting each other acted worse than the most savage animals. He himself had witnessed firsthand the baleful effects of war, particularly in the civil wars that plagued his time. Though wars were evil, they nonetheless fell within the purview of divine providence. God used war to punish the wicked, or to test the virtue of the good. In wars that served particular ends of divine justice, God of course was ultimately in charge, but he chose *boni*, good men found in the appropriate rank in human society, to wage wars under divine auspices. Such *boni*, unlike ancient and some contemporary Romans, eschewed the pursuit of power and *gloria* for their own sakes. Most such wars had occurred in Old Testament times, but in the battle of the Frigidus the Christian emperor Theodosius, a contemporary example of a *bonus*, had fought after receiving assurance of divine support, a support manifested during the battle itself by a providential wind that was like the miracles in the battles of the Old Testament. As for the "just war" of the Romans, it was at best a necessary evil, at worst a pretext for crime.

In line with his general rejection of secular conceptions of war, Augustine derided the potent Roman political idea of *victoria*, preferring to reserve the term "victory" for that of Christians over death, particularly the final victory at the Resurrection in the battle, never to be resolved in this lifetime, against internal vices. He sought to demystify *victoria* for both pagans and Christians. It could be deceptive as well as barren, was motivated by the lust for power and glory, and was purchased at the cost of monstrous savagery and bloodshed. Its personification as Victoria revealed a goddess that was both useless and superfluous, who in the end did not even exist. No, the outcome of war rested in the hands of the one, true God.

Augustine sought to transpose into a Christian key not only *victoria* but also the *pax* that success in war was supposed to achieve. Being the product of wicked and disordered desires, the earthly peace that concluded war was bound to be unjust and disordered as well. Though earthly peace was transitory and imperfect, human beings nonetheless yearned for it, a longing born of the vestiges of the prelapsarian experience of perfect peace still remaining in human nature. The Christians who were citizens of the city of God, now in hope, later in reality, rejected the prideful presumption of imposing the peace of subjugation on others, but sought a perfect peace, not ultimately attainable in this lifetime, through a harmonious order.

Augustine's view of the social and political realities of the mortal human sphere might seem at times bloody-minded and bleak, since he justified state-sponsored killing in the administration of justice and in war, and denied that peace was ever truly possible on earth. Yet the dark cast of such views, especially that regarding the earthly peace, can be overstated because of the polemical context in which they often appear. In *Contra Faustum* Augustine argued in opposition to Manichaean pacifism—and incidentally the pacifism of some contemporary Christians—that war was sometimes necessary in furtherance of the ends of divine providence, and that Christians were not required to avoid military service, since it was not prohibited in Scripture. In *The City of God* Augustine was writing against those pagans who bemoaned the apparent disappearance of *victoria* and the Roman peace in the wake of the sack of Rome, arguing that *victoria* was an ugly illusion and that the benefits of the Roman peace were grossly exaggerated. Such were his theoretical arguments, at least. But we can see especially in his letters where Augustine gets down to "real world" cases. There what seems at times a hard-nosed rigidity is often softened by mercy and humanity. In every instance we know from his letters where real as opposed to theoretical capital punishment was involved, Augustine counseled mercy, even for Donatists who had killed and mutilated Catholic clergy. And when war was at his very doorstep and the possibility of earthly peace presented itself, Augustine grasped for it as avidly as any other mere mortal.

In his time, Augustine's was one voice among many of contemporary Christians who touched on matters of war and military service, at a time when fellow Christians were, in increasing numbers, becoming implicated in the violence and bloodshed of the Roman state, and were working out various attitudes and behaviors in response to this new situation. In his measured and much-qualified appraisal of the values of the Roman state, the earthly city, Augustine usually took a position on these issues somewhere between that of the "accommodationists" and the pacifistic views of someone like Paulinus of Nola. Yet not only did such a finely differentiated set of ideas seem to have little discernible influence on contemporaries, but it is also a fact that there is no hint of their having any influence on anyone for more than four centuries after Augustine's death in 430.

Orosius's history *Seven Books Against the Pagans*, which appeared in 417 or 418,[1] provides a contemporary illustration of how relatively isolated and ineffective the Augustinian vision of war and peace actually was in his own time and place, even in the case of a work written at Augustine's instigation.

Augustine had wanted a historical catalog of earlier Roman disasters to put the recent sack of Rome into its proper perspective. But Orosius exceeded his mandate, and in so doing he showed how the exquisite equilibrium of forces in Augustine's somber portrait of the earthly city could be simplified to the point of becoming unrecognizable. Orosius did see war itself as an evil, as had Augustine.[2] As did Augustine, and for much the same reasons, Orosius also regarded Roman civil wars as being especially lamentable.[3] As also with Augustine, Orosius extolled the benefits of peace, by his reckoning a precious-enough commodity especially in pre-Christian times.[4] Orosius likewise thought that the Roman ideals of just war and *victoria* were largely a sham.[5] But unlike Augustine, Orosius argued that the coming of Christ had brought a measure of peace to the world, ameliorating somewhat the savagery of war since the Incarnation.[6] In line with his view that wars had lately somehow "improved," Orosius thought that truly just wars had been fought in his own day.[7] Orosius more enthusiastically embraced than Augustine the notion of divine intervention at the battle of the Frigidus, and in addition qualified the earlier civil war against Magnus Maximus as having been undertaken "for just and necessary reasons."[8] Orosius's view of war, then, resembles less that of Augustine than that of the Eusebian "accommodationists," the audience for and purveyors of Theodosian propaganda, apologists for a Christian empire. From their perspective, on the issues generated by Christian engagement with war and military service, Augustine's stance, had they even known of it, would have seemed more of an isolated outlier than had been Tertullian's.

Controversies and differing attitudes regarding these issues appear in Tertullian's earliest extant and explicit Christian engagement with them, and become more widespread and visible in the late fourth century as increasing numbers of Christians confronted those issues for the first time. However slowly and hesitantly, over time early Christian writers witness the working-out of not only a *modus vivendi* with the state, but of a *modus cogitandi* that could express the event of war in a Christian idiom, as a regrettable necessity in the unfolding

---

1. On the date, see now A. T. Fear, trans., *Orosius: Seven Books of History Against the Pagans* (Liverpool: Liverpool University Press, 2010), intro., 5–7, in an introduction that well summarizes scholarship on Orosius.

2. Orosius I.1.12 (*CSEL* 5, 7).

3. II.4.4; V.19.12–13; 22; VII.6.8 (88, 329–30, 337–39, 448).

4. III.1.3; IV.12.8 (136, 239).

5. V.1, 5.13 (276–79, 290).

6. III.8.8 (153–54).

7. V.22.7 (338).

8. VII.35.2 (525).

of the greater providential plan. The era of Theodosian war propaganda shows this "accommodationist" stance reflected in political culture, and to the extent that later political culture in the early medieval West inherited a tradition with late antique roots, so too were inherited the views accommodating Christianity to war and military service.

And yet, at the opposite pole, I have not found one scintilla of evidence for a corresponding pacifistic tradition in these early centuries of church history. A modern pacifist like Jean-Michel Hornus might regard St. Martin as a spiritual forebear because of his anti-militarism.[9] This is the same St. Martin who two centuries after his death a Frankish nobleman invoked as he drove a lance into an opponent's throat, the same St. Martin who two centuries further on was invoked to provide divine support for Charlemagne's Frankish army.[10] But if there was no pacifistic tradition per se in late antiquity or in the early medieval West, how does one explain the fact that a sometimes rigorous anti-militarism was prominent in some circles in the West, including those influenced by contemporary ascetic currents, and at the see of Saint Peter itself, for a century and more after Constantine? How does one otherwise account for what looks like the reappearance around 700 in Anglo-Saxon England of the ancient Christian sensibility of blood pollution from killing even in duly authorized wars? Could it be that this Christian stance against blood violence and participation in it had persisted as an often-dormant genetic inheritance at the core of Christianity itself?

The identity of the central "genetic material" of both the accommodationist and pacifistic poles is almost too obvious. It surfaces with Tertullian's criticism of co-religionists who contended that the example of Old Testament warriors made it permissible for Christians to bear arms and wage war, a stance approved almost two centuries later by Ambrose of Milan, who held up those same Old Testament heroes as exemplars of martial courage, in that respect worthy substitutes for pagan heroes.[11] In the opposition between the accommodationist and pacifistic poles there was played out the "tension between the letter and the spirit, the inward and the outward, the Old Testament and the New" that was a more general tendency visible in the church of the period.[12] In that same dynamic there was also played out the tension

9. Jean-Michel Hornus, *It Is Not Lawful for Me to Fight*, trans. Alan Kreider and Oliver Coburn (Scottdale, PA: Herald Press, 1980), 195, 198.

10. *Gregorii episcopi Turonensis Libri Historiarum X*, ed. Bruno Krusch, Wilhelm Levison, Walther Holtzmann, *MGH: SRM* I/1 (Hanover, 1937–51), V.25, 231–32; *CCL* 162, *Corpus benedictionum pontificalium* no. 721, 285–86.

11. Tertullian: chapter 2, notes 8, 11, 12 above; Ambrose: chapter 3, notes 98 to 108 above.

between the individual and the corporate aspects of Christianity. Augustine had revalued *victoria* as fulfilling a social good akin to that of Israel's victories in the Old Testament.[13] But in confession, exclusion from the Eucharist during penance, and reconciliation—what could be more individual? Even here, the accommodationist tendency worked to corporatize the individual, as in the penitential fast of the victors after Fontenoy, whereby blood guilt could be diluted and transferred to the army as a whole.[14] So in effect, there *was* a pacifistic tradition in late antique and medieval Christianity, passed along in the oftentimes-inconvenient words of the New Testament.

In the previous pages civil wars have repeatedly been referenced like a leitmotiv. Civil wars recur repeatedly in the history of early Christian thought on war because such conflicts often involve core issues of identity. In an age when Christianity permeated realms today more reserved for the secular (oftentimes the difference being more a matter of degree!), such core issues of identity could easily resolve into determining who was truly on God's side. Such a question was, of course, moot in the case of outsiders, so wars with them were usually unproblematic and requiring little to no justification. Even in the days of the pre-Constantinian church, when Christians were often at odds with the pagan majority, non-Roman enemies were considered quite beyond the pale. In the case of Fontenoy, the urgency of determining who was on God's side in an extreme political crisis helps to explain the elision of notions of human and divine justice in the ordeal by war. Viewed from a later perspective, the *Brüderkrieg* of the early 840s acted as a choke-point in the transmission of Augustinian texts on war and military service, in which some texts were included and others excluded. A similar choke-point occurred in the late eleventh century, in historical circumstances that were in key respects similar to those of the *Brüderkrieg*. For the conflicts between the papacy and the German emperor can be regarded as a civil war of Christendom itself, fought to decide who would be at its head, a civil war where popes had to justify their resort to arms.

---

12. Rob Meens, "The uses of the Old Testament in early medieval canon law," *The Uses of the Past in the Early Middle Ages*, ed. Yitzhak Hen and Matthew Innes (Cambridge: Cambridge University Press, 2000), 76. Frederick Russell, *The Just War in the Middle Ages* (Cambridge: Cambridge University Press, 1975), 31, also notes how Carolingian scholars recognized the tensions between the Old and the New Testaments in their reflections on war (31).

13. Chapter 8, n. 63.

14. Chapter 9, n. 3.

Since Roman times, civil wars had been regarded as unholy affairs.[15] Yet from the civil wars of the Late Republic to the African general Boniface's revolt in the last days of the Western empire, the rhetoric of just war appeared most often precisely in the context of civil wars. Claims to be fighting in a just cause vindicated the resort to arms in the war most difficult to justify, appealed to the sentiments of would-be supporters and sympathizers, and reassured those already supportive that they were doing the right thing. And as had been the case since the ancient Romans, victory could be interpreted as divine vindication for one's cause. This idea was given medieval imprimatur by the pseudo-Augustinian Letter 13 to Boniface, cited first to that effect in the *CDS* in the ninth century, and later by Anselm and Ivo in the late eleventh. It verges on the ludicrous to link the justification of an ordeal with a supposed earlier Augustinian formulation of the just war, particularly since Augustine did not actually write that letter. In fact, leaving aside the bogus letter, no one up until the twelfth century even implicitly associated Augustine with the just war idea. Ivo did define the just war, but took his definition from Isidore's *Etymologies*.[16] After first repeating Isidore's definition via Ivo, Gratian was the first to cite "Augustine's" definition of the just war from the *Quaestiones in Heptateuchum*.[17]

Seven centuries separate the works of Augustine from his first explicit association with the idea of just war, not because his complex formulation of the idea had in the interim slumbered in obscurity,[18] but because Augustine had not formulated his own just war idea in the first place. As we saw in chapter 7, the just-referenced definition of the just war cited by Gratian was actually not Augustine's, but Cicero's. Further, in its original context the "definition" acted as a negative point of comparison when set beside wars, mostly in the Old Testament, directly instigated by God for the purposes of divine, not human, justice.[19]

As to the supposed Augustinian requirement that just wars were waged only with the goal of restoring peace, it is true that in his *Epist.* 189 to Boniface he had advised the general that "peace should be a matter of choice, war a matter of necessity. . . . For peace is not sought to stir up war, but war is waged to obtain peace."[20] Yet the idea that peace should be the aim of war was not unique

15. Chapter 4, n. 33.

16. *Decretum* 10.116 (*PL* 161:727A) = *Isidori Hispalensis episcopi Etymologiarum sive Originum libri XX*, ed. W. M. Lindsay (Oxford: Clarendon, 1911), t. II, *lib.* XVIII.2.

17. Gratian, *Decretum*, II c.23 q.2 c.1, 2 (col. 894).

18. Russell (n. 12 above), 27.

19. Chapter 7, notes 96 to 103.

20. *Epist.* 189.6 (*CSEL* 57, 135).

to Augustine or to Christians, but was found among pagans as well, including, again, Cicero. The ubiquity of this understanding did not result from some ethical principle shared by Christians and pagans, but from a common human nature that continually sought the restoration of peace, driven by its vestigial remembrance of prelapsarian tranquility. Even so, the peace obtained by war was necessarily disordered and unjust.[21]

Another feature recent writers have attributed to Augustine's supposed just war doctrine is the notion, seemingly absurd on the face of it, that just war amounted to a harsh corrective for sinners that was actually motivated by Christian love, that one could literally and justifiably "kill with kindness." In his 1963 book on Augustine's political and social ideas, Herbert Deane argued that it was Augustine's stance that wars against criminal nations when waged without a spirit of revenge or of taking pleasure in its violence are acts of love and benevolence.[22] Frederick Russell in 1975 assembled a cache of Augustinian quotes to show that for Augustine, "[l]ove for one's neighbor could legitimate his death."[23] William Stevenson in 1987, while cautioning that the love which would lead to a just war had to be an ideal, right kind of love that was mortally unattainable, nonetheless contended that in a just war "anything is permitted as long as it results from an attitude of right love . . . if war is waged in the spirit of love, no particular course of action is ruled out."[24]

It is true that Augustine had a number of times cited the example of a father disciplining his son with harsh correction to show that "there can be love in punishment," and had explicitly likened that model to the actions of governors and kings in using punishment to maintain societal order. In his commentary on the Sermon on the Mount, Augustine noted that in the past the saints had punished some sinners with death in order to instill fear in would-be sinners and to prevent those punished from committing even worse sins had they lived, adding that anyone so punishing "should punish with the disposition of a father punishing his little boy."[25] But although Augustine like many another Christian writer in later times could subsume under the state's *ius gladii* both the exercise of domestic justice and the waging of war, all the above examples explicitly involve the state's right to inflict capital punishment. As we have

---

21. Chapter 8, notes 119 to 123.

22. Herbert A. Deane, *The Political and Social Ideas of St. Augustine* (New York: Columbia University Press, 1963), 164–65.

23. Russell (n. 12 above), 17–18.

24. William R. Stevenson Jr., *Christian Love and Just War: Moral Paradox and Political Life in St. Augustine and His Modern Interpreters* (Macon, GA: Mercer University Press, 1987), 104–13.

25. Chapter 6, notes 112 to 117.

seen, Augustine knew very well what war was, and considered it one of the evils of postlapsarian life; tellingly, he did not include capital punishment in the lists of evils that included war.[26] Almost everything he wrote regarding what should motivate leaders to initiate wars and soldiers to fight them involved the simple and straightforward duty to obey the orders of one's superior: the leader should initiate war in obedience to God, and the soldier should fight in war in obedience to his legitimate superior. There is no mention of the need to fight with love in one's heart.

In only one instance does Augustine come close to saying something of that sort. In his letter to Marcellinus refuting the pagan Volusianus's charge that the pacifistic counsels of Christ were incompatible with the empire's need to defend itself against its enemies, Augustine had countered that were the empire defended by an army that truly followed Christ's commandments, then "even wars themselves would not be waged without kindness."[27] But as noted above in discussing this passage, this seems in context an (not unique) instance of polemical overkill on Augustine's part; not only was he countering Volusianus's unrealistic evocation of Christian quietism with an equally unrealistic picture of a thoroughly Christian army in a thoroughly Christian society, he was at the same time that he wrote this letter beginning *The City of God*, in which the earthly city was depicted as being ultimately irredeemable.[28]

Augustinian statements presuming that wars are fought in obedience to legitimate authority do accord with later medieval understandings of the just war, conceptually culminating in the first of Thomas Aquinas's three requirements for a war to be just, that it be ordered and waged by *auctoritas principis*.[29] But to follow Thomas and others in regarding this requirement as Augustinian in origin is to put the cart before the horse. Apart from the use of just war rhetoric in the propaganda of civil wars, insofar as we can speak of the term in Augustine's day in the context of what passed then for political theory it would consist of the simple formulation that any war initiated by the emperor was just ipso facto (and no doubt perilous to contend otherwise!). The continuity of political culture in Western Europe meant that a war waged by an early medieval king or emperor, a *publicum bellum*, was likewise considered to be just ipso facto: there is no sign whatsoever that

26. Chapter 7, notes 1 to 5.

27. *Epist.* 138.14 (*CSEL* 44, 139–40).

28. Chapter 6, n. 203.

29. *S. Thomae de Aquino Summae Theologiae Secunda Secundae* (Ottawa: Commissio Piana, 1953), vol. 3, col. 1632a–1634a. Thomas here cites *Contra Faustum* 22.75 (*CSEL* 25, 673), a passage discussed in chapter 7, notes 119 to 121.

Augustinian sentiments influenced that conception. What made the locus of the political authority to wage war problematic, and hence a topic for discussion among medieval canonists and theologians, was the devolution of public power after the Carolingian era. In the wrestling of high medieval canonists and theologians with the problem of who could initiate war, one sees clearly the actual role of Augustinian authority in the creation of the medieval *iura belli*.[30] For the issues that discussion treated and indeed the very juridical categories into which that discussion resolved existed *prior* to the extraction of Augustinian texts to support the conclusions arrived at.

Augustine did not author a doctrine of just war. Or, he can only be said to have done so insofar as he was made into *one* of the Christian authorities on war through selective and decontextualized citations from his works performed by later medieval canonists and theologians. But while this process not only reshaped but even distorted Augustine's actual views on the just war of the state, these later writers *did* more or less accurately convey his views on the morality of military service. The *CDS* and especially Ivo of Chartres, followed by Gratian, cite Augustine on the proposition that military service is not displeasing to God and that soldiers acting under legitimate authority can kill without sin in the performance of their official duties, Ivo thereby showing how by the end of the eleventh century canonical authority had dispensed with the notion that killing in war required penance.[31] Augustine was led to this opinion by his conviction that obedience to legitimate authority conduced to the preservation of societal order, an order that was ultimately divinely ordained. This may be a sound theological exegesis of the Pauline sentiment in Romans 13 on a Christian's duty to submit to the authority of the state. But does such a stance adequately address the psychological and spiritual issues attendant to killing in war as well as it does the detached theological?

In an article in 1988, and again in a book published in 1993, Bernard Verkamp argued that the provisions in the Penitential of Theodore and works influenced by it for the penance of a warrior who had killed in even a duly authorized war reflect an early medieval recognition that soldiers returning from war needed to undergo penance as a way to deal with the feelings of guilt and shame engendered by killing in war. Verkamp drew on firsthand

---

30. On the discussion regarding the legitimate authority to wage just wars, see Russell, 68–71, 100–105, 138–55.

31. Augustine *Epist.* 47.5 (*CSEL* 34, 135 = *CDS* 8; Anselm 13.18; Ivo, *Decretum* 10.1; Gratian, *Decretum* II c.23 q.5 c.8); 189 (*CSEL* 57, 131–35 = *CDS* 6; Anselm 13.4; Ivo, *Decretum* 10.126; Gratian, *Decretum* II c.23 q.1 c.3); *DCD* 1.21 (*CCL* 47, 23 = *CDS* 4; Ivo, *Decretum* 10.4; Gratian, *Decretum* II c.23 q.5 c.9.4); 1.26 (*CCL* 47, 27 = *CDS* 7; Ivo, *Decretum* 10.98; Gratian, *Decretum* II c.23 q.5 c.13).

twentieth-century accounts to show how prevalent were feelings of guilt and shame among soldiers who had killed other human beings, even in cases where they had killed in self-defense or in the prosecution of lawful orders. According to Verkamp, early medieval penance addressed a similar sense of contamination felt by early medieval warriors. He went on to argue that the modern prevalence of a "therapeutic" approach to the psychological anguish felt by, for example, returning Vietnam veterans—who were typically abruptly reintegrated into civilian society without any attempt at providing for them a transitional experience—ignored the moral aspects of their pain, which would be better addressed by some process akin to early medieval penance.[32] Further evidence on the psychological cost suffered by those who had killed in war was provided in a book published in 1995 by retired U.S. Army Lieutenant Colonel Dave Grossman.[33] Grossman in his historical survey found that not only have many soldiers throughout history failed to use their weapons in a manner calculated to kill their opponent, but also that soldiers in battle often resorted to "posturing" behavior, which in the age of gunpowder weapons resulted in men deliberately firing too high.[34] Grossman concludes that most individuals have an almost instinctive aversion to killing another human being, even in the circumstances of war.[35] When for whatever reason a soldier is able to overcome that aversion and kill someone, especially if done close-up, "[w]ith very few exceptions . . . [he] reaps a bitter harvest of guilt."[36] Grossman agrees with Verkamp that modern psychology is ill-equipped to deal with a returning soldier's moral pain and guilt.[37]

Did early medieval soldiers suffer guilt for having killed in battle, as Grossman argues is the historical norm? And was the provision of penance for such soldiers, as Verkamp argued, a response to their dealing with feelings of guilt and shame? The only early medieval evidence bearing on the question relates to individuals in the highest levels of a warrior aristocracy, including kings. There was the abdication of Charles Martel's son Carloman on account of his involvement in a bloodbath.[38] Bede's depiction of Cædwalla of Wessex in

32. Bernard J. Verkamp, "Moral treatment of returning warriors in the early middle ages," *Journal of Religious Ethics* 16, no. 2 (1988): 223–49; idem, *The Moral Treatment of Returning Warriors in Early Medieval and Modern Times* (Scranton, PA: University of Scranton Press, 1993).

33. Dave Grossman, *On Killing: The Psychological Cost of Learning to Kill in War and Society* (New York: Back Bay Books, 1995).

34. Grossman, 5–15.

35. Grossman, 39.

36. Grossman, 89.

37. Grossman, 96.

38. Chapter 9, n. 42.

his *Ecclesiastical History* presents the king as *pars pro toto* for all the later Anglo-Saxon kings who followed his example of expiatory pilgrimage to Rome. When Cædwalla arrived at Rome in late 688 or early 689, he had reigned for only two years over Wessex; though still young, he arrived at St. Peter's a man broken in body, and conceivably in spirit, by the wounds he'd suffered in a desperate, genocidal war he had led against the inhabitants of the Isle of Wight.[39]

Easily the best contemporary evidence for something like what Verkamp has hypothesized is in Felix's *Life of Saint Guthlac*, written in about 730.[40] Guthlac had died in 714 after having lived as a hermit in the East Anglian fens for fifteen years. Guthlac, whose family according to Felix belonged to a Mercian royal lineage, had since the age of fifteen led an armed gang in devastating raids on Mercia's enemies, enriching themselves in the process. After nine uninterrupted years of the warrior life, Guthlac in a rare moment of repose was ruminating on the uncertainties in his life of violence,

> when suddenly, marvellous to tell, a spiritual flame, as though it had pierced his breast, began to burn in this man's heart. For when, with wakeful mind, he contemplated the wretched deaths and the shameful ends of the ancient kings of his race in the course of the past ages, and also the fleeting riches of this world and the contemptible glory of this temporal life, then in imagination the form of his own death revealed itself to him; and, trembling with anxiety at the inevitable finish of this brief life, he perceived that its course daily moved to that end. As he thought over these and similar things, suddenly by the prompting of the divine majesty, he vowed that, if he lived until the next day, he himself would become a servant of Christ.[41]

The next day Guthlac bade farewell to his companions and at the age of twenty-four entered the monastery of Repton. There for the next two years, in addition to learning all that went with monastic discipline, he worked to expiate the sins of his previous life. At the end of his monastic formation Guthlac went to Crowland in the East Anglian fens to live the life of a religious hermit.[42]

---

39. Bede, *HE* IV.15, 16: V.7 (382–85, 470–71).

40. *Felix's Life of Saint Guthlac*, ed. and trans. Bertram Colgrave (Cambridge: Cambridge University Press, 1956).

41. *Life of Saint Guthlac* 18 (80, 82; Colgrave trans., 81, 83).

42. *Life of Saint Guthlac* 19–24 (82, 84, 86; Colgrave trans., 83, 85, 87).

Although Felix seems a bit uneasy about describing his hero's life as a warrior, it is clear from his account that Guthlac personally witnessed killing in war, and likely personally participated in it. It is also true that Felix does not explicitly ascribe Guthlac's conversion to guilt for having slain in battle. Whether Guthlac suffered from such guilt has to be inferred from Felix's account, but it is certainly a reasonable supposition. Audrey Meaney has suggested that from a psychological perspective Guthlac's "desire to retreat from the world after undergoing the horrors of warfare is by no means unusual."[43]

There is a temptation, eventually overcome, that happened during Guthlac's years as a hermit and is psychologically congruent with his having suffered guilt for his previous life as a warrior. Guthlac had just entered upon his eremitic life when one day the devil shot a "poisoned arrow of despair" into the saint's mind.

> [T]hen every feeling of the soldier of Christ was disturbed by it, and he began to despair about what he had undertaken, and turning things over in his troubled mind he knew not in what place to rest. For when he remembered that the sins he had committed in the past were of immense weight, it seemed to him that he could not be cleansed from them. He began indeed to despair so utterly that he thought he had undertaken an infinite and insupportable labour.[44]

Bertram Colgrave, the editor and translator of the *Life of Guthlac*, links Guthlac's despair here to the sin of "accidia," common to beginners in the monastic life, who are overwhelmed by the magnitude of their previous sins and become bereft of any hope of ever being free of them.[45] But it is also true that this same sense of having done something that has left one feeling irredeemably contaminated, unable ever again to regain the purity of one's earlier life, is so commonly reported among modern soldiers who have killed in war that citation seems superfluous.

Such feelings resulting from having killed in war are today classified under the perhaps too-broad rubric of post-traumatic stress disorder or PTSD, a diagnosis first applied en masse to veterans of the Vietnam War. Philip Caputo in his Vietnam memoir wrote of the pity and guilt many veterans feel for the

---

43. Audrey L. Meaney, "Felix's *Life of Guthlac*: History or Hagiography?," in *Æthelbald and Offa: Two Eighth-Century Kings of Mercia*, ed. David Hill and Margaret Worthington (Oxford: Basingstoke, 2005), 77.

44. *Life of Saint Guthlac* 29 (96; Colgrave trans., 97).

45. *Life of Saint Guthlac*, 184.

enemy they had killed. Psychologists have also reported a need for forgiveness and purification among many Vietnam veterans.[46] One Vietnam veteran, Claude Anshin Thomas, was so traumatized by the numbers of Vietnamese he had casually killed as a helicopter gunner that in expiation he became a Buddhist monk.[47] What seems an increase in blood guilt among American veterans of Vietnam and later wars is likely at least in part a result of the effectiveness of military training inspired by the work of S. L. A. Marshall after World War Two, who had found what a small percentage of soldiers had actually fired their weapons at the enemy. Modern U.S. military training rarely speaks of killing the enemy, but of "engaging targets." The training has been successful in increasing the rate of fire, "but it does not prepare them to deal with their own consciences."[48] Perhaps unsurprisingly, the psychologist Rachel McNair's analysis of data from the National Vietnam Veterans Readjustment Study in the 1980s found that soldiers who had killed in combat, or believed that they had, suffered higher rates of PTSD.

The problem has been exacerbated in the conditions of the wars in Iraq and Afghanistan, wars resembling more the realities of early medieval combat in that they have more often involved close-up killing. Major Peter Kilner, a former West Point philosophy instructor, who in 2003 was in Iraq to help write an official history of the war, believes that most infantrymen there have "looked down the barrel and shot at people, and many have killed." A former student told him in Iraq, "There's just too much killing. They shoot, we return fire, and they're all dead." One veteran said that coping with having killed is a spiritual, not a psychological task. "You recognize you did the unthinkable. You blasted away a piece of yourself, violated some trust with God."[49] Another veteran claimed, "I have done so much immoral shit during the last month that life is never going to seem the same."[50] One soldier talked about trying to scrub blood off his hands that wasn't there. Another veteran shot himself, leaving a suicide note that read: "I am not a good person. I have done bad things. I have taken lives. Now it's time to take mine."[51]

46. Verkamp, *The Moral Treatment of Returning Warriors* (n. 32 above), 70.

47. Claude Anshin Thomas, *At Hell's Gate: A Soldier's Journey from War to Peace* (Boston and London: Shambhala, 2006).

48. Ilona Meagher, *Moving a Nation to Care: Post-Traumatic Stress Disorder and America's Returning Troops* (New York: IG Publishing, 2007), 86.

49. Dan Baum, "The Price of Valor," *The New Yorker*, July 12, 2004.

50. Meagher (n. 48 above), 110.

51. *Wartorn: 1861-2010*, directed by Jon Alpert and Ellen Goosenberg Kent (HBO Documentary Films, 2010).

Although the separation of church and state and the religious pluralism of most modern societies make it impractical to revive early medieval penitential practices to address these veterans' psychological and spiritual wounds, Verkamp in the last chapter of his book did speak to the possibility and the reality of implementing something similar today. The penitential steps of examination of conscience, of confession, of heartfelt contrition, and of expiatory amendment or restitution, for example, can be and have been used with many veterans employing a variety of modalities and with some "success." One Vietnam veteran reported having a mystical experience of God's mercy when participating in the communal "Kyrie eleison" of a Lutheran liturgy of reconciliation. He spoke of how the personal surrender involved enabled him to feel a spiritual kinship with the "'poor in spirit' of the Sermon on the Mount, the ones who have nothing to offer, nothing to claim, no resources, and therefore can only call upon the mercy of God, neither able nor presumptuous enough to name in advance what it is they need."[52]

On the issue of soldiers' guilt for having killed in war, Augustine's theological exegesis may have been sound, but his psychological insight flawed.

What, then, might we moderns profitably derive from Augustine's actual views on war and military service? In this area in which Augustine is still largely seen by modern commentators as the architect of a Christian just war theory, opinions have largely resolved into two camps. "Hawks" have eagerly appropriated Augustinian authority for a just war "checklist" that when completed eliminates moral doubts about the justice of a war, while "doves" have excoriated Augustine for supposedly betraying the early church's pacifist stance. Besides buying in to the erroneous notion of an Augustinian paternity for the just war doctrine, both camps have also missed the dark cast of his actual views on war. Although all wars ultimately served providential ends, in his mind that did not make them any the less evil. Wars with a stronger divine imprimatur than usual could be fought by good men, but such men were few and far between.

Augustine was no pacifist. For him, as we saw in his *Epist.* 189 to Boniface, war was at times a harsh necessity. Perhaps his attitude toward even wars that men find the most justified is summed up best by Sam Hynes, a U.S. Marine pilot during World War Two, who said of that conflict, the "good war": "I don't think there is such a thing as a good war. There are sometimes necessary wars."[53] Our best glimpse of Augustine's most heartfelt view of war and military

52. Verkamp, *The Moral Treatment of Returning Warriors* (n. 32 above), 102–14.

53. *The War*, directed by Ken Burns and Lynn Novick (Florentine Films, 2006).

service is found in a story he tells in Book 19 of *The City of God* regarding the dilemma of a judge. In an effort to avoid putting an innocent man to death, the judge is nevertheless forced to torture the man to determine his culpability, thereby inflicting suffering on the innocent. And if the man chooses to end his suffering by confessing to a crime he did not commit, the judge ends up executing an innocent man, "so as a result he has both tortured an innocent man to find out whether he is and killed him without finding out." Since there are such dark places in the life of human society, Augustine asks, "will any wise man sit in judgment, or will he not dare to?" But, he concludes, he will so sit. "For the bonds of human society constrain him and compel him to his duty, the neglect of which he considers wrong." Considers wrong, even though, Augustine goes on to point out, sometimes the innocent don't confess but die under torture anyway. How can such a judge, doing what the demands of human society call him to do in the exercise of justice, a duty that men consider an honor and a privilege, but a duty that, if the judge has any shred of conscience, involves him in misery and a hatred for his own part in it, how can such a judge, if there is any religiosity at all in him, do anything but cry out to God: "From my necessities deliver Thou me!"?[54]

---

54. *DCD* 19.6 (*CCL* 48, 670, 671).

Bibliography

PRIMARY SOURCES

The Acts of the Christian Martyrs, intro., text and trans. Herbert Musurillo (Oxford: Clarendon, 1972).

Ambrose of Milan. *De Fide ad Gratianum Augustum* (*CSEL* 78).

— *De obitu Theodosii* 10, ed. Otto Faller, *CSEL* 73, 369–401.

— *De officiis*, ed. and trans. Ivor J. Davidson (Oxford: Oxford University Press, 2001)

— *De paenitentia*, ed. Otto Faller, *CSEL* 73, 117–206.

Anselm of Lucca. Edith Pásztor, "Lotta per le investiture e 'ius belli': la posizione di Anselmo di Lucca," *Sant' Anselmo, Mantova e la lotta per le investiture. Atti del convegno internazionale di studi (Mantova 23–24–25 maggio 1986)*, ed. Paolo Golinelli (Bologna: Pàtron, 1987), 375–421.

Aquinas, Thomas. *S. Thomae de Aquino Summae Theologiae Secunda Secundae* (Ottawa: Commissio Piana, 1953).

Augustine. (See the table below, "Augustine's Texts Cited.")

Basil of Caesarea. *Saint Basile: Lettres*, ed. and trans. Yves Courtonne (Paris: Budé, 1961).

Bede. *Bede's Ecclesiastical History of the English People*, ed. Bertram Colgrave and R. A. B. Mynors (Oxford: Clarendon, 1969).

Capitula diversarum sententiarum pro negociis rei publice consulendis, Paris, Bib. nat. lat. nouv. acq. 1632, fol. 78^V–89^V.

Cicero. *M. Tulli Ciceronis de officiis*, ed. M. Winterbottom (Oxford: Clarendon, 1994).

— *M. Tulli Ciceronis de re publica*, ed. J. G. F. Powell (Oxford: Clarendon, 2006).

Claudian. *Claudii Claudiani Carmina*, ed. J. B. Hall (Leipzig: Teubner, 1985).

Corippus. *Flavii Cresconii Corippi Iohannidos seu de bellis Libycis libri VIII*, ed. J. Diggle and F. R. D. Goodyear (Cambridge: Cambridge University Press, 1970).

Epigrammata Damasiana, ed. A. Ferrua (Vatican City, 1942).

Eusebius of Caesarea. *Historia Ecclesiastica* (*GCS, Eusebius Werke II*, ed. E. Schwartz [Greek], T. Mommsen [Latin] [Leipzig, 1903]).

— *Demonstratio Evangelica* (*GCS, Eusebius Werke VII*, ed. I. A. Heikel [Leipzig, 1913]).

— *ΕΥΣΕΒΙΟΥ ΤΟΥ ΠΑΜΦΙΛΟΥ ΕΙΣ ΚΩΝΣΤΑΝΤΙΝΟΝ ΤΟΝ ΒΑΣΙΛΕΑ ΤΡΙΑΚΟΝΤΑΕΤΗΡΙΚΟΣ*, ed. I. A. Heikel, *GCS* 7.

— *Über das Leben des Kaisers Konstantins* (*GCS* 1/1, ed. F. Winkelmann [Berlin, 1975])

Felix. *Felix's Life of Saint Guthlac*, ed. and trans. Bertram Colgrave (Cambridge: Cambridge University Press, 1956).

Gratian. *Corpus iuris canonici* I, *Decretum magistri Gratiani*, ed. Emil Friedberg (Leipzig, 1879).

Grotius, Hugo. *De iure praedae commentarius, Vol. II, The Collotype Reproduction of the original manuscript of 1604 in the handwriting of Grotius* (Buffalo, NY: William S. Hein & Co., 1995).

— *Hugonis Grotii De iure belli ac pacis libri tres* (Amsterdam, 1646).

Halitgar, Penitential of H. J. Schmitz, *Die Bussbücher und das kanonische Bussverfahren*, II [Graz, 1958 (reprint)]).

Hastings penitential ordinance. *Councils & Synods, with other documents relating to the English Church*, ed. D. Whitelock et al., I:2 (Oxford: Clarendon, 1981), 583–84.

Hrabanus Maurus. *Poenitentium liber ad Otgarium* (*PL* 112: 1397–1424).

Hymni Latini antiquissimi LXXV, ed. Walther Bulst (Heidelberg: F. H. Kerle, 1956).

Isidore of Seville. *Etymologiarum sive Originum libri XX*, ed. W. M. Lindsay (Oxford: Clarendon, 1911).

Ivo of Chartres. *Decretum* (*PL* 161).

Jonas of Bobbio. *Ionae vitae sanctorum Columbani, Vedastis, Iohannis* (*MGH: Scriptores rerum Germanicarum in usum scholarum* 37).

Jordanes. *Getica, MGH: aa* 5.1.

Justin. *M. Iuniani Iustini epitoma historiarum Philippicarum Pompei Trogi*, ed. Otto Seel (Stuttgart: Teubner, 1972).

Lactantius. *Div. Inst.*, *CSEL* 19, 1–672.

— *L. Caeli Firmiani Lactanti Epitome Divinarum Institutionum*, *CSEL* 19, 673–761.

— *De mortibus persecutorum*, ed. & trans. J. L. Creed (Oxford: Clarendon, 1984).

Livy. *Ab urbe condita*, ed. W. Weissenborn, M. Müller, O. Rossbach, 7 vols. (Leipzig: Teubner, 1893–98).

Mansi, J. D. *Sacrorum conciliorum nova et amplissima collectio* (Florence, 1759).

Origen. *ΚΑΤΑ ΚΕΛΣΟΥ (Contra Celsum)*, *GCS, Origenes* II.

Orosius. *Pauli Orosii Historiarum Adversum Paganos Libri VII, CSEL* 5.

XII Panegyrici Latini. Ed. R. A. B. Mynors (Oxford: Clarendon, 1964).

Paulinus of Milan, *Vita Ambrosii,* ed. M. Pellegrino (Rome, 1961).

Penitential of Theodore. W. Finsterwalder, *Die Canones Theodori Cantuariensis und ihre Überlieferungsformen* (Weimar: Hermann Böhlaus, 1929).

Possidius. *Vita Augustini, Vite dei Santi* III, ed. and trans. A. A. R. Bastiaensen, Luca Caneli, and Carlo Carena (Milan: Fondazione Lorenzo Valla, 1975).

Prudentius. *Prudentii Carmina, Peristephanon* I, *CSEL* 61, 291–431.

Pseudo-Augustine. *Epistulae* (*PL* 33: 1093–98).

Rufinus. See Eusebius, *Historia Ecclesiastica.*

Sozomen VII.22.7–8 (*GCS* 50: *Sozomenus Kirchengeschichte,* ed. J. Bidez [Berlin, 1960 (reprint)]).

Sulpicius Severus. *Chron., CSEL* 1, 3–105.

— *Vita Martini, CSEL* 1, 109–37.

— *Dial., CSEL* 1, 152–216.

Tertullian. *Apologeticum* (*CSEL* 69).

— *De corona,* ed. Jacques Fontaine (Paris: Presses Universitaires de France, 1966).

— *De idololatria,* trans. and ed. J. H. Waszink and J. C. M. Van Winden (Leiden: E. J. Brill, 1987).

— *De oratione,* 13, 15 (*CSEL* 20, 180–200).

— *De spectaculis* (*CSEL* 20, 1–29).

Themistius. *Themistii orationes quae supersunt* (Leipzig: Teubner, 1965).

Theodoret. *Theodoret Kirchengeschichte,* ed. L. Parmentier, *GCS* 19 (Leipzig, 1911).

Theodosiani libri XVI cum constitutionibus Sirmondianis, ed. Th. Mommsen (Berlin, 1962 reprint).

La tradition apostolique de saint Hippolyte, ed. B. Botte (Münster: Aschendorff, 1963).

SECONDARY SOURCES

Albert, Sigrid. *Bellum Iustum: Die Theorie des "gerechten Krieges" und ihre praktische Bedeutung für die auswärtigen Auseinandersetzungen Roms in republikanischer Zeit,* Frankfurter Althistorische Studien 10 (Frankfurt: Michael Lassleben, 1980).

Atkins, E. M., and R. J. Dodaro, eds. *Augustine: Political Writings* (Cambridge: Cambridge University Press, 2001).

Babut, E. Ch. *La plus ancienne décrétale* (Paris, 1904).

Bainton, Roland. *Christian Attitudes Toward War and Peace: A Historical Survey and Critical Re-evaluation* (New York and Nashville: Abingdon, 1960).

Barnes, T. D. *Tertullian: A Historical and Literary Study* (Oxford: Clarendon, 1971).

— *Constantine and Eusebius* (Cambridge, MA: Harvard University Press, 1981).

— *Constantine: Dynasty, Religion and Power in the Later Roman Empire* (Chichester: Wiley-Blackwell, 2011).

Bigelmair, Andreas. *Die Beteiligung der Christen am öffentlichen Leben* (Munich, 1902).

Blockley, R. C. *The Fragmentary Classicising Historians of the Later Roman Empire: Eunapius, Olympiodorus, Priscus and Malchus* (Liverpool: Francis Cairns, 1983).

Botermann, Helga. "Ciceros Gedanken zum 'gerechten Krieg' in *de officiis* 1, 34-40," *Archiv für Kulturgeschichte* 69 (1987): 1–29.

Brennecke, Hanns Christof. "'An fidelis ad militiam converti possit [Tertullian, de idolatria 19,1]?' Frühchristliches Bekenntnis und Militärdienst im Widerspruch?," in *Die Weltlichkeit des Glaubens in der Alten Kirche: Festschrift für Ulrich Wickert zum siebzigsten Geburtstag*, ed. Dietmar Wyrwa (Berlin: Walter de Gruyter, 1997), 45–100.

Brown, Peter. "St. Augustine's Attitude to Religious Coercion," *JRS* 54 (1964).

— *Augustine of Hippo: A Biography*, 2nd ed. (Berkeley and Los Angeles: University of California Press, 2000).

— *The Rise of Western Christendom: Triumph and Diversity, A.D. 200-1000*, 2nd ed. (Malden, MA, Oxford, and Melbourne: Blackwell, 2003).

Cadoux, C. John. *The Early Christian Attitude to War: A Contribution to the History of Christian Ethics* (London: Headley Bros., 1919).

Cameron, Alan. *The Last Pagans of Rome* (Oxford: Oxford University Press, 2011).

Cameron, Averil, and Stuart G. Hall, trans. *Eusebius: Life of Constantine* (Oxford: Clarendon, 1999).

Clavadetscher-Thürlemann, Silvia. Πόλεμος δίκαιος *und bellum iustum: Versuch einer Ideengeschichte* (Zürich, 1985).

Corbellini, Clementina. "Il problema della *militia* in Sant' Ambrogio," *Historia* 27 (1978): 630–36.

Daniélou, Jean. *From Shadows to Reality: Studies in the Biblical Typology of the Fathers* (Eng. trans. of *Sacramentum Futuri* [Paris: Beauchesne, 1950] by W. Hibberd) (London: Burns & Oates, 1960).

Deane, Herbert. *The Political and Social Ideas of St. Augustine* (New York and London: Columbia University Press, 1963).

Dix, Gregory. *The Apostolic Tradition of St. Hippolytus* (London: SPCK, 1968).

Dodaro, Robert. "Language and justice in political anthropology in Augustine's *De civitate dei*" (Ph.D. dissertation, Oxford, 1992).

— *Christ and the Just Society in the Thought of Augustine* (Cambridge: Cambridge University Press, 2004).

Douglas, Mary. *Purity and Danger: An Analysis of the Concepts of Pollution and Taboo* (New York: Praeger, 1966).

Drake, H. A. *In Praise of Constantine: A Historical Study and New Translation of Eusebius' Tricennial Orations* (Berkeley and Los Angeles: University of California Press, 1976).

— "The Impact of Constantine on Christianity," in Lenski, *The Age of Constantine*, 111–36.

Drexler, Hans. "Iustum Bellum," *Rheinisches Museum für Philologie* 102, no. 2 (1959): 97–140.

Duval, Yves-Marie. "L'éloge de Théodose dans la *Cité de Dieu* (V, 26, 1): Sa place, sons sens et ses sources," *Recherches augustiniennes* 4 (1966): 135–79.

Erdmann, Carl. *Die Entstehung des Kreuzzugsgedankens* (Stuttgart: W. Kohlhammer, 1935), 14; *The Origin of the Idea of Crusade*, trans. Marshall W. Baldwin and Walter Goffart (Princeton: Princeton University Press, 1977).

Fitzgerald, Allan D., ed.. *Augustine through the Ages: An Encyclopedia* (Grand Rapids: Eerdmans, 1999).

Fontaine, Jacques. "Le culte des martyrs militaires et son expression poétique au IVe siècle: L'idéal évangélique de la non-violence dans le christianisme théodosien," in *Études sur la poésie latine tardive d'Ausone à Prudence* (Paris: Société d'Édition Les Belles Lettres, 1980), 331–61.

Frank, Tenney. "The Import of the Fetial Institutions," *Classical Philology* 7 (1912): 335–42.

Freudenberger, R. "Der Anlass zu Tertullians Schrift 'De corona militis,'" *Historia: Zeitschrift für Alte Geschichte* 19, no. 5 (1970).

Fuchs, Harald. *Augustin und der antike Friedensgedanke: Untersuchungen zum neunzehnten Buch der civitas Dei*, 2nd ed. (Berlin/Zürich: Weidmann, 1965).

Gagé, Jean. "La théologie de la victoire impériale," *Revue Historique* 171 (1933): 1–44.

Geerlings, Wilhelm. "*De civitate dei* XIX als Buch der Augustinischen Friedenslehre," in *Augustinus: De civitate dei*, ed. Christoph Horn (Berlin: Akademie Verlag, 1997), 211–33.

Grossman, Dave. *On Killing: The Psychological Cost of Learning to Kill in War and Society* (New York: Back Bay Books, 1995).

Gruen, E. S. "Augustus and the Ideology of War and Peace," in *The Age of Augustus: Interdisciplinary Conference held at Brown University April 30–May 2, 1982*, ed. Rolf Winkes (Louvain-la-Neuve, Belgium: Art and Archaeology Publications Collège Érasme, 1985), 51–72.

Grünewald, T. *Constantinus Maximus Augustus: Herrschaftspropaganda in der zeitgenössischen Überlieferung* (Stuttgart, 1990).

Hagendahl, Harald. *Augustine and the Latin Classics* 2 (Göteborg: Elanders, 1967).

Haggenmacher, Peter. *Grotius et la doctrine de la guerre juste* (Paris: Presses Universitaires de France, 1983).

Harnack, Adolf von. *Militia Christi: Die christliche Religion und der Soldatenstand in den ersten drei Jahrhunderten* (Tübingen, 1905); trans. David McInnes Gracie as *Militia Christi: The Christian Religion and the Military in the First Three Centuries* (Philadelphia: Fortress Press, 1981).

Harris, William V. *War and Imperialism in Republican Rome, 327–70 B.C.* (Oxford: Clarendon, 1979).

Harrison, Simon. *Augustine's Way into the Will: The Theological and Philosophical Significance of* De Libero Arbitrio (New York: Oxford University Press, 2006).

Hausmaninger, Herbert. "'Bellum iustum' und 'iusta causa belli' im älteren römischen Recht," *Österreichische Zeitschrift für öffentliches Recht* 11 (1961): 335–45.

Hefele, C. J. *Histoire des Conciles* (Paris, 1907).

Hehl, Ernst-Dieter. "War, Peace and the Christian Order," *NCMH* 4:1.

Heim, François. "Le thème de la 'victoire sans combat' chez Ambroise," *Ambroise de Milan: XVIe Centenaire de son élection épiscopale* (Paris, 1974).

— *La Théologie de la victoire de Constantin à Théodose* (Paris: Beauchesne, 1992).

Helgeland, John. "Christians and the Roman Army from Marcus Aurelius to Constantine," *ANRW* 23, no. 1 (1979): 725–834.

Helgeland, John, Robert J. Daly, and J. Patout Burns. *Christians and the Military: The Early Experience* (Philadelphia: Fortress Press, 1985).

Holmes, Robert L. "St. Augustine and the Just War Theory," in *The Augustinian Tradition*, ed. Gareth B. Matthews (Berkeley: University of California Press, 1999), 323–44.

Hornus, Jean-Michel. *Évangile et Labarum: Etude sur l'attitude du christianisme primitif devant les problèmes de l'Etat, de la guerre et de la violence* (Genève: Labor et Fides, 1960); trans. Alan Kreider and Oliver Coburn as *It Is Not Lawful for Me to Fight* (Scottdale, PA: Herald Press, 1980).

Hunter, David. "A Decade of Research on Early Christians and Military Service," *Religious Studies Review* 18, no. 2 (1992): 87–94.

— "The Christian Church and the Roman Army in the First Three Centuries," in *The Church's Peace Witness*, ed. Marlin E. Miller and Barbara Nelson Gingerich (Grand Rapids: Eerdmans, 1994), 161–81.

Inglebert, Hervé. *Les Romains chrétiens face à l'histoire de Rome* (Paris: Brepols, 1996).

Johnson, James Turner. *Ideology, Reason, and the Limitation of War: Religious and Secular Concepts, 1200-1740* (Princeton: Princeton University Press, 1975).

Jones, A. H. M. *The Later Roman Empire, 284-602* (Norman: University of Oklahoma Press, 1964).

Jong, Mayke de. "Transformations of Penance," in *Rituals of Power: From Late Antiquity to the Early Middle Ages*, ed. Frans Theuws and Janet L. Nelson, The Transformation of the Roman World 8 (Leiden, 2000), 185–224.

Kreider, Alan. "Military Service in the Church Orders," *Journal of Religious Ethics* 31, no. 3 (2003): 415–42.

Laehr, Gerhard, and Carl Erdmann, "Ein karolingischer Konzilsbrief und der Fürstenspiegel Hincmars von Reims," *Neues Archiv der Gesellschaft für ältere deutsche Geschichtskunde zur Beförderung einer Gesamtsausgabe der Quellenschriften deutscher Geschichten des Mittelalters* 50 (Berlin, 1935), 106–34.

Laufs, Joachim. *Der Friedensgedanke bei Augustinus: Untersuchungen zum XIX. Buch des Werkes de civitate Dei*, *Hermes* 27 (Wiesbaden: Franz Steiner, 1973).

Leclercq, Henri. "Militarisme," *Dictionnaire d'archéologie chrétienne et de liturgie* (Paris: Letouzey, 1933), 11:1, cols. 1108–81.

Lee, A. D. *War in Late Antiquity: A Social History* (Malden, MA: Blackwell, 2007).

Lenihan, David A. "The Just War Theory in the Work of Saint Augustine," *Augustinian Studies* 19 (1988): 37–70.

— "The Influence of Augustine's Just War: The Early Middle Ages," *Augustinian Studies* 27, no. 1 (1996): 55–93.

Lenski, Noel, ed. *The Age of Constantine* (Cambridge: Cambridge University Press, 2006).

— "The Reign of Constantine," *The Age of Constantine*, 59–90.

Liebeschuetz, J. H. W. G. *Ambrose of Milan: Political Letters and Speeches, Translated Texts for Historians* 43 (Liverpool: Liverpool University Press, 2005).

Mandouze, André. *Saint Augustin: L'aventure de la raison et de la grâce* (Paris, 1968).

Mantovani, Mauro. *Bellum Iustum: Die Idee des gerechten Krieges in der römischen Kaiserzeit* (Bern: Peter Lang, 1990).

Markus, R. A. *Saeculum: History and Society in the Theology of St. Augustine* (Cambridge: Cambridge University Press, 1970).

— "Saint Augustine's Views on the 'Just War,'" *Studies in Church History* 20 (1983): 1–13.

Mattox, John Mark. *Saint Augustine and the Theory of Just War* (London: Continuum, 2006).

Mayer, Cornelius, et al., eds.. *Augustinus-Lexikon* (Basel: Schwabe & Co., 1986–94).

Mazzucco, Clementina. "Origene e la guerra giusta," *Civiltà classica e cristiana* 9, no. 1 (1988): 67–84.

McCormick, Michael. *Eternal Victory: Triumphal Rulership in Late Antiquity, Byzantium, and the Early Medieval West* (Cambridge: Cambridge University Press, 1986).

McLynn, Neil. *Ambrose of Milan: Church and Court in a Christian Capital* (Berkeley: University of California Press, 1994).

Meer, F. Van der. *Augustine the Bishop: The Life and Work of a Father of the Church*, trans. Brian Battershaw and G. R. Lamb (London and New York: Sheed & Ward, 1961).

Moffatt, James. "War," in *Dictionary of the Apostolic Church*, ed. James Hastings (Edinburgh: T. & T. Clark, 1918), vol. II, 646–73.

Morisi, Anna. *La guerra nel pensiero cristiano dalle origini alle crociate* (Florence: G. C. Sansoni, 1963).

Nixon, C. E. V., and Barbara T. Rodgers, *In Praise of Later Roman Emperors: The Panegyrici Latini* (Berkeley, Los Angeles, and Oxford, 1994).

O'Daly, Gerard. *Augustine's City of God: A Reader's Guide* (Oxford: Oxford University Press, 1999).

Palanque, J.-R. *Saint Ambroise et l'Empire romain* (Paris: Boccard, 1933).

Phillipson, Coleman. *The International Law and Custom of Ancient Greece and Rome* (London: Macmillan and Co., 1911).

Pollmann, Karla. "Augustins Transformation der traditionellen römischen Staats- und Geschichtsauffassung," *Augustinus:* De civitate Dei, ed. Christoph Horn (Berlin, 1997), 25–40.

Pucciarelli, Enrico. *I cristiani e il servizio militare: Testimonianze dei primi tre secoli* (Florence: Nardini, 1987).

Regout, Robert H. W. *La doctrine de la guerre juste de saint Augustin à nos jours* (Paris: A. Pedone, 1934).

Rich, J. W. *Declaring War in the Roman Empire in the Period of Transmarine Expansion*, Collection Latomus No. 149 (Brussels: Latomus, 1976).

Rief, Josef. *Der Ordobegriff des jungen Augustinus* (Paderborn: F. Schöningh, 1962).

— *"Bellum" im Denken und in den Gedanken Augustins*, Beiträge zur Friedensethik 7 (Barsbüttel: Institut für Theologie und Frieden, 1990).

Rist, John M. *Augustine: Ancient Thought Baptized* (Cambridge: Cambridge University Press, 1994).

Rordorf, W. "Tertullians Beurteilung des Soldatenstandes," *Vigiliae Christianae* 23 (1969): 105–41.

Rushworth, Alan. "Soldiers and Tribesmen: The Roman Army and Tribal Society in Late Imperial Africa," Ph.D. dissertation, University of Newcastle upon Tyne, November 1992.

Russell, Frederick H. *The Just War in the Middle Ages* (Cambridge: Cambridge University Press, 1975).

Ryan, Edward A. "The Rejection of Military Service by the Early Christians," *Theological Studies* 13 (1952): 1–32.

Schubert, Alois. *Augustins Lex-aeterna-Lehre nach Inhalt und Quellen. Beiträge zur Geschichte der Philosophie des Mittelalters, Texte und Untersuchungen* 24:2 (Münster, 1924).

Shean, John F. *"Militans pro Deo*: The Christianization of the Roman Army" (Ph.D. dissertation, University of Wisconsin-Madison, 1998).

Smith, Anthony D. *The Antiquity of Nations* (Cambridge, UK, and Malden, MA: Polity, 2004).

Southern, Pat, and Karen R. Dixon, *The Late Roman Army* (New Haven: Yale University Press, 1996).

Stancliffe, Clare. *St. Martin and His Hagiographer: History and Miracle in Sulpicius Severus* (Oxford: Clarendon, 1983).

— "Kings Who Opted Out," in Wormald, *Ideal and Reality*, 154–76.

Stephenson, Paul. *Constantine: Unconquered Emperor, Christian Victor* (London: Quercus, 2009).

Swift, Louis J. "St. Ambrose on Violence and War," *Transactions and Proceedings of the American Philological Association* 101 (1970): 533–43.

— *The Early Fathers on War and Military Service* (Wilmington, DE: Michael Glazier, 1983).

Tellenbach, Gerd. "Römischer und christlicher Reichsgedanke in der Liturgie des frühen Mittelalters," *Sitzungsberichte der Heidelberger Akademie der Wissenschaften Philosophisch-historische Klasse* 25 (1934/35).

Vanderpol, Alfred. *Le droit de guerre d'après les théologiens et les canonistes du moyen-âge* (Paris: Tralin, 1911).

— *La guerre devant le Christianisme* (Paris: Tralin, 1912).

— *La doctrine scolastique du droit de guerre* (Paris: A. Pedone, 1919).

Velázquez, Isabel. "*Pro patriae gentisque Gothorum statu* (4th Council of Toledo, canon 75, a. 633)," *Regna and Gentes: The Relationship between Late Antique and Early Medieval Peoples and Kingdoms in the Transformation of the Roman World*, ed. Hans-Werner Goetz, Jörg Jarnut, and Walter Pohl (Leiden and Boston: Brill, 2003), 161–217.

Verkamp, Bernard J. "Moral treatment of returning warriors in the early middle ages," *Journal of Religious Ethics* 16, no. 2 (1988): 223–49.

— *The Moral Treatment of Returning Warriors in Early Medieval and Modern Times* (Scranton, PA: University of Scranton Press, 1993).

Vogel, C. *La discipline pénitentielle en Gaule des origines à la fin du VIIe siècle* (Paris: Letouzey & Ané, 1952).

— "Le péché et la pénitence: Aperçu sur l'évolution historique de la discipline pénitentielle dans l'Église latine," 147–216, in Ph. Delhaye, J. Leclercq, et al., *Pastorale du péché* (Tournai: Desclée, 1961).

Walbank, F. W. "Roman Declarations of War in the Third and Second Centuries B.C.," *Classical Philology* 44 (1949): 15–19.

— *A Historical Commentary on Polybius* (Oxford: Clarendon, 1979).

Walzer, Michael. *Just and Unjust Wars* (New York: Basic Books, 1977).

Watson, Alan. *International Law in Archaic Rome: War and Religion* (Baltimore: Johns Hopkins University Press, 1993).

Wiedemann, Thomas. "The Fetials: A Reconsideration," *Classical Quarterly* 36 (1986): 478–89.

Williams, D. H. *Ambrose of Milan and the End of the Nicene-Arian Conflicts* (Oxford: Clarendon, 1995).

Woolf, Greg. "Roman peace," in *War and Society in the Roman World*, ed. John Rich and Graham Shipley (London and New York: Routledge, 1993), 171–94.

Wormald, Patrick, et al., eds. *Ideal and Reality in Frankish and Anglo-Saxon Society* (Oxford: Basil Blackwell, 1983).

Zecchini, Giuseppe. "S. Ambrogio e le origini del motivo della vittoria incruenta," *Rivista di Storia della Chiesa in Italia* 38, no. 2 (1984): 391–404.

Augustine's Texts Cited

TEXT	MODERN EDITION(S)
Contra Academicos	*CCL* 29, pp. 3–61
Contra Adimantum	*CSEL* 25, pp. 115–90
De bono coniugali	*CSEL* 41, pp. 185–231
De catechizandis rudibus	*CCL* 46, pp. 121–78
De civitate Dei	*CCL* 47, 48, ed. B. Dombart & A. Kalb
Confessions	*CCL* 27
De diversis quaestionibus	*CCL* 44A, pp. 11–249
De doctrina Christiana	*CSEL* 80
Enarrationes in Psalmos (*Enar. in Ps.*)	*CCL* 38: *Enar. in Ps.* 33, 36, 39, 48; *CCL* 39: 60, 67, 72, 74, 75, 84, 90; *CCL* 40: 118, 124, 127, 131, 143, 147, 149; *CSEL* 95.3 also has 124 and 131.
Enchiridion	*CCL* 46, p. 49–114
Epistolae (*Epist.*)	*CSEL* 34: *Epist.* 46, 47, 54, 87, 93, 95, 102, 111; *CSEL* 44: 126, 133, 134, 135, 136, 138, 139, 140, 151, 153; *CSEL* 57: 185, 189, 220, 229
Epist. Divjak	*CSEL* 88
De excidio urbis Romae	*PL* 40: 716–24
Expositio quarundam propositionum ex epistola ad Romanos	*CSEL* 84, pp. 3–52
Contra Faustum	*CSEL* 25
De fide et operibus	*CSEL* 41, pp. 33–97
De Genesi ad litteram	*CSEL* 28:1
De gestis Pelagii	*CSEL* 42, pp. 51–122
In Iohannis Evangelium (*In Iohann. Evang.*)	*CCL* 36
Contra Iulianum	*PL* 44
De libero arbitrio	*CSEL* 29, pp. 211–321
De mendacio	*CSEL* 41, pp. 411–66

De natura boni	*CSEL* 25, pp. 855–89
De ordine	*CCL* 29, pp. 89–137
De peccatorum meritis et remissione et de baptisma parvulorum	*CSEL* 60, p. 3–151
Psalmus contra partem Donati	*CSEL* 51, pp. 3–15
Quaestiones in Heptateuchum	*CSEL* 28:2; *CCL* 33
De quantitate animae	*CSEL* 89, pp. 131–231
Retractationes	*CSEL* 36; *CCL* 57
Sermones (Serm.)	*PL* 38: *Serm.* 1–340; *PL* 39: 351, 352, 356, 357, 359; *SC* 116: *Serm.* 232; *Miscellanea Agostiniana* I (Rome, 1930): *Serm.* 29A, 114A, 260A, 277A, 335A, 359B, 360B. For individual sermons, see also the table in Fitzgerald, pp. 774–89.
De sermone Domini in monte	*CCL* 35
Soliloquies	*CSEL* 89, pp. 3–98
De vera religione	*CSEL* 77, pp. 3–81; *CCL* 32, pp. 187–260

Index of Augustinian Citations

General Index

Abraham, 92, 197, 240, 243
acta martyrum, 37, 58
Adam, 178, 285
Adamantius, on just war, 134–35
Alba Longa, 273–74
Alypius, 165, 167, 207
Ambrose of Milan, 81, 120–22, 167–68, 175, 190–91, 195, 263, 271, 325; and capital punishment, 103–4; on courage, 92–94; disgust at public service, 73; episcopal election, 102–3; on just war, 135–43; on patriotism, 88–92; and penance, 105–10; and Priscillian, 117; reservations, 95–96; as source for Augustine on *ius in bello*, 249–50; source for the Frigidus, 82–84; victory less dependent on strength than faith, 76
Ammianus Marcellinus, 133
Amorites, 237
Ananias, 182
Anselm of Lucca, 313, 316–19, 327
Anthony, Saint, 167
Anulinus, 57
Apostolic Tradition, 47
Apringius, 169, 212, 218
Aquinas, Thomas: 1, 235, 249, 313, 329–30; early basis of Augustinian just war, 9–10; and Haggenmacher, 30; and James Turner Johnson, 24; and Lenihan, 25; and Vanderpol, 16–18
Arbogast, 75
Arcadius, Roman emperor, 85
Arles, Synod of (314), 57–59, 99, 201
Arzuges, 193
Asterius, 80

Attila the Hun, 300
Augustine, 130, 133; on Ambrose's hymnody, 110; biography of, 150–51; on *militia*, 155–212; interpretive issues, 147–50; and just war, 327–30; and military service, 330–36; and origins of just war, 1–2, 5, 9–31, 317; on peace, 278–95; role in history of just war, 34, 48; and Theodosian propaganda, 74, 78, 83; views on war and military service in his own time, 321–24; on *victoria*, 265–77; on war, 213–63
Augustus Caesar, 127, 282
Aurelius of Carthage, 177–78
Avitianus, 115
Ayala, Balthazar, 11–12, 13

Bainton, Roland, 22
Basil of Caesarea, 95, 96, 107–8
Beaufort, L. J. C., 20, 28
Bede, 305–6, 331–32
Bible, 77; in Augustine, 151; and the battle of the Frigidus, 82–83; and just wars, 233–63; on peace, 278–83; and punishment, 181–83; role in determining Christian attitudes to war and military service, 3; role in providential history, 68–70; on suicide and legitimate killing, 195–98; superiority of, in Ambrose, 89; on the tension between Old and New Testaments, 325–26; in Thomas Aquinas, 9; used to justify state service, 35–36; used to describe Christian *victoria*, 65–68; warrior examples in Ambrose, 92–94; as the West's new metanarrative, 305–6;